Wendell Phillips

SPEECHES,

LECTURES, AND LETTERS.

BY

WENDELL PHILLIPS.

Boston:
LEE AND SHEPARD,
149 WASHINGTON STREET.
1872.

EIGHTH THOUSAND.

UNIVERSITY PRESS:
WELCH, BIGELOW, AND COMPANY,
CAMBRIDGE.

SPEECHES,

LECTURES, AND LETTERS.

CONTENTS.

	PAGE
The Murder of Lovejoy	1
Woman's Rights	11
Public Opinion	35
Surrender of Sims	55
Sims Anniversary	71
Philosophy of the Abolition Movement	98
Removal of Judge Loring	154
The Boston Mob	213
The Pilgrims	228
Letter to Judge Shaw and President Walker	237
Idols	242
Harper's Ferry	263
Burial of John Brown	289
Lincoln's Election	294
Mobs and Education	319
Disunion	343
Progress	371
Under the Flag	396
The War for the Union	415
The Cabinet	448
Letter to the Tribune	464
Toussaint l'Ouverture	468
A Metropolitan Police	495
The State of the Country	524

THE MURDER OF LOVEJOY.

On November 7, 1837, Rev. E. P. Lovejoy was shot by a mob at Alton, Illinois, while attempting to defend his printing-press from destruction. When this was known in Boston, William Ellery Channing headed a petition to the Mayor and Aldermen, asking the use of Faneuil Hall for a public meeting. The request was refused. Dr. Channing then addressed a very impressive letter to his fellow-citizens, which resulted in a meeting of influential gentleman at the Old Court Room. Resolutions, drawn by Hon. B. F. Hallett, were unanimously adopted, and measures taken to secure a much larger number of names to the petition. This call the Mayor and Aldermen obeyed.

The meeting was held on the 8th of December, and organized, with the Hon. Jonathan Phillips for Chairman.

Dr. Channing made a brief and eloquent address. Resolutions, drawn by him, were then read and offered by Mr. Hallett, and seconded in an able speech by George S. Hillard, Esq.

The Hon. James T. Austin, Attorney-General of the Commonwealth, followed in a speech of the utmost bitterness, styled by the Boston Atlas a few days after "most able and triumphant." He compared the slaves to a menagerie of wild beasts, and the rioters at Alton to the "*orderly mob*" which threw the tea overboard in 1773,—talked of the "conflict of laws" between Missouri and Illinois,—declared that Lovejoy was "presumptuous and imprudent," and "died as the fool dieth"; in direct and most insulting reference to Dr. Channing, he asserted that a clergyman with a gun in his hand, or one "mingling in the debates of a popular assembly, was marvellously out of place."

The speech of the Attorney-General produced great excitement throughout the Hall. Wendell Phillips, Esq., who had not expected to take part in the meeting, rose to reply. That portion of the assembly which sympathized with Mr. Austin now became so boisterous, that Mr. Phillips had difficulty for a while in getting the attention of the audience.

MR. CHAIRMAN: — We have met for the freest discussion of these resolutions, and the events which gave rise to them. [Cries of "Question," "Hear him," "Go on," "No gagging," etc.] I hope I shall be permitted to express my surprise at the sentiments of the last speaker, — surprise not only at such sentiments from such a man, but at the applause they have received within these walls. A comparison has been drawn between the events of the Revolution and the tragedy at Alton. We have heard it asserted here, in Faneuil Hall, that Great Britain had a right to tax the Colonies, and we have heard the mob at Alton, the drunken murderers of Lovejoy, compared to those patriot fathers who threw the tea overboard! [Great applause.] Fellow-citizens, is this Faneuil Hall doctrine? ["No, no."] The mob at Alton were met to wrest from a citizen his just rights, — met to resist the laws. We have been told that our fathers did the same; and the glorious mantle of Revolutionary precedent has been thrown over the mobs of our day. To make out their title to such defence, the gentleman says that the British Parliament had a *right* to tax these Colonies. It is manifest that, without this, his parallel falls to the ground; for Lovejoy had stationed himself within constitutional bulwarks. He was not only defending the freedom of the press, but he was under his own roof, in arms with the sanction of the civil authority. The men who assailed him went against and over the laws. The *mob*, as the gentleman terms it, — mob, forsooth! certainly we sons of the tea-spillers are a marvellously patient generation! —

the "orderly mob" which assembled in the Old South to destroy the tea were met to resist, not the laws, but illegal exactions. Shame on the American who calls the tea-tax and stamp-act *laws!* Our fathers resisted, not the King's prerogative, but the King's usurpation. To find any other account, you must read our Revolutionary history upside down. Our State archives are loaded with arguments of John Adams to prove the taxes laid by the British Parliament unconstitutional, — beyond its power. It was not till this was made out that the men of New England rushed to arms. The arguments of the Council Chamber and the House of Representatives preceded and sanctioned the contest. To draw the conduct of our ancestors into a precedent for mobs, for a right to resist laws we ourselves have enacted, is an insult to their memory. The difference between the excitements of those days and our own, which the gentleman in kindness to the latter has overlooked, is simply this: the men of that day went for the right, as secured by the laws. They were the people rising to sustain the laws and constitution of the Province. The rioters of our day go for their own wills, right or wrong. Sir, when I heard the gentleman lay down principles which place the murderers of Alton side by side with Otis and Hancock, with Quincy and Adams, I thought those pictured lips [pointing to the portraits in the Hall] would have broken into voice to rebuke the recreant American, — the slanderer of the dead. [Great applause and counter applause.] The gentleman said that he should sink into insignificance if he dared to gainsay the principles of these resolutions. Sir, for the sentiments he has uttered, on soil consecrated by the prayers of Puritans and the blood of patriots, the earth should have yawned and swallowed him up.

[Applause and hisses, with cries of "Take that back." The uproar became so great that for a long time no one could be heard. At length

G. Bond, Esq., and Hon. W. Sturgis came to Mr. Phillips's side at the front of the platform. They were met with cries of "Phillips or nobody," "Make him take back 'recreant,'" "He sha'n't go on till he takes it back." When it was understood they meant to sustain, not to interrupt, Mr. Phillips, Mr. Sturgis was listened to, and said: "I did not come here to take any part in this discussion, nor do I intend to; but I do entreat you, fellow-citizens, by everything you hold sacred, — I conjure you by every association connected with this Hall, consecrated by our fathers to freedom of discussion, — that you listen to every man who addresses you in a decorous manner." Mr. Phillips resumed.]

Fellow-citizens, I cannot take back my words. Surely the Attorney-General, so long and well known here, needs not the aid of your hisses against one so young as I am, — my voice never before heard within these walls!

Another ground has been taken to excuse the mob, and throw doubt and discredit on the conduct of Lovejoy and his associates. Allusion has been made to what lawyers understand very well, — the "conflict of laws." We are told that nothing but the Mississippi River rolls between St. Louis and Alton; and the conflict of laws somehow or other gives the citizens of the former a right to find fault with the defender of the press for publishing his opinions so near their limits. Will the gentleman venture that argument before lawyers? How the laws of the two States could be said to come into conflict in such circumstances I question whether any lawyer in this audience can explain or understand. No matter whether the line that divides one sovereign State from another be an imaginary one or ocean-wide, the moment you cross it the State you leave is blotted out of existence, so far as you are concerned. The Czar might as well claim to control the deliberations of Faneuil Hall, as the laws of Missouri demand reverence, or the shadow of obedience, from an inhabitant of Illinois.

I must find some fault with the statement which has been made of the events at Alton. It has been asked why Lovejoy and his friends did not appeal to the executive, — trust their defence to the police of the city. It has been hinted that, from hasty and ill-judged excitement, the men within the building provoked a quarrel, and that he fell in the course of it, one mob resisting another. Recollect, Sir, that they did act with the approbation and sanction of the Mayor. In strict truth, there was no executive to appeal to for protection. The Mayor acknowledged that he could not protect them. They asked him if it was lawful for them to defend themselves. He told them it was, and sanctioned their assembling in arms to do so. They were not, then, a mob; they were not merely citizens defending their own property; they were in some sense the *posse comitatus*, adopted for the occasion into the police of the city, acting under the order of a magistrate. It was civil authority resisting lawless violence. Where, then, was the imprudence? Is [illegible] doctrine to be sustained here, that it is *imprudent* for men to aid magistrates in executing the laws?

Men are continually asking each other, Had Lovejoy a right to resist? Sir, I protest against the question, instead of answering it. Lovejoy did not resist, in the sense they mean. He did not throw himself back on the natural right of self-defence. He did not cry anarchy, and let slip the dogs of civil war, careless of the horrors which would follow.

Sir, as I understand this affair, it was not an individual protecting his property; it was not one body of armed men resisting another, and making the streets of a peaceful city run blood with their contentions. It did not bring back the scenes in some old Italian cities, where family met family, and faction met faction, and mutually trampled the laws under foot. No; the men in that house were regularly *enrolled*, under the sanction of the Mayor. There being no militia in Alton, about seventy men were enrolled with the approbation of the Mayor. These relieved each other every other night. About thirty men were in arms on the night of the sixth, when the press was landed. The next evening, it was not thought necessary to summon more than half that number; among these was Lovejoy. It was, therefore, you perceive, Sir, the police of the city resisting rioters, — civil government breasting itself to the shock of lawless men.

Here is no question about the right of self-defence. It is in fact simply this: Has the civil magistrate a right to put down a riot?

Some persons seem to imagine that anarchy existed at Alton from the commencement of these disputes. Not at all. "No one of us," says an eyewitness and a comrade of Lovejoy, "has taken up arms during these disturbances but at the command of the Mayor." Anarchy did not settle down on that devoted city till Lovejoy breathed his last. Till then the law, represented in his person, sustained itself against its foes. When he fell, civil authority was trampled under foot. He had "planted himself on his constitutional rights," — appealed to the laws, — claimed the protection of the civil authority, — taken refuge under "the broad shield of the Constitution. When through that he was pierced and fell, he fell as one sufferer in a common catastrophe." He took refuge under the banner of liberty, — amid its folds; and when he fell, its glorious stars and stripes, the emblem of free institutions, around which cluster so many heart-stirring memories, were blotted out in the martyr's blood.

It has been stated, perhaps inadvertently, that Lovejoy or his comrades fired first. This is denied by those who have the best means of knowing. Guns were first fired by the mob. After being twice fired on, those within the building consulted together and deliberately returned the fire. But suppose they did fire first. They had a right so to do; not only the right which every citizen has to defend himself, but the further right which every civil officer has to resist violence. Even if Lovejoy fired the first gun, it would not lessen his claim to our sympathy, or destroy his title to be considered a martyr in defence of a free press. The question now is, Did he act within the Constitution and the laws? The men who fell in State Street on the 5th of March, 1770, did more than Lovejoy is charged with. They were the *first* assailants. Upon some slight quarrel they pelted the troops with every missile within reach. Did this bate one jot of the eulogy with which Hancock and Warren hallowed their memory, hailing them as the first martyrs in the cause of American liberty?

If, Sir, I had adopted what are called Peace principles, I might lament the circumstances of this case. But all you who believe, as I do, in the right and duty of magistrates to execute the laws, join with me and brand as base hypocrisy the conduct of those who assemble year after year on the 4th of July, to fight over the battles of the Revolution, and yet "damn with faint praise," or load with obloquy, the memory of this man, who shed his blood in defence of life, liberty, property, and the freedom of the press!

Throughout that terrible night I find nothing to regret but this, that within the limits of our country, civil authority should have been so prostrated as to oblige a citizen to arm in his own defence, and to arm in vain. The gentleman says Lovejoy was presumptuous and imprudent, — he "died as the fool dieth." And a reverend clergyman of the city * tells us that no citizen has a right to publish opinions disagreeable to the community! If any mob follows such publication, on *him* rests its guilt! He must wait, forsooth, till the people come up to it and agree with

* See Rev. Hubbard Winslow's discourse on *Liberty!* in which he defines "republican liberty" to be "liberty to say and do what the *prevailing* voice and will of the brotherhood will allow and protect."

him! This libel on liberty goes on to say that the want of right to speak as we think is an evil inseparable from republican institutions! If this be so, what are they worth? Welcome the despotism of the Sultan, where one knows what he may publish and what he may not, rather than the tyranny of this many-headed monster, the mob, where we know not what we may do or say, till some fellow-citizen has tried it, and paid for the lesson with his life. This clerical absurdity chooses as a check for the abuses of the press, not the *law*, but the dread of a mob. By so doing, it deprives not only the individual and the minority of their rights, but the majority also, since the expression of *their* opinion may sometimes provoke disturbance from the minority. A few men may make a mob as well as many. The majority, then, have no right, as Christian men, to utter their sentiments, if by any possibility it may lead to a mob! Shades of Hugh Peters and John Cotton, save us from such pulpits!

Imprudent to defend the liberty of the press! Why? Because the defence was unsuccessful? Does success gild crime into patriotism, and the want of it change heroic self-devotion to imprudence? Was Hampden imprudent when he drew the sword and threw away the scabbard? Yet he, judged by that single hour, was unsuccessful. After a short exile, the race he hated sat again upon the throne.

Imagine yourself present when the first news of Bunker Hill battle reached a New England town. The tale would have run thus: "The patriots are routed, — the redcoats victorious, — Warren lies dead upon the field." With what scorn would that *Tory* have been received, who should have charged Warren with *imprudence!* who should have said that, bred a physician, he was "out of place" in that battle, and "died as the *fool dieth*"! [Great applause.] How would the intimation have been received, that Warren and his associates should have waited a better time? But if success be indeed the only criterion of prudence, *Respice finem*, — wait till the end.

Presumptuous to assert the freedom of the press on American ground! Is the assertion of such freedom before the age? So much before the age as to leave one no right to make it because it displeases the community? Who invents this libel on his country? It is this very thing which entitles Lovejoy to greater praise. The disputed right which provoked the Revolution — taxation without representation — is far beneath that for which he died. [Here there was a strong and general expression of disapprobation.] One word, gentlemen. As much as *thought* is better than money, so much is the cause in which Lovejoy died nobler than a mere question of taxes. James Otis thundered in this Hall when the King did but touch his *pocket*. Imagine, if you can, his indignant eloquence, had England offered to put a gag upon his lips. [Great applause.]

The question that stirred the Revolution touched our civil interests. *This* concerns us not only as citizens, but as immortal beings. Wrapped up in its fate, saved or lost with it, are not only the voice of the statesman, but the instructions of the pulpit, and the progress of our faith.

The clergy "marvellously out of place" where free speech is battled for, — liberty of speech on national sins? Does the gentleman remember that freedom to preach was first gained, dragging in its train freedom to print? I thank the clergy here present, as I reverence their predecessors, who did not so far forget their country in their immediate profession as to deem it duty to separate themselves from the struggle of '76, — the Mayhews and Coopers, who remembered they were citizens before they were clergymen.

Mr. Chairman, from the bottom of my heart I thank that brave little band at Alton for resisting. We must remember that Lovejoy had fled from city to city, — suffered the destruction of three presses patiently. At length he took counsel with friends, men of character, of tried integrity, of wide views, of Christian principle. They thought the crisis had come: it was full time to assert the laws. They saw around them, not a community like our own, of fixed habits, of character moulded and settled, but one "in the gristle, not yet hardened into the bone of manhood." The people there, children of our older States, seem to have forgotten the blood-tried principles of their fathers the moment they lost sight of our New England hills. Something was to be done to show them the priceless value of the freedom of the press, to bring back and set right their wandering and confused ideas. He and his advisers looked out on a community, staggering like a drunken man, indifferent to their rights and confused in their feelings. Deaf to argument, haply they might be stunned into sobriety. They saw that of which we cannot judge, the *necessity* of resistance. Insulted law called for it. Public opinion, fast hastening on the downward course, must be arrested.

Does not the event show they judged rightly? Absorbed in a thousand trifles, how has the nation all at once come to a stand? Men begin, as in 1776 and 1640, to discuss principles, to weigh characters, to find out where they are. Haply we may awake before we are borne over the precipice.

I am glad, Sir, to see this crowded house. It is good for us to be here. When Liberty is in danger, Faneuil Hall has the right, it is her duty, to strike the key-note for these United States. I am glad, for one reason, that remarks such as those to which I have alluded have been uttered here. The passage of these resolutions, in spite of this opposition, led by the Attorney-General of the Commonwealth, will show more clearly, more decisively, the deep indignation with which Boston regards this outrage.

WOMAN'S RIGHTS.

THIS speech was made at a Convention held at Worcester, on the 15th and 16th of October, 1851, upon the following resolutions, which were offered by Mr. Phillips: —

"1. *Resolved*, That, while we would not undervalue other methods, the right of suffrage for women is, in our opinion, the corner-stone of this enterprise, since we do not seek to protect woman, but rather to place her in a position to protect herself.

"2. *Resolved*, That it will be woman's fault if, the ballot once in her hand, all the barbarous, demoralizing, and unequal laws relating to marriage and property do not speedily vanish from the statute-book; and while we acknowledge that the hope of a share in the higher professions and profitable employments of society is one of the strongest motives to intellectual culture, we know, also, that an interest in political questions is an equally powerful stimulus; and we see, beside, that we do our best to insure education to an individual, when we put the ballot into his hands; it being so clearly the interest of the community that one upon whose decisions depend its welfare and safety should both have free access to the best means of education, and be urged to make use of them.

"3. *Resolved*, That we do not feel called upon to assert or establish the equality of the sexes, in an intellectual or any other point of view. It is enough for our argument that natural and political justice, and the axioms of English and American liberty, alike determine that rights and burdens, taxation and representation, should be co-extensive; hence women, as individual citizens, liable to punishment for acts which the laws call criminal, or to be taxed in their labor and property for the support of government, have a self-evident and indisputable right, identically the same right that men have, to a direct voice in the enactment of those laws and the formation of that government.

"4. *Resolved*, That the democrat, or reformer, who denies suffrage to women, is a democrat only because he was not born a noble, and one of those levellers who are willing to level only down to themselves.

"5. *Resolved*, That while political and natural justice accord civil equality to woman; while great thinkers of every age, from Plato to Condorcet and Mill, have supported their claim; while voluntary associations, religious and secular, have been organized on this basis, — there is yet a favorite argument against it, that no political community or nation ever existed in which women have not been in a state of political inferiority. But, in reply, we remind our opponents that the same fact has been alleged, with equal truth, in favor of slavery; has been urged against freedom of industry, freedom of conscience, and the freedom of the press; none of these liberties having been thought compatible with a well-ordered state, until they had proved their possibility by springing into existence as facts. Besides, there is no difficulty in understanding why the subjection of woman has been a *uniform custom*, when we recollect that we are just emerging from the ages in which *might* has been always right.

"6. *Resolved*, That, so far from denying the overwhelming social and civil influence of women, we are fully aware of its vast extent; aware, with Demosthenes, that 'measures which the statesman has meditated a whole year may be overturned in a day by a woman'; and for this very reason we proclaim it the very highest expediency to endow her with full civil rights, since only then will she exercise this mighty influence under a just sense of her duty and responsibility; the history of all ages bearing witness that the only safe course for nations is to add open responsibility wherever there already exists unobserved power.

"7. *Resolved*, That we deny the right of any portion of the species to decide for another portion, or of any individual to decide for another individual, what is and what is not its 'proper sphere'; that the proper sphere for all human beings is the largest and highest to which they are able to attain; what this is cannot be ascertained without complete liberty of choice; woman, therefore, ought to choose for herself what sphere she will fill, what education she will seek, and what employment she will follow; and not be held bound to accept, in submission, the rights, the education, and the sphere which man thinks proper to allow her.

"8. *Resolved*, That we hold these truths to be self-evident: 'That all men are created equal; that they are endowed by their Creator with certain inalienable rights; that among these are life, liberty, and the pursuit of happiness; that, to secure these rights, governments are instituted among men, deriving their just powers from the consent of the governed'; and we charge that man with gross dishonesty or ignorance who shall contend that 'men,' in the memorable document from which we quote, does not stand for the human race; that 'life, liberty, and the pursuit of happiness' are the 'inalienable rights' of *half* only of the human species; and that, by 'the governed,' whose consent is affirmed to be the only source of just power, is meant that *half* of mankind only who, in relation to the other, have hitherto assumed the character of *governors*.

"9. *Resolved*, That we see no weight in the argument, that it is necessary to exclude women from civil life because domestic cares and political engagements are incompatible; since we do not see the fact to be so in the case of man; and because, if the incompatibility be real, it will take care of itself, neither men nor women needing any law to exclude them from an occupation when they have undertaken another incompatible with it. Second, we see nothing in the assertion that women themselves do not desire a change, since we assert that superstitious fears, and dread of losing men's regard, smother all frank expression on this point; and further, if it be their real wish to avoid civil life, laws to keep them out of it are absurd, no legislator having ever yet thought it necessary to compel people by law to follow their own inclination.

"10. *Resolved*, That it is as absurd to deny all women their civil rights because the cares of household and family take up all the time of some, as it would be to exclude the whole male sex from Congress, because some men are sailors, or soldiers, in active service, or merchants, whose business requires all their attention and energies."

IN drawing up some of these resolutions, I have used, very freely, the language of a thoughtful and profound article in the *Westminster Review*. It is a review of the proceedings of our recent Convention in this city, and states with singular clearness and force the leading arguments for our reform, and the grounds of our claim in behalf of woman.

I rejoice to see so large an audience gathered to consider this momentous subject. It was well described by Mrs. Rose as the most magnificent reform that has yet been launched upon the world. It is the first organized protest against the injustice which has brooded over the character and the destiny of one half of the human race. Nowhere else, under any circumstances, has a demand ever yet been made for the liberties of one whole half of our race. It is fitting that we should pause and consider so remarkable and significant a circumstance; that we should discuss the question involved with the seriousness and deliberation suitable to such an enterprise. It strikes, indeed, a great and vital blow at the whole social fabric of every nation; but this, to my mind, is no argument against it. The time has been when it was the duty of the reformer to show cause why he appeared to disturb the quiet of the world. But during the discussion of the many reforms that have been advocated, and which have more or less succeeded, one after another, — freedom of the lower classes, freedom of food, freedom of the press, freedom of thought, reform in penal legislation, and a thousand other matters, — it seems to me to have been proved conclusively, that government commenced in usurpation and oppression; that liberty and civilization, at present, are nothing else than the fragments of rights which the scaffold and the stake have wrung from the strong hands of the usurpers. Every step of progress the world has made has been from scaffold to scaffold, and from stake to stake. It would hardly be exaggeration to say, that all the great truths relating to society and government have been first heard in the solemn protests of martyred patriotism, or the loud cries of crushed and starving labor. The law has been always wrong. Government began in tyranny and force, began in the feudalism of the soldier and bigotry of the priest; and the ideas of justice and humanity have been fighting their way, like a thunder-storm, against the organized selfishness of human nature. And this is the last great protest against the wrong of ages. It is no argument to my mind, therefore, that the old social fabric of the past is against us.

Neither do I feel called upon to show what woman's proper sphere is. In every great reform, the majority have always said to the claimant, no matter what he claimed, "You are not fit for such a privilege." Luther asked of the Pope liberty for the masses to read the Bible. The reply was, that it would not be safe to trust the common people with the word of God. "Let them try!" said the great reformer; and the history of three centuries of development and purity proclaims the result. They *have* tried; and look around you for the consequences. The lower classes in France claimed their civil rights, — the right to vote, and to direct representation in the government; but the rich and lettered classes, the men of cultivated intellects, cried out, "You cannot be made fit." The answer was, "Let us try." That France is not, as Spain, utterly crushed beneath the weight of a thousand years of misgovernment, is the answer to those who doubt the ultimate success of this experiment.

Woman stands now at the same door. She says, "You tell me I have no intellect: give me a chance. You tell me I shall only embarrass politics: let me try." The only reply is the same stale argument that said to the Jews of Europe, "You are fit only to make money; you are not fit for the ranks of the army or the halls of Parliament." How cogent the eloquent appeal of Macaulay, — "What right have we to take this question for granted? Throw open the doors of this House of Commons, throw open the ranks of the imperial army, before you deny eloquence to the countrymen of Isaiah or valor to the descendants of the Maccabees." It is the same now with us. Throw open the doors of Congress, throw open those court-houses, throw wide open the doors of your colleges, and give to the sisters of the Motts and the Somervilles the same opportunities for culture that men have, and let the result prove what their capacity and intellect really are. When, I say, woman has enjoyed, for as many centuries as we have, the aid of books, the discipline of life, and the stimulus of fame, it will be time to begin the discussion of these questions, — "What is the intellect of woman?" "Is it equal to that of man?" Till then, all such discussion is mere beating of the air.

While it is doubtless true that great minds, in many cases, make a way for themselves, spite of all obstacles, yet who knows how many Miltons have died "mute and inglorious"? However splendid the natural endowment, the discipline of life, after all, completes the miracle. The ability of Napoleon, — what was it? It grew out of the hope to be Cæsar or Marlborough, — out of Austerlitz and Jena, — out of his battle-fields, his throne, and all the great scenes of that eventful life. Open to woman the same scenes, immerse her in the same great interests and pursuits, and if twenty centuries shall not produce a woman Charlemagne or Napoleon, fair reasoning will then allow us to conclude that there is some distinctive peculiarity in the intellects of the sexes. Centuries alone can lay any fair basis for argument. I believe that, on this point, there is a shrinking consciousness of not being ready for the battle, on the part of *some* of the stronger sex, as they call themselves; a tacit confession of risk to this imagined superiority, if they consent to meet their sisters in the lecture-hall or the laboratory of science. My proof of it is this: that the mightiest intellects of the race, from Plato down to the present time, some of the rarest minds of Germany, France, and England, have successively yielded their assent to the fact that woman is, not perhaps identically, but equally, endowed with man in all intellectual capabilities. It is generally the second-rate men who doubt, — doubt, perhaps, because they fear a fair field: —

"He either fears his fate too much,
Or his deserts are small,
Who fears to put it to the touch,
To gain or lose it all."

But I wish especially to direct your attention to the precise principle which this movement undertakes to urge upon the community. We do not attempt to settle what shall be the profession, education, or employment of woman. We have not that presumption. What we ask is simply this, — what all other classes have asked before: Leave it to woman to choose for herself her profession, her education, and her sphere. We deny to any portion of the species the right to prescribe to any other portion its sphere, its education, or its rights. We deny the right of any individual to prescribe to any other individual his amount of education, or his rights. The sphere of each man, of each woman, of each individual, is that sphere which he can, with the highest exercise of his powers, perfectly fill. The highest act which the human being can do, that is the act which God designed him to do. All that woman asks through this movement is, to be allowed to prove what she can do; to prove it by liberty of choice, by liberty of action, the only means by which it ever can be settled how much and what she can do. She can reasonably say to us: "I have never fathomed the depths of science; you have taught that it was unwomanly, and have withdrawn from me the means of scientific culture. I have never equalled the eloquence of Demosthenes; but you have never quickened my energies by holding up before me the crown and robe of glory, and the gratitude which I was to win. The tools, now, to him or her who can use them. Welcome me, henceforth, brother, to your arena; and let facts — not theories — settle my capacity, and therefore my sphere."

We are not here to-night to assert that woman will

enter the lists and conquer; that she will certainly achieve all that man has achieved; but this we say, "Clear the lists, and let her try." Some reply, "It will be a great injury to feminine delicacy and refinement for woman to mingle in business and politics." I am not careful to answer this objection. Of all such objections, on this and kindred subjects, Mrs. President, I love to dispose in some such way as this: The broadest and most far-sighted intellect is utterly unable to foresee the ultimate consequences of any great social change. Ask yourself, on all such occasions, if there be any element of right and wrong in the question, any principle of clear natural justice that turns the scale. If so, take your part with the perfect and abstract right, and trust God to see that it shall prove the expedient. The questions, then, for me, on this subject, are these: Has God made woman capable — morally, intellectually, and physically — of taking this part in human affairs? Then, what God made her able to do, it is a strong argument that he intended she should do. Does our sense of natural justice dictate that the being who is to suffer under laws shall first personally assent to them? that the being whose industry government is to burden should have a voice in fixing the character and amount of that burden? Then, while woman is admitted to the gallows, the jail, and the tax-list, we have no right to debar her from the ballot-box. "But to go there will hurt that delicacy of character which we have always thought peculiarly her grace." I cannot help that. Let Him who created her capable of politics, and made it just that she should have a share in them, see to it that these rights which he has conferred do not injure the being he created. Is it for any human being to trample on the laws of justice and liberty, from an alleged necessity of helping God govern what he has made? I cannot help God govern his world by telling lies, or doing what my conscience deems unjust. How absurd to deem it necessary that any one should do so! When Infinite Wisdom established the rules of right and honesty, he saw to it that justice should be always the highest expediency.

The evil, therefore, that some timid souls fear to the character of woman, from the exercise of her political rights, does not at all trouble me. "Let education form the rational and moral being, and nature will take care of the woman." Neither do I feel at all disturbed by those arguments addressed to us as to the capacity of woman. I know that the humblest man and the feeblest has the same civil rights, according to the theory of our institutions, as the most gifted. It is never claimed that the humblest shall be denied his civil right, provided he be a man. No. Intellect, even though it reach the Alpine height of a Parker, — ay, setting aside the infamy of his conduct, and looking at him only as an instance of intellectual greatness, to the height of a Webster, — gets no tittle of additional civil right, no one single claim to any greater civil privilege than the humblest individual, who knows no more than the first elements of his alphabet, provided that being is a man (I ought to say, a *white* man). Grant, then, that woman is intellectually inferior to man, — it settles nothing. She is still a responsible, tax-paying member of civil society. We rest our claim on the great, eternal principle, that taxation and representation must be coextensive; that rights and burdens must correspond to each other; and he who undertakes to answer the argument of this Convention must first answer the whole course of English and American history for the last hundred and fifty years. No single principle of liberty has been enunciated, from the year 1688 until now, that does not cover the claim of woman. The State has never laid the basis of right upon the distinction of sex; and no reason has ever been given, except a religious one, — that there are in the records of our religion commands obliging us to make woman an exception to our civil theories, and deprive her of that which those theories give her.

Suppose that woman is essentially inferior to man, — she still has rights. Grant that Mrs. Norton never could be Byron; that Elizabeth Barrett never could have written Paradise Lost; that Mrs. Somerville never could be La Place, nor Sirani have painted the Transfiguration. What then? Does that prove they should be deprived of all civil rights? John Smith never will be, never can be, Daniel Webster. Shall he, therefore, be put under guardianship, and forbidden to vote?

Suppose woman, though equal, to differ essentially in her intellect from man, — is that any ground for disfranchising her? Shall the Fultons say to the Raphaels, "Because you cannot make steam-engines, therefore you shall not vote"? Shall the Napoleons or the Washingtons say to the Wordsworths or the Herschels, "Because you cannot lead armies and govern states, therefore you shall have no civil rights"?

Grant that woman's intellect be essentially different, even inferior, if you choose; still, while our civilization allows her to hold property, and to be the guardian of her children, she is entitled to such education and to such civil rights — voting, among the rest — as will enable her to protect both her children and her estate. It is easy to indulge in *dilettanti* speculation as to woman's sphere and the female intellect; but leave dainty speculation, and come down to practical life. Here is a young widow; she has children, and ability, if you will let her exercise it, to give them the best advantages of education, to secure them every chance of success in life; or, she has property to keep for them, and no friend to rely on. Shall she leave them to sink in the unequal struggles of life? Shall she trust their all to any adviser money can buy, in order to gratify your taste, and give countenance to your nice theories? or shall she use all the powers God has given her for those he has thrown upon her protection? If we consult common sense, and leave theories alone, there is but one answer. Such a one can rightfully claim of society all the civil privileges, and of fashion all such liberty as will best enable her to discharge fully her duties as a mother.

But woman, it is said, may safely trust all to the watchful and generous care of man. She has been obliged to do so hitherto. With what result, let the unequal and unjust legislation of all nations answer. In Massachusetts, lately, a man married an heiress, worth fifty thousand dollars. Dying, about a year after his marriage, he made this remarkably generous and manly will. He left these fifty thousand dollars to her so long as she should remain his widow! [Loud laughter.] These dollars, which he owed entirely to her, which were fairly hers, he left to her, after twelve months' use, on this generous condition, that she should never marry again! Ought a husband to have such unlimited control over the property of his wife, or over the property which they have together acquired? Ought not woman to have a voice in determining what the law shall be in regard to the property of married persons? Often by her efforts, always by her economy, she contributes much to the stock of family wealth, and is therefore justly entitled to a voice in the control and disposal of it. Neither common sense nor past experience encourages her to trust the protection of that right to the votes of men. That

"Mankind is ever weak,
And little to be trusted;
If self the wavering balance strike,
It 's rarely right adjusted," —

is true between the sexes, as much as between individuals.

Make the case our own. Is there any man here willing to resign his own right to vote, and trust his welfare and his earnings entirely to the votes of others? Suppose any class of men should condescendingly offer to settle for us our capacity or our calling, — to vote for us, to choose our sphere for us, — how ridiculously impertinent we should consider it! Yet few have the good sense to laugh at the consummate impertinence with which every bar-room brawler, every third-rate scribbler, undertakes to settle the sphere of the Martineaus and the De Staëls! With what gracious condescension little men continue to lecture and preach on "the female sphere" and "female duties"!

This Convention does not undertake the task of protecting woman. It contends that, in government, every individual should be endowed, as far as possible, with the means of protecting himself. This is far more the truth when we deal with classes. Every class should be endowed with the power to protect itself. Man has hitherto undertaken to settle what is best for woman in the way of education and in the matter of property. He has settled it for her, that her duties and cares are too great to allow her any time to take care of her own earnings, or to take her otherwise legitimate share in the civil government of the country. He has not undertaken to say that the sailor or the soldier, in active service, when he returns from his voyage or his camp, is not free to deposit his vote in the ballot-box. He has not undertaken to say that the manufacturer, whose factories cover whole townships, who is up early and lies down late, who has to borrow the services of scores to help him in the management of his vast estate, — he does not say that such a man cannot get time to study politics, and ought therefore to be deprived of his right to vote with his fellow-citizens. He has not undertaken to say that the lawyer may not vote, though his whole time is spent in the courts, until he knows nothing of what is going on in the streets. O no! But as for woman, her time *must* be all so entirely filled in taking care of her household, her cares must be so extensive, that neither those of soldiers nor sailors nor merchants can be equal to them; she has not a moment to qualify herself for politics! Woman cannot be spared long enough from the kitchen to put in a vote, though Abbott Lawrence can be spared from the counting-house, though General Gaines or Scott can be spared from the camp, though the Lorings and the Choates can be spared from the courts. This is the argument: Stephen Girard cannot go to Congress; he is too busy; therefore, no *man* ever shall. Because General Scott has gone to Mexico, and cannot be President, therefore no *man* shall be. Because A. B. is a sailor, gone on a whaling voyage, to be absent for three years, and cannot vote, therefore no male inhabitant ever shall. Logic how profound! how conclusive! Yet this is the exact reasoning in the case of woman. Take up the newspapers. See the sneers at this movement. "Take care of the children," "Make the clothes," "See that they are mended," "See that the parlors are properly arranged." Suppose we grant it all. Are there no women but housekeepers? no women but mothers? O yes, many! Suppose we grant that the cares of a household are so heavy that they are greater than the cares of the president of a college; that he who has the charge of some hundreds of youths is less oppressed with care than the woman with three rooms and two children; that though President Sparks has time for politics, Mrs. Brown has not. Grant that, and still we claim that you should be true to your theory, and allow to single women those rights which she who is the mistress of a household and mother of a family has no time to exercise.

"Let women vote!" cries one. "Why, wives and daughters might be Democrats, while their fathers and husbands were Whigs. It would never do. It would produce endless quarrels." And the self-satisfied objector thinks he has settled the question.

But, if the principle be a sound one, why not apply it in a still more important instance? Difference of religion breeds more quarrels than difference in politics. Yet we allow women to choose their own religious creeds, although we thereby run the risk of wives being Episcopalians while their husbands are Methodists, or daughters being Catholics while their fathers are Calvinists. Yet who, this side of Turkey, dare claim that the law should compel women to have no religious creed, or adopt that of their male relatives? Practically, this freedom in religion has made no difficulty; and probably equal freedom in politics would make as little.

It is, after all, of little use to argue these social questions. These prejudices never were reasoned up, and, my word for it, they will never be reasoned down. The freedom of the press, the freedom of labor, the freedom of the race in its lowest classes, was never argued to success. The moment you can get woman to go out into the highway of life, and show by active valor what God has created her for, that moment this question is settled forever. One solid fact of a woman's making her fortune in trade will teach the male sex what woman's capacity is. I say, therefore, to women, there are two paths before you in this reform: one is, take all the laws have left you, with a confident and determined hand; the other is, cheer and encourage, by your sympathy and aid, those noble women who are willing to be the pioneers in this enterprise. See that you stand up the firm supporters of those bold and fearless ones who undertake to lead their sisters in this movement. If Elizabeth Blackwell, who, trampling under foot the sneers of the other sex, took her maiden reputation in her hand, and walked the hospitals of Europe, comes back the accomplished graduate of them, to offer her services to the women of America, and to prove that woman, equally with man, is qualified to do the duties and receive the honors and rewards of the healing art, see to it, women, that you greet her efforts with your smiles. Hasten to her side, and open your households to her practice. Demand to have the experiment fairly tried, before you admit that, in your sickness and in your dangers, woman may not stand as safely by your bedside as man. If you will but be true to each other, on some of these points, it is in the power of woman to settle, in a great measure, this question. Why ask aid from the other sex at all? Theories are but thin and unsubstantial air against the solid fact of woman mingling with honor and profit in the various professions and industrial pursuits of life. Would women be true to each other, by smoothing the pathway of each other's endeavors, it is in their power to settle one great aspect of this question, without any statute in such case made and provided. I say, TAKE your rights! There is no law to prevent it, in one half of the instances. If the prejudices of the other sex and the supineness of your own prevent it, there is no help for you in the statute-books. It is for you but to speak, and the doors of all medical hospitals are open for the women by whom you make it known that you intend to be served. Let us have no separate, and therefore necessarily inferior, schools for women. Let us have no poor schools, feebly endowed, where woman must go to gather what help she may, from second-rate professors, in one branch of a profession. No! Mothers, daughters, sisters! say to husband, father, brother, "If this life is dear to you, I intend to trust it, in my hour of danger, to a sister's hand. See to it, therefore, you who are the guides of society and heads of those institutions, if you love your mother, sister, wife, daughter, see to it that you provide these chosen assistants of mine the means to become disciplined and competent advisers in that momentous hour, for I will have no other." When you shall say that, Harvard University, and every other university, and every medical institution, will hasten to open their doors. You who long for the admission of woman to professional life and the higher ranks of intellectual exertion, up, and throw into her scale this omnipotent weight of your determination to be served by her, and by no other! In this matter, what you decide is law.

There is one other light in which this subject is to be considered, — the freedom of ballot; and with a few words upon that, I will close these desultory remarks. As there is no use in educating a human being for nothing, so the thing is an impossibility. Horace Mann says, in the letter which has been read here, that he intends to write a lecture on Woman; and I doubt not he will take the stand which he has always done, that she should be book-taught for some dozen years, and then retire to domestic life, or the school-room. Would he give sixpence for a boy who could only say that he had been shut up for those years in a school? The unfledged youth who comes from college, — what is he? He is a man, and has been subjected to seven years' tutoring; but man though he is, until he has walked up and down the paths of life, until he receives his education in the discipline of the world, in the stimulus of motive, in the hope of gain, in the desire of honor, in the love of reputation, he has got, in nine cases out of ten, no education at all. Profess to educate woman for her own amusement! Profess to educate her in science, that she may go home and take care of her cradle! Teach her the depths of statesmanship and political economy, that she may smile sweetly when her husband comes home! "It is not the education man gets from books," it was well said by your favorite statesman, "but the lessons he learns from life and society, that profit him most highly." "*Le monde est le livre des femmes.*" Of this *book* you deprive her. You give her nothing but man's little printed primers; you make for her a world of dolls, and then complain that she is frivolous. You deprive her of all the lessons of practical out-door life; you deprive her of all the stimulus which the good and great of all nations, all societies, have enjoyed, the world's honors, its gold, and its fame, and then you coolly ask of her, "Why are you not as well disciplined as we are?" I know there are great souls who need no stimulus but love of truth and of growth, whom mere love of labor allures to the profoundest investigations; but these are the exceptions, not the rule. We legislate, we arrange society, for the masses, not the exceptions.

Responsibility is one instrument — a great instrument — of education, both moral and intellectual. It sharpens the faculties. It unfolds the moral nature. It makes the careless prudent, and turns recklessness into sobriety. Look at the young wife suddenly left a widow, with the care of her children's education and entrance into life thrown upon her. How prudent and sagacious she becomes! How fruitful in resources and comprehensive in her views! How much intellect and character she surprises her old friends with! Look at the statesman bold and reckless in opposition; how prudent, how thoughtful, how timid, he becomes, the moment he is in office, and feels that a nation's welfare hangs on his decisions! Woman can never study those great questions that interest and stir most deeply the human mind, until she studies them under the mingled stimulus and check of this responsibility. And until her intellect has been tested by such questions, studied under such influences, we shall never be able to decide what it is.

One great reason, then, besides its justice, why we would claim the ballot for woman, is this: because the great school of this people is the jury-box and the ballot-box. Tocqueville, after travelling in this country, went away with the conviction that, valuable as the jury trial was for the investigation of facts and defence of the citizens, its value even in these respects was no greater than as it was the school of civil education open to all the people. The education of the American citizen is found in his interest in the debates of Congress, — the earnest personal interest with which he seeks to fathom political questions. It is when the mind, profoundly stirred by the momentous stake at issue, rises to its most gigantic efforts, when the great crisis of some national convulsion is at hand, — it is then that strong political excitement lifts the people up in advance of the age, heaves a whole nation on to a higher platform of intellect and morality. Great political questions stir the deepest nature of one half the nation; but they pass far above and over the heads of the other half. Yet, meanwhile, theorists wonder that the first have their whole nature unfolded, and the others will persevere in being dwarfed. Now, this great, world-wide, practical, ever-present education we claim for woman. Never, until it is granted her, can you decide what will be her ability. Deny statesmanship to woman? What! to the sisters of Elizabeth of England, Isabella of Spain, Maria Theresa of Austria; ay, let me add, of Elizabeth Heyrick, who, when the intellect of all England was at fault, and wandering in the desert of a false philosophy, — when Brougham and Romilly, Clarkson and Wilberforce, and all the other great and philanthropic minds of England, were at fault and at a dead-lock with the West India question and negro slavery, — wrote out, with the statesmanlike intellect of a Quaker woman, the simple yet potent charm, — IMMEDIATE, UNCONDITIONAL EMANCIPATION, — which solved the problem, and gave freedom to a race! How noble the conduct of those men! With an alacrity which does honor to their statesmanship, and proves that they recognized the inspired voice when they heard it, they sat down at the feet of that woman-statesman, and seven years under her instruction did more for the settlement of the greatest social question that had ever convulsed England, than had been done by a century, of more or less effort, before. O no! you cannot read history, unless you read it upside down, without admitting that woman, cramped, fettered, excluded, degraded as she has been, has yet sometimes, with one ray of her instinctive genius, done more to settle great questions than all the cumbrous intellect of the other sex has achieved.

It is, therefore, on the ground of natural justice, and on the ground again of the highest expediency, and yet again it is because woman, as an immortal and intellectual being, has a right to all the means of education, — it is on these grounds that we claim for her the civil rights and privileges which man enjoys.

I will not enlarge now on another most important aspect of this question, the value of the contemplated change in a physiological point of view. Our dainty notions have made woman such a hot-house plant, that one half the sex are invalids. The mothers of the next generation are invalids. Better that our women, like the German and Italian girls, should labor on the highway, and share in the toil of harvest, than pine and sicken in the in-door and sedentary routine to which our superstition condemns them. But I leave this sad topic for other hands.

One word more. We heard to-day a very profound and eloquent address as to the course which it is most expedient for woman to pursue in regard to the inadequate remuneration extended to her sex. The woman of domestic life receives but about one third the amount paid to a man for similar or far lighter services. The woman of out-door labor has about the same. The best woman employments are subject to a discount of some forty or fifty per cent on the wages paid to males. It is futile, if it were just, to blame individuals for this. We have all been burdened long by a common prejudice and a common ignorance. The remedy is not to demand that the manufacturer shall pay his workmen more, that the employer of domestics shall pay them more. It is not the capitalist's fault. We inveigh against the wealthy capitalist, but it is not exclusively his fault. It is as much the fault of society itself. It is the fault of that timid conservatism, which sets its face like flint against everything new; of a servile press, which knows so well, by personal experience, how much fools and cowards are governed by a sneer. It is the fault of silly women, ever holding up their idea of what is "*lady-like*" as a Gorgon head to frighten their sisters from earning bread, — themselves, in their folly, the best answer to a weak prejudice they mistake for argument. It is the fault of that pulpit which declares it indecorous in woman to labor, except in certain occupations, and thus crowds the whole mass of working-women into two or three employments, making them rivet each other's chains. Do you ask me the reason of the low wages paid for female labor? It is this. There are about as many women as men obliged to rely for bread on their own toil. Man seeks employment anywhere, and of any kind. No one forbids him. If he cannot make a living by one trade, he takes another; and the moment any trade becomes so crowded as to make wages fall, men leave it, and wages will rise again. Not so with woman. The whole mass of women must find employment in two or three occupations. The consequence is, there are more women in each of these than can be employed; they kill each other by competition. Suppose there is as much sewing required in a city as one thousand hands can do. If the tailors could find only five hundred women to sew, they would be obliged to pay them whatever they asked. But let the case be, as it usually is, that there are five thousand women waiting for that work, unable to turn to any other occupation, and doomed to starve if they fail to get a share of that; we see at once that their labor, being a drug in the market, must be poorly paid for. She cannot say, as man would, "Give me so much, or I will seek another trade." She must accept whatever is offered, and often underbid her sister, that she may secure a share. Any article sells cheap, when there is too much of it in the market. Woman's labor is cheap because there is too much of it in the market. All women's trades are overcrowded, because they have only two or three to choose from. But open to her, now, other occupations. Open to her the studio of the artist, — let her enter there; open to her the office practice, at least, of the lawyers, — let her go there; open to her all in-door trades of society, to begin with, and let women monopolize them. Take from the crowded and starv'ed ranks of the needlewomen of New York some for the arts of design, some for the counter, some to minister in our public libraries, some for our public registries, some to keep merchants' accounts, and some to feel the pulse; and the consequence will be, that, like every other independent laborer, like their male brethren, they may make their own terms, and will be fairly paid for their labor. It is competition in too narrow lists that starves women in our cities; and those lists are drawn narrow by superstition and prejudice.

Woman is ground down, by the competition of her sisters, to the very point of starvation. Heavily taxed, ill-paid, in degradation and misery, is it to be wondered at that she yields to the temptation of wealth? It is the same with men; and thus we recruit the ranks of vice by the prejudices of custom and society. We corrupt the whole social fabric, that woman may be confined to two or three employments. How much do we suffer through the tyranny of prejudice! When we penitently and gladly give to the energy and the intellect and the enterprise of woman their proper reward, their appropriate employment, this question of wages will settle itself; and it will never be settled at all until then.

This question is intimately connected with the great social problem, — the vices of cities. You who hang your heads in terror and shame, in view of the advancing demoralization of modern civilized life, and turn away with horror-struck faces, look back now to these social prejudices, which have made you close the avenues of profitable employment in the face of woman, and reconsider the conclusions you have made! Look back, I say, and see whether you are surely right here. Come up with us and argue the question, and say whether this most artificial delicacy, this childish prejudice, on whose Moloch altar you sacrifice the virtue of so many, is worthy the exalted worship you pay it. Consider a moment. From what sources are the ranks of female profligacy recruited? A few mere giddiness hurries to ruin. Their protection would be in that character and sound common-sense which a wider interest in practical life would generally create. In a few, the love of sensual gratification, grown over-strong, because all the other powers are dormant for want of exercise, wrecks its unhappy victim. The medicine for these would be occupation, awaking intellect, and stirring their highest energies. Give any one an earnest interest in life, something to do, something that kindles emulation, and soon the gratification of the senses sinks into proper subordination. It is idle heads that are tempted to mischief: and she is emphatically idle half of whose nature is unemployed. Why does man so much oftener than woman surmount a few years or months of sensual gratification, and emerge into a worthier life? It is not solely because the world's judgment is so much harder upon her. Man can immerse himself in business that stirs keenly all his faculties, and thus he smothers passion in honorable cares. An ordinary woman, once fallen, has no busy and stirring life in which to take refuge, where intellect will contend for mastery with passion, and where virtue is braced by high and active thoughts. Passion comes back to the "*empty*," though "swept and garnished" chambers, bringing with him more devils than before. But, undoubtedly, the great temptation to this vice is the love of dress, of wealth, and the luxuries it secures. Facts will jostle theories aside. Whether we choose to acknowledge it or not, there are many women, earning two or three dollars a week, who feel that they are as capable as their brothers of earning hundreds, if they could be permitted to exert themselves as freely. Fretting to see the coveted rewards of life forever forbidden them, they are tempted to shut their eyes on the character of the means by which a taste, however short, may be gained of the wealth and luxury they sigh for. Open to man a fair field for his industry, and secure to him its gains, and nine hundred and ninety-nine men out of every thousand will disdain to steal. Open to woman a fair field for her industry, let her do anything her hands find to do, and enjoy her gains, and nine hundred and ninety-nine women out of every thousand will disdain to debase themselves for dress or ease.

Of this great social problem — to cure or lessen the vice of cities — there is no other solution, except what this movement offers you. It is, to leave woman to choose her own employments for herself, responsible, as we are, to the common Creator, and not to her fellow-man. I exhort you, therefore, to look at this question in the spirit in which I have endeavored to present it to you. It is no fanciful, no superficial movement, based on a few individual tastes, in morbid sympathy with tales of individual suffering. It is a great social protest against the very fabric of society. It is a question which goes down — we admit it, and are willing to meet the issue — goes down beneath the altar at which you worship, goes down beneath this social system in which you live. And it is true — no denying it — that, if we are right, the doctrines preached from New England pulpits are wrong; it is true that all this affected horror at woman's deviation from her sphere is a mistake, — a mistake fraught with momentous consequences. Understand us. We blink no fair issue. We throw down the gauntlet. We have counted the cost; we know the yoke and burden we assume. We know the sneers, the lying frauds of misstatement and misrepresentation, that await us. We have counted all; and it is but the dust in the balance and the small dust in the measure, compared with the inestimable blessing of doing justice to one half of the human species, of curing this otherwise immedicable wound, stopping this overflowing fountain of corruption, at the very source of civilized life. Truly, it is the great question of the age. It looks all others out of countenance. It needs little aid from legislation. Specious objections, after all, are not arguments. We know we are right. We only ask an opportunity to argue the question, to set it full before the people, and then leave it to the intellects and the hearts of our country, confident that the institutions under which we live, and the education which other reforms have already given to both sexes, have created men and women capable of solving a problem even more difficult, and meeting a change even more radical, than this.

PUBLIC OPINION.*

MR. PRESIDENT: — I have been thinking, while sitting here, of the different situations of the Antislavery cause now and one year ago, when the last anniversary of this Society was held. To some, it may seem that we had more sources of interest and of public excitement on that occasion than we have now. We had with us, during a portion, at least, of that session, the eloquent advocate of our cause on the other side of the water.† We had the local excitement and the deep interest which the first horror of the Fugitive Slave Bill had aroused. We had, I believe, some fugitives, just arrived from the house of bondage. It may seem to many that, meeting as we do to-day robbed of all these, we must be content with a session more monotonous and less effectual in arousing the community. But when we look over the whole land; when we look back upon what has taken place in our own Commonwealth, at Christiana, at Syracuse; look at the passage through the country of the great Hungarian; at the present state of the public mind, — it seems to me that no year, during the existence of the Society, has presented more encouraging aspects to the Abolitionists. The views which our friend (Parker Pillsbury) has just presented are those upon which, in our most sober calculation, we

* Speech before the Massachusetts Antislavery Society, at the Melodeon, Wednesday evening, January 28, 1852.

† George Thompson, Esq., M. P.

ought to rely. Give us time, and, as he said, talk is all-powerful. We are apt to feel ourselves overshadowed in the presence of colossal institutions. We are apt, in coming up to a meeting of this kind, to ask what a few hundred or a few thousand persons can do against the weight of government, the mountainous odds of majorities, the influence of the press, the power of the pulpit, the organization of parties, the omnipotence of wealth. At times, to carry a favorite purpose, leading statesmen have endeavored to cajole the people into the idea that this age was like the past, and that a "rub-a-dub agitation," as ours is contemptuously styled, was only to be despised. The time has been when, as our friend observed, from the steps of the Revere House — yes, and from the depots of New York railroads — Mr. Webster has described this Antislavery movement as a succession of lectures in school-houses, — the mere efforts of a few hundred men and women to talk together, excite each other, arouse the public, and its only result a little noise. He knew better. He knew better the times in which he lived. No matter where you meet a dozen earnest men pledged to a new idea, — wherever you have met them, you have met the beginning of a revolution. Revolutions are not made: they come. A revolution is as natural a growth as an oak. It comes out of the past. Its foundations are laid far back. The child feels; he grows into a man, and thinks; another, perhaps, speaks, and the world acts out the thought. And this is the history of modern society. Men undervalue the Antislavery movement, because they imagine you can always put your finger on some illustrious moment in history, and say, here commenced the great change which has come over the nation. Not so. The beginning of great changes is like the rise of the Mississippi. A child must stoop and gather away the pebbles to find it. But soon it swells broader and broader, bears on its ample bosom the navies of a mighty republic, fills the Gulf, and divides a continent.

I remember a story of Napoleon which illustrates my meaning. We are apt to trace his control of France to some noted victory, to the time when he camped in the Tuileries, or when he dissolved the Assembly by the stamp of his foot. He reigned in fact when his hand was first felt on the helm of the vessel of state, and that was far back of the time when he had conquered in Italy, or his name had been echoed over two continents. It was on the day when five hundred irresolute men were met in that Assembly which called itself, and pretended to be, the government of France. They heard that the mob of Paris was coming the next morning, thirty thousand strong, to turn them, as was usual in those days, out of doors. And where did this seemingly great power go for its support and refuge? They sent Tallien to seek out a boy lieutenant, — the shadow of an officer, — so thin and pallid that, when he was placed on the stand before them, the President of the Assembly, fearful, if the fate of France rested on the shrunken form, the ashy cheek before him, that all hope was gone, asked, "Young man, can you protect the Assembly?" And the stern lips of the Corsican boy parted only to reply, "I always do what I undertake." Then and there Napoleon ascended his throne; and the next day, from the steps of St. Roche, thundered forth the cannon which taught the mob of Paris, for the first time, that it had a master. That was the commencement of the Empire. So the Antislavery movement commenced unheeded in that "obscure hole" which Mayor Otis could not find, occupied by a printer and a black boy.

In working these great changes, in such an age as ours, the so-called statesman has far less influence than the many little men who, at various points, are silently maturing a regeneration of public opinion. This is a reading and thinking age, and great interests at stake quicken the general intellect. Stagnant times have been when a great mind, anchored in error, might snag the slow-moving current of society. Such is not our era. Nothing but Freedom, Justice, and Truth is of any permanent advantage to the mass of mankind. To these society, left to itself, is always tending. In our day, great questions about them have called forth all the energies of the common mind. Error suffers sad treatment in the shock of eager intellects. "Everybody," said Talleyrand, "is cleverer than anybody"; and any name, however illustrious, which links itself to abuses, is sure to be overwhelmed by the impetuous current of that society which (thanks to the press and a reading public) is potent, always, to clear its own channel. Thanks to the Printing-Press, the people now do their own thinking, and statesmen, as they are styled,—men in office,—have ceased to be either the leaders or the clogs of society.

This view is one that Mr. Webster ridiculed in the depots of New York. The time has come when he is obliged to change his tone; when he is obliged to retrace his steps,—to acknowledge the nature and the character of the age in which he lives. Kossuth comes to this country, penniless, and an exile; conquered on his own soil; flung out as a weed upon the waters; nothing but his voice left;—and the Secretary of State must meet him. Now, let us see what he says of his "rub-a-dub agitation," which consists of the voice only,—of the tongue, which our friend Pillsbury has described. This is that "tongue" which the impudent statesman declared, from the drunken steps of the Revere House, ought to be silenced,—this tongue, which was a "rub-a-dub agitation" to be despised, when he spoke to the farmers of New York.

He says, "We are too much inclined to underrate the power of moral influence." Who is? Nobody but a Revere House statesman. "We are too much inclined to underrate the power of moral influence, and the influence of public opinion, and the influence of the principles to which great men — the lights of the world and of the present age — have given their sanction. Who doubts that, in our struggle for liberty and independence, the majestic eloquence of Chatham, the profound reasoning of Burke, the burning satire and irony of Colonel Barre, had influences upon our fortunes here in America? They had influences both ways. They tended, in the first place, somewhat to diminish the confidence of the British ministry in their hopes of success, in attempting to subjugate an injured people. They had influence another way, because all along the coasts of the country — and all our people in that day lived upon the coast — there was not a reading man who did not feel stronger, bolder, and more determined in the assertion of his rights, when these exhilarating accents from the two Houses of Parliament reached him from beyond the seas."

"I thank thee, Jew!" This "rub-a-dub agitation," then, has influence both ways. It diminishes the confidence of the Administration in its power to execute the Fugitive Slave Law, which it has imposed so insolently on the people. It acts on the *reading men* of the nation, and in that single fact is the whole story of the change. Wherever you have a reading people, there every tongue, every press, is a power. Mr. Webster, when he ridiculed in New York the agitation of the Antislavery body, supposed he was living in the old feudal times, when a statesman was an integral element in the state, an essential power in himself. He must have supposed himself speaking in those ages when a great man outweighed the masses. He finds now that he is living much later, in an age when the accumulated common-sense of the people outweighs the greatest statesman or the most influential individual. Let me illustrate the difference of our times and the past in this matter, by their difference in another respect. The time has been when men cased in iron from head to foot, and disciplined by long years of careful instruction, went to battle. Those were the days of nobles and knights; and in such times, ten knights, clad in steel, feared not a whole field of unarmed peasantry, and a hundred men-at-arms have conquered thousands of the common people, or held them at bay. Those were the times when Winkelried, the Swiss patriot, led his host against the Austrian phalanx, and, finding it impenetrable to the thousands of Swiss who threw themselves on the serried lances, gathered a dozen in his arms, and, drawing them together, made thus an opening in the close-set ranks of the Austrians, and they were overborne by the actual mass of numbers. Gunpowder came, and then any finger that could pull a trigger was equal to the highest born and the best disciplined; knightly armor, and horses clad in steel, went to the ground before the courage and strength which dwelt in the arm of the peasant, as well as that of the prince. What gunpowder did for war, the printing-press has done for the mind, and the statesman is no longer clad in the steel of special education, but every reading man is his judge. Every thoughtful man, the country through, who makes up an opinion, is his jury to which he answers, and the tribunal to which he must bow. Mr. Webster, therefore, does not overrate the power of this "rub-a-dub agitation," which Kossuth has now adopted, "stealing our thunder." [Laughter and applause.] He does not overrate the power of this "rub-a-dub agitation," when he says, "Another great mistake, gentlemen, is sometimes made. [Yes, in Bowdoin Square!] We think nothing powerful enough to stand before despotic power. There is something strong enough, quite strong enough; and if properly exerted, it will prove itself so; and that is, the power of intelligent public opinion." "I thank thee, Jew!" That opinion is formed, not only in Congress, or on hotel steps; it is made also in the school-houses, in the town-houses, at the hearth-stones, in the railroad-cars, on board the steam-boats, in the social circle, in these Antislavery gatherings which he despises. Mark you: *There is nothing powerful enough to stand before it!* It may be a self-styled divine institution; it may be the bank-vaults of New England; it may be the mining interests of Pennsylvania; it may be the Harwich fishermen, whom he told to stand by the Union, because its bunting protected their decks; it may be the factory operative, whom he told to uphold the Union, because it made his cloth sell for half a cent more a yard; it may be a parchment Constitution, or even a Fugitive Slave Bill, signed by Millard Fillmore!!! — no matter, all are dust on the threshing-floor of a reading public, once roused to indignation. Remember this, when you would look down upon a meeting of a few hundreds in the one scale, and the fanatic violence of State Street in the other, that there is NOTHING, Daniel Webster being witness, strong enough to stand against public opinion, — and if the tongue and the press are not parents of that, what is?

Napoleon said, "I fear three newspapers more than a hundred thousand bayonets." Mr. Webster now is of the same opinion. "There is not a monarch on earth," he says, "whose throne is not liable to be shaken by the progress of opinion and the sentiment of the just and intelligent part of the people." "I thank thee, Jew!" We have been told often, that it was nothing but a morbid sentiment that was opposed to the Fugitive Slave Bill, — it was a sentiment of morbid philanthropy. Grant it all. But take care, Mr. Statesman; cure or change it in time, else it will beat all your dead institutions to dust. Hearts and sentiments are alive, and we all know that the gentlest of Nature's growths or motions will, in time, burst asunder or wear away the proudest dead-weight man can heap upon them. If this be the power of the gentlest growth, let the stoutest heart tremble before the tornado of a people roused to terrible vengeance by the sight of long years of cowardly and merciless oppression, and oft-repeated instances of selfish and calculating apostasy. You may build your Capitol of granite, and pile it high as the Rocky Mountains; if it is founded on or mixed up with iniquity, the pulse of a girl will in time beat it down. "There is no monarch on earth whose throne is not liable to be shaken by the sentiment of the just and intelligent part of the people." What is this but a recantation, — doing penance for the impudence uttered in Bowdoin Square? Surely this is the white sheet and lighted torch which the Scotch Church imposed as penance on its erring members. Who would imagine, that the same man who said of the public discussion of the Slavery question, that it must be put down, could have dictated this sentiment, — "It becomes us, in the station which we hold, to let that public opinion, so far as we form it, have free course"? What was the haughty threat we heard from Bowdoin Square a year ago? "This agitation must be put down." Now, "It becomes us, in the station which we hold, to let that public opinion have free course." Behold the great doughface cringing before the calm eye of Kossuth, who had nothing but "rub-a-dub agitation" with which to rescue Hungary from the bloody talons of the Austrian eagle!

This is statesmanship! The statesmanship that says to the Commonwealth of Massachusetts to-day, "Smother those prejudices," and to-morrow, "There is no throne on the broad earth strong enough to stand up against the sentiment of justice." What is that but the "prejudices" of the Commonwealth of Massachusetts against man-hunting? And this is the man before whom the press and the pulpit of the country would have had the Abolitionists bow their heads, and lay their mouths in the dust, instead of holding fast to the eternal principles of justice and right!

It would be idle, to be sure, to base any argument on an opinion of Mr. Webster's. Like the chameleon, he takes his hue, on these subjects, from the air he breathes. He has his "October sun" opinion, and his Faneuil Hall opinions. But the recantation here is at least noticeable; and his testimony to the power of the masses is more valuable as coming from an unwilling witness. The best of us are conscious of being, at times, somewhat awed by the colossal institutions about us, which seem to be opposing our progress. There are those who occasionally weary of this moral suasion, and sigh for something tangible; some power that they can feel, and see its operation. The advancing tide you cannot mark. The gem forms unseen. The granite increases and crumbles, and you can hardly mark either process. The great change in a nation's opinion is the same. We stand here to-day, and if we look back twenty years, we can see a change in public opinion; yes, we can see a great change. Then the great statesmen had pledged themselves not to talk on this subject. They have been made to talk. These hounds have been whipped into the traces of the nation's car, not by *three* newspapers, which Napoleon dreaded, but by *one*. [Cheers.] The great parties of the country have been broken to pieces and crumbled. The great sects have been broken to pieces. Suppose you cannot put your finger upon an individual fact; still, in the great result, you see what Webster tells us in his speech: "Depend upon it, gentlemen, that between these two rival powers, — the autocratic power, maintained by arms and force, and the popular power, maintained by opinion, —

the former is constantly decreasing; and, thank God! the latter is constantly increasing. Real human liberty is gaining the ascendant; — [he must feel sad at that!] — and the part which we have to act in all this great drama is to show ourselves in favor of those rights; to uphold our ascendency, and to carry it on, until we shall see it culminate in the highest heaven over our heads."

Now I look upon this speech as the most remarkable Mr. Webster has ever made on the antislavery agitation to which we are devoted, — as a most remarkable confession, under the circumstances. I read it here and to you, because, in the circle I see around me, the larger proportion are Abolitionists, — men attached to the movement which this meeting represents, — men whose thoughts are occasionally occupied with the causes and with the effects of its real progress. I would force from the reluctant lips of the Secretary of State his testimony to the real power of the masses. I said that the day was, before gunpowder, when the noble, clad in steel, was a match for a thousand. Gunpowder levelled peasant and prince. The printing-press has done the same. In the midst of thinking people, in the long run, there are no so-called "great" men. The accumulated intellect of the masses is greater than the heaviest brain God ever gave to a single man. Webster, though he may gather into his own person the confidence of parties, and the attachment of thousands throughout the country, is but a feather's weight in the balance against the average of public sentiment on the subject of slavery. A newspaper paragraph, a county meeting, a gathering for conversation, a change in the character of a dozen individuals, — these are the several fountains and sources of public opinion. And, friends, when we gather, month after month, at such meetings as these, we should encourage ourselves with considerations of this kind: — that we live in an age of democratic equality; that, for a moment, a party may stand against the age, but in the end it goes by the board; that the man who launches a sound argument, who sets on two feet a startling fact, and bids it travel from Maine to Georgia, is just as certain that in the end he will change the government, as if, to destroy the Capitol, he had placed gunpowder under the Senate-chamber. Natural philosophers tell us, that, if you will only multiply the simplest force into enough time, it will equal the greatest. So it is with the slow intellectual movement of the masses. It can scarcely be seen, but it is a constant movement: it is the shadow on the dial; never still, though never seen to move; it is the tide, it is the ocean, gaining on the proudest and strongest bulwarks that human art or strength can build. It may be defied for a moment, but in the end Nature always triumphs. So the race, if it cannot drag a Webster along with it, leaves him behind and forgets him. [Loud cheers.] The race is rich enough to afford to do without the greatest intellects God ever let the Devil buy. Stranded along the past, there are a great many dried mummies of dead intellects, which the race found too heavy to drag forward.

I hail the almighty power of the tongue. I swear allegiance to the omnipotence of the press. The people never err. "*Vox populi, vox Dei,*" — the voice of the people is the voice of God. I do not mean this of any single verdict which the people of to-day may record. In time, the selfishness of one class neutralizes the selfishness of another. The interests of one age clash against the interests of another; but in the great result the race always means right. The people always mean right, and in the end they will have the right. I believe in the twenty millions — not the twenty millions that live now, necessarily — to arrange this question of slavery, which priests and politicians have sought to keep out of sight

They have kept it locked up in the Senate-chamber, they have hidden it behind the communion-table, they have appealed to the superstitious and idolatrous veneration for the State and the Union to avoid this question, and so have kept it from the influence of the great democratic tendencies of the masses. But change all this, drag it from its concealment, and give it to the people; launch it on the age, and all is safe. It will find a safe harbor. A man is always selfish enough for himself. The soldier will be selfish enough for himself; the merchant will be selfish enough for himself; yes, he will be willing to go to hell to secure his own fortune, but he will not be ready to go there to make the fortune of his neighbor. Rarely is any man willing to sacrifice his own character for the benefit of his neighbor; and whenever we shall be able to show this nation that the interests of a class, not of the whole, the interests of a portion of the country, not of the masses, are subserved by holding our fellow-men in bondage, then we shall spike the guns of the enemy, or get their artillery on our side.

I want you to turn your eyes from institutions to men. The difficulty of the present day and with us is, we are bullied by institutions. A man gets up in the pulpit, or sits on the bench, and we allow ourselves to be bullied by the judge or the clergyman, when, if he stood side by side with us, on the brick pavement, as a simple individual, his ideas would not have disturbed our clear thoughts an hour. Now the duty of each antislavery man is simply this, — Stand on the pedestal of your own individual independence, summon these institutions about you, and judge them. The question is deep enough to require this judgment of you. This is what the cause asks of you, my friends; and the moment you shall be willing to do this, to rely upon yourselves, that moment the truths I have read from the lips of one whom the country regards as its greatest statesman will shine over your path, assuring you that out of this agitation, as sure as the sun shines at noonday, the future character of the American government will be formed.

If we lived in England, if we lived in France, the philosophy of our movement might be different, for there stand accumulated wealth, hungry churches, and old nobles, — a class which popular agitation but slowly affects. To these public opinion is obliged to bow. We have seen, for instance, the agitation of 1848 in Europe, deep as it was, seemingly triumphant as it was for six months, retire, beaten, before the undisturbed foundations of the governments of the Continent. You recollect, no doubt, the tide of popular enthusiasm which rolled from the Bay of Biscay to the very feet of the Czar, and it seemed as if Europe was melted into one republic. Men thought the new generation had indeed come. We waited twelve months, and "the turrets and towers of old institutions — the church, law, nobility, government — reappeared above the subsiding wave." Now there are no such institutions here; — no law that can abide one moment when popular opinion demands its abrogation. The government is wrecked the moment the newspapers decree it. The penny papers of this State in the Sims case did more to dictate the decision of Chief Justice Shaw, than the Legislature that sat in the State-House, or the statute-book of Massachusetts. I mean what I say. The penny papers of New York do more to govern this country than the White House at Washington. Mr. Webster says we live under a government of laws. He was never more mistaken, even when he thought the antislavery agitation could be stopped. We live under a government of men — and morning newspapers. [Applause.] Bennett and Horace Greeley are more really Presidents of the United States than Millard Fillmore. Daniel Webster himself cannot even get a nomination. Why? Because, long ago, the ebbing tide of public opinion left him a wreck, stranded on the side of the popular current.

We live under a government of men. The Constitution is nothing in South Carolina, but the black law is everything. The law that says the colored man shall sit in the jury-box in the city of Boston is nothing. Why? Because the Mayor and Aldermen, and the Selectmen of Boston, for the last fifty years, have been such slaves of colorphobia, that they did not choose to execute this law of the Commonwealth. I might go through the statute-book, and show you the same result. Now if this be true against us, it is true for us. Remember, that the penny papers may be starved into antislavery, whenever we shall put behind them an antislavery public sentiment. Wilberforce and Clarkson had to vanquish the moneyed power of England, the West India interest, and overawe the peerage of Great Britain, before they conquered. The settled purpose of the great middle class had to wait till all this was accomplished. The moment we have the control of public opinion, — the women and the children, the school-houses, the school-books, the literature, and the newspapers, — that moment we have settled the question.

Men blame us for the bitterness of our language and the personality of our attacks. It results from our position. The great mass of the people can never be made to stay and argue a long question. They must be made to feel it, through the hides of their idols. When you have launched your spear into the rhinoceros hide of a Webster or a Benton, every Whig and Democrat feels it. It is on this principle that every reform must take for its text the mistakes of great men. God gives us great scoundrels for texts to antislavery sermons. See to it, when Nature has provided you a monster like Webster, that you exhibit him — himself a whole menagerie — throughout the country. [Great cheering.] It is not often, in the wide world's history, that you see a man so lavishly gifted by nature, and called, in the concurrence of events, to a position like that which he occupied on the seventh of March, surrender his great power, and quench the high hopes of his race. No man, since the age of Luther, has ever held in his hand, so palpably, the destinies and character of a mighty people. He stood like the Hebrew prophet betwixt the living and the dead. He had but to have upheld the cross of common truth and honesty, and the black dishonor of two hundred years would have been effaced forever. He bowed his vassal head to the temptations of the flesh and of lucre. He gave himself up into the lap of the Delilah of slavery, for the mere promise of a nomination, and the greatest hour of the age was bartered away, — not for a mess of pottage, but for the *promise* of a mess of pottage, — a promise, thank God! which is to be broken. [Enthusiastic applause.] I say, it is not often that Providence permits the eyes of twenty millions of thinking people to behold the fall of another Lucifer, from the very battlements of Heaven, down into that "lower deep of the lowest deep" of hell. [Great sensation.] On such a text, how effective should be the sermon!

Let us see to it, that, in spite of the tenderness of American prejudice, in spite of the morbid charity that would have us rebuke the sin, but spare the sinner, in spite of this effeminate Christianity, that would let millions pine, lest one man's feelings be injured, — let us see to it, friends, that we be "harsh as truth and uncompromising as justice"; remembering always, that every single man set against this evil may be another Moses, every single thought you launch may be the thunders of another Napoleon from the steps of another St. Roche; remembering that we live not in an age of individual despotism, when a Charles the Fifth could set up or put down the slave-trade, but surrounded by twenty millions, whose opinion is omnipotent, — that the hundred gathered in a New England school-house may be the hundred who shall teach the rising men of the other half of the continent, and stereotype Freedom on the banks of the Pacific; remembering and worshipping reverentially the great American idea of the omnipotence of "thinking men," of the "sentiment of justice," against which no throne is potent enough to stand, no Constitution sacred enough to endure. Remember this, when you go to an antislavery gathering in a school-house, and know that, weighed against its solemn purpose, its terrible resolution, its earnest thought, Webster himself, and all huckstering statesmen, in the opposite scale, shall kick the beam. Worshipping the tongue, let us be willing, at all times, to be known throughout the community as the all-talk party. The age of bullets is over. The age of men armed in mail is over. The age of thrones has gone by. The age of statesmen — God be praised! *such* statesmen — is over. The age of thinking men has come. With the aid of God, then, every man I can reach I will set *thinking* on the subject of slavery. [Cheers.] The age of reading men has come. I will try to imbue every newspaper with Garrisonianism. [Loud applause.] The age of the masses has come. Now, Daniel Webster counts one. Give him joy of it! — but the "rub-a-dub agitation" counts at least twenty, — nineteen better. Nineteen, whom no chance of nomination tempts to a change of opinions once a twelvemonth; who need no Kossuth advent to recall them to their senses.

What I want to impress you with is, the great weight that is attached to the opinion of everything that can call itself a man. Give me anything that walks erect, and can read, and he shall count one in the millions of the Lord's sacramental host, which is yet to come up and trample all oppression in the dust. The weeds poured forth in nature's lavish luxuriance, give them but time, and their tiny roots shall rend asunder the foundations of palaces, and crumble the Pyramids to the earth. We may be weeds in comparison with these marked men; but in the lavish luxuriance of that nature which has at least allowed us to be "thinking, reading men," I learn, Webster being my witness, that there is no throne potent enough to stand against us. It is morbid enthusiasm this that I have. Grant it. But they tell us that this heart of mine, which beats so unintermittedly in the bosom, if its force could be directed against a granite pillar, would wear it to dust in the course of a man's life. Your Capitol, Daniel Webster, is marble, but the pulse of every humane man is beating against it. God will give us time, and the pulses of men shall beat it down. [Loud and enthusiastic cheering.] Take the mines, take the Harwich fishing-skiffs, take the Lowell mills, take all the coin and the cotton, still the day must be ours, thank God, for the hearts — the hearts are on our side!

There is nothing stronger than human prejudice. A crazy sentimentalism like that of Peter the Hermit hurled half of Europe upon Asia, and changed the destinies of kingdoms. We may be crazy. Would to God he would make us all crazy enough to forget for one moment the cold deductions of intellect, and let these hearts of ours beat, beat, beat, under the promptings of a common humanity! They have put wickedness into the statute-book, and its destruction is just as certain as if they had put gunpowder under the Capitol. That is my faith. That it is which turns my eye from the ten thousand newspapers, from the forty thousand pulpits, from the millions of Whigs, from the millions of Democrats, from the might of sect, from the marble government, from the iron army, from the navy riding at anchor, from all that we are accustomed to deem great and potent, — turns it back to the simplest child or woman, to the first murmured protest that is heard against bad laws. I recognize in it the great future, the first rumblings of that volcano destined to overthrow these mighty preparations, and bury in the hot lava of its full excitement all this laughing prosperity which now rests so secure on its side.

All hail, Public Opinion! To be sure, it is a dangerous thing under which to live. It rules to-day in the desire to obey all kinds of laws, and takes your life. It rules again in the love of liberty, and rescues Shadrach from Boston Court-House. It rules to-morrow in the manhood of him who loads the musket to shoot down — God be praised! — the man-hunter, Gorsuch. [Applause.] It rules in Syracuse, and the slave escapes to Canada. It is our interest to educate this people in humanity, and in deep reverence for the rights of the lowest and humblest individual that makes up our numbers. Each man here, in fact, holds his property and his life dependent on the constant presence of an agitation like this of antislavery. Eternal vigilance is the price of liberty: power is ever stealing from the many to the few. The manna of popular liberty must be gathered each day, or it is rotten. The living sap of to-day outgrows the dead rind of yesterday. The hand intrusted with power becomes, either from human depravity or *esprit de corps*, the necessary enemy of the people. Only by continual oversight can the democrat in office be prevented from hardening into a despot: only by unintermitted agitation can a people be kept sufficiently awake to principle not to let liberty be smothered in material prosperity. All clouds, it is said, have sunshine behind them, and all evils have some good result; so slavery, by the necessity of its abolition, has saved the freedom of the white race from being melted in the luxury or buried beneath the gold of its own success. Never look, therefore, for an age when the people can be quiet and safe. At such times Despotism, like a shrouding mist, steals over the mirror of Freedom. The Dutch, a thousand years ago, built against the ocean their bulwarks of willow and mud. Do they trust to that? No. Each year the patient, industrious peasant gives so much time from the cultivation of his soil and the care of his children to stop the breaks and replace the willow which insects have eaten, that he may keep the land his fathers rescued from the water, and bid defiance to the waves that roar above his head, as if demanding back the broad fields man has stolen from their realm.

Some men suppose that, in order to the people's governing themselves, it is only necessary, as Fisher Ames said, that the "Rights of Man be printed, and that every citizen have a copy." As the Epicureans, two thousand years ago, imagined God a being who arranged this marvellous machinery, set it going, and then sunk to sleep. Republics exist only on the tenure of being constantly agitated. The antislavery agitation is an important, nay, an essential part of the machinery of the state. It is not a disease nor a medicine. No; it is the normal state, — the normal state of the nation. Never, to our latest posterity, can we afford to do without prophets, like Garrison, to stir up the monotony of wealth, and reawake the people to the great ideas that are constantly fading out of their minds, — to trouble the waters, that there may be health in their flow. Every government is always growing corrupt. Every Secretary of State is, by the very necessity of his position, an apostate. [Hisses and cheers.] I mean what I say. He is an enemy to the people, of necessity, because the moment he joins the government, he gravitates against that popular agitation which is the life of a republic. A republic is nothing but a constant overflow of lava. The principles of Jefferson are not up to the principles of to-day. It was well said of Webster, that he knows well the Hancock and Adams of 1776, but he does not know the Hancocks and Adamses of to-day. The republic which sinks to sleep, trusting to constitutions and machinery, to politicians and statesmen, for the safety of its liberties, never will have any. The people are to be waked to a new effort, just as the Church has to be regenerated, in each age. The antislavery agitation is a necessity of each age, to keep ever on the alert this faithful vigilance, so constantly in danger of sleep. We must live like our Puritan fathers, who always went to church, and sat down to dinner, when the Indians were in their neighborhood, with their musket-lock on the one side and a drawn sword on the other.

If I had time or voice to-night, I might proceed to a further development of this idea, and I trust I could make it clear, which I fear I have not yet done. To my conviction, it is Gospel truth, that, instead of the antislavery agitation being an evil, or even the unwelcome cure of a disease in this government, the youngest child that lives may lay his hand on the youngest child that his gray hairs shall see, and say: "The agitation was commenced when the Declaration of Independence was signed; it took its second tide when the Antislavery Declaration was signed in 1833, — a movement, not the cure, but the diet of a free people, — not the homœopathic or the allopathic dose to which a sick land has recourse, but the daily cold water and the simple bread, the daily diet and absolute necessity, the manna of a people wandering in the wilderness." There is no Canaan in politics. As health lies in labor, and there is no royal road to it but through toil, so there is no republican road to safety but in constant distrust. "In distrust," said Demosthenes, "are the nerves of the mind." Let us see to it that these sentinel nerves are ever on the alert. If the Alps, piled in cold and still sublimity, be the emblem of Despotism, the ever-restless ocean is ours, which, girt within the eternal laws of gravitation, is pure only because never still. [Long-continued applause.]

SURRENDER OF SIMS.*

MR. PRESIDENT: I do not feel disposed to talk about Colonization to-night, and I am glad to think that, after the remarks already submitted to us, it is unnecessary anything more should be said on that topic. I mean, the colonization of black men to Africa. I have been *colonized* myself from this hall for some time; and in getting here again, I prefer to go back to the old note, and try to get the "hang of this school-house." [Laughter.] You know Baron Munchausen says, in one of his marvellous stories, that it was so cold one day in Russia, when he began to play a tune on his trumpet, that half of it froze in the instrument before it could get out; and a few months afterwards, he was startled, in Italy, to hear, of a sudden, the rest of the tune come pealing forth. We were somewhat frozen up a while ago in this hall, with George Thompson on the platform; now we want the rest of the tune. [Laughter and cheers.]

The *Mail* of this morning says that we have no right to this hall, because it was refused to the greatest statesman in the land, — to Daniel Webster. I believe this is a mistake. The Mayor and Aldermen went to him, metaphorically, on their knees, and entreated the great man to make use of the old walls. It was the first time Faneuil

* Speech before the Massachusetts Antislavery Society, at Faneuil Hall, Friday evening, January 30, 1852.

Hall ever begged anybody to enter it; but Daniel was pettish, and would not come. Very proper in him, too; it is not the place in which to defend the Fugitive Slave Bill. He did right when he refused to come. Who built these walls? Peter Faneuil's ancestors were themselves fugitives from an edict *almost* as cruel as the Fugitive Slave Law; and only he whose soul and body refuse to crouch beneath inhuman legislation has a right to be heard here, — nobody else. [Cheers.] A Huguenot built this hall, who was not permitted to live on the soil of his own beautiful France, and it may naturally be supposed that he dedicated it to the most ultra, outside idea of liberty. It is a place for the running slave to find a shelter, — not for a recreant statesman. [Deafening cheers.]

This hall has never been made ridiculous but once; never was made the laughing-stock of New England but once. That was about nine months ago, when the "Sims brigade" were left soundly asleep here, in the gray of the morning, while the awkward squad of Marshal Tukey stole down State Street with Thomas Sims, not deigning to ask their permission or their aid, and leaving them to find out, the next morning, that the great deed had been done, without their so much as "hearing a noise." Soldiers asleep in Faneuil Hall, while mischief was doing so near as State Street? O what gallant soldiers they must have been! [Loud laughter and cheers.]

Times have changed since we were here before. The last time I stood on this platform, there sat beside me a heroine worthy to sit in the hall of the old Huguenot, — one Elizabeth Blakeley, a mulatto girl, of Wilmington, N. C., who, loving freedom more than slavery, concealed herself on board a Boston brig, in the little narrow passage between the side of the vessel and the partition that formed the cabin, — two feet eight inches of room. There she lay while her inhuman master, almost certain she was on board the vessel, had it smoked with sulphur and tobacco three times over. Still she bore it. She came North, half frozen, in the most inclement month of the year, — this month. She reached Boston just able to crawl. Where did she come? O those were better times then! She came here. Just able to stand, fresh from that baptism of suffering for liberty, she came *here.* We told her story. And with us that night — within ten feet of where I stand — sat Fredrika Bremer, the representative of the literature of the Old World; and her humane sympathies were moved so much, that the rose-bud she held in her hand she sent (honoring me by sending it by my hand) to the first representative of American slavery she had seen. It was the tribute of Europe's heart and intellect to a heroine of the black race, in Faneuil Hall. Times have changed since. Not to speak of the incense which Miss Bremer has, half ignorantly, I hope, laid on the demon altar of our land, it would not be safe to put that Betsey Blakeley on this platform to-night; it would not be safe for her to appear in a public meeting. What has changed this public opinion? I wish it was some single man. I wish it was some official of the city, that so we could make him the scapegoat of public indignation, let him carry it forth, and thus the fair fame of our city be freed. This, Mr. President, brings me to my subject. The resolutions I wish to speak to are these. I think they ought to be read in Faneuil Hall, at this, the first meeting the Abolitionists have held here since the foul deed of April 12th disgraced the city. I feel that these peddling hucksters of State and Milk Streets owe me full atonement for the foul dishonor they have brought upon the city of my birth.

"*Resolved*, That, as citizens of Boston and the Commonwealth, we record our deep disapprobation and indignant protest against the surrender of Thomas Sims by the city, its sanction of the cowardly and lying policy of the police, its servile and volunteer zeal in behalf of the man-hunters, and its deliberate, wanton, and avowed violation of the laws of the Commonwealth, for the basest of all purposes, — slave-trading, selling a free man into bondage, that State Street and Milk Street might make money."

Next we come to that man [John P. Bigelow] who stood at yonder door, looking on, while George Thompson was mobbed from this platform; who, neither an honorable Mayor nor a gentleman, broke at once his oath of office and his promise as a gentleman to give us this hall for certain eighty dollars to be paid him, and when he had stood by and seen us mobbed out of it, thought he mended his character by confessing his guilt, in not daring to send in a bill!

"*Resolved*, That the circumstances of the case will not allow us to believe that this infamous deed was the act of the City Government only; and then, as Boston-born men, some of us, comforting ourselves in the reflection that the fawning sycophant who disgraced the Mayor's chair was not born on the peninsula whose fair fame he blotted; but all the facts go to show, that in this, as in all his life, he was only the easy and shuffling tool of the moneyed classes, and therefore too insignificant to be remembered with any higher feeling than contempt.

"*Resolved*, That we cherish a deep and stern indignation towards the judges of the Commonwealth, who, in personal cowardice, pitiful subserviency, utter lack of official dignity, and entire disregard of their official oaths, witnessed in silence the violation of laws they were bound to enforce, and disgraced the Bench once honored by the presence of a Sedgwick and a Sewall."

I do not forget that the Church, all the while this melancholy scene was passing, stood by and upheld a merciless people in the execution of an inhuman law, accepted the barbarity, and baptized it "Christian duty."

O no, I do not forget this! But I remember that, in an enterprising, trading city like ours, the merchants are full as much, if not more, responsible for the state of public opinion, than the second-rate men who rather occupy than fill our pulpits, and who certainly seldom tempt the brains of their hearers to violate the command of the Jewish Scriptures, "Thou shalt not do any work on the Sabbath day."

Do you ask why the Abolitionists denounce the traders of Boston? It is because the merchants chose to send back Thomas Sims, — pledged their individual aid to Marshal Tukey, in case there should be any resistance; it is because the merchants did it to make money. Thank God, they have not made any! [Great cheering.] Like the negro who went to hear Whitefield, and rolled in the dust in the enthusiasm of his religious excitement, until they told him it was *not* Whitefield, when he picked himself up, crying out, "Then I dirty myself for nothing," so they dirtied themselves for nothing! [Tremendous cheering.] If only slave-hunting can save them, may bankruptcy sit on the ledger of every one of those fifteen hundred scoundrels who offered Marshal Tukey their aid! [Tumultuous applause.]

There is one thing to be rejoiced at, — it is this: the fact that the police of this city did not dare even to arrest a fugitive slave, calling him such. The dogs of Marshal Tukey that arrested Thomas Sims in Richmond Street had to disguise themselves to do it, — dressed in the costume and called themselves watchmen; and told a lie, — that the arrest was for theft, — in order to keep peace in the street, while they smuggled him into a carriage. Claim, for the honor of Boston, that, when her police became man-hunters, they put their badges in their pockets, and lied, lest their prey should be torn from their grasp, in the first burst of popular indignation. It was the first time in Boston — I hope it will be the last — that the laws were obliged to be executed by lying and behind bayonets, in the night. So much, though it be very little, may still be said for Boston, — that Sims was arrested by lying and disguised policemen; he was judged by a Commissioner who sat behind bayonets; and was carried off in the gray of the morning, after the moon set, and before the sun rose, by a police body armed with swords. She was disgraced, but it was by force; while, the reverse of the Roman rule, *cedant arma togæ*, the robe gave way to the sword. The law was executed; but it was behind bayonets. Such laws do not last long. [Loud cheers.] Courts that sit behind chains seldom sit more than once. [Renewed cheering.]

[A Voice: "The Whigs defend it."]

O, I know that Mr. Choate has been here, — I heard him, and before a Whig caucus, defend the policy of the Fugitive Slave Bill. He told us, while I sat in yonder gallery, of the "infamous ethics,"— the "*infamous ethics*, that from the Declaration of Independence and the Sermon on the Mount deduced the duty of immediate emancipation." The sentiment was received, I am thankful to say, with a solemn silence, though Rufus Choate uttered it to an assembly of Webster Whigs. I heard it said to-day, that the Abolitionists had done nothing, because a fugitive, within the last twelve months, had been taken out of Boston. They have done a great deal since, sixteen or seventeen years ago, Peleg Sprague, standing on this platform, pointed to this portrait, [the portrait of Washington,] and called him "that slaveholder." It is not now considered a merit in Washington that he held slaves; men apologize for it now. I stood in this hall, sixteen years ago, when "Abolitionist" was linked with epithets of contempt, in the silver tones of Otis, and all the charms that a divine eloquence and most felicitous diction could throw around a bad cause were given it; the excited multitude seemed actually ready to leap up beneath the magic of his speech. It would be something, if one must die, to die by such a hand, — a hand somewhat worthy and able to stifle antislavery, if it could be stifled. The orator was worthy of the gigantic task he attempted; and thousands crowded before him, every one of their hearts melted by that eloquence, beneath which Massachusetts had bowed, not unworthily, for more than thirty years. I came here again last fall, — the first time I had been here, in a Whig meeting, since listening to Otis. I found Rufus Choate on the platform. Compared with the calm grace and dignity of Otis, the thought of which came rushing back, he struck me like a monkey in convulsions. [Roars of laughter and cheers.] Alas! I said, if the party which has owned Massachusetts so long, which spoke to me, as a boy, through the lips of Quincy and Sullivan, of Webster and Otis, has sunk down to the miserable sophistry of this mountebank! — and I felt proud of the city of my birth, as I looked over the murmuring multitude beneath me, on whom his spasmodic chatter fell like a wet blanket. [Great laughter and cheering.] He did not dare to touch a second time on the Fugitive Slave Bill. He tried it once, with his doctrine of "infamous ethics," and the men were as silent as the pillars around them. Ah! thought I, *we* have been here a little too often; and if we have not impressed the seal of our sentiments very deeply on the people, they have at least learned that immediate emancipation, though possibly it be a dream, is not "infamous ethics"; and that such doctrine, the Declaration of Independence and the Sermon on the Mount, need more than the flashy rhetoric of a Webster retainer to tear them asunder. [Great cheering.]

The judges of the Commonwealth, — the judges of the Commonwealth, — I have something to say of them. I wish sometimes we lived in England, and I will tell you why. Because John Bull has some degree of self-respect left. There is an innate, dogged obstinacy in him, that would never permit the successors of a Hale, a Buller, a Mansfield, or a Brougham, to stoop beneath any chain that a city constable could put round Westminster Hall. I was once a member of the profession myself, but glad I am so no longer, since the head of it has bowed his burly person to Francis Tukey's chain. [Cheers.] Did he not know that he was making history that hour, when the Chief Justice of the Commonwealth entered his own court, bowing down like a criminal beneath a chain four feet from the soil? Did he not recollect he was the author of that decision which shall be remembered when every other case in Pickering's Reports is lost, declaring the slave Med a free woman the moment she set foot on the soil of Massachusetts, and that he owed more respect to himself and his own fame than to disgrace the ermine by passing beneath a chain? There is something in emblems. There is something, on great occasions, even in the attitude of a man. Chief Justice Shaw betrayed the bench and the courts of the Commonwealth, and the honor of a noble profession, when for any purpose, still more for the purpose of enabling George T. Curtis to act his melancholy farce in peace, he crept under a chain into his own court-room. And, besides, what a wanton and gratuitous insult it was! What danger was there, with two hundred men inside the court-house, and three hundred men around it on the sidewalk? Near five hundred sworn policemen in and around that building, — what need for any chain? It was put there in wanton insult to the feelings of the citizens of Boston, — nothing else; in wanton servility to the Slave Power, — nothing else; in wanton flattery to Daniel Webster. Yes, it was the gratuitousness of the insult that makes it all the more unbearable! And the "old chief," as we loved to call him, made himself, in timid servility, party to the insult and the degradation. How truly American! Ah, our slave system by no means exists only on Southern plantations!

We are said to be unreasonable in this manner of criticising the institutions, laws, and men of our country. It is thought that, as little men, we are bound to tune our voices and bow our heads to the great intellects, as they are called, of the land, — Mr. Webster and others. He tells us, that there are certain important interests concerned in this question, which we are bound to regard, and not abstract theories about the equality of men, and the freedom of humble individuals. Well, all I say to that is, when dollars are to be discussed, let him discuss them with Franklin Haven, in the directors' room of the Merchants' Bank. Let him discuss them over the bursting ledgers of Milk Street, that is the place for dollar talks. But there is no room for dollars in Faneuil Hall. The idea of liberty is the great fundamental principle of this spot, — that a man is worth more than a bank-vault. [Loud cheers.]

I know Mr. Webster has, on various occasions, intimated that this is not statesmanship in the United States; that the cotton-mills of Lowell, the schooners of Cape Cod, the coasters of Marblehead, the coal and iron mines of Pennsylvania, and the business of Wall Street are the great interests which this government is framed to protect. He intimated, all through the recent discussion, that property is the great element this government is to stand by and protect, — the test by which its success is to be appreciated. Perhaps it is so; perhaps it is so; and if the making of money, if ten per cent a year, if the placing of one dollar on the top of another, be the highest effort of human skill; if the answer to the old Puritan catechism, "What is the chief end of man?" is to be changed, as, according to modern state craft it ought to be, why, be it so. Nicholas of Russia made a catechism for the Poles, in which they are taught that Christ is next below God, and the Emperor of all the Russias is next below Christ. So, judging by the tenor of his recent speeches, Daniel has got a new catechism, "What is the chief end of man?" The old one of the Westminster divines, of Selden and Hugh Peters, of Cotton and the Mathers, used to answer, "To glorify God and enjoy him forever"; that is Kane-treason, now. The "chief end of man"?—why, it is to save the Union!

A Voice.—"Three cheers for the Union!"

Mr. Phillips.—Feeble cheers those!—[Great applause]—and a very thankless office it is to defend the Union on that lay. Did you ever read the fable of the wolf and the house-dog? The one was fat, the other gaunt and famine-struck. The wolf said to the dog, "You are very fat." "Yes," replied the dog, "I get along very well at home." "Well," said the wolf, "could you take me home?" "O, certainly." So they trotted along together; but as they neared the house, the wolf caught sight of several ugly scars on the neck of the dog, and, stopping, cried, "Where did you get those scars on your neck? they look very sore and bloody." "O," said the dog, "they tie me up at night, and I have rather an inconvenient iron collar on my neck. But that 's a small matter; they feed me well." "On the whole," said the wolf, "taking the food and the collar together, I prefer to remain in the woods." Now, if I am allowed to choose, I do not like the collar of Daniel Webster and Parson Dewey, and there are certain ugly scars I see about their necks. I should not like, Dr. Dewey, to promise to return my mother to slavery; and, Mr. Webster, I prefer to be lean and keep my "prejudices," to getting fat by smothering them. I do not like your idea of the Yankee character, which seems to be too near that of the Scotchman, of whom Dr. Johnson said, that, if he saw a dollar on the other side of hell, he would make a spring for it at the risk of falling in. [Laughter.] Under correction of these great statesmen and divines, I cannot think this the *beau ideal* of human perfection. I do not care whether the schooners of Harwich, under slaveholding bunting, catch fish and keep them or not; I do not care whether the mills of Abbott Lawrence make him worth two millions or one, whether the iron and coal mines of Pennsylvania are profitable or not, if, in order to have them profitable, we must go down on our marrow-bones and thank Daniel Webster for saving his Union, call Mayor Bigelow an honorable man and Mayor, and acknowledge Francis Tukey as Chief Justice of the Commonwealth. I prefer hunger and the woods to the hopeless task of maintaining the sincerity of Daniel Webster, or bending under the chain of Francis Tukey. [Tremendous cheering.]

Sir, I have something to say of this old Commonwealth. I went up one day into the Senate-chamber of Massachusetts, in which the Otises, the Quincys, and the Adamses, Parsons and Sedgwick, Sewall and Strong, have sat and spoke in times gone by, — in which the noblest legislation in the world, on many great points of human concern, has made her the noblest State in the world, — the good old Commonwealth of Massachusetts, — and I stood there to see this impudent City Marshal tell the Senate of Massachusetts that he knew he was trampling on the laws of the Commonwealth, and that he intended to do so, as Mayors told him to! And there was not spirit enough in the Free Soil party, — no, nor in the Democratic party, — there was not self-respect enough in the very Senators who were sworn to maintain these laws, to defend them against this insolent boast of a city constable. Now, fellow-citizens, you may, and probably do, think me a fanatic; till you judge men and things on different principles, I do not care much what you think me; I have outgrown that interesting anxiety: but I tell you this, if I see the Commonwealth upside down, I mean to keep my neck free enough from collars to say so; and I think it is upside down when a city constable dictates law in the Senate-chamber of Massachusetts. [Loud cheers.]

Mr. President, let me add one thing more. For Francis Tukey I have no epithet of contempt or of indignation. He may, and does, for aught I know, perform his duties as City Marshal efficiently and well. I know he would, had he been present, have done his duty, and his deputy stood ready to do it that night in George Thompson's presence, if we had really had a Mayor, and not a lackey in the Mayor's chair. [Great laughter and cheering.] I find little fault, comparatively, with the City Marshal of Boston, that he did the infamous duty which the merchants of Boston set him. The fault that I rather choose to note is, that the owner of the brig Acorn can walk up State Street, and be as honored a man as he was before; that John H. Pearson walks our streets as erect as ever, and no merchant shrinks from his side. But we will put the fact that he owned that brig, and the infamous uses he made of it, so blackly on record, that his children — yes, HIS CHILDREN — will gladly, twenty years hence, forego all the wealth he will leave them to blot out that single record. [Enthusiastic applause.] The time shall come when it will be thought the unkindest thing in the world for any one to remind the son of that man that his father's name was John H. Pearson, and that he owned the Acorn. [Renewed cheering.]

[At this point a voice called out, "Three cheers for John H. Pearson." After what had been said from the platform, such a call was not likely to be very warmly responded to; but one or two voices were raised, and Mr. Phillips continued.]

Yes, it is fitting that the cheer should be a poor one, when, in the presence of that merchant [pointing to the portrait of John Hancock], of that merchant who led the noblest movement for civil liberty ever made on this side the ocean, — when in his presence you attempt to cheer this miserable carrier of slaves, who calls himself, and alas! according to the present average of State Street, has a right to call himself, a Boston merchant.

I want to remark one other change, since we were shut out of Faneuil Hall. It is this. Within a few months, I stood in this hall, when Charles Francis Adams was on the platform; — a noble representative, a worthy son, let me say in passing, of the two Adamses who hung here above him. While here he had occasion to mention the name of Daniel Webster, as I have once or twice to-night, and it was received with cheer on cheer, four, five, and six times repeated during the course of his speech. In fact, he could hardly go on for the noisy opposition. That was at a time when some men were crazy enough to think that Daniel would yet be nominated for the Presidency; but those gaudy soap-bubbles have all burst. ["Three cheers for Daniel Webster."] Yes, three cheers for Sir Pertinax M'Sycophant, who all his life long has been bowing down to the Slave Power to secure the Presidency; willing to sacrifice his manhood for the *promise* of a mess of pottage, and destined to be outwitted at last. [Cheers.] Three cheers for the man who, after "many great and swelling words" against Texas, when finally the question of the Mexican war was before the Senate, did not dare to vote, but dodged the question, afraid to be wholly Southerner or Northerner, and striving in vain to outdo Winthrop in facing both ways. [Cheers.] Three cheers for the man who went into Virginia, and, under an "October sun" of the Old Dominion, pledged himself — the recreant New-Englander! — to silence on the slave question; a pledge infamous enough in itself, but whose infamy was doubled when he broke it only to speak against the slave on the 7th of March, 1850. Three cheers for him! [They were given, but so faintly, that a shout of derision went up from the whole audience.] Three cheers for the statesman who said on the steps of the Revere House that "this agitation must be put down," and the agitationists have entered Faneuil Hall before him. [Great applause.] Three cheers for the man who could afford no better name to the Abolitionists than "rub-a-dub agitators," till Kossuth found no method but theirs to chain the millions to himself; and then this far-sighted statesman discovered that "there were people inclined to underrate the influence of public opinion." [Laughter.] Three cheers for the man who gave the State a new motive to send Horace Mann back to Washington, lest we should be thought guilty abroad of shocking bad taste in the old imperial tongue of the Romans. [Laughter.] Three cheers for the man — (O, I like to repeat the Book of Daniel!) — three cheers for "the Whig, the Massachusetts Whig, the Faneuil Hall Whig," who came home to Massachusetts, — his own Massachusetts, the State he thought he owned, body and soul, — who came home to Massachusetts, and lobbied so efficiently as to secure the election of Charles Sumner to the Senate of the United States. [Loud cheers.]

[A voice: "Three cheers for Charles Sumner." Overwhelming applause. "Three cheers for Webster." Mr. Phillips continued: —]

Faintly given, those last; but I do not much care, Mr. Chairman, which way the balance of cheers goes in respect to the gentleman whose name has just been mentioned [Mr. Webster]. It is said, you know, that when Washington stood before the surrendering army of Cornwallis, some of the American troops, as Cornwallis came forward to surrender his sword, began, in very bad taste, to cheer. The noble Virginian turned to them and said, "Let posterity cheer for us"; and they were silent. Now, if Daniel Webster has done anything on the subject of slavery which posterity will not have the kindness to forget, may he get cheers for it, fifty years hence, and in this hall; using my Yankee privilege, however, "I rather guess" some future D'Israeli will be able to put that down in continuation of his grandfather's chapter of "events that never took place." I much, I very much doubt, whether, fifty years hence, Massachusetts will not choose men with back-bones to send to Washington; not men who go there to yield up to the great temptations, social and political, of the capital, the interests and the honor of Massachusetts and New England. I believe, no matter whether the Abolitionists have done much or little, that the average of political independence has risen within the last ten or fifteen years. I know that strange sounds have been heard from the House of Representatives and the Senate within the last ten or fifteen years: that the old tone so often breathed there of Northern submission has very much changed since John Quincy Adams vindicated free speech on the floor of that House. I read just now a speech worthy, in some respects, of Faneuil Hall, from the lips of Robert Rantoul, in rebuke of a recreant Abolitionist from the banks of the Connecticut (George T. Davis). I know not what may be the future course of Mr. Rantoul on this question; I know not how erect he may stand hereafter; but I am willing to give him good credit in the future, so well paid has been this his first bill of exchange. [Great cheering.] He has done, at least, his duty to the constituency he represented. He looked North for his instructions. The time has been when no Massachusetts representative looked North; we saw only their backs. They have always looked to the Southern Cross; they never turned their eyes to the North Star. They never looked back to the Massachusetts that sent them. Charles Allen and Horace Mann, no matter how far they may be from the level of what we call antislavery, show us at least this cheering sign. While speaking, they have turned their faces toward Massachusetts. They reflect the public opinion of the State they represent. They look to Faneuil Hall, not to "the October sun of the Old Dominion." Now, Mr. Chairman, if we can come to this hall, year after year; if we can hold these meetings; if we can sustain any amount of ridicule for the sake of antislavery; if we can fill yonder State-House with legislative action that shall vindicate the old fame of the State; if we can fill every town-house and school-house in the State with antislavery agitation, — then the eyes of every caucus and every political meeting, and of Congress, will all turn North, and, God willing, they shall see a North worth looking at. We will have better evidence than the somewhat apocryphal assurance of Mr. Webster, at Marshfield, in '48, that the North Star is at last discovered. There will not only be a shrine, but worshippers. [Cheers.]

I have not the voice to detain this meeting any longer. I am rejoiced to find myself again in Faneuil Hall. I am glad it has so happened that the very first meeting of the Massachusetts Antislavery Society since April 12th, 1851, has been within these walls, and that the first note of their rebuke of the city government, and of the Milk Street interest whose servant it stooped to be, has been from the platform of Faneuil Hall. [Applause.]

SIMS ANNIVERSARY.*

MR. CHAIRMAN: There is a resolution on your table to this effect: —

"*Resolved, Therefore,* That we advise all colored persons, liable to these arrests, to leave the United States, unless they are fully resolved to take the life of any officer who shall attempt, under any pretext, to seize them; and we urge the formation in every town of vigilance committees, prepared to secure to every person claimed as a slave the fullest trial possible, and to avail themselves fearlessly, according to their best judgment, of all the means God and Nature have put into their hands, to see that substantial justice be done."

To this Mr. Garrison moves as an amendment the following: —

"*Resolved,* That if 'resistance to tyrants,' by bloody weapons, 'is obedience to God,' and if our Revolutionary fathers were justified in wading through blood to freedom and independence, then every fugitive slave is justified in arming himself for protection and defence, — in taking the life of every marshal, commissioner, or other person who attempts to reduce him to bondage; and the millions who are clanking their chains on our soil find ample warrant in rising *en masse,* and asserting their right to liberty, at whatever sacrifice of the life of their oppressors.

"*Resolved,* That the State in which no fugitive slave can remain in safety, and from which he must flee in order to secure

* Speech at the Melodeon, on the First Anniversary of the Rendition of Thomas Sims, April 12, 1852.

his liberty in another land, is to be held responsible for all the crimes and horrors which cluster about the slave-system and the slave-trade, — and that State is the Commonwealth of Massachusetts."

I incline to the first form, rather than to that suggested by my friend, though such is my conviction of the soundness of his judgment and his rare insight into all the bearings of our cause, that I distrust my own deliberate judgment, when it leads me to a different conclusion from his.

I am, however, strongly impressed with the conviction, that the friends of the cause and the fugitives among us need some advice; and that we cannot make a better use of this occasion than to discuss what that advice shall be. Mr. Garrison's amendment seems to me too ambiguous; it contents itself with announcing an important principle, but suggests nothing, and advises nothing.

Why, Mr. Chairman, do we assemble here on such a melancholy occasion as the present? This, instead of last Thursday, should be our Fast Day, if there were any reason for us to fast at all, — for on this day, twelve months ago, the Abolitionists of the Commonwealth suffered a great, a melancholy defeat. On that day, unexpectedly to many, a man was carried back to slavery from the capital of the State. It was an event which surprised some of our fellow-citizens, and all the rest of New England, which relied too fondly on the reputation Massachusetts had won as an antislavery community. Either the flavor of our old religion, or some remnant of the spirit of 1649 and 1776, had made the city of the Puritans a house of refuge to the fugitive. They had gathered here, and in our neighborhood, by hundreds. There are traditions of attempts to seize one now and then, — sometimes of trials in open court; and it is possible that, in the general indifference, a few may have been carried back quietly by some underling official, though we have no certain knowledge of any case where the victim was not finally saved. Thomas Sims is the first man that the city of Boston ever openly bound and fettered, and sent back to bondage. I have no heart to dwell on so horrible an outrage: — that sad procession, in the dim morning, through our streets, — the poor youth, — his noble effort to break his chains, — mocked with one short hour of freedom, and then thrust back to the hell he had escaped, by brother men, in the prostituted names of justice and religion. We sit down with the single captive, and weep with him as the iron enters into his soul, — too sad to think, for the moment, of the disgrace of our city, or even the wickedness of its rulers. Pity swallows up indignation. We might be forgiven if for the moment we mistook our sadness for despair, and even fancied the event disastrous to others than the victim. But not so. Liberty knows nothing but victories. In a cause like ours, to which every attribute of the Most High is pledged, "everything helps us." Selfish commerce, huckstering politics, and the mocking priest, might turn from such a scene and congratulate each other, saying, "Our mountain stands strong"; but we knew that emotions were stronger than statutes, more lasting than ledgers, and not to be frozen down even by creeds, and that all New England would erelong gather itself to answer the last sad question of this hapless victim, as he stepped on the piratical deck of the Acorn, — "Is this Massachusetts liberty?"

What, then, is the use of such a celebration as this? It seems to me the only possible use that could, in any circumstances, be made of such an occasion, would be to record our protest against the deed, with an indignant rebuke of its perpetrators, and to direct our eyes forward to see what we can now do for men in like jeopardy with Sims. Our protest and our rebuke have been already uttered. It is needless to repeat them. The individuals who so infamously misused their little brief authority have, some of them, faded from the public eye, — melted back into the mass of their fellow-slaves. Their names are not worth recalling, for they are not of mark enough to point a moral. Let them pass, all of them; — the judge who stood head and shoulders above the rest in brutal bearing and the arts of a demagogue; the commissioner, whom the atmosphere of noble enthusiasm about him never betrayed, during all that eventful week, into even the semblance of an honorable emotion; the counsellor who pledged a word, till then undoubted, to that lie for which no guaranty but his could have won even a momentary credence, and the belief of which snapped the last tiny thread of hope that bound the hapless victim to the altar of Massachusetts criminal law.

Yes, let them pass. The few whom charity may hope sinned, unable to "discern between their right hand and their left hand," and the many who did just right enough to prove they knew their duty, but wallowed in the wrong so greedily as to show how much they loved it. Let History close the record. Let her allow that "on the side of the oppressor there was power," — power "to frame mischief by a law"; that on that side were all the *forms* of law, and behind those forms, most of the elements of control: wealth, greedy of increase, and anxious for order, at any sacrifice of principle, — priests prophesying smooth things, and arrogating to themselves the name of Christianity, — ambition, baptizing itself statesmanship, — and that unthinking patriotism, child of habit and not of reason, which mistakes government for liberty and law for justice. And, on the other hand, let her allow that, though the Abolitionists were heedful of the hour, and fearless against the prelates of the Church,

"to plead her cause,
And from our judges vindicate the laws," —

while they "did not spare the tyrant one hard word," — they were strictly law-abiding citizens. While judges and executives deserted their posts, the Abolitionists violated no law. They begged for nothing but the law, — they wearied themselves to obtain the simple legal rights guaranteed to them and to all by the State. The city government, in direct defiance of the statute of 1843, aided, both directly and indirectly, in the arrest and detention of a person claimed as a slave. To effect this purpose, they violated the commonest rights of the citizens, — shut them out of their own court-house, — subjected them from day to day to needless, illegal, and vexatious arrests. Judges were "Artful Dodgers," and sheriffs refused all processes. The Abolitionists exhausted every device, besieged every tribunal, implored the interference of every department, to obtain the bare execution of the law of the Commonwealth. And let History say beside, that meantime they fearlessly declared that resistance would be better than submission; while not so absurd as to throw one man, or a score of men, against a government in arms, they proclaimed that they would have been glad to see the people rise against the law, — that nothing which a handful of men could do for such an end was wanting, — that they denounced the church sanctioning the deed as "a synagogue of Satan," and the law, whether constitutional or not, as mere tyranny and wickedness, its executioners worse than murderers, — that, knowing the value of a true law and real order, they said and believed, that rather than one man should be sent back to slavery, better, far better, human laws should be trampled under foot, and the order of society broken every day.

When the pulpit preached slave-hunting, and the law bound the victim, and society said, "Amen! this will make money," we were "fanatics," — "enthusiasts," — "seditious, — "disorganizers," — "scorners of the pulpit," —

"traitors." Genius of the Past! drop not from thy tablets one of these honorable names. We claim them all as our surest title-deeds to the memory and gratitude of mankind. We indeed thought man more than constitutions, humanity and justice of more worth than law. Seal up the record! If Boston is proud of her part, let her rest assured we are not ashamed of ours!

All this has been said so often, that it is useless to dwell on it now. The best use that we can now make of this occasion, it seems to me, is to look about us, take our bearings, and tell the fugitives, over whom yet hangs this terrible statute, what course, in our opinion, they should pursue.

And, in the first place, it is neither frank nor honest to keep up the delusive idea that a fugitive slave can be protected in Massachusetts. I hope I am mistaken; I shall be glad to be proved incorrect; but I do not believe there is any such antislavery sentiment here as is able to protect a fugitive on whom the government has once laid its hand. We were told this afternoon, from this platform, that there were one hundred and fifty men in one town ready to come with their muskets to Boston, — all they waited for was an invitation. I heard, three weeks before the Sims case, that there were a hundred in one town in Plymouth County pledged to shoulder their muskets in such a cause. We saw nothing of them. I heard, three weeks after the Sims rendition, that there were two hundred more in the city of Worcester ready to have come, had they been invited. We saw nothing of them. On such an occasion, from the nature of the case, there cannot be much previous concert; the people must take their own cause into their own hands. Intense earnestness of purpose, pervading large classes, must instinctively perceive the crisis, and gather all spontaneously for the first act which is to organize revolution. When the Court was in pursuit of John

Hampden, we are not told that the two thousand men who rode up to London the next morning, to stand between their representative and a king's frown, waited for an invitation. They assembled of their own voluntary and individual purpose, and *found* themselves in London. Whenever there is a like determination throughout Massachusetts, it will need no invitation. When, in 1775, the British turned their eyes toward Lexington, the same *invitation* went out from the Vigilance Committee of Mechanics in Boston, as in our case of April, 1851. Two lanterns on the North Church steeple telegraphed the fact to the country; Revere and Prescott, as they rode from house to house in the gray light of that April morning, could tell little what others would do, — they flung into each house the startling announcement, "The red-coats are coming!" and rode on. None that day issued orders, none obeyed aught but his own soul. Though Massachusetts rocked from Barnstable to Berkshire, when the wire flashed over the land the announcement that a slave lay chained in the Boston court-house, there was no answer from the antislavery feeling of the State. It is sad, therefore, but it seems to me honest, to say to the fugitive in Boston, or on his way, that, if the government once seize him, he cannot be protected here. I think we are bound, in common kindness and honesty, to tell them that there are but two ways that promise any refuge from the horrors of a return to bondage: one is to fly, — to place themselves under the protection of that government, which, with all her faults, has won the proud distinction that slaves cannot breathe her air, — the fast-anchored isle of empire, where tyrants and slaves may alike find refuge from vengeance and oppression. AND THIS IS THE COURSE I WOULD ADVISE EVERY MAN TO ADOPT. THIS, UNLESS THERE ARE, IN HIS PARTICULAR CASE, IMPERATIVE REASONS TO THE CONTRARY, IS HIS DUTY. If this course be impossible, then the other way is to arm himself, and by resistance secure in the Free States a trial for homicide, — trusting that no jury will be able so far to crush the instincts of humanity as not to hold him justified.

But some one may ask, Why countenance, even by a mention of it, this public resistance, — you, whose whole enterprise repudiates force? Because this is a very different question from that great issue, the abolition of slavery. On that point, I am willing to wait. I can be patient, no matter how often that is defeated by treacherous statesmen. The cause of three millions of slaves, the destruction of a great national institution, must proceed slowly; and, like every other change in public sentiment, we must wait patiently for it, and there the best policy is, beyond all question, the policy of submission; for that gains, in time, on public sympathy. But this is a different case. Who can ask the trembling, anxious fugitive to stop and submit patiently to the overwhelming chances of going back, that his fate may, in some indirect manner, and far-off hour, influence for good the destiny of his fellow-millions? Such virtue must be self-moved. Who could stand and ask it of another? True, Thomas Sims returned is a great public event, calculated to make Abolitionists; but the game sickens me when the counters are living men. We have no right to use up fugitives for the manufacture of antislavery sentiment. There are those who hang one man to benefit another, and to create a wholesome dread of crime. I shrink from using human life as raw material for the production of any state of public opinion, however valuable. I do not think we have a right to use up fugitive slaves in this pitiless way, in order to extend or deepen an antislavery sentiment. At least, I have no right to use them so, without their full consent. It seems to me, therefore, we are bound to tell those who have taken refuge under the laws of Massachusetts, what they must expect here. The time was when we honestly believed they might expect protection. That time, in my opinion, has passed by. I do not certainly know that there will be any taken this year or next. I do not know when they may choose again to take another man from Boston. But I *do* know, that just so soon as any other miscreant Webster [hisses and cheers] shall think it necessary to lay another fugitive slave on the altar of his Presidential chances, just so soon will another be taken from the streets of Boston. I note those hisses. Do not understand me that Mr. Webster himself will ever find it worth while again to ask this act of vassal service from his retainers. O no! wait a few months, and his fate will be that of Buckingham: —

> "wicked but in will, of means bereft,
> He left not faction, but of that was left."

But even though he die or be shelved, the race of traitors will not be extinct; and it is a sickening dread for these two or three hundred men and women to live with this law, worse than the sword of Damocles, hanging over their heads. I believe the Abolitionists of the country owe it to their brethren to tell them what policy should rule their conduct in the present crisis. To be sure, you may ask them to stay, and, when they are taken, to submit, and let the fact appeal to the sympathies of the country, which will result in kindling public indignation; and if they choose, from deep religious convictions, to make themselves thus the food of antislavery growth, God bless them for the heroic self-sacrifice which dictates such a course. But I cannot ask of a poor, friendless, broken-hearted fellow-creature such a momentous sacrifice. I do say, in private, to every one that comes to me, "But one course is left for you. There is no safety for you here; there is no law for you here. The hearts of the judges are stone, the hearts of the people are stone. It is in vain that you appeal to the Abolitionists. They may be ready, may be able, ten years hence." But the "brace of Adamses," to which our friend [Theodore Parker] alluded this morning, if they had mistaken 1765 for 1775, would have ended at the scaffold instead of the Declaration of Independence and the treaty of 1783. We must bide our time, and we must read, with anointed eyes, the signs of our time. If public opinion is wrong, we want to know it; know it, that we may remodel it. We will ourselves trample this accursed Fugitive Slave Law under foot. [Great cheering.] But we are a minority at present, and cannot do this to any great practical effect; we are bound to suggest to these unfortunates who look to us for advice, some feasible plan. This, in my view, should be our counsel: "Depart if you can,—if you have time and means. As no one has a right to ask that you stay, and, if arrested, submit, in order that your case may convert men to antislavery principles; so you have no right, capriciously, to stay and resist, merely that your resistance may rouse attention, and awaken antislavery sympathy. It is a grave thing to break into the bloody house of life. The mere expectation of good consequences will not justify you in taking a man's life. You have a perfect right to live where you choose. No one can rightfully force you away. There may be important and sufficient reasons, in many cases, why you should stay and vindicate your right at all hazards. But in common cases, where no such reasons exist, it is better that you surrender your extreme right to live where you choose, than assert it in blood, and thus *risk* injuring the movement which seeks to aid your fellows. Put yourselves under the protection of the British flag; appeal to the humanity of the world. Do not linger here." Does any friend of the cause exclaim, "You take away the great means of antislavery agitation! The sight of a slave carried back to bondage is the most eloquent appeal the antislavery cause can make to the sympathies of the public." I know it! but the gain is all too dear when it is bought by the sacrifice of one man, thrust back to the hell of American bondage. Still, circumstances may prevent flight, imperative reasons may exist why he should remain here: he may be seized before he succeeds in escaping. I say to him, then, There is a course left, if you have the courage to face it. There is one appeal left, which has not yet been tried; it may avail you; I cannot insure you even that. It has now reached that pass when even the chance of a Boston gibbet may be no protection from a Georgia plantation; but if I were in your place, I would try! [Tremendous cheering.] The sympathies of the people will gather round you, if put on trial for such an act. The mortal hatred which would set the hounds of the law, thirsty for our blood, on keener scent, if we stood charged with legal offences, would not reach you. I do not know that the state-prison would be any refuge from the jail at Savannah or Charleston; but there may be something in an appeal to a Massachusetts jury impanelled to try a man's INALIENABLE right to liberty, the pursuit of happiness, and to protect himself; and I hope — I dare not hope much, but I do hope — that there is still humanity enough to bring you in "not guilty." There is another point. I really believe if a jury of Boston merchants should steel themselves to a verdict of guilty, that a Governor sitting in the seat of Samuel Adams or Henry Vane would never dare to sign the warrant, until he had secured a passage on board a Cunard steamer. I think, therefore, that it is possible an appeal to the criminal jurisdiction of the State might save a man. Perhaps it might be just that final blow which would stun this drunken nation into sobriety, and make it heed, at last, the claims of the slave.

Mark me! I do not *advise* any one to take the life of

his fellow, — to brave the vengeance of the law, and run the somewhat, after all, unequal risk of the hard technical heart of a Massachusetts jury. Such an act must be, after all, one's own impulse. To burst away from all civil relations, to throw one's self back on this great primal right of self-protection, at all hazards, must be the growth of one's own thought and purpose. I can only tell the sufferer the possibilities that lie before him, — tell him what I would do in his case, — tell him that what I would do myself I would countenance another in doing, and aid him to the extent of my power.

The antislavery cause is a wonder to many. They wonder that it does not succeed faster. We see William Cobbett, with his Political Register, circulating seventy thousand copies per week, appeal to the workingmen of Great Britain, and in a few years he carries his measures over the head of Parliament. Cobden talks the farmers of England, in less than ten years, out of a tyranny that had endured for generations. The difference is, we have no such selfish motives to appeal to. We appeal to white men, who cannot see any present interest they have in the slave question. It is impossible to stir them. They must ascend to a level of disinterestedness which the masses seldom reach, before we can create any excitement in them on the question of slavery. I do not know when that point will be gained. If we shall ever be able to reach, through the press, the millions of non-slaveholding white men in the Southern States, I think we shall have a parallel then to the course of English agitation; for we can then appeal to the selfish interest of white men, able to vote, to speak, and to act on this subject. But at present we have to make men interested, indignant, enthusiastic for others, not for themselves. The slave question halts and lingers, because it cannot get the selfishness of men on its side; and that, after all, has been the lever by which the greatest political questions have been carried.

There is one other motive; that is, fear. Cobbett and his fellows gathered the people of Great Britain in public meetings of two hundred thousand men; and though the Duke of Wellington ordered his Scotch Greys to rough-grind their swords, as at Waterloo, he feared to order them drawn in the face of two hundred thousand Englishmen. That gathering was for their own rights. Cross the Channel, and you come to the Irish question. How was that dealt with? By fear. When Ireland got no sympathy from the English people, she so ordered her affairs that the dread of anarchy, anchored so close to Liverpool and Bristol, forced the government to treat the question, and they treated it by submission.

Now, I read my lesson in the light of this historical experience. I cannot yet move the selfishness of the white man to help me. On this question I cannot get it on my side. It is just possible that the fugitive slave, taking his defence into his own right hand, and appealing to the first principle of natural law, may so excite the sympathy of some and the fears of others, as to gain the attention of all, and force them to grapple with this problem of slavery and the Fugitive Slave Bill. The time may come when Massachusetts may not be willing to have her cities scenes of bloodshed, in order that one over-ambitious man may gain his point, and smooth his path to the Presidency; or that a human being should be hurried into bondage, that rich men may add field to field and house to house.

I have striven to present this point as slowly, as fully, as deliberately as possible, because I know it is an important one. It is, in some sense, the launching of a new measure in the antislavery enterprise, to countenance the fugitive, who has tried in vain every avenue of escape, in standing even at last at bay, and protecting himself. But

I know of no pledge of the antislavery cause against it. Our enterprise is pledged to nothing but the abolition of slavery. When we set out, we said we would do our work under the government and under the Church. We tried it. We found that we could not work in either way; we found it necessary to denounce the Church and withdraw from the government. We did what we could to work through both. We saw that it was expedient to work through them both, if we could. Finding it impossible, we let experience dictate our measures. We came out. Consistency — *consistency* bade us come out. CONSISTENCY, — we cannot always sail due east, though our destination be Europe. It is no violation of consistency, therefore, (if that were of any consequence,) for us to adopt a measure like this, though it was not at first contemplated.

I go further. I do not believe that, if we should live to the longest period Providence ever allots to the life of a human being, we shall see the total abolition of slavery, unless it comes in some critical conjuncture of national affairs, when the slave, taking advantage of a crisis in the fate of his masters, shall dictate his own terms. How did French slavery go down? How did the French slave-trade go down? When Napoleon came back from Elba, when his fate hung trembling in the balance, and he wished to gather around him the sympathies of the liberals of Europe, he no sooner set foot in the Tuileries than he signed the edict abolishing the slave-trade, against which the Abolitionists of England and France had protested for twenty years in vain. And the trade went down, because Napoleon felt that he must do something to gild the darkening hour of his second attempt to clutch the sceptre of France. How did the slave system go down? When, in 1848, the Provisional Government found itself in the Hôtel de Ville, obliged to do something to draw to itself the sympathy and liberal feeling of the French nation, they signed an edict — it was the first from the nascent Republic — abolishing the death-penalty and slavery. The storm which rocked the vessel of state almost to foundering, snapped forever the chain of the French slave. Look, too, at the history of Mexican and South American emancipation; you will find that it was, in every instance, I think, the child of convulsion.

The hour will come — God hasten it! — when the American people shall so stand on the deck of their Union, "built i' th' eclipse, and rigged with curses dark." If I live to see that hour, I shall say to every slave, Strike now for Freedom! [Long-continued and deafening cheers.] The balance hangs trembling; it is uncertain which scale shall kick the beam. Strain every nerve, wrestle with every power God and nature have put into your hands, for your place among the races of this Western world"; and that hour will free the slave. The Abolitionist who shall stand in such an hour as that, and keep silence, will be recreant to the cause of three million of his fellow-men in bonds. I believe that probably is the only way in which we shall ever, any of us, see the downfall of American slavery. I do not shrink from the toast with which Dr. Johnson flavored his Oxford Port, — "Success to the first insurrection of the blacks in Jamaica!" I do not shrink from the sentiment of Southey, in a letter to Duppa, — "There are scenes of tremendous horror which I could smile at by Mercy's side. An insurrection which should make the negroes masters of the West Indies is one." I believe both these sentiments are dictated by the highest humanity. I know what anarchy is. I know what civil war is. I can imagine the scenes of blood through which a rebellious slave-population must march to their rights. They are dreadful. And yet, I do not know that, to an enlightened mind, a scene of civil war is any more sickening than the thought of a hundred and fifty years of slavery. Take the broken hearts, the bereaved mothers, the infant wrung from the hands of its parents, the husband and wife torn asunder, every right trodden under foot, the blighted hopes, the imbruted souls, the darkened and degraded millions, sunk below the level of intellectual life, melted in sensuality, herded with beasts, who have walked over the burning marl of Southern slavery to their graves, and where is the battle-field, however ghastly, that is not white — white as an angel's wing — compared with the blackness of that darkness which has brooded over the Carolinas for two hundred years? [Great sensation.] Do you love mercy? Weigh out the fifty thousand hearts that have beaten their last pulse amid agonies of thought and suffering fancy faints to think of, and the fifty thousand mothers who, with sickening senses, watch for footsteps that are not wont to tarry long in their coming, and soon find themselves left to tread the pathway of life alone, — add all the horrors of cities sacked and lands laid waste, — that is war, — weigh it now against some young, trembling girl sent to the auction-block, some man like that taken from our court-house and carried back into Georgia; multiply this individual agony into three millions; multiply that into centuries; and that into all the relations of father and child, husband and wife; heap on all the deep moral degradation both of the oppressor and the oppressed, — and tell me if Waterloo or Thermopylæ can claim one tear from the eye even of the tenderest spirit of mercy, compared with this daily system of hell amid the most civilized and Christian people on the face of the earth!

No, I confess I am not a non-resistant. The reason why I advise the slave to be guided by a policy of peace is because he has no chance. If he had one, — if he had as good a chance as those who went up to Lexington seventy-seven years ago, — I should call him the basest recreant that ever deserted wife and child if he did not vindicate his liberty by his own right hand. [Cheers.] And I am not by any means certain that Northern men would not be startled — would not be wholesomely startled — by one or two such cases as a scoundrel Busteed shot over his perjured affidavit. If a Morton or a Curtis could be shot on the commissioner's bench by the hand of him they sought to sacrifice, I have no doubt that it would have a wholesome effect. [Great applause.] Is there a man here who would, if he had arms in his hands, either himself go to Georgia, or let any one near and dear to him go there, without sending somebody before him to a lighter and cooler place than a Georgian plantation?

I am not dealing with the cause of three millions of slaves. I am not dealing with the question of a great sin and wrong existing among us. I believe I understand the philosophy of reform. I understand the policy of waiting. I know that, in reforming great national abuses, we cannot expect to be in haste; that the most efficient protection for the three million of slaves is to eradicate the prejudice of the twenty millions of whites who stand above them. I have learnt all that. But, Mr. Chairman, the question to which I speak is a very different one. It is this. "I, William Crafts, an independent, isolated individual in myself, am no more called to secure the safety of three million of slaves than you are. I, William Crafts, have succeeded in getting to Boston. I have reached what is called free territory. It happens that there are strong and sufficient reasons why I cannot leave these shores, or cannot YET leave them. I have got possession of arms. I have inquired of the most intelligent men, and they tell me that the laws afford me no protection. I have asked of the highest authorities on government my duty in this emergency, and they tell me, one and all, from Grotius down to Lord Brougham, that when government ceases to protect, the citizen ceases to owe allegiance.* Very well. My case stands by itself. It is for me to decide to-night whether I will go back to Georgia to-morrow. It is no special comfort to assure me that, half a century hence, somebody will go down to Faneuil Hall, — some Robert C. Winthrop, perhaps, converted for the occasion, — and pronounce an oration on the jubilee of American freedom. It is no answer to tell me that, in order to this, it is considered by some people to be a great thing that the fugitive should go willingly and quietly back to slavery. There comes up to me a man who says he is an officer, and has a parchment warrant in his pocket. Somebody has given him authority to seize me. I am not to be bullied by institutions. I am not to be frightened by parchments. Forms and theories are nothing to me. Majorities are nothing. You have outlawed me from your law. You have exiled me from your protection. I am a descendant of Esau, — every man's hand against me, my hand against every man. I have no time or means of escape, no defence, except I make it. If I make it, I secure the hour of liberty and escape. I decide to make it. I shoot the miscreant, and thus gain time to pass from the spot where I was to have been arrested, to freedom under the flag of England or on the deck of a vessel." Let him who fully knows his own heart and strength, and feels, as he looks down into his child's cradle, that he could stand by and

* "Protection, your Lordships are aware, affording security of person and property, is the first law of the state. The Legislature has no right to claim obedience to its laws, the Crown has no right to demand allegiance from its subjects, if the Legislature and the Crown do not afford, in return for both, protection for person and property. Without protection, the Legislature would abdicate its functions, if it demanded obedience; without protection, the Crown would be a usurper of its right to enforce allegiance." — *Lord Brougham's Debate on the Irish Coercion Bill*, 1833.

see that little nestling one borne away, and submit, — let him cast the first stone. But all you whose blood is wont to stir over Naseby and Bunker Hill will hold your peace, unless you are ready to cry, with me, *Sic semper tyrannis!* So may it ever be with slave-hunters!

Mr. Chairman, it seems to me that the man who is not conscientiously a non-resistant, is not only entitled, he is bound, to use every means that he has or can get to resist arrest in the last resort. What is the slave, when he is once surrendered? He goes back to degradation worse than death. If he has children, they are to perpetuate that degradation. He has no right to sacrifice himself or them to that extent. These are considerations which it is just as well to state, and to bring before the community. I know my friend, Mr. Garrison, differs from me on this question. You will listen to him. I shall not quarrel if you agree with his judgment, and leave me alone. I am talking to-night to the men who say they were ready to take up their muskets in defence of Thomas Sims, or Shadrach, or somebody else. It is very well for fiction — for a Harriet Beecher Stowe — to paint a submissive slave, and draw a picture that thrills your hearts. You are very sensitive over "Uncle Tom's Cabin." Your nerves are very sensitive; see that your consciences are as sensitive as your nerves. If your hearts answered instead of your nerves, you would rise up every one of you Abolitionists, ready to sacrifice everything rather than a man should go back to slavery. Let me see that effect, and then I will reckon the value of the tears that have answered to the wand of this magician; but till then, they are but the tears of a nervous reader under high excitement. Would those tears could crystallize into sentiment, crystallize into principle, — into Christian principle, out of which the weapon of antislavery patience and perseverance and self-sacrifice is to be wrought! Guard yourselves, friends, against the delusive idea, that the tears and sad eyes you see about you are harbingers of a better hour for Massachusetts than this day twelve months saw darken over her fame. It may be so; but there is no certainty that it will. We are to speak to practical Massachusetts. I do not shrink from going before the farmers, the mechanics, and the workingmen, — the thinking men of Massachusetts, — and urging upon them the consideration that the State, by solemn act, has proclaimed to every one that her soil is not holy enough to protect the fugitive, and that, so far as she is concerned, the only thing left, the only possibility, the only chance remaining for the fugitive, lies in his own courage and good right arm. The city of John Hancock has proved that her soil is not holy enough to protect the fugitive; Faneuil Hall, where "still the eloquent air breathes, burns," with Otis and Adams, is not holy enough to shelter the fugitive; Bunker Hill, red with the blood of the noblest men who ever fell in the cause of civil liberty, is not too sacred for fettered feet; the churches, planted, as we have been told to-day, in tears, in prayers, and in blood, have no altar-horns for the fugitive; the courts, even that which first naturalized Lord Mansfield's decision, drawing a nice distinction between slaves *brought* and slaves *escaping*, — judges loving humanity so well, even in the humblest suitor, that, like their noble predecessors in the great case of DeVere, they "caught hold of a twig or a twine thread to uphold it"; — that, too, has shut its doors on the fugitive, — yes, against that very child Med, should she again be seized, in whose behalf they settled this proud rule. I would say all this to the men about me, and add, — There is one gleam of hope. It is just possible that the floor of the State's prison may have a magic charm in it. That may save the fugitive, if he can once entitle himself to a place there. When, therefore, the occasion shall demand, let us try it! [Great cheering.] It is a sad thought, that the possibility of a gibbet, the chance of imprisonment for life, is the only chance which can make it prudent for a fugitive to remain in Massachusetts.

You will say this is bloody doctrine, — anarchical doctrine; it will prejudice people against the cause. I know it will. Heaven pardon those who make it necessary! Heaven pardon the judges, the merchants, and the clergy, who make it necessary for hunted men to turn, when they are at bay, and fly at the necks of their pursuers! It is not our fault! I shrink from no question, however desperate, that has in it the kernel of possible safety for a human being hunted by twenty millions of slave-catchers in this Christian republic of ours. [Cheers.] I am willing to confess my faith. It is this: that the Christianity of this country is worth nothing, except it is or can be made capable of dealing with the question of slavery. I am willing to confess another article of my faith: that the Constitution and government of this country is worth nothing, except it is or can be made capable of grappling with the great question of slavery. I agree with Burke: "*I have no idea of a liberty unconnected with honesty and justice. Nor do I believe that any good constitutions of government or of freedom can find it necessary for their security to doom any part of the people to a permanent slavery. Such a constitution of freedom, if such can be, is in effect no more than another name for the tyranny of the strongest faction;* and factions in republics have been and are full as capable as monarchs of the most cruel oppression and injustice." That is the language of Edmund Burke to the electors of Bristol; I agree with it! [Applause.] The greatest praise government can win is, that its citizens know their rights, and dare to maintain them. The best use of good laws is to teach men to trample bad laws under their feet.

On these principles, I am willing to stand before the community in which I was born and brought up, — where I expect to live and die, — where, if I shall ever win any reputation, I expect to earn and to keep it. As a sane man, a Christian man, and a lover of my country, I am willing to be judged by posterity, if it shall ever remember either this meeting or the counsels which were given in its course. I am willing to stand upon this advice to the fugitive slave — baffled in every effort to escape, or bound here by sufficient ties, exiled from the protection of the law, shut out from the churches — to PROTECT HIMSELF, and make one last appeal to the humane instincts of his fellow-men. Friends, it is time something should be said on these points. Twenty-six cases — twenty-six slave cases, under this last statute, have taken place in the single State of Pennsylvania. I do not believe one man in a hundred who hears me supposed there were half a dozen cases there. So silently, so much a matter of course, so much without any public excitement, have those slaves been surrendered! Should the record be made up for the other States, it would probably be in proportion. Recollect, beside, the cases of kidnapping, not by any means unfrequent, which are so much facilitated by the existence of laws like this. For slaves to stay among us and be surrendered may excite commiseration; but remember, and this is a very important consideration, familiarity with such scenes begets indifference; the tone of public sentiment is lowered; soon cases pass as matters of course, and the community, burnt over with previous excitement, is doubly steeled against all active sympathy with the sufferers. What was usurpation yesterday is precedent to-morrow. When we asked the Supreme Court of Massachusetts to interfere in Sims's behalf, on the ground that the law of 1850 was unconstitutional, they declined, because the law was much the same as that of 1793, ard that was constitutional, because SO HELD and SUBMITTED TO. Surely, tyranny should have no such second acquiescence to plead. Yet that public feeling, so alert, so indignant at the outset, already droops and grows cold. Government stands ever a united, powerful, and organized body, always in session, its temptations creeping over the dulled senses, the wearied zeal, or the hour of want. The sympathies of a people for the down-trodden and the weak are scattered, evanescent, now excited, now asleep. The assembly which is red-hot to-day has vanished to-morrow. The indignation that lowers around a court-house in chains is scattered in a month. The guerilla troops of reform are now here, and now crumbled away. On the other hand, permanently planted, with a boundless patronage, which sways everything, stands government, with hands ever open, and eyes that never close, biding cunningly its time; always concentrated; and, of course, too often able to work its will, for a time, against any amount of popular indignation or sympathy.

Do not misunderstand me. I know the antislavery cause will triumph. The mightiest intellects, the Websters and the Calhouns of the Whig and Democratic parties, — they have no more effect upon the great mass of the public mind, in the long run, than the fly's weight had on the chariot-wheel where he lighted. But that is a long battle. I am speaking now of death or life, to be dealt out in a moment. I am dealing with a family about to be separated, standing, as many of you have been called again and again to do, by the hearth, or at the table, where that family circle were never to assemble again; broken and scattered to the four winds; the wife in agony, her husband torn from her side, her children gathering around, vainly asking, "Where are we to go, mother?" Open those doors! How many of them might you open in these Northern States within the last two years! How many of these utterly indescribable scenes might you have witnessed within that brief period! This law has executed itself. Twenty-six have been sent back from Pennsylvania; only one from Boston; only a dozen, perhaps, from New York. Yes; but, in the mean time, the dread that they might be seized has broken up hundreds of happy families. It has been executed: and when I remember that Northern traitor who made its enactment possible, I sometimes think that the vainest man who ever lived never dreamed, in the hour of his fondest self-conceit, that he had done the human race as much good as Daniel Webster has wrought it sorrow and despair. [Great applause.] I do not think you fully appreciate the state of dread in which the colored population has lived for months.

Mark, too, the infamous characteristics of these cases! It is not their frequency, after all, that should cause the most apprehension, but the objectional incidents and very dangerous precedents they establish. It is not that the slave act is law. That is not half the enormity of the fact. It is, that not only is the slave statute held to be law, but that there is really no law beside it in the Free States, — to execute it, all other laws are set aside and disregarded. The commonest and best settled principles have been trodden under foot. Almost all these persons have been arrested by a lie. Sims was, — Long was, — Preston was. In the case at Buffalo, the man was arrested by a bloodthirsty attack, — knocked down in the streets. The atrocious haste, the brutal haste of Judge Kane, in the case of Hannah Kellam, language fails in describing, — indignation stands dumb before the cold and brutal wickedness. Many of these cases have been a perversion, not only of all justice, but of all law. Take a single and slight instance. The merciful and safe rule has always been, that an officer, arresting any one wrongfully, shall not be permitted to avail himself of his illegal act for the service of a true warrant while he has the man in custody. This would be not only a sanction, but an encouragement, of illegal detention. But, in several of these cases, the man has been seized on some false pretence, known to be a sham, and then the authorities allowed those having him in custody to waive the prosecution of the pretended claim, and serve upon him the real warrant. The same disgraceful proceeding was allowed in the Latimer case in this city, his master arresting him as a thief, and afterwards dismissing that process, and claiming him as a slave. This dangerous precedent has been followed in many of these late cases. The spirit of the rule, and in some cases its letter, would have set the prisoner free, and held void all the proceedings.

Amid this entire overthrow of legal safeguards, this utter recklessness of all the checks which the experience of ages has invented for the control of the powerful and the protection of the weak, it is idle to dream of any colored person's being safe. They stand alone, exposed to the whole pelting of this pitiless storm. I wish there existed here any feeling on this subject adequate to the crisis. Is there such? Do you point me to the past triumphs of the antislavery sentiment of Massachusetts? The list is short, we know it by heart. Yes, there has been enough of feeling and effort to send Charles Sumner to the Senate. Let us still believe that the event will justify us in trusting him, spite of his silence there for four long months, — silence when so many ears have been waiting for the promised words. There is an antislavery sentiment here of a certain kind. Test it, and let us see what it is worth. There is antislavery sentiment enough to crowd our Legislature with Free-Soilers. True. Let us wait for some fruit, correspondent to their pledges, before we rejoice too loudly. Heaven grant us the sight of some before we be forced to borrow from our fathers a name for these legislative committees of Free-Soilers. In 1765 there were certain Parliamentary committees, to whom were referred the petitions of the Colonists, and many good plans of relief, and that was the last heard of either petition or plan. Our fathers called them "committees of oblivion." I hope we may never need that title again; and wherever we find the untarnished name of Sewall, we need have no apprehension.

Yes, there is antislavery sentiment sufficient to put many persons on their good behavior, — sufficient to bring Orville Dewey to his knees, and make him attempt to lie himself out of a late delicate embarrassment. [Great applause.] That, to be sure, is the only way for a true-bred American to apologize! Some men blame us for the personality of our attacks, — for the bad taste of actually naming a sinner on such a platform as this. Never doubt its benefits again. Did not the reverend doctor "go to and fro in the earth, and walk up and down in it," offering to return his own mother into slavery for our dear Union; and was he not rewarded by our national government with a chaplaincy in the navy, — as most men thought to secure him a trip to the Mediterranean, and repose his wearied virtue? Where could public rumor more appropriately send him than to that very spot on the Naples coast, where his great and only exemplar, Nero, devoted his mother to a kinder fate than this Christian imitator designed for a "venerable relative"! Could he have passed his life at Bauli, the genius of the place would have protected her well-deserving son, and all had been well. But here a certain "rub-a-dub agitation" had done so much mischief, that even the Unitarian denomination could not uphold its eminent leader till he had *explained* that he did not mean his "venerable relative," he only meant his son! How clear the lesson to that son not to treat others as they treat him, —

since then he might be led to do what even his father deems inhuman, namely, return his "venerable relative" into slavery to save a Union! Does Dr. Dewey indeed think it "extravagant and ridiculous to consent" to return one's mother to slavery? On what principle, then, it has been well asked, does he demand that every *colored son* submit patiently to have it done? Does his Bible read that God did not make of one blood all nations?

Yes, we have antislavery feeling and character enough to humble a Dewey; we want more, — want enough to save a Sims, — to give safe shelter to Ellen Crafts. "Hide the outcast, bewray not him that wandereth," is the simplest lesson of common humanity. The Commonwealth, which, planted by exiles, proclaimed by statute in 1641 her welcome to "*any stranger who might fly to her from the tyranny or oppression of their persecutors*," — the State which now seeks "PEACE IN LIBERTY," should not content herself with this: her rebuke of the tyrant, her voice of welcome to the oppressed, should be uttered so loud as to be heard throughout the South. It should not be necessary to *hide* the outcast. It ought not to be counted merit now that one does not lift hand against him. O no! fidelity to ancient fame, to present honor, to duty, to God, demands that the fugitive from the oppressions of other lands should be able to go up and down our highway in peace, — tell his true name, meet his old oppressor face to face, and feel that a whole Commonwealth stands between him and all chance of harm.

"*God save the Commonwealth of Massachusetts!*" How coldly, often, does the old prayer fall from careless lips! How sure to reach the ear of Him, who heareth the sighing of the prisoner, when it shall rise, in ecstasy of gratitude, from the slave-hut of the Carolinas, or from the bursting heart of the fugitive, who, after deadly peril, rests at last beneath the shadow of her protection!

PHILOSOPHY OF THE ABOLITION MOVEMENT.*

MR. CHAIRMAN: I have to present, from the business committee, the following resolution: —

"*Resolved*, That the object of this society is now, as it has always been, to convince our countrymen, by arguments addressed to their hearts and consciences, that slaveholding is a heinous crime, and that the duty, safety, and interest of all concerned demand its immediate abolition, without expatriation."

I wish, Mr. Chairman, to notice some objections that have been made to our course ever since Mr. Garrison began his career, and which have been lately urged again, with considerable force and emphasis, in the columns of the London Leader, the able organ of a very respectable and influential class in England. I hope, Sir, you will not think it waste of time to bring such a subject before you. I know these objections have been made a thousand times, that they have been often answered, though we generally submitted to them in silence, willing to let results speak for us. But there are times when justice to the slave will not allow us to be silent. There are many in this country, many in England, who have had their attention turned, recently, to the antislavery cause. They are asking, "Which is the best and most efficient

* Speech before the Massachusetts Antislavery Society, at the Melodeon, Boston, January 27, 1853.

method of helping it?" Engaged ourselves in an effort for the slave, which time has tested and success hitherto approved, we are very properly desirous that they should join us in our labors, and pour into this channel the full tide of their new zeal and great resources. Thoroughly convinced ourselves that our course is wise, we can honestly urge others to adopt it. Long experience gives us a right to advise. The fact that our course, more than all other efforts, has caused that agitation which has awakened these new converts, gives us a right to counsel them. They are our spiritual children: for their sakes, we would free the cause we love and trust from every seeming defect and plausible objection. For the slave's sake, we reiterate our explanations, that he may lose no tittle of help by the mistakes or misconceptions of his friends.

All that I have to say on these points will be to you, Mr. Chairman, very trite and familiar; but the facts may be new to some, and I prefer to state them here, in Boston, where we have lived and worked, because, if our statements are incorrect, if we claim too much, our assertions can be easily answered and disproved.

The charges to which I refer are these: that, in dealing with slaveholders and their apologists, we indulge in fierce denunciations, instead of appealing to their reason and common sense by plain statements and fair argument; — that we might have won the sympathies and support of the nation, if we would have submitted to argue this question with a manly patience; but, instead of this, we have outraged the feelings of the community by attacks, unjust and unnecessarily severe, on its most valued institutions, and gratified our spleen by indiscriminate abuse of leading men, who were often honest in their intentions, however mistaken in their views; — that we have utterly neglected the ample means that lay around us to convert the nation, submitted to no discipline, formed no plan, been guided by

no foresight, but hurried on in childish, reckless, blind, and hot-headed zeal, — bigots in the narrowness of our views, and fanatics in our blind fury of invective and malignant judgment of other men's motives.

There are some who come upon our platform, and give us the aid of names and reputations less burdened than ours with popular odium, who are perpetually urging us to exercise charity in our judgments of those about us, and to consent to argue these questions. These men are ever parading their wish to draw a line between themselves and us, because *they must be permitted* to wait, — to trust more to reason than feeling, — to indulge a generous charity, — to rely on the sure influence of simple truth, uttered in love, &c., &c. I reject with scorn all these implications that *our* judgments are uncharitable, — that *we* are lacking in patience, — that *we* have any other dependence than on the simple truth, spoken with Christian frankness, yet with Christian love. These lectures, to which you, Sir, and all of us, have so often listened, would be impertinent, if they were not rather ridiculous for the gross ignorance they betray of the community, of the cause, and of the whole course of its friends.

The article in the Leader to which I refer is signed "Ion," and may be found in the Liberator of December 17, 1852. The writer is cordial and generous in his recognition of Mr. Garrison's claim to be the representative of the antislavery movement, and does entire justice to his motives and character. The criticisms of "Ion" were reprinted in the Christian Register, of this city, the organ of the Unitarian denomination. The editors of that paper, with their usual Christian courtesy, love of truth, and fair-dealing, omitted all "Ion's" expressions of regard for Mr. Garrison and appreciation of his motives, and reprinted only those parts of the article which undervalue his sagacity and influence, and indorse the common objections to

his method and views. You will see in a moment, Mr. President, that it is with such men and presses "Ion" thinks Mr. Garrison has not been sufficiently wise and patient, in trying to win their help for the antislavery cause. Perhaps, were he on the spot, it would tire even his patience, and puzzle even his sagacity, to make any other use of them than that of the drunken Helot, — a warning to others how disgusting is mean vice. Perhaps, were he here, he would see that the best and only use to be made of them is to let them unfold their own characters, and then show the world how rotten our politics and religion are, that they naturally bear such fruit. "Ion" quotes Mr. Garrison's original declaration, in the Liberator: —

"I am aware that many object to the severity of my language; but is there not cause for severity? I *will* be as harsh as truth, and as uncompromising as justice. I am in earnest, — I will not equivocate, — I will not excuse, — I will not retreat a single inch, — AND I WILL BE HEARD.

"It is *pretended* that I am retarding the cause of emancipation by the coarseness of my invective and the precipitancy of my measures. *The charge is not true.* On this question, my influence, humble as it is, is felt at this moment to a considerable extent, and shall be felt in coming years, — not perniciously, but beneficially, — not as a curse, but as a blessing; and posterity will bear testimony that I was right. I desire to thank God that he enables me to disregard 'the fear of man, which bringeth a snare,' and to speak his truth in its simplicity and power."

"Ion" then goes on to say: —

"This is a defence which has been generally accepted on this side of the Atlantic, and many are the Abolitionists among us whom it has encouraged in honesty and impotence, and whom it has converted into conscientious hinderances. . . . .

"We would have Mr. Garrison to say, 'I will be as harsh as *progress*, as uncompromising as *success*.' If a man speaks for his own gratification, he may be as 'harsh' as he pleases; but if he speaks for the down-trodden and oppressed, he must be content to put a curb upon the tongue of holiest passion, and speak only as harshly as is compatible with the amelioration of the evil he proposes to redress. Let the question be again repeated: Do you seek for the slave vengeance or redress? If you seek retaliation, go on denouncing. But distant Europe honors William Lloyd Garrison because it credits him with seeking for the slave simply redress. We say, therefore, that 'uncompromising' policy is not to be measured by absolute justice, but by practical amelioration of the slave's condition. Amelioration as fast as you can get it, — absolute justice as soon as you can reach it."

He quotes the sentiment of Confucius, that he would choose for a leader "a man who would maintain a steady vigilance in the direction of affairs, who was capable of forming plans, and of executing them," and says: —

"The philosopher was right in placing wisdom and executive capacity above courage; for, down to this day, our popular movements are led by heroes who *fear* nothing, and who *win* nothing. . . . .

"There is no question raised in these articles as to the work to be done, but only as to the mode of *really* doing it. The platform resounds with announcements of principle, which is but *asserting* the right, while nothing but contempt is showered on policy, which is the *realization* of right. The air is filled with all high cries and spirited denunciations; indignation is at a premium; and this is called advocacy. . . . . But to calculate, to make sure of your aim, is to be descried as one who is too cold to feel, too genteel to strike."

Further on, he observes: —

"If an artillery officer throws shell after shell which never reach the enemy, he is replaced by some one with a better eye and a surer aim. But in the artillery battle of opinion, *to mean* to hit is quite sufficient; and if you have a certain grand indifference as to whether you hit or not, you may count on public applause. . . . .

"A man need be no less militant, as the soldier of facts, than as the agent of swords. But the arena of argument needs discipline, no less than that of arms. It is this which the anti-slavery party seem to me not only to overlook, but to despise. They do not put their valor to drill. Neither on the field nor the platform has courage any inherent capacity of taking care of itself."

The writer then proceeds to make a quotation from Mr. Emerson, the latter part of which I will read : —

"Let us withhold every *reproachful*, and, if we can, every *indignant* remark. In this cause, we must renounce our temper, and the risings of pride. If there be any man who thinks the ruin of a race of men a small matter compared with the last decorations and completions of his own comfort, — who would not so much as part with his ice-cream to save them from rapine and manacles, — I think I must not hesitate to satisfy *that* man that also his cream and vanilla are safer and cheaper by placing the negro nation on a fair footing, than by robbing them. If the Virginian piques himself on the picturesque luxury of his vassalage, on the heavy Ethiopian manners of his house-servants, their silent obedience, their hue of bronze, their turbaned heads, and would not exchange them for the more intelligent but precarious hired services of whites, I shall not refuse to show *him* that, when their free papers are made out, it will still be their interest to remain on his estates ; and that the oldest planters of Jamaica are convinced that it is cheaper to pay wages than to own slaves."

The critic takes exception to Mr. Garrison's approval of the denunciatory language in which Daniel O'Connell rebuked the giant sin of America, and concludes his article with this sentence : —

"When William Lloyd Garrison praises the great Celtic monarch of invective for this dire outpouring, he acts the part of the boy who fancies that the terror is in the war-whoop of the savage, unmindful of the quieter muskets of the civilized infantry, whose unostentatious execution blows whoop and tomahawk to the Devil."

Before passing to a consideration of these remarks of "Ion," let me say a word in relation to Mr. Emerson. I do not consider him as indorsing any of these criticisms on the Abolitionists. His services to the most radical antislavery movement have been generous and marked. He has never shrunk from any odium which lending his name and voice to it would incur. Making fair allowance for his peculiar taste, habits, and genius, he has given a generous amount of aid to the antislavery movement, and never let its friends want his cordial "God-speed."

"Ion's" charges are the old ones, that we Abolitionists are hurting our own cause, — that, instead of waiting for the community to come up to our views, and endeavoring to remove prejudice and enlighten ignorance by patient explanation and fair argument, we fall at once, like children, to abusing everything and everybody, — that we imagine zeal will supply the place of common sense, — that we have never shown any sagacity in adapting our means to our ends, have never studied the national character, or attempted to make use of the materials which lay all about us to influence public opinion, but by blind, childish, obstinate fury and indiscriminate denunciation, have become "honestly impotent, and conscientious hinderances."

These, Sir, are the charges which have uniformly been brought against all reformers in all ages. "Ion" thinks the same faults are chargeable on the leaders of all the "popular movements" in England, which, he says, "are led by heroes who *fear* nothing and who *win* nothing." If the leaders of popular movements in Great Britain for the last fifty years have been *losers*, I should be curious to know what party, in "Ion's" opinion, have won? My Lord Derby and his friends seem to think Democracy has made, and is making, dangerous headway. If the men who, by popular agitation, outside of Parliament, wrung from a powerful oligarchy Parliamentary Reform, and the Abolition of the Test Acts, of High Post Rates, of Catholic Disability, of Negro Slavery and the Corn Laws, did "not win anything," it would be hard to say what winning is. If the men who, without the ballot, made Peel their tool and conquered the Duke of Wellington, are considered unsuccessful, pray what kind of a thing would success be? Those who now, at the head of that same middle class, demand the separation of Church and State, and the Extension of the Ballot, may well guess, from the fluttering of Whig and Tory dove-cotes, that soon they will "win" that same "nothing." Heaven grant they may enjoy the same *ill success* with their predecessors! On our side of the ocean, too, we ought deeply to sympathize with the leaders of the temperance movement in their entire want of success! If "Ion's" mistakes about the antislavery cause lay as much on the surface as those I have just noticed, it would be hardly worth while to reply to him; for as to these, he certainly exhibits only "the extent and variety of his misinformation."

His remarks upon the antislavery movement are, however, equally inaccurate. I claim, before you who know the true state of the case, — I claim for the antislavery movement with which this society is identified, that, looking back over its whole course, and considering the men connected with it in the mass, it has been marked by sound judgment, unerring foresight, the most sagacious adaptation of means to ends, the strictest self-discipline, the most thorough research, and an amount of patient and manly argument addressed to the conscience and intellect of the nation, such as no other cause of the kind, in England or this country, has ever offered. I claim, also, that its course has been marked by a cheerful surrender of all individual claims to merit or leadership, — the most cordial welcoming of the slightest effort, of every honest attempt, to lighten or to break the chain of the slave. I need not waste time by repeating the superfluous confession that we are men, and therefore do not claim to be perfect. Neither would I be understood as denying that we use denunciation, and ridicule, and every other weapon that the human mind knows. We must plead guilty, if there be guilt in not knowing how to separate the sin from the sinner. With all the fondness for abstractions attributed to us, we are not yet capable of that. We are fighting a momentous battle at desperate odds, — one against a thousand. Every weapon that ability or ignorance, wit, wealth, prejudice, or fashion can command, is pointed against us. The guns are shotted to their lips. The arrows are poisoned. Fighting against such an array, we cannot afford to confine ourselves to any one weapon. The cause is not ours, so that we might, rightfully, postpone or put in peril the victory by moderating our demands, stifling our convictions, or filing down our rebukes, to gratify any sickly taste of our own, or to spare the delicate nerves of our neighbor. Our clients are three millions of Christian slaves, standing dumb suppliants at the threshold of the Christian world. They have no voice but ours to utter their complaints, or to demand justice. The press, the pulpit, the wealth, the literature, the prejudices, the political arrangements, the present self-interest of the country, are all against us. God has given us no weapon but the truth, faithfully uttered, and addressed, with the old prophets' directness, to the conscience of the individual sinner. The elements which control public opinion and mould the masses are against us. We can but pick off here and there a man from the triumphant majority. We have facts for those who think, arguments for those who reason; but he who cannot be reasoned out of his prejudices must be laughed out of them; he who cannot be argued out of his selfishness must be shamed out of it by the mirror of his hateful self held up relentlessly before his eyes. We live in a land where every man makes broad his phylactery, inscribing thereon, "All men are created equal," — "God hath made of one blood all nations of men." It seems to us that in such a land there must be, on this question of slavery, sluggards to be awakened, as well as doubters to be convinced. Many more, we verily believe, of the first than of the last. There are far more dead hearts to be quickened, than confused intellects to be cleared up, — more dumb dogs to be made to speak, than doubting consciences to be enlightened. [Loud cheers.] We have use, then, sometimes, for something beside argument.

What is the denunciation with which we are charged? It is endeavoring, in our faltering human speech, to declare the enormity of the sin of making merchandise of men, — of separating husband and wife, — taking the infant from its mother, and selling the daughter to prostitution, — of a professedly Christian nation denying, by statute, the Bible to every sixth man and woman of its population, and making it illegal for "two or three" to meet together, except a white man be present! What is this harsh criticism of motives with which we are charged? It is simply holding the intelligent and deliberate actor responsible for the character and consequences of his acts. Is there anything inherently wrong in such denunciation or such criticism? This we may claim, — we have never judged a man but out of his own mouth. We have seldom, if ever, held him to account, except for acts of which he and his own friends were proud. All that we ask the world and thoughtful men to note are the principles and deeds on which the American pulpit and American public men plume themselves. We always allow our opponents to paint their own pictures. Our humble duty is to stand by and assure the spectators that what they would take for a knave or a hypocrite is really, in American estimation, a Doctor of Divinity or Secretary of State.*

The South is one great brothel, where half a million of women are flogged to prostitution, or, worse still, are degraded to believe it honorable. The public squares of half our great cities echo to the wail of families torn asunder at the auction-block; no one of our fair rivers that has not closed over the negro seeking in death a refuge from a life too wretched to bear; thousands of fugitives skulk along our highways, afraid to tell their names, and trembling at the sight of a human being; free men are kidnapped in our streets, to be plunged into that hell of slavery; and now and then one, as if by mir-

* A paragraph from the New England Farmer, of this city, has gone the rounds of the press, and is generally believed. It says: —

"We learn, on reliable authority, that Mr. Webster confessed to a warm political friend, a short time before his death, that the great mistake of his life was the famous Seventh of March Speech, in which, it will be remembered, he defended the Fugitive Slave Law, and fully committed himself to the Compromise Measures. Before taking his stand on that occasion, he is said to have corresponded with Professor Stuart, and other eminent divines, to ascertain how far the religious sentiment of the North would sustain him in the position he was about to assume."

Some say this "warm political friend" was a clergyman! Consider a moment the language of this statement, the form it takes on every lip and in every press. "The great *mistake* of his life"! Seventy years old, brought up in New England churches, with all the culture of the world at his command, his soul melted by the repeated loss of those dearest to him, a great statesman, with a heart, according to his admirers, yet tender and fresh, — one who bent in such agony over the death-bed of his first daughter, — he looks back on this speech, which his friends say changed the feelings of ten millions of people, and made it possible to enact and execute the Fugitive Slave Law. He sees that it flooded the hearth-stones of thousands of colored men with wretchedness and despair, — crazed the mother, and broke the heart of the wife, — putting the virtue of woman and the liberty of man in the power of the vilest, — and all, as he at least

acle, after long years, returns to make men aghast with his tale. The press says, "It is all right"; and the pulpit cries, "Amen." They print the Bible in every tongue in which man utters his prayers; and get the money to do so by agreeing never to give the book, in the language our mothers taught us, to any negro, free or bond, south of Mason and Dixon's line. The press says, "It is all right"; and the pulpit cries, "Amen." The slave lifts up his imploring eyes, and sees in every face but ours the face of an enemy. Prove to me now that harsh rebuke, indignant denunciation, scathing sarcasm, and pitiless ridicule are wholly and always unjustifiable; else we dare not, in so desperate a case, throw away any weapon which ever broke up the crust of an ignorant prejudice, roused a slumbering conscience, shamed a proud sinner, or changed, in any way, the conduct of a

now saw, for nothing. Yet one who, according to his worshippers, was "the grandest growth of our soil and our institutions," looked back on such an act, and said — what? With one foot in the grave, said what of it? "I did wrong"? "I committed a foul outrage on my brother man"? "I sported too carelessly with the welfare of the poor"? Was there no moral chord in that heart, "the grandest growth of our soil and our institutions"? No! He said, "I made a mistake!" Not, "I was false in my stewardship of these great talents and this high position!" No! But on the chess-board of the political game, I made a bad move! I threw away my chances! A gambler, I did not understand my cards! And to whom does he offer this acknowledgment? To a clergyman! the representative of the moral sense of the community! What a picture! We laugh at the lack of heart in Talleyrand, when he says, "It is worse than a crime, a blunder." Yet all our New-Englander can call this momentous crime of his life is — a *mistake!*

Whether this statement be entirely true or not, we all know it is exactly the tone in which all about us talk of that speech. If the statement be true, what an entire want of right feeling and moral sensibility it shows in Mr. Webster! If it be unfounded, still the welcome it has received, and the ready belief it has gained, show the popular appreciation of him, and of such a crime. Such is the public with which Abolitionists have to deal.

human being. Our aim is to alter public opinion. Did we live in a market, our talk should be of dollars and cents, and we would seek to prove only that slavery was an unprofitable investment. Were the nation one great, pure church, we would sit down and reason of "righteousness, temperance, and judgment to come." Had slavery fortified itself in a college, we would load our cannons with cold facts, and wing our arrows with arguments. But we happen to live in the world, — the world made up of thought and impulse, of self-conceit and self-interest, of weak men and wicked. To conquer, we must reach all. Our object is not to make every man a Christian or a philosopher, but to induce every one to aid in the abolition of slavery. We expect to accomplish our object long before the nation is made over into saints or elevated into philosophers. To change public opinion, we use the very tools by which it was formed. That is, all such as an honest man may touch.

All this I am not only ready to allow, but I should be ashamed to think of the slave, or to look into the face of my fellow-man, if it were otherwise. It is the only thing which justifies us to our own consciences, and makes us able to say we have done, or at least tried to do, our duty.

So far, however you distrust my philosophy, you will not doubt my statements. That we have denounced and rebuked with unsparing fidelity will not be denied. Have we not also addressed ourselves to that other duty, of arguing our question thoroughly? — of using due discretion and fair sagacity in endeavoring to promote our cause? Yes, we have. Every statement we have made has been doubted. Every principle we have laid down has been denied by overwhelming majorities against us. No one step has ever been gained but by the most laborious research and the most exhausting argument. And no question has ever, since Revolutionary days, been so thoroughly investigated or argued here, as that of slavery. Of that research and that argument, of the whole of it, the old-fashioned, fanatical, crazy Garrisonian antislavery movement has been the author. From this band of men has proceeded every important argument or idea which has been broached on the antislavery question from 1830 to the present time. [Cheers.] I am well aware of the extent of the claim I make. I recognize, as fully as any one can, the ability of the new laborers, — the eloquence and genius with which they have recommended this cause to the nation, and flashed conviction home on the conscience of the community. I do not mean, either, to assert that they have in every instance borrowed from our treasury their facts and arguments. Left to themselves, they would probably have looked up the one and originated the other. As a matter of fact, however, they have generally made use of the materials collected to their hands. But there are some persons about us, sympathizers to a great extent with "Ion," who pretend that the antislavery movement has been hitherto mere fanaticism, its only weapon angry abuse. They are obliged to assert this, in order to justify their past indifference or hostility. At present, when it suits their purpose to give it some attention, they endeavor to explain the change by alleging that now it has been taken up by men of thoughtful minds, and its claims are urged by fair discussion and able argument. My claim, then, is this: that neither the charity of the most timid of sects, the sagacity of our wisest converts, nor the culture of the ripest scholars, though all have been aided by our twenty years' experience, has yet struck out any new method of reaching the public mind, or originated any new argument or train of thought, or discovered any new fact bearing on the question. When once brought fully into the struggle, they have found it necessary to adopt the same means, to rely on the same arguments, to hold up the same men and the same measures to public reprobation, with the same bold rebuke and unsparing invective that we have used. All their conciliatory bearing, their painstaking moderation, their constant and anxious endeavor to draw a broad line between their camp and ours, have been thrown away. Just so far as they have been effective laborers, they have found, as we have, their hands against every man, and every man's hand against them. The most experienced of them are ready to acknowledge that our plan has been wise, our course efficient, and that our unpopularity is no fault of ours, but flows necessarily and unavoidably from our position. "I should suspect," says old Fuller, "that his preaching had no salt in it, if no galled horse did wince." Our friends find, after all, that men do not so much hate us as the truth we utter and the light we bring. They find that the community are not the honest seekers after truth which they fancied, but selfish politicians and sectarian bigots, who shiver, like Alexander's butler, whenever the sun shines on them. Experience has driven these new laborers back to our method. We have no quarrel with them, — would not steal one wreath of their laurels. All we claim is, that, if they are to be complimented as prudent, moderate, Christian, sagacious, statesmanlike reformers, we deserve the same praise; for they have done nothing that we, in our measure, did not attempt before. [Cheers.]

I claim this, that the cause, in its recent aspect, has put on nothing but timidity. It has taken to itself no new weapons of recent years; it has become more compromising, — that is all! It has become neither more persuasive, more learned, more Christian, more charitable, nor more effective than for the twenty years preceding. Mr. Hale, the head of the Free Soil movement, after a career in the Senate that would do honor to any man, — after a six years' course which entitles him to the respect and confidence of the antislavery public, — can put his name, within the last month, to an appeal from the city of Washington, signed by a Houston and a Cass, for a monument to be raised to Henry Clay! If that be the test of charity and courtesy, we cannot give it to the world. [Loud cheers.] Some of the leaders of the Free Soil party of Massachusetts, after exhausting the whole capacity of our language to paint the treachery of Daniel Webster to the cause of liberty, and the evil they thought he was able and seeking to do, — after that, could feel it in their hearts to parade themselves in the funeral procession got up to do him honor! In this we allow we cannot follow them. The deference which every gentleman owes to the proprieties of social life, that self-respect and regard to consistency which is every man's duty, — these, if no deeper feelings, will ever prevent us from giving such proofs of this newly-invented Christian courtesy. [Great cheering.] We do not *play* politics; antislavery is no half-jest with us; it is a terrible earnest, with life or death, worse than life or death, on the issue. It is no lawsuit, where it matters not to the good feeling of opposing counsel which way the verdict goes, and where advocates can shake hands after the decision as pleasantly as before. When we think of such a man as Henry Clay, his long life, his mighty influence cast always into the scale against the slave, — of that irresistible fascination with which he moulded every one to his will; when we remember that, his conscience acknowledging the justice of our cause, and his heart open on every other side to the gentlest impulses, he could sacrifice so remorsely his convictions and the welfare of millions to his low ambition; when we think how the slave trembled at the sound of his voice, and that, from a multitude of breaking hearts there went up nothing but gratitude to God when it pleased him to

8

call that great sinner from this world, — we cannot find it in our hearts, we could not shape our lips to ask any man to do him honor. [Great sensation.] No amount of eloquence, no sheen of official position, no loud grief of partisan friends, would ever lead us to ask monuments or walk in fine processions for pirates; and the sectarian zeal or selfish ambition which gives up, deliberately and in full knowledge of the facts, three million of human beings to hopeless ignorance, daily robbery, systematic prostitution, and murder, which the law is neither able nor undertakes to prevent or avenge, is more monstrous, in our eyes, than the love of gold which takes a score of lives with merciful quickness on the high seas. Haynau on the Danube is no more hateful to us than Haynau on the Potomac. Why give mobs to one, and monuments to the other?

If these things be necessary to courtesy, I cannot claim that we are courteous. We seek only to be honest men, and speak the same of the dead as of the living. If the grave that hides their bodies could swallow also the evil they have done and the example they leave, we might enjoy at least the luxury of forgetting them. But the evil that men do lives after them, and example acquires tenfold authority when it speaks from the grave. History, also, is to be written. How shall a feeble minority, without weight or influence in the country, with no jury of millions to appeal to, — denounced, vilified, and contemned, — how shall we make way against the overwhelming weight of some colossal reputation, if we do not turn from the idolatrous present, and appeal to the human race? saying to your idols of to-day, "Here we are defeated; but we will write our judgment with the iron pen of a century to come, and it shall never be forgotten, if we can help it, that you were false in your generation to the claims of the slave!" [Loud cheers.]

At present, our leading men, strong in the support of

large majorities, and counting safely on the prejudices of the community, can afford to despise us. They know they can overawe or cajole the Present; their only fear is the judgment of the Future. Strange fear, perhaps, considering how short and local their fame! But however little, it is their all. Our only hold upon them is the thought of that bar of posterity, before which we are all to stand. Thank God! there is the elder brother of the Saxon race across the water, — there is the army of honest men to come! Before that jury we summon you. We are weak here, — out-talked, out-voted. You load our names with infamy, and shout us down. But our words bide their time. We warn the living that we have terrible memories, and that their sins are never to be forgotten. We will gibbet the name of every apostate so black and high that his children's children shall blush to bear it. Yet we bear no malice, — cherish no resentment. We thank God that the love of fame, "that last infirmity of noble mind," is shared by the ignoble. In our necessity, we seize this weapon in the slave's behalf, and teach caution to the living by meting out relentless justice to the dead. How strange the change death produces in the way a man is talked about here! While leading men live, they avoid as much as possible all mention of slavery, from fear of being thought Abolitionists. The moment they are dead, their friends rake up every word they ever contrived to whisper in a corner for liberty, and parade it before the world; growing angry, all the while, with us, because we insist on explaining these chance expressions by the tenor of a long and base life. While drunk with the temptations of the present hour, men are willing to bow to any Moloch. When their friends bury them, they feel what bitter mockery, fifty years hence, any epitaph will be, if it cannot record of one living in this era some service rendered to the slave! These, Mr. Chairman, are the reasons why we take care that "the memory of the wicked shall rot."

I have claimed that the antislavery cause has, from the first, been ably and dispassionately argued, every objection candidly examined, and every difficulty or doubt anywhere honestly entertained treated with respect. Let me glance at the literature of the cause, and try not so much, in a brief hour, to prove this assertion, as to point out the sources from which any one may satisfy himself of its truth.

I will begin with certainly the ablest and perhaps the most honest statesman who has ever touched the slave question. Any one who will examine John Quincy Adams's speech on Texas, in 1838, will see that he was only seconding the full and able exposure of the Texas plot, prepared by Benjamin Lundy, to one of whose pamphlets Dr. Channing, in his "Letter to Henry Clay," has confessed his obligation. Every one acquainted with those years will allow that the North owes its earliest knowledge and first awakening on that subject to Mr. Lundy, who made long journeys and devoted years to the investigation. His labors have this attestation, that they quickened the zeal and strengthened the hands of such men as Adams and Channing. I have been told that Mr. Lundy prepared a brief for Mr. Adams, and furnished him the materials for his speech on Texas.

Look next at the right of petition. Long before any member of Congress had opened his mouth in its defence, the Abolition presses and lecturers had examined and defended the limits of this right with profound historical research and eminent constitutional ability. So thoroughly had the work been done, that all classes of the people had made up their minds about it long before any speaker of eminence had touched it in Congress. The politicians were little aware of this. When Mr.

Adams threw himself so gallantly into the breach, it is said he wrote anxiously home to know whether he would be supported in Massachusetts, little aware of the outburst of popular gratitude which the Northern breeze was even then bringing him, deep and cordial enough to wipe away the old grudge Massachusetts had borne him so long. Mr. Adams himself was only in favor of receiving the petitions, and advised to refuse their prayer, which was the abolition of slavery in the District. He doubted the power of Congress to abolish. His doubts were examined by Mr. William Goodell, in two letters of most acute logic, and of masterly ability. If Mr. Adams still retained his doubts, it is certain at least that he never expressed them afterward. When Mr. Clay paraded the same objections, the whole question of the power of Congress over the district was treated by Theodore D. Weld in the fullest manner, and with the widest research, — indeed, leaving nothing to be added: an argument which Dr. Channing characterized as "demonstration," and pronounced the essay "one of the ablest pamphlets from the American press." No answer was ever attempted. The best proof of its ability is, that no one since has presumed to doubt the power. Lawyers and statesmen have tacitly settled down into its full acknowledgment.

The influence of the Colonization Society on the welfare of the colored race was the first question our movement encountered. To the close logic, eloquent appeals, and fully sustained charges of Mr. Garrison's Letters on that subject no answer was ever made. Judge Jay followed with a work full and able, establishing every charge by the most patient investigation of facts. It is not too much to say of these two volumes, that they left the Colonization Society hopeless at the North. It dares never show its face before the people, and only lingers in some few nooks of sectarian pride, so secluded from the influence of present ideas as to be almost fossil in their character.

The practical working of the slave system, the slave laws, the treatment of slaves, their food, the duration of their lives, their ignorance and moral condition, and the influence of Southern public opinion on their fate, have been spread out in a detail and with a fulness of evidence which no subject has ever received before in this country. Witness the works of Phelps, Bourne, Rankin, Grimke, the "Antislavery Record," and, above all, that encyclopædia of facts and storehouse of arguments, the "Thousand Witnesses" of Mr. Theodore D. Weld. He also prepared that full and valuable tract for the World's Convention called "Slavery and the Internal Slave-Trade in the United States," published in London, 1841. Unique in antislavery literature is Mrs. Child's "Appeal," one of the ablest of our weapons, and one of the finest efforts of her rare genius.

The Princeton Review, I believe, first challenged the Abolitionists to an investigation of the teachings of the Bible on slavery. That field had been somewhat broken by our English predecessors. But in England, the proslavery party had been soon shamed out of the attempt to drag the Bible into their service, and hence the discussion there had been short and somewhat superficial. The proslavery side of the question has been eagerly sustained by theological reviews and doctors of divinity without number, from the half-way and timid faltering of Wayland up to the unblushing and melancholy recklessness of Stuart. The argument on the other side has come wholly from the Abolitionists; for neither Dr. Hague nor Dr. Barnes can be said to have added anything to the wide research, critical acumen, and comprehensive views of Theodore D. Weld, Beriah Green, J. G. Fee, and the old work of Duncan.

On the constitutional questions which have at various times arisen, — the citizenship of the colored man, the soundness of the "Prigg" decision, the constitutionality of the old Fugitive Slave Law, the true construction of the slave-surrender clause, — nothing has been added, either in the way of fact or argument, to the works of Jay, Weld, Alvan Stewart, E. G. Loring, S. E. Sewall, Richard Hildreth, W. I. Bowditch, the masterly essays of the Emancipator at New York and the Liberator at Boston, and the various addresses of the Massachusetts and American Societies for the last twenty years. The idea of the antislavery character of the Constitution, — the opiate with which Free Soil quiets its conscience for voting under a proslavery government, — I heard first suggested by Mr. Garrison in 1838. It was elaborately argued that year in all our antislavery gatherings, both here and in New York, and sustained with great ability by Alvan Stewart, and in part by T. D. Weld. The antislavery construction of the Constitution was ably argued in 1836, in the "Antislavery Magazine," by Rev. Samuel J. May, one of the very first to seek the side of Mr. Garrison, and pledge to the slave his life and efforts, — a pledge which thirty years of devoted labors have nobly redeemed. If it has either merit or truth, they are due to no legal learning recently added to our ranks, but to some of the old and well-known pioneers. This claim has since received the fullest investigation from Mr. Lysander Spooner, who has urged it with all his unrivalled ingenuity, laborious research, and close logic. He writes as a lawyer, and has no wish, I believe, to be ranked with any class of antislavery men.

The influence of slavery on our government has received the profoundest philosophical investigation from the pen of Richard Hildreth, in his invaluable essay on "Despotism in America," — a work which deserves a place by the side of the ablest political disquisitions of any age.

Mrs. Chapman's survey of "Ten Years of Antislavery Experience," was the first attempt at a philosophical discussion of the various aspects of the antislavery cause, and the problems raised by its struggles with sect and party. You, Mr. Chairman, [Edmund Quincy, Esq.,] in the elaborate Reports of the Massachusetts Antislavery Society for the last ten years, have followed in the same path, making to American literature a contribution of the highest value, and in a department where you have few rivals and no superior. Whoever shall write the history either of this movement, or any other attempted under a republican government, will find nowhere else so clear an insight and so full an acquaintance with the most difficult part of his subject.

Even the vigorous mind of Rantoul, the ablest man, without doubt, of the Democratic party, and perhaps the ripest politician in New England, added little or nothing to the storehouse of antislavery argument. The grasp of his intellect and the fulness of his learning every one will acknowledge. He never trusted himself to speak on any subject till he had dug down to its primal granite. He laid a most generous contribution on the altar of the antislavery cause. His speeches on our question, too short and too few, are remarkable for their compact statement, iron logic, bold denunciation, and the wonderful light thrown back upon our history. Yet how little do they present which was not familiar for years in our antislavery meetings!

Look, too, at the last great effort of the idol of so many thousands, Mr. Senator Sumner, — the discussion of a great national question, of which it has been said that we must go back to Webster's Reply to Hayne, and Fisher Ames on the Jay Treaty, to find its equal in Congress, — praise which we might perhaps qualify, if any adequate report were left us of some of the noble orations of Adams. No one can be blind to the skilful use he has made of his materials, the consummate ability with which he has marshalled them, and the radiant glow which his genius has thrown over all. Yet, with the exception of his reference to the antislavery debate in Congress, in 1817, there is hardly a train of thought or argument, and no single fact in the whole speech, which has not been familiar in our meetings and essays for the last ten years.

Before leaving the halls of Congress, I have great pleasure in recognizing one exception to my remarks, Mr. Giddings. Perhaps he is no real exception, since it would not be difficult to establish his claim to be considered one of the original Abolition party. But whether he would choose to be so considered or not, it is certainly true that his long presence at the seat of government, his whole-souled devotedness, his sagacity and unwearied industry, have made him a large contributor to our antislavery resources.

The relations of the American Church to slavery, and the duties of private Christians, — the whole casuistry of this portion of the question, so momentous among descendants of the Puritans, — have been discussed with great acuteness and rare common-sense by Messrs. Garrison, Goodell, Gerritt Smith, Pillsbury, and Foster. They have never attempted to judge the American Church by any standard except that which she has herself laid down; — never claimed that she should be perfect, but have contented themselves by demanding that she should be consistent. They have never judged her except out of her own mouth, and on facts asserted by her own presses and leaders. The sundering of the Methodist and Baptist denominations, and the universal agitation of the religious world, are the best proof of the sagacity with which their measures have been chosen, the cogent arguments they have used, and the indisputable facts on which their criticisms have been founded.

In nothing have the Abolitionists shown more sagacity or more thorough knowledge of their countrymen than in the course they have pursued in relation to the Church. None but a New-Englander can appreciate the power which church organizations wield over all who share the blood of the Puritans. The influence of each sect over its own members is overwhelming, often shutting out, or controlling, all other influences. We have Popes here, all the more dangerous because no triple crown puts you on your guard. The Methodist priesthood brings the Catholic very vividly to mind. That each local church is independent of all others, we have been somewhat careful to assert, in theory and practice. The individual's independence of all organizations which place themselves between him and his God, some few bold minds have asserted in theory, but most even of those have stopped there.

In such a land, the Abolitionists early saw, that, for a moral question like theirs, only two paths lay open: to work through the Church, — that failing, to join battle with it. Some tried long, like Luther, to be Protestants, and yet not come out of Catholicism; but their eyes were soon opened. Since then we have been convinced that, to come out from the Church, to hold her up as the bulwark of slavery, and to make her shortcomings the main burden of our appeals to the religious sentiment of the community, was our first duty and best policy. This course alienated many friends, and was a subject of frequent rebuke from such men as Dr. Channing. But nothing has ever more strengthened the cause, or won it more influence; and it has had the healthiest effect on the Church itself. British Christians have always sanctioned it, whenever the case has been fairly presented to them.

Mr. John Quincy Adams, a man far better acquainted with his own times than Dr. Channing, recognized the soundness of our policy. I do not know that he ever uttered a word in public on the delinquency of the churches; but he is said to have assured his son, at the time the Methodist Church broke asunder, that other men might be more startled by the *éclat* of political success, but nothing, in his opinion, promised more good, or showed more clearly the real strength of the antislavery movement, than that momentous event.*

In 1838, the British Emancipation in the West Indies opened a rich field for observation, and a full harvest of important facts. The Abolitionists, not willing to wait for the official reports of the government, sent special agents through those islands, whose reports they scattered, at great expense and by great exertion, broadcast through the land. This was at a time when no newspaper in the country would either lend or sell them the aid of its columns to enlighten the nation on an experiment so vitally important to us. And even now, hardly a press in the country cares or dares to bestow a line or communicate a fact toward the history of that remarkable revolution. The columns of the Antislavery Standard, Pennsylvania Freeman, and Ohio Bugle have been for years full of all that a thorough and patient advocacy of our cause demands. And the eloquent lips of many whom I see around me, and whom I need not name here, have done their share toward pressing all these topics on public attention. There is hardly any record of these labors of the living voice. Indeed, from the nature of the case, there cannot be any adequate one. Yet, unable to command a wide circulation for our

* Henry Clay attached the same importance to the ecclesiastical influence and divisions. See his "Interview with Rev. Dr. Hill, of Louisville, Ky.," *Antislavery Standard*, July 14, 1860

books and journals, we have been obliged to bring ourselves into close contact with the people, and to rely mainly on public addresses. These have been our most efficient instrumentality. For proof that these addresses have been full of pertinent facts, sound sense, and able arguments, we must necessarily point to results, and demand to be tried by our fruits. Within these last twenty years it has been very rare that any fact stated by your lecturers has been disproved, or any statement of theirs successfully impeached. And for evidence of the soundness, simplicity, and pertinency of their arguments we can only claim that our converts and co-laborers throughout the land have at least the reputation of being specially able "to give a reason for the faith that is in them."

I remember that when, in 1845, the present leaders of the Free Soil party, with Daniel Webster in their company, met to draw up the Anti-Texas Address of the Massachusetts Convention, they sent to Abolitionists for antislavery facts and history, for the remarkable testimonies of our Revolutionary great men which they wished to quote. [Hear! hear!] When, many years ago, the Legislature of Massachusetts wished to send to Congress a resolution affirming the duty of immediate emancipation, the committee sent to William Lloyd Garrison to draw it up, and it stands now on our statute-book as he drafted it.

How vigilantly, how patiently, did we watch the Texas plot from its commencement! The politic South felt that its first move had been too bold, and thenceforward worked underground. For many a year, men laughed at us for entertaining any apprehensions. It was impossible to rouse the North to its peril. David Lee Child was thought crazy, because he would not believe there was no danger. His elaborate "Letters on Texan Annexation" are the ablest and most valuable contribution that has been made towards a history of the whole plot. Though we foresaw and proclaimed our conviction that annexation would be, in the end, a fatal step for the South, we did not feel at liberty to relax our opposition, well knowing the vast increase of strength it would give, at first, to the Slave Power. I remember being one of a committee which waited on Abbott Lawrence, a year or so only before annexation, to ask his countenance to some general movement, without distinction of party, against the Texas scheme. He smiled at our fears, begged us to have no apprehensions; stating that his correspondence with leading men at Washington enabled him to assure us annexation was impossible, and that the South itself was determined to defeat the project. A short time after, Senators and Representatives from Texas took their seats in Congress!

Many of these services to the slave were done before I joined his cause. In thus referring to them, do not suppose me merely seeking occasion of eulogy on my predecessors and present co-laborers. I recall these things only to rebut the contemptuous criticism which some about us make the excuse for their past neglect of the movement, and in answer to "Ion's" representation of our course as reckless fanaticism, childish impatience, utter lack of good sense, and of our meetings as scenes only of excitement, of reckless and indiscriminate denunciation. I assert that every social, moral, economical, religious, political, and historical aspect of the question has been ably and patiently examined. And all this has been done with an industry and ability which have left little for the professional skill, scholarly culture, and historical learning of the new laborers to accomplish. If the people are still in doubt, it is from the inherent difficulty of the subject, or a hatred of light, not from want of it.

So far from the antislavery cause having lacked a manly and able discussion, I think it will be acknowledged hereafter that this discussion has been one of the noblest contributions to a literature really American. Heretofore, not only has our tone been but an echo of foreign culture, but the very topics discussed and the views maintained have been too often pale reflections of European politics and European philosophy. No matter what dress we assumed, the voice was ever "the voice of Jacob." At last we have stirred a question thoroughly American; the subject has been looked at from a point of view entirely American; and it is of such deep interest, that it has called out all the intellectual strength of the nation. For once, the nation speaks its own thoughts, in its own language, and the tone also is all its own. It will hardly do for the defeated party to claim that, in this discussion, all the ability is on their side.

We are charged with lacking foresight, and said to exaggerate. This charge of exaggeration brings to my mind a fact I mentioned, last month, at Horticultural Hall. The theatres in many of our large cities bring out, night after night, all the radical doctrines and all the startling scenes of "Uncle Tom." They preach immediate emancipation, and slaves shoot their hunters to loud applause. Two years ago, sitting in this hall, I was myself somewhat startled by the assertion of my friend, Mr. Pillsbury, that the theatres would receive the gospel of antislavery truth earlier than the churches. A hiss went up from the galleries, and many in the audience were shocked by the remark. I asked myself whether I could indorse such a statement, and felt that I could not. I could not believe it to be true. Only two years have passed, and what was then deemed rant and fanaticism, by seven out of ten who heard it, has proved true. The theatre, bowing to its audience, has preached immediate emancipation, and given us the whole of "Uncle Tom"; while the pulpit is either silent or hostile, and in the columns of the theological papers the work is subjected to criticism, to reproach, and its author to severe rebuke. Do not, therefore, friends, set down as extravagant every statement which your experience does not warrant. It may be that you and I have not studied the signs of the times quite as accurately as the speaker. Going up and down the land, coming into close contact with the feelings and prejudices of the community, he is sometimes a better judge than you are of its present state. An Abolitionist has more motives for watching and more means of finding out the true state of public opinion, than most of those careless critics who jeer at his assertions to-day, and are the first to cry, "Just what *I* said," when his prophecy becomes fact to-morrow.

Mr. "Ion" thinks, also, that we have thrown away opportunities, and needlessly outraged the men and parties about us. Far from it. The antislavery movement was a patient and humble suppliant at every door whence any help could possibly be hoped. If we now repudiate and denounce some of our institutions, it is because we have faithfully tried them, and found them deaf to the claims of justice and humanity. Our great Leader, when he first meditated this crusade, did not

"At once, like a sunburst, his banner unfurl."

O no! he sounded his way warily forward. Brought up in the strictest reverence for church organizations, his first effort was to enlist the clergymen of Boston in the support of his views. On their aid he counted confidently in his effort to preach immediate repentance of all sin. He did not go, with *malice prepense*, as some seem to imagine, up to that "attic" where Mayor Otis with difficulty found him. He did not court hostility or seek exile. He did not sedulously endeavor to cut himself off from the sympathy and countenance of the community about him. O no! A fervid disciple of the American Church, he conferred with some of the leading clergy of the city, and laid before them his convictions on the subject of slavery.* He painted their responsibility, and tried to induce them to take from his shoulders the burden of so mighty a movement. He laid himself at their feet. He recognized the colossal strength of the Clergy; he knew that against their opposition it would be almost desperate to attempt to relieve the slave. He entreated them, therefore, to take up the cause. But the Clergy turned away from him! They shut their doors upon him! They bade him compromise his convictions, — smother one half of them, and support the colonization movement, making his own auxiliary to that, or they would have none of him. Like Luther, he said: "Here I stand; God help me; I can do nothing else!" But the men who joined him were not persuaded that the case was so desperate. They returned, each to his own local sect, and remained in them until some of us, myself among the number, — later converts to the antislavery movement, — thought they were slow and faltering in their obedience to conscience, and that they ought to have cut loose

* "The writer accompanied Mr. Garrison, in 1829, in calling upon a number of prominent ministers in Boston, to secure their co-operation in this cause. *Our expectations of important assistance from them were, at that time, very sanguine.*" — Testimony of William Goodell, in a recent work entitled "Slavery and Antislavery."

In an address on Slavery and Colonization, delivered by Mr. Garrison in the Park Street Church, Boston, July 4, 1829, (which was subsequently published in the National Philanthropist,) he said: "I call on the ambassadors of Christ, everywhere, to make known this proclamation, 'Thus saith the Lord God of the Africans, Let this people go, that they may serve me.' I ask them to 'proclaim liberty to the captive, and the opening of the prison to them that are bound.' I call on the churches of the living God to LEAD in this great enterprise."

much sooner than they did. But a patience, which old sympathies would not allow to be exhausted, and associations, planted deeply in youth, and spreading over a large part of manhood, were too strong for any mere argument to dislodge them. So they still persisted in remaining in the Church. Their zeal was so fervent, and their labors so abundant, that in some towns large societies were formed, led by most of the clergymen, and having almost all the church-members on their lists. In those same towns now you will not find one single Abolitionist, of any stamp whatever. They excuse their falling back by alleging that we have injured the cause by our extravagance and denunciation, and by the various other questions with which our names are associated. This might be a good reason why they should not work with us, but does it excuse their not working at all? These people have been once awakened, thoroughly instructed in the momentous character of the movement, and have acknowledged the rightful claim of the slave on their sympathy and exertions. It is not possible that a few thousand persons, however extravagant, could prevent devoted men from finding some way to help such a cause, or at least manifesting their interest in it. But they have not only left us, they have utterly deserted the slave, in the hour when the interests of their sects came across his cause. Is it uncharitable to conjecture the reason? At the early period, however, to which I have referred, the Church was much exercised by the persistency of the Abolitionists in not going out from her. When I joined the antislavery ranks, sixteen years ago, the voice of the clergy was: "Will these *pests* never leave us? Will they still remain to trouble us? If you do not like us, there is the door!" When our friends had exhausted all entreaty, and tested the Christianity of that body, they shook off the dust of their feet, and came out of her.

At the outset, Mr. Garrison called on the head of the Orthodox denomination, — a man compared with whose influence on the mind of New England that of the statesman whose death you have just mourned was, I think, but as dust in the balance, — a man who then held the Orthodoxy of Boston in his right hand, and who has since taken up the West by its four corners, and given it so largely to Puritanism, — I mean the Rev. Dr. Lyman Beecher. Mr. Garrison was one of those who bowed to the spell of that matchless eloquence which then fulmined over our Zion. He waited on his favorite divine, and urged him to give to the new movement the incalculable aid of his name and countenance. He was patiently heard. He was allowed to unfold his plans and array his facts. The reply of the veteran was, "Mr. Garrison, I have too many irons in the fire to put in another." My friend said, "Doctor, you had better take them all out and put this one in, if you mean well either to the religion or to the civil liberty of our country." [Cheers.]

The great Orthodox leader did not rest with merely refusing to put another iron in his fire; he attempted to limit the irons of other men. As President of Lane Theological Seminary, he endeavored to prevent the students from investigating the subject of slavery. The result, we all remember, was a strenuous resistance on the part of a large number of the students, led by that remarkable man, Theodore D. Weld. The right triumphed, and Lane Seminary lost her character and noblest pupils at the same time. She has languished ever since, even with such a President. Why should I follow Dr. Beecher into those ecclesiastical conventions where he has been tried, and found wanting, in fidelity to the slave? He has done no worse, indeed he has done much better, than most of his class. His opposition has always been open and manly.

But, Mr. Chairman, there is something in the blood which, men tell us, brings out virtues and defects, even when they have lain dormant for a generation. Good and evil qualities are hereditary, the physicians say. The blood whose warm currents of eloquent aid my friend solicited in vain in that generation has sprung voluntarily to his assistance in the next, — both from the pulpit and the press, — to rouse the world by the vigor and pathos of its appeals. [Enthusiastic cheers.] Even on that great triumph I would say a word. Marked and unequalled as has been that success, remember, in explanation of the phenomenon, — for "Uncle Tom's Cabin" is rather an event than a book, — remember this: if the old antislavery movement had not roused the sympathies of Mrs. Stowe, the book had never been written; if that movement had not raised up hundreds of thousands of hearts to sympathize with the slave, the book had never been read. [Cheers.] Not that the genius of the author has not made the triumph all her own; not that the unrivalled felicity of its execution has not trebled, quadrupled, increased tenfold, if you please, the number of readers; but there must be a spot even for Archimedes to rest his lever upon, before he can move the world, [cheers,] and this effort of genius, consecrated to the noblest purpose, might have fallen dead and unnoticed in 1835. It is the antislavery movement which has changed 1835 to 1852. Those of us familiar with antislavery literature know well that Richard Hildreth's "Archy Moore," now "The White Slave," was a book of eminent ability; that it owed its want of success to no lack of genius, but only to the fact that it was a work born out of due time; that the antislavery cause had not then aroused sufficient numbers, on the wings of whose enthusiasm even the most delightful fiction could have risen into world-wide influence and repute. To the cause which had changed 1835 to 1852 is due somewhat of the influence of "Uncle Tom's Cabin."

The Abolitionists have never overlooked the wonderful power which the wand of the novelist was yet to wield in their behalf over the hearts of the world. Fredrika Bremer only expressed the common sentiment of many of us, when she declared that "the fate of the negro is the romance of our history." Again and again, from my earliest knowledge of the cause, have I heard the opinion, that in the debatable land between Freedom and Slavery, in the thrilling incidents of the escape and sufferings of the fugitive, and the perils of his friends, the future Walter Scott of America would find the "border-land" of his romance, and the most touching incidents of his "sixty years since"; and that the literature of America would gather its freshest laurels from that field.

So much, Mr. Chairman, for our treatment of the Church. We clung to it as long as we hoped to make it useful. Disappointed in that, we have tried to expose its paltering and hypocrisy on this question, broadly and with unflinching boldness, in hopes to purify and bring it to our aid. Our labors with the great religious societies, with the press, with the institutions of learning, have been as untiring, and almost as unsuccessful. We have tried to do our duty to every public question that has arisen, which could be made serviceable in rousing general attention. The Right of Petition, the Power of Congress, the Internal Slave-Trade, Texas, the Compromise Measures, the Fugitive Slave Law, the motions of leading men, the tactics of parties, have all been watched and used with sagacity and effect as means to produce a change in public opinion. Dr. Channing has thanked the Abolition party, in the name of all the lovers of free thought and free speech, for having vindicated that right, when all others seemed ready to surrender it, — vindicated it at the cost of reputation, ease, property, even life itself. The only blood that has ever been shed, on this side the ocean, in defence of the freedom of the press, was the blood of Lovejoy, one of their number. In December, 1836, Dr. Channing spoke of their position in these terms: —

"Whilst, in obedience to conscience, they have refrained from opposing force to force, they have still persevered, amidst menace and insult, in bearing their testimony against wrong, in giving utterance to their deep convictions. Of such men, I do not hesitate to say, that they have rendered to freedom a more essential service than any body of men among us. The defenders of freedom are not those who claim and exercise rights which no one assails, or who win shouts of applause by well-turned compliments to Liberty in the days of her triumph. They are those who stand up for rights which mobs, conspiracies, or single tyrants put in jeopardy; who contend for liberty in that particular form which is threatened at the moment by the many or the few. To the Abolitionists this honor belongs. The first systematic effort to strip the citizen of freedom of speech they have met with invincible resolution. From my heart I thank them. I am myself their debtor. I am not sure that I should this moment write in safety, had they shrunk from the conflict, had they shut their lips, imposed silence on their presses, and hid themselves before their ferocious assailants. I know not where these outrages would have stopped, had they not met resistance from their first destined victims. The newspaper press, with a few exceptions, uttered no genuine indignant rebuke of the wrong-doers, but rather countenanced by its gentle censures the reign of force. The mass of the people looked supinely on this new tyranny, under which a portion of their fellow-citizens seemed to be sinking. A tone of denunciation was beginning to proscribe all discussion of slavery; and had the spirit of violence, which selected associations as its first objects, succeeded in this preparatory enterprise, it might have been easily turned against any and every individual, who might presume to agitate the unwelcome subject. It is hard to say to what outrage the fettered press of the country might not have been reconciled. I thank the Abolitionists that, in this evil day, they were true to the rights which the multitude were ready to betray. Their purpose to suffer, to die, rather than surrender their dearest liberties, taught the lawless that they had a foe to contend with whom it was not safe to press, whilst, like all manly appeals, it called forth reflection and sympathy in the better portion of the community. In the name of freedom and humanity, I thank them."

No one, Mr. Chairman, deserves more of that honor than he whose chair you now occupy. Our youthful city can boast of but few places of historic renown; but I know of no one which coming time is more likely to keep in memory than the roof which Francis Jackson offered to the antislavery women of Boston, when Mayor Lyman confessed he was unable to protect their meeting, and when the only protection the laws could afford Mr. Garrison was the shelter of the common jail.

Sir, when a nation sets itself to do evil, and all its leading forces, wealth, party, and piety, join in the career, it is impossible but that those who offer a constant opposition should be hated and maligned, no matter how wise, cautious, and well planned their course may be. We are peculiar sufferers in this way. The community has come to hate its reproving Nathan so bitterly, that even those whom the relenting part of it is beginning to regard as standard-bearers of the antislavery host think it unwise to avow any connection or sympathy with him. I refer to some of the leaders of the political movement against slavery. They feel it to be their mission to marshal and use as effectively as possible the present convictions of the people. They cannot afford to encumber themselves with the odium which twenty years of angry agitation have engendered in great sects sore from unsparing rebuke, parties galled by constant defeat, and leading men provoked by unexpected exposure. They are willing to con-

fess, privately, that our movement produced theirs, and that its continued existence is the very breath of their life. But, at the same time, they would fain walk on the road without being soiled by too close contact with the rough pioneers who threw it up. They are wise and honorable, and their silence is very expressive.

When I speak of their eminent position and acknowledged ability, another thought strikes me. Who converted these men and their distinguished associates? It is said we have shown neither sagacity in plans, nor candor in discussion, nor ability. Who, then, or what, converted Burlingame and Wilson, Sumner and Adams, Palfrey and Mann, Chase and Hale, and Phillips and Giddings? Who taught the Christian Register, the Daily Advertiser, and that class of prints, that there were such things as a slave and a slaveholder in the land, and so gave them some more intelligent basis than their mere instincts to hate William Lloyd Garrison? [Shouts and laughter.] What magic wand was it whose touch made the toadying servility of the land start up the real demon that it was, and at the same time gathered into the slave's service the professional ability, ripe culture, and personal integrity which grace the Free Soil ranks? We never argue! These men, then, were converted by simple denunciation! They were all converted by the "hot," "reckless," "ranting," "bigoted," "fanatic" Garrison, who never troubled himself about facts, nor stopped to argue with an opponent, but straightway knocked him down! [Roars of laughter and cheers.] My old and valued friend, Mr. Sumner, often boasts that he was a reader of the Liberator before I was. Do not criticise too much the agency by which such men were converted. That blade has a double edge. Our reckless course, our empty rant, our fanaticism, has made Abolitionists of some of the best and ablest men in the land. We are inclined to go on, and see if even with such poor tools we cannot make some more. [Enthusiastic applause.] Antislavery zeal and the roused conscience of the "godless come-outers" made the trembling South demand the Fugitive Slave Law, and the Fugitive Slave Law "provoked" Mrs. Stowe to the good work of "Uncle Tom." That is something! [Cheers.] Let me say, in passing, that you will nowhere find an earlier or more generous appreciation, or more flowing eulogy, of these men and their labors, than in the columns of the Liberator. No one, however feeble, has ever peeped or muttered, in any quarter, that the vigilant eye of the Pioneer has not recognized him. He has stretched out the right hand of a most cordial welcome the moment any man's face was turned Zionward. [Loud cheers.]

I do not mention these things to praise Mr. Garrison, I do not stand here for that purpose. You will not deny — if you do, I can prove it — that the movement of the Abolitionists converted these men. Their constituents were converted by it. The assault upon the right of petition, upon the right to print and speak of slavery, the denial of the right of Congress over the District, the annexation of Texas, the Fugitive Slave Law, were measures which the antislavery movement provoked, and the discussion of which has made all the Abolitionists we have. The antislavery cause, then, converted these men; it gave them a constituency; it gave them an opportunity to speak, and it gave them a public to listen. The antislavery cause gave them their votes, got them their offices, furnished them their facts, gave them their audience. If you tell me they cherished all these principles in their own breasts before Mr. Garrison appeared, I can only say, if the antislavery movement did not give them their ideas, it surely gave the courage to utter them.

In such circumstances, is it not singular that the name

of William Lloyd Garrison has never been pronounced on the floor of the United States Congress linked with any epithet but that of contempt! No one of those men who owe their ideas, their station, their audience, to him, have ever thought it worth their while to utter one word in grateful recognition of the power which called them into being. When obliged, by the course of their argument, to treat the question historically, they can go across the water to Clarkson and Wilberforce, — yes, to a safe salt-water distance. [Laughter.] As Daniel Webster, when he was talking to the farmers of Western New York, and wished to contrast slave labor and free labor, did not dare to compare New York with Virginia, — sister States, under the same government, planted by the same race, worshipping at the same altar, speaking the same language, — identical in all respects, save that one in which he wished to seek the contrast; but no; he compared it with Cuba, [cheers and laughter,] — the contrast was so close! [Renewed cheers.] Catholic — Protestant; Spanish — Saxon; despotism — municipal institutions; readers of Lope de Vega and of Shakespeare; mutterers of the Mass — children of the Bible! But Virginia is too near home! So is Garrison! One would have thought there was something in the human breast which would sometimes break through policy. These noble-hearted men whom I have named must surely have found quite irksome the constant practice of what Dr. Gardiner used to call "that despicable virtue, prudence"! [Laughter.] One would have thought, when they heard that name spoken with contempt, their ready eloquence would have leaped from its scabbard to avenge even a word that threatened him with insult. But it never came, — never! [Sensation.] I do not say I blame them. Perhaps they thought they should serve the cause better by drawing a broad black line between themselves and him. Perhaps they thought the Devil could be cheated; — I do not think he can. [Laughter and cheers.]

We are perfectly willing — I am, for one — to be the dead lumber that shall make a path for these men into the light and love of the people. We hope for nothing better. Use us freely, in any way, for the slave. When the temple is finished, the tools will not complain that they are thrown aside, let who will lead up the nation to "put on the topstone with shoutings." But while so much remains to be done, while our little camp is beleaguered all about, do nothing to weaken his influence, whose sagacity, more than any other single man's, has led us up hither, and whose name is identified with that movement which the North still heeds, and the South still fears the most. After all, Mr. Chairman, this is no hard task. We know very well, that, notwithstanding this loud clamor about our harsh judgment of men and things, our opinions differ very little from those of our Free Soil friends, or of intelligent men generally, when you really get at them. It has even been said, that one of that family which has made itself so infamously conspicuous here in executing the Fugitive Slave Law, a judge, whose earnest defence of that law we all heard in Faneuil Hall, did himself, but a little while before, arrange for a fugitive to be hid till pursuit was over. I hope it is true, — it would be an honorable inconsistency. And if it be not true of him, we know it is of others. Yet it is base to incite others to deeds, at which, whenever we are hidden from public notice, our own hearts recoil! But thus we see that when men lay aside the judicial ermine, the senator's robe, or the party collar, and sit down in private life, you can hardly distinguish their tones from ours. Their eyes seem as anointed as our own. As in Pope's day, —

> "At all we laugh they laugh, no doubt;
> The only difference is, we dare *laugh out.*"

Caution is not always good policy in a cause like ours. It is said that, when Napoleon saw the day going against him, he used to throw away all the rules of war, and trust himself to the hot impetuosity of his soldiers. The masses are governed more by impulse than conviction; and even were it not so, the convictions of most men are on our side, and this will surely appear, if we can only pierce the crust of their prejudice or indifference. I observe that our Free Soil friends never stir their audience so deeply as when some individual leaps beyond the platform, and strikes upon the very heart of the people. Men listen to discussions of laws and tactics with ominous patience. It is when Mr. Sumner, in Faneuil Hall, avows his determination to disobey the Fugitive Slave Law, and cries out, "I was a man before I was a Commissioner," — when Mr. Giddings says of the fall of slavery, quoting Adams, "Let it come; if it must come in *blood*, yet I say let it come!" — that their associates on the platform are sure they are wrecking the party, — while many a heart beneath beats its first pulse of antislavery life.

These are brave words. When I compare them with the general tone of Free Soil men in Congress, I distrust the atmosphere of Washington and of politics. These men move about, Sauls and Goliaths among us, taller by many a cubit. There they lose port and stature. Mr. Sumner's speech in the Senate unsays no part of his Faneuil Hall pledge. But, though discussing the same topic, no one would gather from any word or argument that the speaker ever took such ground as he did in Faneuil Hall. It is all through, the *law*, the *manner* of the surrender, not the surrender itself, of the slave, that he objects to. As my friend Mr. Pillsbury so forcibly says, so far as anything in the speech shows, he puts the slave behind the jury trial, behind the *habeas corpus* act, and behind the new interpretation of the Constitution, and says to the slave claimant: "You must get through all these, before you reach him; but if you *can* get through all these, you may have him!" It was no tone like this which made the old Hall rock! Not if he got through twelve jury trials, and forty *habeas corpus* acts, and constitutions built high as yonder monument, would he permit so much as the shadow of a little finger of the slave claimant to touch the slave! [Loud applause.] At least, so he was understood. In an elaborate discussion, by the leader of the political antislavery party, of the whole topic of fugitive slaves, you do not find one protest against the surrender itself, one frank expression on the constitutional clause, or any indication of the speaker's final purpose, should any one be properly claimed under that provision. It was under no such uncertain trumpet that the antislavery host was originally marshalled. The tone is that of the German soldiers whom Napoleon routed. They did not care, they said, for the defeat, but only that they were not beaten according to rule. [Laughter and cheers.] Mr. Mann, in his speech of February 15, 1850, says: "*The States being separated*, I would as soon return my own brother or sister into bondage, as I would return a fugitive slave. Before God, and Christ, and all Christian men, they are my brothers and sisters." What a condition! from the lips, too, of a champion of the Higher Law! Whether the States be separate or united, neither my brother nor any other man's brother shall, with my consent, go back to bondage. [Enthusiastic cheers.] So speaks the *heart*, — Mr. Mann's version is that of the politician.

Mr. Mann's recent speech in August, 1852, has the same non-committal tone to which I have alluded in Mr. Sumner's. While professing, in the most eloquent terms, his loyalty to the Higher Law, Mr. Sutherland asked: "Is there, in Mr. Mann's opinion, any conflict between that Higher Law and the Constitution? If so, what is it? If not so, why introduce an irrelevant topic into the debate?" Mr. Mann avoided any reply, and asked not to be interrupted! Is that the frankness which becomes an Abolitionist? Can such concealment help any cause? The design of Mr. Sutherland is evident. If Mr. Mann had allowed there was no conflict between the Higher Law and the Constitution, all his remarks were futile and out of order. But if he asserted that any such conflict existed, how did he justify himself in swearing to support that instrument? — a question our Free Soil friends are slow to meet. Mr. Mann saw the dilemma, and avoided it by silence!

The same speech contains the usual deprecatory assertions that Free-Soilers have no wish to interfere with slavery in the States; that they "consent to let slavery remain where it is." If he means that he, Horace Mann, a moral and accountable being, "consents to let slavery remain where it is," all the rest of his speech is sound and fury, signifying nothing. If he means that he, Horace Mann, as a politician and party man, consents to that, but, elsewhere and otherwise, will do his best to abolish this "all-comprehending wickedness of slavery, in which every wrong and every crime has its natural home," then he should have plainly said so. Otherwise, his disclaimer is unworthy of him, and could have deceived no one. He must have known that all the South care for is the action, not in what capacity the deed is done.

Mr. Giddings is more careful in his statement; but, judged by his speech on the "Platforms," how little does he seem to understand either his own duty or the true philosophy of the cause he serves! He says: —

"We, Sir, would drive the slave question from discussion in this hall. It never had a constitutional existence here. Separate this government from all interference with slavery; let the Federal power wash its hands from that institution; let us purify ourselves from its contagion; leave it with the States, who alone have the power to sustain it, — then, Sir, will agitation cease in regard to it here; then we shall have nothing more to do with it; our time will be no more occupied with it; and, like a band of freemen, a band of brothers, we could meet here, and legislate for the prosperity, the improvement of mankind, for the elevation of our race."

Mr. Sumner speaks in the same strain. He says: —

"The time will come when courts or Congress will declare, that nowhere under the Constitution can man hold property in man. For the republic, such a decree will be the way of peace and safety. As slavery is banished from the national jurisdiction, it will cease to vex our national politics. It may linger in the States as a local institution, but it will no longer endanger national animosities when it no longer demands national support. . . . . . For himself, he knows no better aim under the Constitution than to bring the government back to the precise position which it occupied" when it was launched.

This seems to me a very mistaken strain. Whenever slavery is banished from our national jurisdiction, it will be a momentous gain, a vast stride. But let us not mistake the half-way house for the end of the journey. I need not say that it matters not to Abolitionists under what special law slavery exists. Their battle lasts while it exists anywhere, and I doubt not Mr. Sumner and Mr. Giddings feel themselves enlisted for the whole war. I will even suppose, what neither of these gentlemen states, that their plan includes, not only that slavery shall be abolished in the District and Territories, but that the slave basis of representation shall be struck from the Constitution, and the slave-surrender clause construed away. But even then, does Mr. Giddings or Mr. Sumner really believe that slavery, existing in its full force in the States, "will cease to vex our national politics"? Can they point to any State where a powerful oligarchy, possessed of immense wealth, has ever existed, without attempting to meddle in the government? Even now, does not manufacturing, banking, and commercial capital perpetually vex our politics? Why should not slave capital exert the same influence? Do they imagine that a hundred thousand men, possessed of two thousand millions of dollars, which they feel the spirit of the age is seeking to tear from their grasp, will not eagerly catch at all the support they can obtain by getting the control of the government? In a land where the dollar is almighty, "where the sin of not being rich is only atoned for by the effort to become so," do they doubt that such an oligarchy will generally succeed? Besides, banking and manufacturing stocks are not urged by despair to seek a controlling influence in politics. They know they are about equally safe, whichever party rules, — that no party wishes to legislate their rights away. Slave property knows that its being allowed to exist depends on its having the virtual control of the government. Its constant presence in politics is dictated, therefore, by despair, as well as by the wish to secure fresh privileges. Money, however, is not the only strength of the Slave Power. That, indeed, were enough, in an age when capitalists are our feudal barons. But, though driven entirely from national shelter, the slaveholders would have the strength of old associations, and of peculiar laws in their own States, which gives those States wholly into their hands. A weaker prestige, fewer privileges, and less comparative wealth, have enabled the British aristocracy to rule England for two centuries, though the root of their strength was cut at Naseby. It takes ages for deeply-rooted institutions to die; and driving slavery into the States will hardly be our Naseby. Whoever, therefore, lays the flattering unction to his soul, that, while slavery exists anywhere in the

States, our legislators will sit down "like a band of brothers," — unless they are all slaveholding brothers, — is doomed to find himself wofully mistaken. Mr. Adams, ten years ago, refused to sanction this doctrine of his friend, Mr. Giddings, combating it ably and eloquently in his well-known reply to Ingersoll. Though Mr Adams touches on but one point, the principle he lays down has many other applications.

But is Mr. Giddings willing to sit down with slaveholders, "like a band of brothers," and not seek, knowing all the time that they are tyrants at home, to use the common strength to protect their victims? Does he not know that it is impossible for Free States and Slave States to unite under any form of Constitution, no matter how clean the parchment may be, without the compact resulting in new strength to the slave system? It is the unimpaired strength of Massachusetts and New York, and the youthful vigor of Ohio, that, even now, enable bankrupt Carolina to hold up the institution. Every nation must maintain peace within her limits. No government can exist which does not fulfil that function. When we say the Union will maintain peace in Carolina, that being a Slave State, what does "peace" mean? It means keeping the slave beneath the heel of his master. Now, even on the principle of two wrongs making a right, if we put this great weight of a common government into the scale of the slaveholder, we are bound to add something equal to the slave's side. But no, Mr. Giddings is content to give the slaveholder the irresistible and organic help of a common government, and bind himself to utter no word, and move not a finger, in his civil capacity, to help the slave! An Abolitionist would find himself not much at home, I fancy, in that "band of brothers"!

And Mr. Sumner "knows no better aim, under the Constitution, than to bring back the government" to where it was in 1789! Has the voyage been so very honest and prosperous a one, in his opinion, that his only wish is to start again with the same ship, the same crew, and the same sailing-orders? Grant all he claims as to the state of public opinion, the intentions of leading men, and the form of our institutions at that period; still, with all these checks on wicked men, and helps to good ones, here we are, in 1853, according to his own showing, ruled by slavery, tainted to the core with slavery, and binding the infamous Fugitive Slave Law like an honorable frontlet on our brows! The more accurate and truthful his glowing picture of the public virtue of 1789, the stronger my argument. If even all those great patriots, and all that enthusiasm for justice and liberty, did not avail to keep us safe in such a Union, what will? In such desperate circumstances, can his statesmanship devise no better aim than to try the same experiment over again, under precisely the same conditions? What new guaranties does he propose to prevent the voyage from being again turned into a piratical slave-trading cruise? None! Have sixty years taught us nothing? In 1660, the English thought, in recalling Charles II., that the memory of that scaffold which had once darkened the windows of Whitehall would be guaranty enough for his good behavior. But, spite of the spectre, Charles II. repeated Charles I., and James outdid him. Wiser by this experience, when the nation, in 1689, got another chance, they trusted to no guaranties, but so arranged the very elements of their government that William III. *could not* repeat Charles I. Let us profit by the lesson. These mistakes of leading men merit constant attention. Such remarks as those I have quoted, uttered from the high places of political life, however carefully guarded, have a sad influence on the rank and file of the party. The antislavery awakening has cost too many years and too much labor to risk letting its energy be turned into a wrong channel, or balked by fruitless experiments. Neither the slave nor the country must be cheated a second time.

Mr. Chairman, when I remember the grand port of these men elsewhere, and witness this confusion of ideas, and veiling of their proud crests to party necessities, they seem to me to lose in Washington something of their old giant proportions. How often have we witnessed this change! It seems the inevitable result of political life under any government, but especially under ours; and we are surprised at it in these men, only because we fondly hoped they would be exceptions to the general rule. It was Chamfort, I think, who first likened a republican senate-house to Milton's Pandemonium; — another proof of the rare insight French writers have shown in criticising republican institutions. The Capitol at Washington always brings to my mind that other Capitol, which in Milton's great epic "rose like an exhalation" "from the burning marl," — that towering palace, "with starry lamps and blazing cressets" hung, — with "roof of fretted gold" and stately height, its hall "like a covered field." You remember, Sir, the host of archangels gathered round it, and how thick the airy crowd

> "Swarmed and were straitened; till, the signal given,
> Behold a wonder! They but now who seemed
> In bigness to surpass earth's giant sons,
> Now less than smallest dwarfs, in narrow room
> Throng numberless, like that pygmean race
> Beyond the Indian mount; or fairy elves,
> Whose midnight revels, by a forest side
> Or fountain, some belated peasant sees.
> . . . . .
> Thus incorporeal spirits to smallest forms
> Reduced their shapes immense, and were at large,
> Though without number still, amid the hall
> Of that infernal court."

Mr. Chairman, they got no further than the hall

[Cheers.] They were not, in the current phrase, "*a healthy party*"*!* The healthy party — the men who made no compromise in order to come under that arch — Milton describes further on, where he says:

> "But far within,
> And in their own dimensions, like themselves,
> The great seraphic lords and cherubim,
> In close recess and secret conclave, sat;
> A thousand demigods on golden seats
> Frequent and full."

These were the healthy party! [Loud applause.] These are the Casses and the Houstons, the Footes and the Soulés, the Clays, the Websters, and the Douglases, that bow no lofty forehead in the dust, but can find ample room and verge enough under the Constitution. Our friends go down there, and must be dwarfed into pygmies before they can find space within the lists! [Cheers.]

It would be superfluous to say that we grant the entire sincerity and true-heartedness of these men. But in critical times, when a wrong step entails most disastrous consequences, to "mean well" is not enough. Sincerity is no shield for any man from the criticism of his fellow-laborers. I do not fear that such men as these will take offence at our discussion of their views and conduct. Long years of hard labor, in which we have borne at least our share, have resulted in a golden opportunity. How to use it, friends differ. Shall we stand courteously silent, and let these men play out the play, when, to our thinking, their plan will slacken the zeal, balk the hopes, and waste the efforts of the slave's friends? No! I know Charles Sumner's love for the cause so well, that I am sure he will welcome my criticism whenever I deem his counsel wrong; that he will hail every effort to serve our common client more efficiently. [Great cheering.] It is not his honor nor mine that is at issue; not his feeling nor mine that is to be consulted. The only question for either of us is, What in these golden moments can be done? where can the hardest blow be struck? [Loud applause.] I hope I am just to Mr. Sumner; I have known him long, and honor him. I know his genius, I honor his virtues; yet if, from his high place, he sends out counsels which I think dangerous to the cause, I am bound to raise my voice against them. I do my duty in a private communication to him first, then in public to his friends and mine. The friendship that will not bear this criticism is but the frost-work of a winter's morning, which the sun looks upon and it is gone. His friendship will survive all that I say of him, and mine will survive all that he shall say of me; and this is the only way in which the antislavery cause can be served. Truth, success, victory, triumph over the obstacles that beset us, — this is all either of us wants. [Cheers.]

If all I have said to you is untrue, if I have exaggerated, explain to me this fact. In 1831, Mr. Garrison commenced a paper advocating the doctrine of immediate emancipation. He had against him the thirty thousand churches and all the clergy of the country, — its wealth, its commerce, its press. In 1831, what was the state of things? There was the most entire ignorance and apathy on the slave question. If men knew of the existence of slavery, it was only as a part of picturesque Virginia life. No one preached, no one talked, no one wrote about it. No whisper of it stirred the surface of the political sea. The Church heard of it occasionally, when some colonization agent asked funds to send the blacks to Africa. Old school-books tainted with some antislavery selections had passed out of use, and new ones were compiled to suit the times. Soon as any dissent from the prevailing faith appeared, every one set himself to crush it. The pulpits preached at it; the press denounced it; mobs tore down houses, threw presses into the fire and the stream, and shot the editors; religious conventions tried to smother it; parties arrayed themselves against it. Daniel Webster boasted in the Senate, that he had never introduced the subject of slavery to that body, and never would. Mr. Clay, in 1839, makes a speech for the Presidency, in which he says, that to discuss the subject of slavery is moral treason, and that no man has a right to introduce the subject into Congress. Mr. Benton, in 1844, laid down his platform, and he not only denies the right, but asserts that he never has and never will discuss the subject. Yet Mr. Clay, from 1839 down to his death, hardly made a remarkable speech of any kind, except on slavery. Mr. Webster, having indulged now and then in a little easy rhetoric, as at Niblo's and elsewhere, opens his mouth in 1840, generously contributing his aid to both sides, and stops talking about it only when death closes his lips. Mr. Benton's six or eight speeches in the United States Senate have all been on the subject of slavery in the Southwestern section of the country, and form the basis of whatever claim he has to the character of a statesman, and he owes his seat in the next Congress somewhat, perhaps, to anti-slavery pretensions! The Whig and Democratic parties pledged themselves just as emphatically against the anti-slavery discussion, — against agitation and free speech. These men said: "It sha'n't be talked about, it won't be talked about!" These are *your statesmen!* — men who understand the present, that is, and mould the future! The man who understands his own time, and whose genius moulds the future to his views, he is a statesman, is he not? These men devoted themselves to banks, to the tariff, to internal improvements, to constitutional and financial questions. They said to slavery: "Back! no entrance here! We pledge ourselves against you." And then there came up a humble printer-boy, who whipped them into the traces, and made them talk, like Hotspur's starling, nothing BUT slavery. He scattered all these gigantic shadows, — tariff, bank, constitutional questions, financial questions, — and slavery, like the colossal head in Walpole's romance, came up and filled the whole political horizon! [Enthusiastic applause.] Yet you must remember he is not a statesman; he is a "fanatic." He has no discipline, — Mr. "Ion" says so; he does not understand the "discipline that is essential to victory"! This man did not understand his own time, — he did not know what the future was to be, — he was not able to shape it, — he had no "prudence," — he had no "foresight"! Daniel Webster says, "I have never introduced this subject, and never will," — and died broken-hearted because he had not been able to talk enough about it. Benton says, "I will never speak of slavery," and lives to break with his party on this issue! Mr. Clay says it is "moral treason" to introduce the subject into Congress, and lives to see Congress turned into an antislavery debating-society, to suit the purpose of one "too powerful individual"!

These were statesmen, mark you! Two of them have gone to their graves covered with eulogy; and our national stock of eloquence is all insufficient to describe how profound and far-reaching was the sagacity of Daniel Webster! Remember who it was that said, in 1831, "I am in earnest, — I will not equivocate, — I will not excuse, — I will not retreat a single inch, — *and I will be heard!*" [Repeated cheers.] That speaker has lived twenty-two years, and the complaint of twenty-three millions of people is, "Shall we never hear of anything but slavery?" [Cheers.] I heard Dr. Kirk, of Boston, say in his own pulpit, when he returned from London, — where he had been as a representative to the "Evangelical Alliance," — "I went up to London, and they asked me what I thought of the question of immediate emancipation. They examined us all. Is an American never to travel anywhere in the world but men will throw this troublesome question in his face?" Well, it is all HIS fault [pointing to Mr. Garrison]. [Enthusiastic cheers.]

Now, when we come to talk of statesmanship, of sagacity in choosing time and measures, of endeavor, by proper means, to right the public mind, of keen insight into the present and potent sway over the future, it seems to me that the Abolitionists, who have taken — whether for good or for ill, whether to their discredit or to their praise — this country by the four corners, and shaken it until you can hear nothing but slavery, whether you travel in railroad or steamboat, whether you enter the hall of legislation or read the columns of a newspaper, — it seems to me that such men may point to the present aspect of the nation, to their originally avowed purpose, to the pledges and efforts of all your great men against them, and then let you determine to which side the credit of sagacity and statesmanship belongs. Napoleon busied himself, at St. Helena, in showing how Wellington ought not to have conquered at Waterloo. The world has never got time to listen to the explanation. Sufficient for it that the Allies entered Paris. In like manner, it seems hardly the province of a defeated Church and State to deny the skill of measures by which they have been conquered.

It may sound strange to some, this claim for Mr. Garrison of a profound statesmanship. Men have heard him styled a mere fanatic so long, that they are incompetent to judge him fairly. "The phrases men are accustomed," says Goethe, "to repeat incessantly, end by becoming convictions, and ossify the organs of intelligence." I cannot accept you, therefore, as my jury. I appeal from Festus to Cæsar; from the prejudice of our streets to the common sense of the world, and to your children.

Every thoughtful and unprejudiced mind must see that such an evil as slavery will yield only to the most radical treatment. If you consider the work we have to do, you will not think us needlessly aggressive, or that we dig down unnecessarily deep in laying the foundations of our enterprise. A money power of two thousand millions of dollars, as the prices of slaves now range, held by a small body of able and desperate men; that body raised into a political aristocracy by special constitutional provisions; cotton, the product of slave labor, forming the basis of our whole foreign commerce, and the commercial class thus subsidized; the press bought up, the pulpit reduced to vassalage, the heart of the common people chilled by a bitter prejudice against the black race; our leading men bribed, by ambition, either to silence or open hostility; — in such a land, on what shall an Abolitionist rely? On a few cold prayers, mere lip-service, and never from the heart? On a church resolution, hidden often in its records, and meant only as a decent cover for servility in daily practice? On political parties, with their superficial influence at best, and seeking ordinarily only to use existing prejudices to the best advantage? Slavery has deeper root here than any aristocratic institution has in Europe; and politics is but the common pulse-beat, of which revolution is the fever-spasm. Yet we have seen European aristocracy survive storms which seemed to reach down to the primal strata of European life. Shall we, then, trust to mere politics, where even revolution has failed? How shall the stream rise above its fountain? Where shall our church organizations or parties get strength to attack their great parent and moulder, the Slave Power? Shall the thing formed say to him that formed it, Why hast thou made me thus? The old jest of one who tried to lift himself in his own basket, is but a tame picture of the man who imagines that, by working solely through existing sects and parties, he can destroy slavery. Mechanics say nothing but an earthquake, strong enough to move all Egypt, can bring down the Pyramids.

Experience has confirmed these views. The Abolitionists who have acted on them have a "short method" with all unbelievers. They have but to point to their own success, in contrast with every other man's failure. To waken the nation to its real state, and chain it to the consideration of this one duty, is half the work. So much we have done. Slavery has been made the question of this generation. To startle the South to madness, so that every step she takes, in her blindness, is one step more toward ruin, is much. This we have done. Witness Texas and the Fugitive Slave Law. To have elaborated for the nation the only plan of redemption, pointed out the only exodus from this "sea of troubles," is much. This we claim to have done in our motto of IMMEDIATE, UNCONDITIONAL EMANCIPATION ON THE SOIL. The closer any statesmanlike mind looks into the question, the more favor our plan finds with it. The Christian asks fairly of the infidel, "If this religion be not from God, how do you explain its triumph, and the history of the first three centuries?" Our question is similar. If our agitation has not been wisely planned and conducted, explain for us the history of the last twenty years! Experience is a safe light to walk by, and he is not a rash man who expects success in future from the same means which have secured it in times past.

REMOVAL OF JUDGE LORING.*

MR. CHAIRMAN AND GENTLEMEN: The petitions offered you on any one topic are usually all in the same words. On the present occasion, I observe on your table twelve or fourteen different forms. This is very significant. It shows they do not proceed from a central committee, which has been organized to rouse the Commonwealth. They speak the instinctive, irrepressible wish of all parts of the State. It is the action of persons of different parties, sects, and sections, moving independently of each other, but seeking the same object. Some persons have sneered at these petitions because women are found among the signers. Neither you, Gentlemen, nor the Legislature, will maintain that women, that is, just one half of the Commonwealth, have no right to petition. A civil right, which no one denies even to foreigners, will not certainly be denied to the women of Massachusetts. And is there any one thoughtless enough to affirm that this is not a proper occasion for women to exercise their rights? These petitions ask the removal of a *Judge of Probate*. Probate judges are the guardians of widows and orphans. Women have a peculiar interest in the character of such judges. He chooses an exceedingly bad occasion to laugh, who laughs when the women of the

* Argument before the Committee on Federal Relations of the Massachusetts Legislature, in Support of the Petitions for the Removal of Edward Greely Loring from the Office of Judge of Probate, February 20, 1855.

Commonwealth ask you to remove a Judge of Probate, who has shown that he is neither a humane man nor a good lawyer. In the whole of my remarks, Gentlemen, I beg you to bear in mind that we, the petitioners, are asking you to remove, not a judge merely, but a Judge of *Probate*. A magistrate who is, in a peculiar sense, the counsellor of the widow and the fatherless.

The family, in the moment of terrible bereavement and distress, must first stand before him. To his discretion and knowledge are committed most delicate questions, large amounts of property, and very dear and vastly important family relations. Surely, that should not be a rude hand which is thrust among chords that have just been sorely wrung. Surely, he should be a wise and most trustworthy man who is to settle questions on many of which, from the nature of the case, there can, practically, be no appeal. His court is not watched by a jury. It is silent and private, and has little publicity in its proceedings. He should be, therefore, most emphatically a magistrate able to stand alone; whose rigid independence cannot be overawed or swayed by cunning or able individuals about him; one skilful in the law, and who, while he holds the scales of justice most exactly even, has a tender and humane heart; one whose generous instincts need no prompting from without.

Some object that this petition asks you to do an act fatal, they say, to the independence of the judiciary. The petitioners are asked whether they do not know the value and importance of an independent judiciary. Mr. Chairman, we are fully aware of its importance. We know as well as our fellow-citizens the unspeakable value of a high-minded, enlightened, humane, independent, and just judge; one whom neither "fear, favor, *affection*, nor hope of reward" can turn from his course. It is *because* we are so fully impressed with this, that we appear before you.

Taking our history as a whole, we are proud of the Bench of Massachusetts. You have given no higher title than that of a Massachusetts Judge to Sewall, to Sedgwick, to Parsons. Take it away, then, from one who volunteers, hastens, to execute a statute which the law as well as the humanity of the nineteenth century regards as infamous and an outrage. We come before you, not to attack the Bench, but to strengthen it, by securing it the only support it can have under a government like ours, — the confidence of the people. You cannot legislate judges into the confidence of the people. You cannot preach them into it; confidence must be earned. To make the name of judge respected, it must be worthy of respect, — must never be borne by unworthy men. It never will be either respected or respectable while this man bears it. I might surely ask his removal in the names of the Judges of Massachusetts, who must feel that this man is no fit fellow for them. The special reasons why we deem him an unfit judge, I shall take occasion to state by and by. At present, I will only add, that it is not, as report says, merely because he differs from us on the question of slavery, that we ask his removal. It is not for an honest or for any other difference of opinion that we ask it; but, as we shall presently take occasion to state, for far other and very grave reasons.

I do not know, Gentlemen, what course of remark the remonstrant, or his counsel, may adopt; but I have thought it necessary to say so much, in order that they may understand our position, and thus avoid any needless enlargement upon our want of respect for the function, or appreciation of the value, of an independent, high-minded judiciary. You will see, in the course of my remarks, that it is because this incumbent has sinned in that very respect that we appear here.

Gentlemen, these petitions, though variously worded,

all ask you to "take proper steps for the removal of Edward Greely Loring from office," — "*proper steps.*" It is for the Legislature to decide what the "proper steps" are.

In offering some remarks on the proper method of procedure in this case, you will bear in mind that I necessarily, perhaps, go over more ground than the progress of this discussion may show to have been necessary; because, of course, I must be entirely ignorant what ground the remonstrant, or his counsel, will take. I must, therefore, cover *all* the ground.

You are of course aware, Gentlemen, that, originally, all judges were appointed by the king, and held their offices as long and on such conditions as he pleased to prescribe. Some held as long as they behaved well, — *during good behavior*, as our Constitution translates the old law Latin, *quamdiu se bene gesserint;* others held during the pleasure of the king, *durante bene placito*, as the phrase is. This, of course, made the judges entirely the creatures of the king. To prevent this, and secure the independence of the judges, after the English Revolution of 1689, it was fixed by the Act of Settlement, as it is called, that the king should not have the power to remove judges, but that they should hold their offices "*during good behavior.*" They were still, however, removable by the king, on address from both Houses of Parliament.

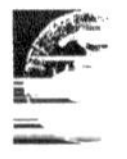

Hallam, in his Constitutional History, states very tersely the exact state of the English law, and it is precisely the law of this Commonwealth also, in these words: "No judge can be dismissed from office except in consequence of a conviction for some offence, OR *the address of both Houses of Parliament*, which is tantamount to an act of Legislature." (Const. Hist., Am. edit., p. 597.)

To come now to our Commonwealth. There are, as I just intimated, two ways of removing a judge known to the Constitution: one is, by impeachment; and the other is, by address of the Legislature to the Governor. A judge who commits a crime, whether in his official capacity or not, may be punished by indictment, precisely as any other man may, — this principle may be left out of the question. A judge, who, sitting on the bench, transgresses the laws in his official capacity, may be impeached by the House of Representatives before the Senate, as a Court of Impeachment, and removed. (Const. Mass., Chap. I. Sec. 2, Art. 8.)

The petitioners do not ask you to impeach Judge Loring. Why? Because they do not come here to say that he has been guilty of *official misconduct.* To render a judge liable to impeachment, he must be proved to have misconducted *in his official capacity.* I shall not go into the niceties of the law of impeachment. One would suppose, from the arguments of the press at the present time, and their comments on Mr. Loring's remonstrance, that a judge could not be impeached unless he had violated some express law. This is not so. It has been always held, that a judge may be guilty of *official misconduct*, and liable to impeachment, who had not violated any positive statute. It is enough that the act violates the principles of the common law. All authorities agree in this, and some would seem to lay down the rule still more broadly. (See Story on the Const., Bk. III. ch. 10, §§ 796 – 798, and Shaw's argument when counsel against Prescott, Prescott's Trial, p. 180.) As the Constitution confines the process of impeachment to cases of *official misconduct*, and as we do not pretend that Mr. Loring, *sitting as a Judge of Probate*, has been guilty of any such, I pass from this point.

But the Constitution provides another form, which is, that a judge may be removed from office by address of both Houses to His Excellency the Governor. In the first place, Gentlemen, let me read to you the source of this power. " All judicial officers, duly appointed, commissioned, and sworn, shall hold their offices during good behavior, excepting such concerning whom there is a different provision made in this Constitution: *Provided*, nevertheless, the Governor, with consent of the Council, may remove them upon address of both Houses of the Legislature." (Const. of Mass., Chap. III. Art. 1.) "*Provided, nevertheless*, the Governor, with consent of the Council, may remove them upon the address of both Houses of the Legislature." Now, Gentlemen, looking on the face of this, it would be naturally inferred that, notwithstanding his "good behavior," and without alleging any violation of it, a judge could, nevertheless, be removed by address; that an "address" need not be based on a charge of official misconduct, — that an "address" need not be based on a charge of illegal conduct, in any capacity. This seems so clear, that I should have left this point without further remark, if Mr. Loring had not placed upon your files a remonstrance against the prayer of these petitioners, which remonstrance (I shall not occupy your time by reading it) is based upon the principle, that it would be a hard and unjust procedure if either house should address the Governor against him, seeing that he has not violated any State law, or done anything that was illegal, or that was prohibited by the laws of Massachusetts, and alleging that he has only acted in conformity with the official oath of all officers of the State to support the Constitution of the United States. The defence of the remonstrant, as far as we are informed of it, is, that he ought not to be removed, because he has violated no *law* of Massachusetts. To that plea, Gentlemen, I shall simply reply: the method of removing a judge by "address" does not require that the House or Senate should be convinced that he has violated any law whatever. Grant all Mr. Loring states in his remonstrance, — that he has broken no law, that he stands legally impeccable before you; which, in other words, is simply to say that he cannot be indicted. If he had violated a law, he could be indicted; he comes to this house and says, in effect, "Gentlemen, I cannot be indicted; *therefore*, I ought not to be removed." The reply of the petitioners is, A man may be unfit for a judge long before he becomes fit for the state-prison. Their reply is, (leaving for the time all question of impeachment,) It is not necessary that a judge should render himself liable to indictment, in order to be subject to be removed by "address." He can be removed (as my brother who preceded me [Seth Webb, Jr., Esq.] has well said) for any cause which the Legislature, in its discretion, thinks a fitting cause for his removal. Even if he has not violated any law of the Commonwealth, written or unwritten, still he may be removed, if the Legislature thinks the public interest demands it. The matter is entirely within your discretion. My proof of this is, first, the language of the Constitution. The Constitution says: "The Senate shall be a court with full authority to hear and determine all impeachments made by the House of Representatives against any officer or officers of the Commonwealth, for misconduct and mal-administration in their offices." (Chap. I. Sec. 2, Art. 8.) Now, suppose it true, as some claim, that such *misconduct* must amount to a violation of positive law, that nothing short of that will justify impeachment; the mere fact that the Constitution provides another way would be *prima facie* evidence that it meant to lay a broader foundation for removal; else, why *two* methods? If, in his office, he had outraged the laws of the State, he could be impeached. Is not one remedy sufficient? Why does the Constitution provide another? Because the people, through their Constitution, meant to say, "We will not have judges that cannot be removed unless they have violated a statute. We will provide, that in case of any misconduct, any unfitting character, any incapacity or loss of confidence, the supreme power of the Legislature may intervene and remove them." If impeachment applies only to *official* misconduct, expressly prohibited by statute, as seems to be claimed, then, from the existence of another additional method in the Constitution, one would naturally infer that this other power referred to misconduct *not* official, and *not* expressly prohibited by statute. In addition to the mere letter of the Constitution, and the inference from the fact of two powers being granted, we have the action of the Commonwealth in times past. I have not time for historical details, but the power of address, whenever it has been used in this Commonwealth, has been used to remove judges who had not violated any law. Judge Bradbury was removed, I think, for mental incapacity, resulting from advancing age. Of course, intellectual inefficiency is not impeachable; it is not such "misconduct or mal-administration" as renders a man liable to impeachment; but the Constitution, in order to cover the whole ground, has left with the Legislature the power to remove an inefficient judge, — a judge who has grown too old to perform his duties.

But it happens that this clause of the Constitution has been passed upon, — not, indeed, by the Supreme Court, but I may say by equally high authority. It has been expounded by some of the ablest men the Commonwealth ever knew, and in circumstances which preclude the idea of prejudice or passion. It is fortunate for these petitioners, in regard to this claim of the power of the Legislature (which it is said Mr. Loring's friends intend to deny, and which his remonstrance does practically deny), — it is fortunate for them, that in the Constitutional Convention of Massachusetts, in 1820, this clause of the Constitution was deliberately discussed. It was discussed, Gentlemen, not when there was a case before the Commonwealth, when men were divided into parties, when personal sympathy or antipathy might bias men's judgments, but when the debaters were in the most unimpassioned state of mind; — statesmen, endeavoring to found the laws of the Commonwealth on the best basis. The discussion was long and able. I shall read you the sentiments of different gentlemen who took part in that discussion, for this purpose, — to show you that this Legislature has an unlimited power of removal for any cause, — whether the law has been violated or not, — whether acts were done by a judge in his official capacity or any other. Allow me to remind you, Gentlemen, that there are two questions you are bound to ask. The first is, *Can* we remove a judge who is not guilty of any *official misconduct*, of any violation of statute law, in any capacity? The second is, If we have the power, *ought* we to exercise it in the present case? 1st. Have we this power? 2d. Ought we to exercise it?

I propose to read you extracts from the speeches in the Massachusetts Convention of 1820, to show that the Legislature has, in the judgment of our ablest lawyers and statesmen, an unlimited authority to ask the removal of judges whenever it sees fit, and for any cause the Legislature thinks sufficient; that the PEOPLE, the original source of all power, have not parted with their sovereignty in this respect, — did not intend to part with it, and did not part with it. When I have convinced you, if I shall succeed in convincing you, that you have this authority, I shall, with your permission, say a few words to enforce the other point, that you ought to exercise it according to the prayer of the petitioners.

In the first place, I read the clause of the Constitution: "The Governor, with consent of the Council, may remove them [judicial officers] upon the address of both houses of the Legislature." The Constitutional Convention, which met in 1820, appointed a committee to take this clause into consideration. That committee consisted of Messrs. Story of Salem (Judge Story, of the Supreme Court of the United States), John Phillips of Boston (Judge of the Common Pleas Court of Massachusetts, and President of the Senate), Martin of Dorchester, Cummings of Salem (Judge of the Common Pleas), Levi Lincoln of Worcester (afterwards Judge of our Supreme Court and Governor of the Commonwealth), Andrews of Newburyport, Holmes of Rochester, Hills of Pittsfield, Austin of Charlestown (High Sheriff of Middlesex County), Leland of Roxbury (afterwards Judge of Probate for Norfolk County), Kent of West Springfield, Shaw of Boston (present Chief Justice of the Commonwealth), Marston of Barnstable, Austin of Boston (since Attorney-General of the Commonwealth), and Bartlett of Medford, — a committee highly respectable for the ability and position of its members. Permit me to read a section of their Report (p. 136): —

"By the first article of the Constitution, any judge may be removed from his office by the Governor, with the advice of the Council, upon the address of a bare majority of both Houses of the Legislature. The committee are of opinion that this provision has a tendency materially to impair the independence of the judges, and to destroy the efficacy of the clause which declares they shall hold their offices during good behavior. The tenure of good behavior seems to the committee indispensable to guard judges, on the one hand, from the effects of sudden resentments and temporary prejudices entertained by the people, and, on the other hand, from the influence which ambitious and powerful men naturally exert over those who are dependent upon their good-will. A provision which should at once secure to the people a power of removal in cases of palpable misconduct or incapacity, and at the same time secure to the judges a reasonable permanency in their offices, seems of the greatest utility; and such a provision will, in the opinion of the committee, be obtained by requiring that the removal instead of being upon the address of a *majority*, shall be upon the address of *two thirds* of the members present of each House of the Legislature."

The committee, you see, Gentlemen, acknowledge that there is unlimited power; they think that power dangerous; they advise that it should be limited — how? Observe, even this committee, although they say they think it dangerous, do not advise it should be stricken out; but they advise it should be limited by requiring a two-thirds vote, and this is all.

Remember, Gentlemen, that I read the following extracts, not to show the opinion of this Convention as to the value or the danger of this power; I merely wish to show you that, in the opinion of the ablest lawyers of the State, the Constitution, as it then stood, (and *it stands now precisely as it stood then*,) gave to this Legislature unlimited authority to remove judges, for any cause they saw fit; and that, while all the speakers were fully aware of its liability to abuse, no speaker denied its unlimited extent, or proposed to strike the power from the Constitution. After that report had been put in, the Convention proceeded to take it up for discussion.

The first gentleman who joins, to any purpose, in the debate, is Samuel Hubbard, Esq., perhaps, beyond all comparison, the fairest-minded as well as one of the ablest lawyers of the Suffolk bar; and let me add, that, after a life passed in the most responsible practice of his profession, he finished it on the bench of the Supreme Court. His testimony is the more valuable, because Mr. Hubbard thought this provision eminently dangerous. But he says: —

"The Constitution was defective in not sufficiently securing the independence of judges. He asked if a judge was free when the Legislature might have him removed *when it pleased*. . . . . The tenure of office of judges was said to be during good behavior. Was this the case, when the Legislature might deprive them of their office, *although they had committed no crime?* .... No justice of the peace was allowed to be deprived of his office without a hearing, but here the judges of the highest court might be dismissed without an opportunity of saying a word in their defence."

Then comes Chief Justice Lemuel Shaw: —

"The general principle was, that they should be independent of the other persons during good behavior. What is meant by good behavior? The faithful discharge of the duties of the office. If not faithful, they were liable to trial by impeachments. But cases might arise when it might be desirable to remove a judge from office *for other causes.* He may become incapable of performing the duties of the office without fault. He may lose his reason, or be *otherwise incapacitated.* It is the theory of our government, that no man shall receive the emoluments of office without performing the services, though he is incapacitated by the providence of God. It is necessary, therefore, that there should be provision for this case. But in cases when it applies, the reason will be so manifest as to command a general assent. It must be known so as to admit of no doubt, if a judge has lost his reason, or become incapable of performing his duties. As it does not imply misbehavior, if the reason cannot be made manifest so as to command the assent of a great majority of the Legislature, of two thirds at least, there can be no necessity for the removal. *By the Constitution as it stands, the judges hold their offices at the will of the majority of the Legislature.* He confessed with pride and pleasure that the power had not been abused. But it was capable of being abused. If so, it ought to be guarded against. That could be done by requiring the voice of two thirds of each branch of the Legislature."

Then comes William Prescott, a name well known here and the world over. He was a man of English make; taciturn, of few words, no diffuse American talker. He spoke little, but each word was worth gold. His rare civil virtues, great ability, and eminently judicial mind added lustre to a name that was heard in the van of Bunker Hill fight.

"What security have they [judges] by the Constitution? They hold their offices as long as they behave well, and nc longer. They are impeached when guilty of misconduct. It is the duty of the House of Representatives, constituting the grand inquest of the Commonwealth, to make inquiry, — for the Senate to try, and, if guilty, to remove them from office. There may be other cases in which they ought to be removed, when not guilty of misconduct in office, but for infirmity. Provision is made for these cases, that the two branches of the Legislature, concurring with the Governor and Council, may remove judges from office. He did not object to this provision, if it was restrained so as to preserve the independence of the judges. They should be independent of the Legislature and of the Governor and Council. But now there is no security. The two other departments may remove them without inquiry, — without putting any reason on record. It is in their power to say that the judges shall no longer hold their offices, and that others more agreeable shall be put in their places. He asked, was this independence?"

There may be "other cases" in which they ought to be removed when not guilty of misconduct in office, but from infirmity. Is not that exactly what the petitioners claim? There being no misconduct in office, no violation of the precise statutes of the Commonwealth, comes the case described by Mr. Prescott, where a judge ought to be dismissed for "infirmity"; for we maintain that there was here a cruel "infirmity." "He did not object to this provision" if properly restrained, (that was the old Federalist; the man who never was inclined to trust the people too far; the man who was in favor of a strong government!) — "he did not object to this provision"; all he asked was a two-thirds vote.

Then comes Mr. Daniel Davis of Boston. You may not have known him, Gentlemen; but those of us who are older remember him as the Solicitor-General for the Commonwealth of Massachusetts. He says: —

"If the resolutions were before the committee in a form

which admitted of amendment, he would propose to alter it in such manner that the officer to be removed should have a right to be heard. No reason need now be given for the removal of a judge, but that the Legislature do not like him."

He did not deny the power, did not question its utility; all he wanted was, that the officer should be heard. "No reason need be given, but that the Legislature do not like him." Is not this unlimited power? The claim of Mr. Loring is, substantially, that you abuse your power, unless you charge, and prove, that he has offended against a statute "in such case made and provided." Mr. Daniel Davis says: "No reason need be given for the removal of a judge, but that the Legislature do not like him." That is his idea of the power of this Legislature.

Then comes Mr. Henry H. Childs of Pittsfield. I do not know his history. He did not want the Constitution changed at all; he did not ask even the two-thirds vote. Mr. Childs says: —

"It was in violation of an important principle of the government, that the majority of the Legislature, together with the Governor, should not have the power of removal from office. This power was in accordance with the principle of the Bill of Rights. It was imperative in the advocates of this resolution to show that it was necessary to intrench this department of the government for its security. They had not shown it; on the contrary, we were in the full tide of successful experiment. The founders of the Constitution intended to put the judiciary on the footing of the fullest independence consistent with their responsibility."

"This power was in accordance with the provisions of the Bill of Rights." What are these? Section V. of the Bill of Rights reads thus: —

"All power residing originally in the people, and being derived from them, the several magistrates and officers of government, vested with authority, whether legislative, executive, or judicial, are their substitutes and agents, and are at all times accountable to them."

Mr. Loring knew under what condition he was taking office. He knew this provision in the Declaration of Rights, that the people retain all power, and that all magistrates "vested with authority, whether legislative, executive, or judicial, are their substitutes and agents, and are at all times accountable to them," — in office and out of it. Section VIII. says further: —

"In order to prevent those who are vested with authority from becoming oppressors, the people have a right, at such periods and in such manner as they shall establish by their frame of government, to cause their public officers to return to private life; and to fill up vacant places by certain and regular elections and appointments."

No man has a right to criticise here the manner in which the removal is effected. Let them go elsewhere than to this tribunal, if they say it is a bad power. The people retain the right, at such periods and in such manner as they shall establish by their frame of government, to cause their public officers to return to private life.

This is the principle of our Declaration of Rights. Mr. Childs says: "The founders of the Constitution intended to put the judiciary on the footing of the fullest independence consistent with their responsibility." Mr. Chairman, I beseech you, in the progress of this discussion, if the remonstrant shall ring changes on the necessity of maintaining the independence of the judiciary, to remember this remark, that "the founders of the Constitution intended to put the judiciary on the footing of the fullest independence *consistent with their responsibility*," — no more.

Then Mr. Cummings of Salem, afterwards Judge, rose. He says: —

"In this State, they cannot be removed on address of the

Legislature, but with the consent of the Council. Was not this a sufficient guard? Another part of the Constitution protects them when acused of crimes. This provision is not intended to embrace cases of crime, — it is only for cases when they become incompetent to discharge their duties. May not the people, by a majority, determine whether judges are incompetent?"

Mr. Loring says, "Show me my crime!" Mr. Cummings says, "This provision is not intended to embrace cases of crime."

Levi Lincoln of Worcestor comes next. He was then a Democrat, — since Governor, and Judge:

"He was entirely satisfied with the Constitution as it was. He had never heard till now, and was now surprised to hear, that there was any want of independence in the judiciary. He had heard it spoken of in charges, sermons, and discourses in the streets, as one of the most valuable features of the Constitution, that it established an independent judiciary. He inquired, Was it dependent on the Legislature? It was not on the Legislature nor on the Executive. No judge could be removed but by the concurrent act of four co-ordinate branches of the government, — the House of Representatives, the Senate, with a different organization from the House, the Governor, and the Council. Was it to be supposed that all these should conspire together to remove a useful judge? But it was argued that future Legislatures might be corrupt. This was a monstrous supposition. He would rather suppose that a judge might be corrupt. It was more natural that a single person should be corrupt than a numerous body. The proposed amendment was said to be similar to provisions of other governments. There was no analogy, because other governments are not constituted like ours. It was said that judges have estates in their offices, — he did not agree to this doctrine. The office was not made for the judge, nor the judge for the office; but both for the people. There was another tenure, — the confidence of the people. It was that which had hitherto occurred here. Have we, then, less reason to confide in posterity than our ancestors had to confide in us?"

Then follows Mr. Daniel Webster. He had recently come to the State. Joining in the debate, he says: —

"As the Constitution now stands, all judges are liable to be removed from office by the Governor, with the consent of the Council, on the address of the two Houses of the Legislature. It is not made necessary that the two Houses should give any reasons for their address, or that the judge should have an opportunity to be heard. I look upon this as against common right, as well as repugnant to the general principles of the government. . . . . .

"If the Legislature may remove judges at pleasure, assigning no cause for such removal, of course it is not to be expected that they would often find decisions against the constitutionality of their own acts."

These are Webster's words; and you will remember, Mr. Chairman, that the Constitution stands, in 1855, just as it stood when Webster was speaking. I cite the language to show what Mr. Webster understood to be the Constitution of Massachusetts, — that you could remove a judge without giving *any* reason, "at your pleasure," without hearing him. Now, what does he propose to do? Does he propose to strike out that provision? No, Sir! He does not even propose a two-thirds vote.

"In Pennsylvania, the judges may be removed, 'for any reasonable cause,' on the address of two thirds of the two Houses. In some of the States, three fourths of each House is required. The new Constitution of Maine has a provision, with which I should be content; which is, that no judge shall be liable to be removed by the Legislature till the matter of his accusation has been made known to him, and he has had an opportunity of being heard in his defence."

He says that the Constitution gives you the power to remove, and all he asks is, that, before doing it, you should allow the judge an opportunity to be heard.

The fact is, Gentlemen, you have, according to Mr. Webster, the power to shut that door, and, without assigning any reason whatever, vote a judge out of office, and send him word that he is out, — the Constitution does not guarantee him anything else than that. Webster wanted it amended; the Convention submitted a proposition for amendment; but the people declined to accept it. This absolute sovereignty of Massachusetts, which, ever since the Colonies, had been held on to by the people, — of that they were unwilling to yield a whit.

The debate continues, and Mr. Childs again joins in it.

"The object in giving the power to the Legislature was, that judges might be removed when it was the *universal sentiment of the community that they were disqualified for the office* although they could not be convicted on impeachment."

Can you ask anything more definite than that? Nobody denied it. "The object in giving this power to the Legislature was, that judges might be removed, when it was the universal sentiment of the community that they were disqualified for the office, although they could not be convicted on impeachment."

Gentlemen, I would not weary your patience with long extracts; I am giving you only the general current of the discussion. The next speaker is James Trecothick Austin, — the name of one who will not be suspected of being too favorable to the rights of the people; it is not often that I have an opportunity to quote him on my side. "Nobody objects to this provision," said Mr. Austin. There sat Prescott, Shaw, Webster, Story, Lincoln, — the men whom you look up to as the lights of this Commonwealth; but — "nobody objects to this provision"!

"Nobody objects to this provision. The House of Representatives is the grand inquest, — they are tried by the Senate, and have the right of being heard. But the Constitution admits that there may be cases in which judges may be removed without supposing a crime. But how is it to be done by this resolution? There are to be two trials, when for the greater charge of a high crime he has only one. It so obstructs the course of proceeding, that it will never be used. He would suppose the case, not of mental disability, but the loss of public confidence. He knew that such cases were not to be anticipated. But he would look to times when the principle might be brought into operation, when the judge, by indulging strong party feelings, or from any other cause, should so far have lost the confidence of the community that his usefulness should be destroyed. He ought in such cases to be removed; but if witnesses were to be summoned to prove specific charges, it would be impossible to remove him. A man may do a vast deal of mischief, and yet evade the penalty of the law, — a judge may act in such a manner that an intelligent community may think their rights in danger, and yet commit no offence against any written or unwritten law. Men are more likely to act in such manner as to render themselves unworthy to be trusted, than so as to subject themselves to trial. The great argument for the amendment is, that it is necessary to secure the independence of the judiciary. He was in favor of the principle, but it had its limitations. While we secure the independence of the judges, we should remember that they are but men, and sometimes mere partisans."

The remonstrant here says, I have not touched a statute. Mr. Austin says, No matter whether you have or not; "a man may do a vast deal of mischief, and yet evade the penalty of the law." Then he says he has heard a great deal of the weakness of the judiciary. He says the judiciary is not weak. Should you chance to see the remonstrant appear here, attended by eminent legal relatives and friends, you will remember this: —

"The court were besides attended by a splendid and powerful retinue, — the bar. They have great influence from their talents, learning, and *esprit de corps*, and as an appendage to the court, they give them a great and able support. He did not admit that the judiciary was a weak branch of the government, but, on the contrary, it was a strong branch."

Then comes Judge Story. If anybody ever was, I

may say, a little crazy on the subject of the independence of the judges, it was the late able and learned Judge Story, — at least during the last half of his life. What does he say? He says: —

"The Governor and Council might remove them [judges] on the address of a majority of the Legislature, not for crimes and misdemeanors, for that was provided for in another manner, but for no cause whatever, — no reason was to be given. A powerful individual, who has a cause in court which he is unwilling to trust to an upright judge, may, if he has influence enough to excite a momentary prejudice, and command a majority of the Legislature, obtain his removal. He does not hold the office by the tenure of good behavior, but at the will of a majority of the Legislature, and they are not bound to assign any reason for the exercise of their power. *Sic volo, sic jubeo, stet pro ratione voluntas.* (Thus I wish it; thus I order: let my will stand for a reason.) This is the provision of the Constitution, and it is only guarded by the good sense of the people. He had no fear of the voice of the people, when he could get their deliberate voice, — but he did fear from the Legislature, if the judge has no right to be heard."

That is the opinion of the learned Judge Story as to the power of the Legislature. "I have no fear of the voice of the people," says Judge Story. All he proposed was, that the judge should have an opportunity to be heard.

What was the result of this discussion? The Convention proposed to the people — what? That no judge should ever be removed without notice. The people voted on that amendment, voted NAY, and declined to insert it in the Constitution.

Now, Gentlemen, what is my argument? Here is a debate on this clause, not by men heated with passion, not by men with party purposes to serve, but by men acting as statesmen, in the coolest, most deliberate, and temperate mood, — men of various parties, Whig and Democratic, —

and every one of them asserts, without a dissenting voice, that this provision is inserted for the purpose of giving the Legislature the power to remove a judge, when he has not violated any law of the Commonwealth. In addition to this, Gentlemen, I will read the remark of Chief Justice Shaw, when he was counsel for the House against Judge Prescott, of Groton, who was removed on impeachment, you will recollect, in 1821. On that occasion, Judge Shaw was counsel for the House of Representatives, and made some comments on this provision, which, as his opinion has a deserved weight in matters of constitutional law, it is well to read here. He says: —

"It is true, that, by another course of proceeding, warranted by a different provision of the Constitution, any officer may be removed by the Executive, at the will and pleasure of a bare majority of the Legislature; a will which the Executive in most cases would have little power and inclination to resist. The Legislature, without either allegation or proof, has but to pronounce the *sic volo, sic jubeo,* and the officer is at once deprived of his place, and of all the rank, the powers and emoluments, belonging to it. And yet, perhaps, this provision (whether wise or not I will not now stop to consider) is hardly sufficient to justify the extraordinary alarm which has been so eloquently expressed for the liberty and security of the people, or to affix upon the Constitution the charge of containing features more odious and oppressive than those of Turkish despotism. The truth is, that the security of our rights depends rather upon the general tenor and character, than upon particular provisions of our Constitution. The love of freedom and of justice, — so deeply engraven upon the hearts of the people, and interwoven in the whole texture of our social institutions, — a thorough and intelligent acquaintance with their rights, and a firm determination to maintain them, — in short, those moral and intellectual qualities without which social liberty cannot exist, and over which despotism can obtain no control, — these stamp the character and give security to the rights of the free people of this

Commonwealth. So long as such a character is maintained, no danger perhaps need be apprehended from the arbitrary course of proceeding, under the provision of the Constitution, to which I have alluded. But, Sir, we have never for a moment imagined that the proceedings on this impeachment could be influenced or affected by that provision. The two modes of proceeding are altogether distinct, and, in my humble apprehension, were designed to effect totally distinct objects. No, Sir; had the House of Representatives expected to attain their object by any means short of the allegation, proof, and conviction of criminal misconduct, an address, and not an impeachment, would have been the course of proceeding adopted by them."

These well-considered and weighty sentences of Chief Justice Shaw show his idea of the extent of your power, and will relieve your minds of any undue apprehension as to the danger of its exercise.

The people of Massachusetts have always chosen to keep their judges, in some measure, dependent on the popular will. It is a Colonial trait, and the sovereign State has preserved it. Under the King, though he appointed the judges, the people jealously preserved their hold on the bench, by keeping the salaries year by year dependent on the vote of the popular branch of the Legislature. This control was often exercised. When Judge Oliver took pay of the King, they impeached him. (See Washburn's Judicial History of Massachusetts, 139, 160.) When the Constitution was framed, the people chose to keep the same sovereignty in their own hands. Independence of judges, therefore, in Massachusetts, Gentlemen, means, in the words of Mr. Childs, "the fullest independence consistent *with their responsibility*."

The opinions I have read you derive additional weight from the fact, that all the speakers were aware of the grave nature of this power, and some painted in glowing colors how liable to abuse it was. Still not one proposed to take it from you. The most anxious only asked to check it by requiring a two-thirds vote. This proposition the Convention refused to accept; the utmost the Convention would recommend to the people was, that the judge should have notice and liberty to defend himself. Even this limitation on your power the people refused to adopt. They were fully warned, and deliberately, on mature reflection, decided that it was safe and wise to intrust you with *unlimited discretion* in this respect. With such a page in our history, it is not competent for the press or the friends of Judge Loring to argue that no such power ought to have been given you, and that it is too dangerous to be used. The people alone have the right to decide that question, and *they have decided it.* When, after full deliberation, they gave you the power, they said, in effect, that occasions might arise requiring its exercise, and on such fitting occasions they wished it exercised. Doubtless, Gentlemen, this is a grave power, and one to be used only on important occasions. We are bound to show you, not light and trifling reasons for the removal of Judge Loring, but such grave and serious reasons, such weighty cause, as will justify your interference, and make this use of your authority strengthen rather than weaken the proper independence of the bench.

Indeed, the power is in itself a wise, good, and necessary one, and should be lodged somewhere in every government. The Boston papers, in all their arguments on this point, take it for granted that the people are to be always under guardianship, — that government is a grand Probate Court to prevent the people — the insane and always under-age people — from wasting their own property and cutting their own throat. Not such is the theory of republican institutions. The true theory is, that the people came of age on the fourth day of July, 1776, and *can be trusted* to manage their own affairs. The people, with their practical common-sense, instinctive feeling of right and wrong, and manly love of fair play, are the true conservative element in a just government. It is true, the people are not always right; but it is true, also, that the people are not often wrong, — less often, surely, than their leaders. The theory of our government is, that the purity of the bench is a matter which concerns every individual. Whenever, therefore, guilt, recklessness, or incapacity shield themselves on the bench, by technical shifts and evasions, against direct collision with the law, it is meant that the reserved power of the people shall intervene, and save the State from harm.

It is easy to conceive many occasions for the exercise of such a power. How many men among us, by gross misconduct in railroad or banking companies, have incurred the gravest disapprobation, and yet avoided legal conviction? Suppose such men had been at the same time judges, will any one say they should have been continued on the bench? Yet, on the remonstrant's theory, it would be an "abuse of power" to impeach or "address" them off the bench! Suppose a judge by great private immorality incurs utter contempt, — is drunk every day in the week except Probate Court day, — shall he, because he is cunning enough to evade statutes, still hide himself under the ermine? Suppose a Judge of Probate should open his court on the days prescribed by the statute, and close it in half an hour, as your Judge Loring did when he shut up the Probate Court of Suffolk on Monday, the 29th of May, to hurry forward the kidnapping of Anthony Burns. Suppose some judge should thus keep his court open only five minutes each probate day the whole year through. He violates no statute, though he puts a stop to all business; yet, according to the arguments of the press and the remonstrant, it would be a *gross abuse of power* to impeach him, or address the Governor for his removal, since he has violated no law!

Not such was the good old doctrine. In the Prescott case, Judge Shaw went so far as to contend that a judge might not only be removed by address, but *impeached* "for misconduct and mal-administration in office, ... of such a nature that the ordinary tribunals would not take notice of or punish them, in their usual course of proceedings, and according to the laws of the land, and for which, therefore, the offender would not be indictable." (Prescott's Case, p. 180.)

You may think, Gentlemen, that I have occupied too much time in proving the unlimited extent of your power. But it seemed necessary, since the press which defends the remonstrant, and he also, though they do not in words deny your unlimited authority, do so in effect. They claim that you destroy the independence of the bench, and *abuse* your power, if you exercise it in any case but a clear violation of law. This is a practical annihilation of the power. This claim loses sight of the very nature and intent of the power, which is well stated by Mr. Austin, when he says that a judge who has lost the confidence of the community ought to be removed, though you can prove no specific charges against him, — though he may have violated no law, written or unwritten. Or, in words said to have been used by Mr. Rufus Choate in a recent case, "A judicial officer may be removed if found intellectually incapable, or if he has been left to commit some great enormity, so as to show himself morally deranged."

This unlimited power, then, Gentlemen, is one that you undoubtedly possess. It is one that the people deliberately planned and intended that you should possess. It is one which the nature of the government makes it necessary you should possess, and that, on fitting occasion, you should have the courage to use. True, it is a grave power. But what is all government but the exercise of grave powers? "When the sea is calm, all boats alike show mastership in floating." The merit of a government is, that it helps us in critical times. All the checks and ingenuity of our institutions are arranged to secure for us in these halls men wise and able enough to be trusted with grave powers, and bold enough to use them when the times require. Let not, then, this bugbear of the liability of this power to abuse, deter you from using it at all. Lancets and knives are dangerous instruments. The usefulness of surgeons is, that, when lancets are *needed*, somebody may know how to use them and save life.

Has, then, a proper case occurred for the exercise of this power? In other words, ought you now to exercise it? The petitioners think you ought, and for the following reasons

First. When Judge Loring issued his warrant in the Burns case, he acted in defiance of the solemn convictions and settled purpose of Massachusetts, — convictions and purpose officially made known to him, with all the solemnity of a statute.

In order to do him the fullest justice on this point, allow me to read a sentence from his remonstrance: —

"And I respectfully submit, that when (while acting as a Commissioner) I received my commission as Judge of Probate, no objection was made by the Executive of the Commonwealth, or by any other branch of the government, to my further discharge of the duties of a Commissioner; nor at the passage of the act of 1850, when the jurisdiction aforesaid was given to the Commissioners of the Circuit Courts of the United States, nor at any time since, was I notified that the government of Massachusetts, or either the executive or legislative branch thereof, regarded the two offices as incompatible, or were of opinion that the same qualities and experience which were employed for the rights and interests of our own citizens should not be employed for the protection of all legal rights of alleged fugitives from service or labor under the United States act of 1850.

"I make these latter remarks only for the purpose of bringing respectfully to the notice and clear apprehension of your honorable bodies the extreme injustice and want of equity that would be involved in the removal of a judge from office, for the past discharge of other official duties, not by law made incompatible with his duties as judge, against his exercise of which no official objection had ever been raised, and which were created and imposed on him by that law of the land which is the supreme law of Massachusetts."

Gentlemen, this is a mere evasion. He was made Judge of Probate in 1847. He then knew, as well as you and I do, that Massachusetts *did* regard the conduct of any one of her magistrates in aiding in the return of a fugitive slave as something disgraceful and infamous. He had solemn and *official* intimation of this. My proof is the statute of March 24, 1843, entitled, "An Act further to protect personal liberty": —

"SECT. 1. *No judge of any court of record of this Commonwealth*, and no justice of the peace, shall hereafter take cognizance or grant a certificate in cases that may arise under the third section of an act of Congress, passed February twelfth, seventeen hundred and ninety-three, and entitled, 'An Act respecting fugitives from justice, and persons escaping from the service of their masters,' to any person who claims any other person as a fugitive slave within the jurisdiction of the Commonwealth.

"SECT. 2. No sheriff, deputy sheriff, coroner, constable, jailer, or *other officer of this Commonwealth* shall hereafter arrest or detain, or aid in the arrest or detention or imprisonment, in any jail or other building belonging to this Commonwealth, or to any county, city, or town thereof, of any person, for the reason that he is claimed as a fugitive slave.

"SECT. 3. Any justice of the peace, sheriff, deputy sheriff, coroner, constable, or jailer, who shall offend against the provisions of this law, by in any way acting, directly or indirectly under the power conferred by the third section of the act of Congress aforementioned, shall forfeit a sum not exceeding one thousand dollars for every such offence, to the use of the county where said offence is committed, or shall be subject to imprisonment not exceeding one year in the county jail." (Approved, March 24, 1843.)

The intent of that statute is clear and unmistakable. It expresses the determined will of the Commonwealth, that no magistrate of hers shall accept from the United States any authority, or take any part, directly or indirectly, in returning fugitive slaves to their masters. It means to set a stigma on slave-catching in this Commonwealth. It thunders forth its command, that no officer shall hold the broad seal of the State in one hand, and reach forth the other for a slave-catcher's fee. This is the heart and gist of the statute. He that runneth may read.

Technically construed, it may be said only to forbid that a judge, *acting as a judge*, should issue a slave warrant; and it may be claimed that Mr. Loring did not transgress it, since he issued his warrant, not *as a judge*, but as a slave commissioner. Technically speaking, this may be so, and an inferior court of justice would be bound so to regard it. But you are not sitting as *nisi prius* lawyers, bound by quiddling technicalities; you are statesmen, looking with plain, manly sense at the essence of things. Have you any doubt what Massachusetts intended when she enacted that statute? Have you any doubt that Mr. Loring knew what Massachusetts meant? Why does the Constitution give you this power of removing judges by address? To meet just such cases as this; when some individual has violated the spirit and essence of a law, but cannot be technically held by impeachments. Remember what Mr. Austin says, describing just this case in the extract I have twice quoted from his speech in the

Convention. If you allow yourselves to be diverted from the exercise of the power by such technicalities, you forget the very purpose for which it was given, and practically annihilate it.

It is not true, then, as Mr. Loring claims, that, when he received his commission, "no objection was made by the Executive of the Commonwealth, or of any other branch of the government, to his further discharge of the duties of a Commissioner,"—meaning the duty of catching slaves. The statute of 1843, then in full force and effect, was clear and official notice to him what "objection" the Commonwealth had to the returning of slaves.

But it is said the statute was passed in 1843, and only prohibited officers from acting under the slave act of 1793; it cannot have any reference to the slave act of 1850, since this was not in existence in 1843, and Mr. Loring's action in the Burns case was under the act of 1850.

This is another technical evasion, but not as good even as the first; because, in the Sims case, (7 Cushing, 285,) which Mr. Loring cites, Judge Shaw holds the act of 1850 constitutional, because it is so *precisely* like the act of 1793; and Mr. Loring, in his Burns judgment, takes the same view. Now, if the two acts are so precisely alike that the constitutionality of one proves the constitutionality of the other, then they are such twins as to be both within the meaning and intent of our statute of 1843.

When the counsel of Sims and Burns wished to argue the unconstitutionality of the act of 1850, on the ground that it went far beyond anything judicially recognized in the act of 1793, then Judges Shaw and Loring find the two acts so much alike that the argument is unnecessary. When Mr. Loring's friends would defend him, then these two acts are so different, that our law of 1843 can apply only to the first! To plunge an innocent and free man like Burns into slavery, against law and evidence, these statutes are just alike; to save Judge Loring from the act of 1843, they are different as white and black!*

But even this technicality is of no avail. The *official* action of the State has forever closed this door of escape.

While Congress was discussing the Fugitive Slave Bill, which was finally passed September 18, 1850, our Legislature passed the following resolutions, which the Governor approved, May 1, 1850: —

"*Resolved*, That the sentiments of the people of Massachusetts, as expressed in their legal enactments, in relation to the delivering up of fugitive slaves, remain unchanged; and inasmuch as the legislation necessary to give effect to the clause of the Constitution relative to this subject is within the exclusive jurisdiction of Congress, we hold it to be the duty of that body to pass such laws only in regard thereto as will be sustained by the public sentiment of the Free States, where such laws are to be enforced, and which shall especially secure to all persons, whose surrender may be claimed as having escaped from labor and service in other States, the right of having the validity of such claim determined by a jury in the State where such claim is made.

"*Resolved*, That the people of Massachusetts, in the maintenance of these their well-known and invincible principles, expect that all their officers and representatives will adhere to them at all times, on all occasions, and under all circumstances." (Approved, May 1, 1850.)

* I might have pushed this argument further. The act of 1850 is styled "An Act to *amend, and supplementary to*, the Act entitled 'An Act respecting Fugitives,' &c., approved Feb. 12, 1793." It is, then, properly a part of the act of 1793, and acting under it is not only substantially within the prohibition of our statute of 1843, but perhaps is, *in strict law*, included in that prohibition. At any rate, how do the statutes of 1793 and 1850 differ? In 1793, Congress enacted that certain State officers should be *ex officio* slave-catchers. Massachusetts, in 1843, forbade her magistrates to accept the authority. In 1850, Congress makes it necessary that a man should have a separate commission to entitle him to catch slaves. Massachusetts reiterates her orders. In defiance of these, Judge Loring accepts a commission. Is the case not substantially within the meaning of the act of 1843?

Observe, the Commonwealth reaffirms the principle of her former *legal enactments*, — that is, the act of 1843; and expects all her "officers to adhere to them *at all times, on all occasions, and under all circumstances*."

What shall we say now to Mr. Loring's claim, that neither when he received the commission as Judge of Probate, nor at any time since, was he notified "by the government of Massachusetts, or by the executive or legislative branch thereof," that slave-catching and bearing office under Massachusetts were incompatible! Are not these resolutions substantially a re-enactment of the statute of 1843, distinctly applying to the Fugitive Slave Bill of 1850, and officially warning all officers that the State expected them to abstain from taking part in the execution of that act, as much as of the act of 1793?

Look at the case, Gentlemen. A sovereign State issues her mandate, that no magistrate of hers shall aid in catching slaves. Seven years later, she solemnly reiterates the order, and directs her officers to remember it on all occasions. In open, contemptuous defiance of all this, one of her judges adjourns his own court to hold one that dooms a man to bondage. The Legislature meet and talk of removing him. But the judge, in a tone of indignant innocence, exclaims: "What! turn me out for a mere difference of opinion! Have I not evaded the law? If you remove such an innocent and law-abiding judge as I am, you will destroy the independence of the bench!" Yes, truly; that sort of independence which consists in defying the State in order to serve a party, or minister to the ambition of friends.

Some men allege that the same reasoning would condemn Judge Shaw for refusing to set Sims free, by *habeas corpus*, from the grasp of the claimant. But surely he must be stone blind who sees no difference between a judge like Shaw, who, thinking he has no power to arrest the

Slave Act when once set in motion, refuses to interfere, and a judge like Loring, who actually sets the Slave Act in motion, and personally executes it! The statute of 1843 only orders our officers not to aid in catching slaves. It does not order them to prevent everybody else from catching slaves. Loring actually hunted a slave, and sent him to Virginia. Shaw only declared himself unauthorized to prevent George T. Curtis from hunting fugitive slaves. Surely, there is some slight difference here.

In consenting, then, to act as a Slave Commissioner, while holding the office of a Probate Judge, Mr. Loring defied the well-known, settled, religious convictions of the State, *officially* made known to him. The question was one of vital, practical morality of the gravest importance; one where justice was on one side and infamy on the other. He cannot complain if you consider this heedless or heartless choice of the infamous side, this open defiance, on so momentous a matter, sufficient cause for his removal.

My second reason is, that the very method of the trial of Anthony Burns shows Mr. Loring unfit to be continued longer on the bench. I am not now dealing with the point that he *did* act; I have said that his mere acting in the case was a defiance of the Commonwealth; but I now say, that the *manner* of his acting is another ground for which he ought to be removed, and shows him to be unfit for the office of a judge.

Anthony Burns was arrested at eight o'clock on Wednesday evening. He was hurried to the court-house, and concealed there within four walls. He was not allowed to see anybody but the slave claimant, the Marshal, and the police. At nine o'clock on Thursday morning, our Judge of Probate, Mr. Edward G. Loring, the Slave Commissioner, appeared in his court-room, with the slave claimant and his witnesses, the alleged fugitive, the Marshal, and the police. He proceeded to trial. Trembling, ignorant, confused, astounded, friendless, not knowing what to say or where to look, that unhappy man, Burns, sat, handcuffed, with a policeman on each side. The Commissioner proceeded to try him. By accident, Mr. Richard H. Dana, Jr. had heard that such a trial was to be held, and had reached the court-room. By accident, another learned counsel, who sits by my side (Charles M. Ellis, Esq.), heard that such a scene was enacting, and hurried to the court-house. I heard of it in the street. Mr. Theodore Parker was notified, and we went to the court-room. We found Robert Morris, Esq., already there. Mr. Morris, a member of the bar, had attempted to speak to Burns, — the policemen forbade him. The melancholy farce had proceeded for about half an hour. In two hours more, so far as any one could then see, the judgment would have been given, the certificate signed, the victim beyond our reach. There sat the Judge of Probate, clothed with the ermine of Massachusetts; before him cowered the helpless object of cruel legislation, — the crushed victim of an inhuman system. Mr. Dana had moved the court before to defer the trial; but the Commissioner proceeded to examine the witness. After a short time, Mr. Dana rose, (he had no right to rise, technically speaking, — he rose as a citizen merely, not as counsel,) and I read you what he said : —

"May it please your Honor: I rise to address the court as *amicus curiæ*, for I cannot say that I am regularly of counsel for the person at the bar. Indeed, from the few words I have been enabled to hold with him, and from what I can learn from others who have talked with him, I am satisfied that he is not in a condition to determine whether he will have counsel or not, or whether or not and how he shall appear for his defence. He declines to say whether any one shall appear for him, or whether he will defend or not.

"Under these circumstances, I submit to your Honor's judgment, that time should be allowed to the prisoner to recover himself from the stupefaction of his sudden arrest, and his novel and distressing situation, and have opportunity to consult with friends and members of the bar, and determine what course he will pursue. . . . . .

"He does not know what he is saying. I say to your Honor, as a member of the bar, on my personal responsibility, that from what I have seen of the man, and what I have learnt from others who have seen him, that he is not in a fit state to decide for himself what he will do. He has just been arrested and brought into this scene, with this immense stake of freedom or slavery for life at issue, surrounded by strangers, — and even if he should plead guilty to the claim, the court ought not to receive the plea under such circumstances.

"It is but yesterday that the court at the other end of the building refused to receive a plea of guilty from a prisoner. The court never will receive this plea in a capital case, without the fullest proof that the prisoner makes it deliberately, and understands its meaning and his own situation, and has consulted with his friends. In a case involving freedom or slavery for life, this court will not do less. . . . . .

"I know enough of this tribunal to know that it will not lend itself to the hurrying off a man into slavery to accommodate any man's personal convenience, before he has even time to recover his stupefied faculties, and say whether he has a defence or not. Even without a suggestion from an *amicus curiæ*, the court would, of its own motion, see to it that no such advantage was taken.

"The counsel for the claimant says, that, if the man were out of his mind, he would not object. Out of his mind! Please your Honor, if you had ever reason to fear that a prisoner was not in full possession of his mind, you would fear it in such a case as this. But I have said enough. I am confident your Honor will not decide so momentous an issue against a man without counsel and without opportunity."

Again, in his argument, alluding to the same scene, Mr. Dana says: —

"Burns was arrested suddenly, on a false pretence, coming home at nightfall from his day's work, and hurried into custody, among strange men, in a strange place, and suddenly, whether claimed rightfully or claimed wrongfully, he saw he was claimed as a slave, and his condition burst upon him in a flood of terror. This was at night. You saw him, Sir, the next day, and you remember the state he was then in. You remember his stupefied and terrified condition. You remember his hesitation, his timid glance about the room, even when looking in the mild face of justice. How little your kind words reassured him. Sir, the day after the arrest, you felt obliged to put off his trial two days, because he was not in a condition to know or decide what he would do."

Mr. Ellis rose also, and protested against the trial. Gentlemen, what a scene! A man clothed in the ermine of Massachusetts has before him a helpless man, — in the words of Mr. Dana, "terrified, stupefied, intimidated," — and begins to try him. If the Chief Justice of the Commonwealth should find the veriest vagrant from the streets indicted for murder by twenty-three jurors, and solemnly and legally set before him, he would not take upon himself to proceed to trial without the man had counsel, — every lawyer knows this. And yet this man, who ought to have shown the discretion and humanity of a judge, was proceeding in a trial so enormous and fearful, that counsel coming in by accident felt urged to rise in their places and interrupt him, protesting, as citizens of Massachusetts, that this mockery of justice should not go on. You have a Judge of Probate who needs to have accident fill his court-room with honest men, to call him back to his duty. The petitioners say that such a man is not fit to sit upon the Bench of Massachusetts. Do we exaggerate the importance of the occasion? Let me read a single sentence from Dr. Channing: —

"This Constitution was not established to send back slaves to chains. The article requiring this act of the Free States was forced on them by the circumstances of the times, and submitted to as a hard necessity. It did not enter into the essence of the instrument; whilst the security of freedom was its great, living, all-pervading idea. We see the tendency of slavery to warp the Constitution to its purposes, in the law for restoring the flying bondman. Under this, not a few, having not only the same natural but legal rights with ourselves, have been subjected to the lash of the overseer.

"But a higher law than the Constitution protests against the act of Congress on this point. According to the law of nature, no greater crime against a human being can be committed than to make him a slave. . . . . .

"To condemn a man to perpetual slavery is as solemn a sentence as to condemn him to death. Before being thus doomed, he has a right to all the means of defence which are granted to a man who is tried for his life. All the rules, forms, solemnities, by which innocence is secured from being confounded with guilt, he has a right to demand. In the present case, the principle is eminently applicable, that many guilty should escape, rather than that one innocent man should suffer; because the guilt of running away from an 'owner' is of too faint a color to be seen by some of the best eyes, whilst that of enslaving the free is of the darkest hue."

Dr. Channing would have all the forms and solemnities of justice, usual in cases where life hangs on the issue, rigidly observed, when a slave case is to be determined. Your Judge of Probate arrests a man at night; no one knows of it; at the earliest hour in the morning that a court ever sits, he opens his court; this poor, trembling, friendless victim, who hardly dared to look up and meet his eye, is brought before him, and he proceeds to try him. Strangers come in and say, he is too stupefied to be tried. Still the judge goes on, and they sit awhile, their blood boiling within them, till they feel compelled to rise, and solemnly protest against this insult to all the forms of justice; and the court, after the repeated protests of two members of the bar, at length consents to put off that trial, allow the unhappy man to recover himself, consult with friends, and decide what course to pursue.

Why, Gentlemen, if a man has committed murder, and has been indicted by a jury, the statute provides that he shall have time allowed him to prepare for his defence, have a copy of his indictment, and a list of the witnesses against him; and when it is all done, the Supreme Court would not touch the case until they had assigned him counsel. They would fear to draggle their ermine in blood. But here is a Massachusetts Judge of Probate with whom it is but the accident of an accident, but the impudence of counsel, so to speak, that prevents such an outrage as Mr. Dana's protest describes. Now, your petitioners ask, in the name of Massachusetts, for a judge who can be safely trusted in a private chamber with an innocent man.

I recall the scene in that court-room, while our hope that the judge would postpone that case hung trembling in the balance. We were none of us sure that even the indignant, unintermitted protests of these members of the bar would secure the postponement of that trial. Think of the difference in this case! You are trying Mr. Loring for continuance in his office. He comes here with all the advantages of education, wealth, social position, professional discipline, everything on his side, and can choose when he will be tried. Around him are troops of friends. Influential journals defend his rights. But that poor victim — what a contrast! According to Dr. Channing, it was as much as life that hung in the balance. The old English law says that the judge is counsel for the prisoners. There were no such promptings here as led the judge to say, "I shall not try that man unless he has counsel, and all the safeguards and checks of a judicial examination." The hapless victim, too ignorant at the best to know his own rights or how to defend them, was then stunned by the overwhelming blow, — by the arrest, and the sight of the horrible pit into which he was to be plunged. Over his prostrate body this Massachusetts judge of the fatherless and widow opens his court, and begins to hold the mockery of a trial! If you continue him in office, you should appoint some one, — some "flapper," as Dean Swift says, — some humane man, to wait upon his court, and for the honor of the State remind him when it will be but decent to remember justice and mercy, for he is not fit to go alone.

Do you ask us what course Mr. Loring should have adopted? We answer, the same course that any merely decent judge would adopt in such a case. Here was a man arrested some twelve hours before on a false pretence, and kept shut up from all his friends. All this Mr. Loring knew, or was bound to know, since such has been the constant practice in all slave cases, here and elsewhere. The first duty of a just judge was to tell the man, truly and plainly, what he was arrested for, — see that his friends had free access to him, and fix some future day to commence his trial, leaving time sufficient to consult and prepare a defence. This is what the statutes of every civilized state ordain, in cases where even ten dollars are in dispute. The first word that William Brent, the witness, was allowed to speak on the stand in such circumstances was the death-knell to any claim Mr. Loring might have to be thought a humane man, a good lawyer, or a just judge. A statute which the whole civilized world regards as the most infamous on record is executed by men who claim to be lawyers, judges, and Christians, with a violence and haste which doubles its mischief. These slave commissioners, while constantly prating of the "painful duty" their allegiance to law entails on them, contrive to add by their haste to the brutality and cruelty even of the Slave Act. Knowing the cruel nature of the statute he was executing, and the routine of lies and close confinement always found in slave cases, Mr. Loring's first duty, after his court was open, was to adjourn it for three days, at least, taking measures that Burns should meantime see friends and counsel, to consult on his defence. All Mr. Loring's friends can say for him is, that he was only acting as all other slave commissioners act, and that no harm was done, since the Abolitionists came in and secured Burns a trial! As if the infamous slave-prisons of Curtis and Ingraham were precedents for any court to follow! As if any man was proved fit to be a judge by alleging that strangers prevented his doing all the mischief he intended!

The case was adjourned to Saturday.

Where do we next meet this specimen of Massachusetts humanity and judicial decorum?

It was necessary some one should see Burns to arrange for his having counsel. The United States Marshal refused us admission to the cell. On Friday I went to Mr. Loring at Cambridge, where he was Law Lecturer in Harvard College, and asked him for an order directing the Marshal to allow me to see the prisoner. He sits down and writes a letter, authorizing me to cross that barrier and see Burns; and as he hands it to me, he says: "Mr. Phillips, the case is so clear, that I do not think you will be justified in placing any obstacles in the way of this man's going back, AS HE PROBABLY WILL"!! What right had he to think Burns would go back? He had heard only one witness; yet he says, "*The case is so clear, that I do not think you will be justified in placing any obstacles in the way of this man's going back*, AS HE PROBABLY WILL"!!!

Suppose, Mr. Chairman, that, in the case of Dr. Webster, after he had been indicted, but before he had been put on trial, the Chief Justice of the Commonwealth had said to Mr. Sohier, or any other of the counsel: "Sir, I do not think you will be justified in placing any obstacles in the way of this man's being hung, *as he probably will!*" What would be thought of the judge who should proceed to try a man for his life, after expressing such an opinion on the case to be brought before him? Yet such was the mood of mind of this Judge of Probate, that, without hearing argument or testimony, — only the disjointed story of a single witness, interrupted by the protests of Messrs. Dana and Ellis, — the mere *disjecta membra* of a trial, — nothing, — he had so far made up his mind, that he could warn me from attempting to do anything to save the man from the doom to which he was devoted, on the ground of the probability of his being given up! "A judge who proceeds on half evidence will not do quarter justice," says an old English essayist. What proportion, then, of justice may we expect from a judge who decides on no evidence at all?

I ask (I was going to say) the judges of the Commonwealth of Massachusetts, — men of fair fame and judicial reputation, — whether a person of that temper of mind is fit to sit by their side? I ask any man who loves the honor of the Bench, who desires to see none but high-minded, conscientious, humane, just judges, whether the petitioners who ask for the removal of such an individual are attacking or supporting the honor of the Bench of Massachusetts, — its real strength and independence? It seems to me that we are cutting off a corrupt member, and securing for the rest the only source of strength, the confidence of the Commonwealth. The Bench is not weakened when we remove a bad judge, but when we retain him.

Gentlemen, it is not in the power of this Legislature –

respectfully be it said — it is not in the power of this Legislature to command the respect of this Commonwealth for a Bench on which sits Edward Greely Loring. You may refuse to remove him; but you cannot make the people respect a Bench upon which he sits. If any man here loves the judiciary, and wishes to secure its independence and its influence with the people, let him aid us to cut off the offending member.

Thirdly. Gentlemen, where is your Judge next heard of? He is next heard of at midnight, on Saturday, the 27th of May, drawing up a bill of sale of Anthony Burns, which now exists in his own handwriting! Before the trial was begun, he sits down and writes a bill of sale: —

"Know all men by these presents, — That I, Charles F. Suttle, of Alexandria, in Virginia, in consideration of twelve hundred dollars, to me paid, do hereby release and discharge, quitclaim and convey to Antony Byrnes, his liberty; and I hereby manumit and release him from all claims and services to me forever, hereby giving him his liberty to all intents and effects forever.

"In testimony whereof, I have hereto set my hand and seal, this twenty-seventh day of May, in the year of our Lord eighteen hundred and fifty-four."

Gentlemen, suppose, while Dr. Webster sat in the dock, before the trial commenced, Chief Justice Shaw had summoned Mrs. Webster to his side, and said, "I advise you to get a petition to the Governor to have your husband pardoned; I think he will be found guilty!" Why, he would have been scouted from one end of the Commonwealth to the other. Suppose a deed of land was in dispute, and before the case began, the judge should call one of the claimants before him and say, "I advise you to compromise this matter, for I think your deed is not worth a straw!" Who would trust his case to such a judge? But here is a man put before a judge to be tried on an issue which Dr. Channing says is as solemn as that of life or death, and the judge is found at midnight, with the pregnant intimation that that man must be bought, or he is not safe! What right had he to say that? Mr. Chairman, the case may have been so clear even then, before it was half begun, that every man in the Commonwealth, save one, would have been obliged to say that Burns was a fugitive; but there was one pair of lips that honor and official propriety ought to have sealed, and those were the lips of the judge who was trying the case. Yet he is the very man who is found babbling! He seemed to be utterly lost to all the proprieties of his position. Colonel Suttle selling Burns on the 27th of May! What even legal right in Burns had Colonel Suttle then to convey? None. No law knew of any. Yet the very judge trying the case volunteers to suppose a title based on his own decision, which ought then to have been unknown, even to himself. Suffolk Court-House is turned into a slave-auction block; and the Slave Commissioner, the trial hardly commenced, jumps upon the stand, — not needing to lay aside whatever judicial robes a Slave Commissioner may be supposed to wear!

Fourthly. The Commissioner knew how general was the opinion among lawyers, that a writ of replevin might be served after his judgment and before the affidavit of the claimant was made. He knew the anxiety of the friends of Burns to test the possibility of thus legally securing his release by Massachusetts law. But in the Commissioner's hot haste and obstinate determination to have every law except those of this Commonwealth obeyed to the letter, he arranged and conspired with Colonel Suttle and the United States Marshal to have all the papers executed in such secrecy, and so exactly at the same moment, as to deprive Burns of all chance from this measure. How eminently worthy such plotting as this of a Massachusetts judge! — of one who assures you that he has scrupulously obeyed the *laws of Massachusetts!*

Well, Gentlemen, it is said, — I cannot state it on any thing but rumor, — that, as the crowning act of his unjudicial conduct, he communicated his decision to one party twenty hours before he communicated it to the other, so that Messrs. Smith, Hallett, Thomas, Suttle, & Co. had time to send down into Dock Square and have bullets cast for the soldiers who were to be employed to assist the slave-hunter; had time to inform the newspapers in the city what they intended to do; — while Messrs. Dana and Ellis, counsel for the prisoner, were allowed to go to their homes in utter ignorance whether that decision would be one way or another. Where can you find, in the whole catalogue of judicial enormities, an instance when a judge revealed his decision to one party and concealed it from the other? If he thought it necessary, on any grounds of public security or from private reasons of propriety, to inform them what his decision was to be, he should have said: "Gentleman, I can meet you only in open court, in the presence of counsel on both sides. I cannot speak to you, Mr. Thomas, unless Mr. Dana or Mr. Ellis is here. Call them, and then I will tell you what my decision is to be." At four o'clock on Thursday, the Commissioner made known his decision to the slave-claimant's counsel; on Friday, at nine o'clock, to Messrs. Dana and Ellis, and the world!!

What a picture! Put aside that it was a slave case; forget, if you will, for a moment, that he was committing an act which the Commonwealth says is *ipso facto* infamous, and declares that no man shall do it and hold office. The old law of Scotland declared that a butcher should not sit upon a jury; he was incapacitated by his profession. The Commonwealth of Massachusetts, by the statute of 1843, says that any Slave Commissioner is unfit to sit upon the bench. Mr. Loring cannot see it, although it was written and signed, re-enacted and signed again,— although he was doing an act which the butchers of our city, to their honor be it said, would not sanction, two days afterwards. He puts this man into a room, bewildered, terrified, unfriended,—so unfit for trial, that strangers deem it their duty repeatedly to protest against the proceedings of the court. Having gone through that mockery of half an hour's trial, he takes occasion to express his deliberate opinion of what the result is to be to counsel. Having done that, he makes his conduct still more flagrant by drawing up a bill of sale of the man who was still on trial before him. There was but one man in the State of Massachusetts who could not have drawn that bill of sale, as I before said; yet *he* was the man to draw it! After that, he proceeds to collogue, to conspire, with one party, and tell them his decision, twenty hours before he informs the other. Gentlemen, I submit to you, as a citizen of Massachusetts, that this is conduct unfitting for the bench; that there is, not to speak of inhumanity, an utter unfitness to try questions of any kind, an utter recklessness of judicial character and regard for propriety in such conduct, which might cause the very stones in the street to rise and plead for the majesty of the laws against such a judge. The petitioners say to you, that such a man is not fit to wear the ermine of the Commonwealth of Massachusetts. Do they say too much? I am to die in this city; many of the petitioners are to die here. Our wills are to go into his hands. Our children and widows are to go before him. We cannot trust him; and we ask you to remove him, under that provision of the Constitution which gives you unlimited power to remove a judge who is unfit for the duties of his office.

It is not necessary, Mr. Chairman, that I detain you long on the charge that Mr. Loring "wrested the law to the support of injustice, tortured evidence to help the strong against the weak, and administered a merciless statute in a merciless manner." You have in your hands the able arguments of Messrs. Ellis and Dana, as well as that remarkable "Decision which Judge Loring might have given," originally published in the Boston Atlas. These make it needless for me to enlarge on the law points. Allow me, however, a few brief remarks.

1st. To use my own statement prepared for another occasion, "the Fugitive Slave Act leaves the party claimant his choice between two processes; one under its sixth section; the other under the tenth.

"The sixth section obliges the claimant to prove three points: (1.) that the person claimed *owes* service; (2.) that he has *escaped;* and, (3.) that the party before the court is the *identical one* alleged to be a slave.

"The tenth section makes the claimant's certificate *conclusive* as to the first two points, and only leaves the *identity to be proved.*

"In this case, the claimant, by offering proof of service and escape, made his election of the sixth section.

"Here he failed, — failed to prove service, failed to prove escape. Then the Commissioner allowed him to swing round and take refuge in the tenth, leaving identity only to be proved; and this he proved by the prisoner's confession, made in terror, if at all; wholly denied by him, and proved only by the testimony of a witness of whom we know nothing, but that he was contradicted by several witnesses as to the only point to which he affirmed, capable of being tested."

2d. As to the point of identity. Colonel Suttle proved that the person at the bar was his Anthony Burns by the testimony of one witness. Of this witness, it may be emphatically said, we knew nothing. He was never in the State before, and we hope he never will be again. He swore that Burns escaped from Richmond, March 24, 1854. To contradict him, six witnesses volunteered their testimony. They were not sought out; they came accidentally or otherwise into court, and offered, unsolicited, their testimony, that they had seen the man at the bar in Boston for three or four weeks before the day of alleged escape. These were witnesses of whose daily life and unimpeached character ample evidence existed. Everybody knew them. Six to one! They were Boston mechanics and bookkeepers; one a city policeman, one an officer in the regiment, and member of the Common Council. Surely, it was evident, either that the record was wrong, that the Virginia witness was wrong, or that this prisoner was not the man Colonel Suttle claimed as his slave.* Out of either door, there was chance for the judge to find his way to release Burns. At any rate, there was reasonable doubt, and the person claimed was therefore entitled to his release. But no; Mr. Loring lets one unknown slave-hunter outweigh six well-known and honest men, tramples on the rule that in such cases all doubts are to be held in favor of the prisoner, and surrenders his victim to bondage.

Observe, Gentlemen, in this connection, the exceeding importance of granting time to prepare for trial, the omission of which, on the part of Mr. Loring, I have commented on. If this case had been finished on Thursday, as it would have been but for the interference of others, these witnesses would not have been heard of till after Burns was out of the State. But after the two efforts of his counsel had succeeded in getting delay till Monday, the facts of the case became known through the city, and,

* After the surrender of Burns, it was discovered that the statements of these six witnesses were exactly correct. Burns came to Boston early in February, and Suttle's witness made a mistake of a month in the date of Burns's exit from Virginia.

having heard them, these witnesses volunteered their testimony. Now, if the ascertaining of pertinent facts be the purpose of a trial, which it surely is in all courts, except those of slave commissioners, the consideration I have stated is a very important one. Though Mr. Loring chose to disregard this evidence, it was due to the law and to the satisfaction of the community, that, even in his court, it should be heard.

3d. But as to the sole point to be proved, under the tenth section, identity, the evidence Mr. Loring relies on is the confession of the poor victim when first arrested. No confession is admissible when made in terror.

This confession was made at night; and even twelve hours after, Mr. Loring was forced himself to admit that the prisoner was so stupefied and terrified, he was in no fit state to be tried. Yet he admitted his confessions made in a still more terrified hour! The only witness, also, to this alleged confession, was this same unknown slave-hunter, unless we count one of the ruffians who guarded Burns.

But if the confession be taken at all, the whole must be taken. Now, in this confession, sworn to by Colonel Suttle's own witness, Burns said he did not run away, but fell asleep on board a ship, where he was at work with his master's permission, and was brought away. This statement being brought in by Colonel Suttle's own witness, must be taken by this claimant as true. He cannot be allowed to doubt or contradict it. If it be true, then Burns was not a fugitive slave, and so not within the Fugitive Slave Law provisions. Our own Supreme Court has decided (see 7 Cushing, 298) that a slave on board a national vessel with his master, by express permission of the Navy Secretary, who had been landed in Boston in consequence of Navy orders, against the wish of the master, and of course by no action of the slave, could not be reclaimed. To be brought from a Slave State is no escape, within the meaning of the law. If taken at all, the whole confession must be taken. If the whole be taken, then the claimant himself has proved that his alleged slave did not escape. If not taken in the whole, then it cannot be taken at all, not even under the tenth section, and then there is no evidence as to identity; and the whole case falls to the ground.

Surely somewhere among all these wide gaping chasms in the claimant's case, this poor judge, who pleads he was obliged to do infamous work and accept the case, might have found chance of escape, if he were a learned and humane man!

Mr. Loring contends that he was obliged to issue the warrant in consequence of the oath he took when appointed Judge of Probate, to support the Constitution of the United States. He says: —

"When I was appointed Judge of Probate, I was, by the authority of the people of Massachusetts, bound by an official oath to support the Constitution of the United States; this is to be done only by fulfilling the provisions of the Constitution, and of those laws of the United States which are constitutionally made to carry the Constitution into effect. And on the authority of the Supreme Judicial Court of Massachusetts, I confidently claim that, in my action under the United States Act of 1850, I exactly complied with the official oath imposed on me by the authority of the people of Massachusetts."

A simple illustration will show the absurdity of this claim. If the "official oath" to the Constitution of the United States, which he says Massachusetts required him as Judge of Probate to take, really binds him to execute all the laws of the Union, in every capacity, then such execution becomes a part of his *official duty*, since it was as a Judge of Probate, and only as such, that he took the "official oath." It follows, then, that if Marshal Freeman should direct Judge Loring to aid in catching a slave, and he should refuse, the House of Representatives could impeach him for *official misconduct.* I think no one but a Slave Commissioner will maintain that this is law.

Mr. Loring contends that he was bound to issue the warrant, holding as he did the office of Commissioner! Who obliged him to hold the office? Could he not have resigned, as many—young Kane of Philadelphia, and others—did, when first the infamous act made it possible that he should be insulted by an application for such a warrant? There was a time when all of us would have deemed such an application an insult to Edward G. Loring. Could he not have resigned when the application was made, as Captain Hayes of our police did, when called on to aid in doing the very act which Mr. Loring had brought like a plague on the city? Could he not have declined to issue the warrant or take part in the case, as B. F. Hallett was reported to have done in the case of William and Ellen Crafts?

But whether he could or not matters not to you, Gentlemen. Massachusetts has a right to say what sort of men she will have on her bench. She does not complain if vile men will catch slaves. She only claims that they shall not, at the same time, be officers of hers. Mr. Loring had his choice, to resign his judgeship or his commissionership. He chose to act as Commissioner, and, of course, took the risk of losing the other office whenever the State should rise to assert her laws. Nobody can complain that he is not allowed to hold a Probate Court one hour and a Slave Court the next. Certainly, it is not too much to claim for Massachusetts the poor right to say, that when the "legalized robber," "the felonious slave-trader," (these are Channing's words,) comes here, he shall not be able to select agents for his merciless work from those sitting on our bench and clothed in our ermine.

One single line of this remonstrance goes far to show

the hollowness of all the rest: "In this conviction, the Commissioners, *refusing all pecuniary compensation*, have performed their duties to the Constitution and the law." If the "pieces of silver" are clean, and have no spot of blood, why do all our Commissioners refuse to touch them? And why, when accused of executing this merciless statute, (all men seem to think it an *accusation*,) does each one uniformly plead in extenuation or atonement that he refused the fee? Is it any real excuse for doing an infamous act, that one did it for nothing? There is something strange in this. Ah, Gentlemen, not all the special pleading in the world, not "all the perfumes of Arabia, can sweeten" that accursed gold.

There is one paragraph in this remonstrance which deserves notice, as showing either great ignorance or great heedlessness in one who claims to sit on a judicial bench. Mr. Loring says; —

"In the year 1851, the Act of Congress of 1850 was declared, by the unanimous opinion of the Justices of the Supreme Judicial Court of the Commonwealth of Massachusetts, to be a constitutional law of the United States, passed by Congress in execution of the fourth article of the Constitution of the United States, and as such the supreme law of Massachusetts (7 Cush. Rep. 285); and in exposition of the subject, after reference to the nature of the Constitution of the United States, as a compromise of mutual rights, creating mutual obligations and duties, it was declared (page 319): 'In this spirit and with these views steadily in prospect, it seems to be the duty of all judges and magistrates to expound and apply these provisions in the Constitution and laws of the United States, and in this spirit it behooves all persons bound to obey the laws of the United States to consider and regard them.' And this authoritative direction as to the duties of the magistrates and people of Massachusetts was given in direct reference to the fourth article of the Constitution of the United States, the United States Act of 1850, and the laws of Massachusetts, as they then were and have ever since been."

Observe the language: "It was declared," by the court, of course, and it is an "authoritative direction as to the duties of magistrates." You conclude, Gentlemen, as every reader would, and would have a right to conclude, that this sentence, quoted from the 319th page of Cushing's Reports, is part of a decision of our Supreme Court. Not at all, Gentlemen; it is only a note to a decision, written, to be sure, by Judge Shaw, but on his private responsibility, and no more an "authoritative direction" to magistrates and people than any casual remark of Judge Shaw to his next-door neighbor as they stand together on the sidewalk. In his decision in the Burns case, Mr. Loring refers to the Sims case, above cited, (7 Cushing, 285,) "as the unanimous opinion of the judges of the Supreme Court of Massachusetts," and then quotes this same sentence as part of the opinion, terming it "the wise words of our revered Chief Justice IN THAT CASE." Could this important mistake, twice made, on solemn occasions, be mere inadvertence? If he knew no better, he seems hardly fit for a judge. If any of his friends should claim he did know better, then, surely, he must have intended to deceive, and that does not much increase his fitness for the bench.

Mr. Chairman, there is one view of the Burns case which has not, I believe, been suggested. It is this. Massachusetts declares that the fugitive slave is constitutionally entitled to a jury trial. It is the general conviction of the North. Mr. Webster had once prepared an amendment to the Fugitive Slave Act securing jury trial. A Commissioner of humane and just instincts would be careful, therefore, to remember that the present act, on the contrary, made him both judge and jury. Now does any man in the Commonwealth believe that a jury would have ever sent Burns into slavery with six witnesses against one as to his identity, and his confession as much in his favor as against him? Mr. Loring knows, this day, that he sent into slavery a man whom no jury that could be impanelled in Massachusetts would have condemned. I might add, whom no judge but himself, now on our bench, would have condemned on the same evidence.

The friends of Mr. Loring, in the streets, tell us it is hard to hold him accountable for this decision; that all the world knows he did not make it, — powerful relatives and friends dictated it to him. Gentlemen, the apology seems worse even than our accusation. A man whose own heart does not lead him to be a slave-catcher allow himself to be made the tool of others for such business! Besides, does this excuse prove him so very fit, after all, to sit on the Probate Bench? What if he should allow able relatives to dictate his decisions there also?

Gentlemen, I have not enlarged, as I might have done, on the general principle that, without alleging special misconduct, the mere fact of Mr. Loring's consenting to act at all as a Slave Commissioner is sufficient cause for his removal from the office of a Massachusetts judge. To consent actively to aid in hunting slaves here and now shows a hardness of heart, a merciless spirit, a moral blindness, an utter spiritual death, which totally unfit a man for the judicial office. No such man ought or can expect to preserve the confidence of the community, which is essential to his usefulness as a judge. Neither can Mr. Loring claim that he had not full warning such would be the case. To our shame we must confess, that the State has submitted to the execution of the Slave Act within her limits. But, thank God! we are justified in claiming that she submitted in sad, reluctant, sullen silence; that while she offered no resistance to the law, as such, she proclaimed, in the face of the world, her loathing and detestation of a slave-hunter. In the words of Channing: —

"The great difficulty in the way of the arrangement now proposed is the article of the Constitution requiring the surrender and return of fugitive slaves. A State, obeying this, seems to me to contract as great guilt as if it were to bring slaves from Africa. No man, who regards slavery as among the greatest wrongs, can in any way reduce his fellow-creatures to it. The flying slave asserts the first right of a man, and should meet aid rather than obstruction. . . . . *No man among us, who values his character, would aid the slave-hunter. The slave-hunter here would be looked on with as little favor as the felonious slave-trader.* Those among us who dread to touch slavery in its own region, lest insurrection and tumults should follow change, still feel that the fugitive who has sought shelter so far can breed no tumult in the land which he has left, and that, of consequence, no motive but the unhallowed love of gain can prompt to his pursuit; and when they think of slavery as perpetuated, not for public order, but for gain, they abhor it, *and would not lift a finger to replace the flying bondsman beneath the yoke.*"

The Legislature, the press, the pulpit, the voice of private life, every breeze that swept from Berkshire to Barnstable, spoke contempt for the hound who joined that merciless pack. Every man who touched the Fugitive Slave Act was shrunk from as a leper. Every one who denounced it was pressed to our hearts. Political sins were almost forgotten, if a man would but echo the deep religious conviction of the State on this point. When Charles Sumner, himself a Commissioner, proclaimed beforehand his determination not to execute the Fugitive Slave Act, exclaiming, in Faneuil Hall, "I was a man before I was a Commissioner!" all Massachusetts rose up to bless him, and say, Amen! The other Slave Commissioner who burdens the city with his presence cannot be said to have lost the respect and confidence of the community, seeing he never had either. But slave-hunting was able to sink even him into a lower depth than he had before reached.

The hunting of slaves is, then, a sufficient cause for

removal from a Massachusetts bench. Indeed, I should blush for the State if it were not so. I am willing this case should stand forever as a precedent. Let it be considered as settled, that when a judge violates the well-known, mature, religious conviction of the State on a grave and vital question of practical morality, having had full warning, such violation shall be held sufficient cause for his removal. This principle will do no shadow of harm to the independence of the bench. Mr. Chairman, as I have before remarked, the bench is weakened when we retain a bad judge, not when we remove him.

I am glad that the facts of this case are such that we can remove Mr. Loring without violating in the least tittle the proper independence of the judiciary; that Massachusetts can fix the seal of her detestation on the Slave Act by so solemn a deed, without danger to her civil polity. But, Mr. Chairman, I frankly confess that, if the case had been otherwise, if it had been necessary to choose between two alternatives, (while I value as highly as any man can an independent judge,) better, far better, in my opinion, to have for judges dependent honest men, than independent slave-catchers.

Dr. Channing, sitting in his study, says that "no man among us who values his character would aid the slave-hunter." We ask you to remove from judicial office the man who has done it, — done it unnecessarily, done it in hot haste, done it against law. We ask you not to have slave-hunters on the bench of our old Commonwealth. Read Channing's last, dying words: —

"There is something worse than to be a slave. It is to make other men slaves. Better be trampled in the dust than trample on a fellow-creature. Much as I shrink from the evils inflicted by bondage on the millions who bear it, I would sooner endure them than inflict them on a brother. Freemen of the mountains! as far as you have power, remove from yourselves, from our dear and venerable mother, the Commonwealth of Massachusetts, and from all the Free States, the baseness and guilt of ministering to slavery, of acting as the slaveholder's police, of lending him arms and strength to secure his victim. . . . . Should a slave-hunter ever profane these mountainous retreats by seeking here a flying bondman, regard him as a *legalized robber.* Oppose no force to him; you need not do it. Your contempt and indignation will be enough to disarm the 'man-stealer' of the unholy power conferred on him by unrighteous laws."

This is the picture of a slave-hunter, which a dispassionate man leaves as his legacy to his fellow-citizens. Gentlemen, we assert that such a man is not fit to sit upon the bench. We have a right to claim that you shall give us honorable, just, high-minded, conscientious judges, — men worthy the respect and confidence of the community. You cannot have such, if you have men who consent to act as United States Slave Commissioners. You never can enact a United States Commissioner into respect. You may pile your statutes as high as Wachusett, they will suffice to disgrace the State, they cannot make a Slave Commissioner a respectable man.

We have, it seems to us, a right to ask of Massachusetts this act, — it being clearly within her just authority, — as a necessary and righteous expression of the feeling of the State. The times are critical. South Carolina records her opinion of slavery in a thousand ways. She violates the United States Constitution to do it, expelling Mr. Hoar from her borders, and barring him out with fine and imprisonment. Young Wisconsin makes the first page of her State history glorious by throwing down her gauntlet against this slave-hunting Union, in defence of justice and humanity. Some of us had hoped that our beloved Commonwealth would have placed that crown of oak on her own brow. Her youngest daughter has earned it first. God speed her on her bright pathway to success and immortal honor! Shall Massachusetts alone be mute, when the world gathers to this great protest against a giant sin, to this holy crusade of humanity?

Say not, we claim something extreme and fanatical. We say only, what the State enacted in 1843 and reiterated in 1850, that to be a Massachusetts magistrate and a slave-hunter are incompatible offices. Surely, public opinion has not gone back since 1850. Surely, the Nebraska outrage has not reconciled you to the Slave Power. We dare be as much opposed to slavery and slave-hunting now as we were before that insult. Tell the nation that Massachusetts throws no sanction around the Slave Law by allowing her officers to join in executing it. She marks her sense of its merciless nature by refusing her broad seal to any one who upholds it.

Judge Loring says, "I only obeyed the United States law in returning the fugitive." Let Massachusetts say to him, "Do it! do it freely! do it as often as you please! Return a fugitive slave every day! But, when you do, remember you shall skulk through the streets like a leper from whose side every man shrinks. Remember, you shall hold no commission of mine. No, the humblest work that the lowliest official performs, since it is honest, is too holy to be polluted by you. We do not deny your right. It is, unfortunately, your right, as a citizen of the United States, to take your part in slave hunts; but the Commonwealth has also, we thank God, still the right to say that her judges shall be decent men, at least. Make your choice! You wish to be United States Commissioner? — be it; but no longer be officer of mine!" What! shall our judges be men whose names it makes one involuntarily shudder to meet in our public journals? — whose hand many an honest man would blush to be seen to touch in the streets?

Indeed, Mr. Chairman, I do not exaggerate. Grant that

Burns was Colonel Suttle's slave, and what are the facts? A brave, noble man, born, unhappily, in a Slave State, has shown his fitness for freedom better than most of us have done. At great risk and by great effort obtained he this freedom; but we were only free born. He hides himself in Boston. By hard work he earns his daily bread. With patient assiduity, he sits at the feet of humble teachers, in school and pulpit, and tries to become really a man. The heavens smile over him. He feels that all good men must wish him success in his blameless efforts to make himself more worthy to stand at their side. Weeks roll on, and the heart which stood still with terror at every lifting of the door-latch begins to grow more calm. He has finished his day's work; and, under the free stars, wearied, but full of joyful hope that words could never express, he seeks his home, — happy, however humble, as it is his, and it is free. In a moment, the cup is dashed from his lips. He is in fetters, and a slave. The dear hope of knowledge, manhood, and worthy Christian life seems gone. To read is a crime now, marriage a mockery, and virtue a miracle. Who shall describe the horrible despair of that moment? How the world must have seemed to shut down over him as a living tomb! What hand dealt that terrible blow? This poor man, against mountain obstacles, is struggling to climb up to be more worthy of his immortality. What hand is it, that, in this Christian land, starts from the cloud and thrusts him back? It is the hand of one whom your schools have nurtured with their best culture, sitting at ease, surrounded with wealth; one whom your commission appoints to protect the fatherless, and mete out justice between man and man. Men! Christians! is there one of you who would, for worlds, take upon his conscience the guilt of thus crushing a hapless, struggling soul? Is the man who could, in obedience to any human law, be guilty of such an act, fit to be judge over Christian people?

Gentlemen, the petitioners have no feeling of revenge toward Mr. Edward G. Loring. Let the general government reward him with thousands, if it will. To us he is only an object of pity. There was an hour when one man trembled before him, — when one hapless victim, with more than life at stake, trembled before this man's want of humanity and ignorance of law. That hour has passed away. To-day he is but a weed on the great ocean of humanity. To us he is nothing; but we, with you, are the Commonwealth of Massachusetts; and for the honor of the State, for the sake of justice, in the name of humanity, we claim his removal. We have a right to a judiciary worthy of the respect of the community. We cannot respect him. Do not give us a man whose judicial character is made up of party bias, personal predilection, bad law, and a reckless disregard of human rights, and whose heart was too hard to melt before the mute eloquence of a hapless and terrified man, — do not commit to such a one the widows and orphans of the Commonwealth! Do not place such a man on a bench which only able and humane and Christian men have occupied before! Do not let him escape the deserved indignation of the community, by the technical construction of a statute! The Constitution has left you, as the representatives of the original sovereignty of the people, the power to remove a judge, when you think he has lost the confidence and respect of his constituents. Exercise it! Say to the United States, "The Constitution allows the return of fugitive slaves. Find your agents where you will; you shall not find them on the Supreme or any inferior Bench of Massachusetts. You shall never gather round that infamous procedure any respectability derived from the magistracy of the Commonwealth. If it is to be done, let it be done by men whom it does not harm the honor or the interest of Massachusetts to have dishonored and made infamous!"

Mr. Chairman, give free channel to the natural instincts of the Commonwealth, and let us — let us be at liberty to despise the slave-hunter, without feeling that our children's hopes and lives are prejudiced thereby! When you have done it, — when you have pronounced on this hasty, reckless, inhuman court its proper judgment, the verdict of official reprobation, — you will secure another thing. The next Slave Commissioner who opens his court will remember that he opens it in Massachusetts, where a man is not to be robbed of his rights as a human being merely because he is black. You will throw around the unfortunate victim of a cruel law, which you say you cannot annul, all the protection that Massachusetts incidentally can. And, doing this, you will do something to prevent seeing another such sad week as that of last May or June, in the capital of the Commonwealth. Although you cannot blot out this wicked clause in the Constitution, you will render it impossible that any but reckless, unprincipled, and shameless men shall aid in its enforcement. Such men cannot long uphold a law in this Commonwealth.

The petitioners ask both these things; claiming especially to have proved that you can do this work, and that, if you love justice or mercy, you ought to do it.

THE BOSTON MOB.*

MR. PRESIDENT: I feel that I have very little right on this platform to-day. I stand here only to express my gratitude to those who truly and properly occupy it, for what we all owe them — the women and the men — who stood by our honor, and so nobly did our duties, when we forgot it and them twenty years ago.

At this hour, twenty years ago, I was below in the street; — I thank God I am inside the house now! I was not in the street as one of the mob, but as a spectator. I had come down from my office in Court Street to see what the excitement was. I did not understand antislavery then; that is, I did not understand the country in which I lived. We have all learned much since then; learned what antislavery means, — learned what a republican government really is, — learned the power of the press and of money, which I, at least, did not know then. I remember saying to the gentleman who stood next to me in the street: "Why does not the Mayor call out the regiment?" (I belonged to it then.) "We would cheerfully take arms in such a case as this. It is a very shameful business. Why does he stand there arguing? Why does he not call for the guns?" I did not then know that the men who should have borne them were the

* Speech before the Antislavery Meeting held in Stacy Hall, Boston, on the Twentieth Anniversary of the Mob of October 21, 1835.

mob; that all there was of government in Boston was in the street; that the people, our final reliance for the execution of the laws, were there, in "broadcloth and broad daylight," in the street. Mayor Lyman knew it; and the only honorable and honest course open to him was, to have said, "If I cannot *be* a magistrate, I will not *pretend* to be one."

I do not know whether to attribute the Mayor's disgraceful conduct to his confused notion of his official duties, or to a cowardly unwillingness to perform what he knew well enough to be his duty. A superficial observer of the press and pulpit of that day would be inclined to consider it the result of ignorance, and lay the blame at the door of our republican form of government, which thrusts up into important stations dainty gentlemen like Lyman, physicians never allowed to doctor any body but the body politic, or cunning tradesmen who have wriggled their slimy way to wealth, — men who in a trial hour not only know nothing of their own duties, but do not even know where to go for advice. And for the preachers, I am inclined to think this stolid ignorance of civil rights and duties may be pleaded as a disgraceful excuse, leaving them guilty only of meddling in matters far above their comprehension. But one who looks deeper into the temper of that day will see plainly enough that the Mayor and the editors, with their companions "in broadcloth," were only blind to what they did not wish to see, and knew the right and wrong of the case well enough, only, like all half-educated people, they were but poorly able to comprehend the vast importance of the wrong they were doing. The mobs which followed, directed against others than Abolitionists, the ripe fruit of the seed here planted, opened their eyes somewhat.

Mr. Garrison has given us specimens enough of the press of that day. There was the Daily Advertiser, of course on the wrong side, — respectable when its opponents are strong and numerous, and quite ready to be scurrilous when scurrility is safe and will pay, — behind whose editorials a keen ear can always catch the clink of the dollar, — entitled to be called the Rip Van Winkle of the press, should it ever, like Rip, wake up; the Advertiser condescended, strangely enough, to say, that it was *not surprised* (!) that papers abroad considered the meeting of mobocrats in the street below *a riot* (!); but the *wiser Advertiser* itself regarded it "*not so much as a riot as the prevention of a riot*"! It "*considered the whole transaction as the triumph of law over lawless violence, and the love of order over riot and confusion*"!! Dear, dreamy Van Winkle! and he goes on to "*rejoice*" at the exceeding "moderation" of the populace, that they did not murder Mr. Garrison on the spot! And this is the journal which Boston literature regards as its organ, and which Boston wealth befools itself by styling "respectable"!

Next came the scurrilous Gazette, which, it is said, repented of its course when it found that Northern subscribers fell off and Southerners continued to despise it as before; and which, outliving public forbearance and becoming bankrupt, earned thus the right to be melted into the Daily Advertiser.

With them in sad alliance marched the Courier, — always strong and frank, whichever side it took, and even of whose great merit and bravery between that time and this, it is sufficient praise to say, that it was enough to outweigh its great wrong in 1835, and its vile servility now.

With rare daring, the Christian Register, the organ of the Unitarians, snatched the palm of infamy. In a moment of forgetful frankness, remembering, probably, the coward course of its own sect, it counselled hypocrisy; suiting manner to matter, it *hints* to the Abolitionists, that they should imitate the example, as, with laughable ignorance, it avers, of the early Christians of Trajan's day, and meet in secret, if the "*vanity*" of the ladies would allow! The coward priest forgot, if he ever knew, that the early Christians met in secret beneath the pavements of Rome, only to pray for the martyrs whose crosses lined the highways, whose daring defied Paganism at its own altars, and whose humanity stopped the bloody games of Rome in the upper air; that they met beneath the ground, not so much to hide themselves, as to get strength for attacks on wicked laws and false altars.

Infamy, however, at that day, was not a monopoly of one sect. Hubbard Winslow, a Pharisee of the Pharisees, strictly Orthodox, a bigot in good and regular standing, shortly after this preached a sermon to illustrate and defend the doctrine, that no man, under a republican government, has a right to promulgate any opinion but such as "a majority of the brotherhood would allow and protect"; and he is said to have boasted that Judge Story thanked him for such a discourse!

The Mayor played a most shuffling and dishonorable part. For some time previous, he had held private conferences with leading Abolitionists, urging them to discontinue their meetings, professing, all the while, entire friendship, and the most earnest determination to protect them in their rights at any cost. The Abolitionists treated him, in return, with the utmost confidence. They yielded to his wishes, so far as to consent to do nothing that would increase the public excitement, with this exception, that they insisted on holding meetings often enough to assert their *right* to meet. Yet, while they were thus honorably avoiding everything which would needlessly excite the public mind, going to the utmost verge of submission and silence that duty permitted, — while the Abolitionists, with rare moderation, were showing this magnanimous forbearance and regard to the weakness of public authority and the reckless excitement of the public, — the Mayor himself, in utter violation of official decorum and personal honor, accepted the chair of the public meeting assembled in Faneuil Hall, and presided over that assembly, — an assembly which many intended should rouse a mob against the Abolitionists, and which none but the weak or wilfully blind could avoid seeing must lead to that result. In his opening speech to that factious meeting, the Mayor, under oath at that moment to protect every citizen in his rights, and doubly bound just then by private assurances to these very Abolitionists, forgot all his duty, all his pledges, so far as to publicly *warn them of the danger of their meeting*, — a warning or threat, the memory of which might well make him tremblingly anxious to save Garrison's life, since of any blood shed that day, every law, divine and human, would have held the Mayor guilty.

Such was the temper of those times. The ignorant were not aware, and the wise were too corrupt to confess, that the most precious of human rights, free thought, was at stake. These women knew it, felt the momentous character of the issue, and consented to stand in the gap. Those were trial hours. I never think of them without my shame for my native city being swallowed up in gratitude to those who stood so bravely for the right. Let us not consent to be ashamed of the Boston of 1835. Those howling wolves in the streets were not Boston. These brave men and women were Boston. We will remember no other.

I never open the statute-book of Massachusetts without thanking Ellis Gray Loring and Samuel J. May, Charles Follen and Samuel E. Sewall, and those around me who stood with them, for preventing Edward Everett from blackening it with a law making free speech an indictable offence. And we owe it to fifty or sixty women, and a dozen or two of men, that free speech was saved, in 1835, in the city of Boston. Indeed, we owe it mainly to one man. If there is one here who loves Boston, who loves her honor, who rejoices to know that, however fine the thread, there *is* a thread which bridges over that dark and troubled wave, and connects us by a living nerve with the freemen of the Revolution, — that Boston, though betrayed by her magistrates, her wealth, her press, and her pulpits, never utterly bowed her neck, let him remember that we owe it to you, Sir, [Mr. Francis Jackson,] who offered to the women not allowed to meet here, even though the Mayor was in this hall, the use of your house; and one sentence of your letter deserves to be read whenever Boston men are met together to celebrate the preservation of the right of free speech in the city of Adams and Otis. History, which always loves courage, will write it on a page whiter than marble and more incorruptible than gold. You said, Sir, in answer to a letter of thanks for the use of your house: —

"If a large majority of this community choose to turn a deaf ear to the wrongs which are inflicted upon their countrymen in other portions of the land, — if they are content to turn away from the sight of oppression, and 'pass by on the other side,' — so it must be.

"But when they undertake in any way to impair or annul my right to speak, write, and publish upon any subject, and more especially upon enormities which are the common concern of every lover of his country and his kind, — so it must not be, — so it shall not be, if I for one can prevent it. Upon this great right let us hold on at all hazards. And should we, in its exercise, be driven from public halls to private dwellings, one house at least shall be consecrated to its preservation. And if, in defence of this sacred privilege, which man did not give me, and shall not (if I can help it) take from me, this roof and these walls shall be levelled to the earth, — let them fall, if they must. They cannot crumble in a better cause. They will appear of very little value to me, after their owner shall have been whipped into silence."

This was only thirty days after the mob. I need not read the remainder of that letter, which is in the same strain.

We owe it to one man that a public meeting was held, within a month, by these same women, in the city of Boston. But to their honor be it rememembered, also, — a fact which Mr. Garrison omitted to state, — that when Mayor Lyman urged them to go home, they left this hall in public procession and went "home" to the house of Mrs. M. W. Chapman, in West Street, to organize and finish their meeting that very afternoon. To Mrs. Chapman's pen we owe the most living picture of that whole scene, and her able, graphic, and eloquent reports of the proceedings of the Female Antislavery Society, and specially of this day, have hung up to everlasting contempt the "men of property and standing," — the "respectable" men of Boston.

Let us open, for a moment, the doors of the hall which stood here, and listen to the Mayor receiving his lesson in civil duty from the noble women of this society.

Mr. Lyman. — Go home, ladies, go home.

President. — What renders it necessary we should go home?

Mr. Lyman. — I am the Mayor of the city, and I cannot now explain; but will call upon you this evening.

President. — If the ladies will be seated, we will take the sense of the meeting.

Mr. Lyman. — Don't stop, ladies, go home.

President. — Will the ladies listen to a letter addressed to the Society, by Francis Jackson, Esq.?

Mr. Lyman. — Ladies, do you wish to see a scene of bloodshed and confusion? If you do not, go home.

One of the Ladies. — Mr. Lyman, your personal friends

are the instigators of this mob; have you ever used your personal influence with them?

Mr. Lyman. — I know no personal friends; I am merely an official. Indeed, ladies, you must retire. It is dangerous to remain.

Lady. — If this is the last bulwark of freedom, we may as well die here as anywhere.

There is nothing braver than that in the history of the Long Parliament, or of the Roman Senate.

At that Faneuil Hall meeting, one of "the family" was present, — one of that family which was never absent when a deed of infamy was to be committed against the slave, — a family made up mostly of upstart attorneys, who fancy themselves statesmen, because able to draw a writ or pick holes in an indictment. Mr. Thomas B. Curtis read the resolutions; and then followed three speeches, by Harrison Gray Otis, Richard Fletcher, and Peleg Sprague, unmatched for adroit, ingenious, suggestive argument and exhortation to put down, legally or violently, — each hearer could choose for himself, — all public meetings on the subject of slavery in the city of Boston. Everything influential in the city was arrayed against this society of a few women. I could not but reflect, as I sat here, how immortal principle is. Rev. Henry Ware, Jr. read the notice of this society's meeting from Dr. Channing's pulpit, and almost every press in the city woke barking at him next morning for what was called his "impudence." He is gone to his honored grave; many of those who met in this hall in pursuance of that notice are gone likewise. They died, as Whittier so well says,

> "their brave hearts breaking slow,
> But, self-forgetful to the last,
> In words of cheer and bugle glow,
> Their breath upon the darkness passed."

In those days, as we gathered round their graves, and

resolved that, the "narrower the circle became, we would draw the closer together," we envied the dead their rest. Men ceased to slander them in that sanctuary; and as we looked forward to the desolate vista of calamity and toil before us, and thought of the temptations which beset us on either side from worldly prosperity which a slight sacrifice of principle might secure, or social ease so close at hand by only a little turning aside, we almost envied the dead the quiet sleep to which we left them, the harvest reaped, and the seal set beyond the power of change. And of those who assaulted them, many are gone. The Mayor so recreant to his duty, or so lacking in knowledge of his office, is gone; the Judge before whom Mr. Garrison was arraigned, at the jail, the next day after the mob, is gone; the Sheriff who rode with him to the jail is gone; the city journals have changed hands, being more than once *openly* bought and sold. The editor of the *Atlas*, whose zeal in the cause of mob violence earned it the honor of giving its name to the day, — "the *Atlas* mob" many called it, — is gone; many of the prominent actors in that scene, twenty years ago, have passed away; the most eloquent of those whose voices cried "Havoc!" at Faneuil Hall has gone, — Mr. Otis has his wish, that the grave might close over him before it closed over the Union, which God speed in his good time; — but the same principle fills these same halls, as fresh and vital to-day, as self-fixed and resolute to struggle against pulpit and press, against wealth and majorities, against denunciation and unpopularity, and certain in the end to set its triumphant foot alike on man and everything that man has made.

Here stands to-day the man whom Boston wealth and Boston respectability went home, twenty years ago this night, and gloried in having crushed. The loudest boasters are gone. He stands to-day among us, these very

walls, these ideas which breathe and burn around us, saying for him, "I still live." If, twenty or twice twenty years hence, he too shall have passed away, may it not be till his glad ear has caught the jubilee of the emancipated millions whom his life has been given to save!

This very Female Antislavery Society which was met here twenty years ago did other good service but a few months after, in getting the Court of Massachusetts to recognize that great principle of freedom, that a slave, *brought into a Northern State*, is free. It was in the well-known Med case. We owe that to the Boston Female Antislavery Society. To-day, Judge Kane, and the Supreme Court, which alone can control him, are endeavoring to annihilate that principle which twenty years ago was established. How far and how soon they may be successful, God only knows.

Truly, as Mr. Garrison has said, the intellectual and moral growth of antislavery has been great within twenty years; but who shall deny that, in the same twenty years, the political, the organic, the civil growth of slavery has been more than equal? We stand here to-day with a city redeemed — how far? Just so far as this meeting commemorates, — the right of free speech is secured. Thank God! in twenty years, we have proved that an antislavery meeting is not only possible, but respectable, in Massachusetts, — that is all we have proved. Lord Erskine said a newspaper was stronger than government. We have got many newspapers on our side. Ideas will, in the end, beat down anything; — we have got free course for ideas.

But let us not cheer ourselves too hastily, for the government, the wealth, the public opinion, of this very city in which we meet, remain to-day almost as firmly anchored as ever on the side of slavery. Vanes turn only when the wind shifts, so the *Daily Advertiser* has not changed a whit,

— not a whit. The same paper that spoke doubtful words before October 21st, hoped the meeting would be stopped, and afterwards could not quite decide whether there was a mob or not, but was glad the ladies were not allowed to hold their meeting, — that same paper would doze through the same shameless part to-day. That paper, which represented then so well the mobocrats in broadcloth, has passed from a father wearied in trying to hold Massachusetts back, to his son, — whose accession, to reverse James the First's motto, "no day followed," — and it is published to-day with the same spirit, represents the same class, actuated exactly with the same purpose. If there is strength outside the city, in the masses, enough to rebuke that class and that press and that purpose, and give the State of Massachusetts more emphatically to some kind of antislavery, it is still a struggle. I would not rejoice, therefore, too much. We must discriminate. "To break your leg twice over the same stone is your own fault," says the Spanish proverb.

I came here to-day to thank God that Boston never wanted a person to claim his inalienable right to utter his thoughts on the subject of slavery, nor a spot upon which he could do it; — that is all my rejoicing to-day. And in that corner-stone of individual daring, of fidelity to conscience, I recognize the possibility of the emancipation of three millions of slaves. But that possibility is to be made actual by labors as earnest and unceasing, by a self-devotion as entire, as that which has marked the twenty years we have just passed.

I find that these people, who have made this day famous, were accused in their own time of harsh language and over-boldness, and great disparagement of dignities. These were the three charges brought against the Female Antislavery Society in 1835. The women forgot their homes, it was said, in endeavoring to make the men do their duty. It was a noble lesson which the sisters and mothers of that time set the women of the present day, — I hope they will follow it.

There was another charge brought against them, — it was, that they had no reverence for dignitaries. The friend who sits here on my right (Mrs. Southwick) dared to rebuke a slaveholder with a loud voice, in a room just before, if not then, consecrated by the presence of Chief Justice Shaw, and the press was astonished at her boldness. I hope, though she has left the city, she has left representatives behind her who will dare rebuke any slave-hunter, or any servant of the slave-power, with the same boldness, frankness, and defiance of authorities, and contempt of parchment.

Then there was another charge brought against their meetings, that they indulged in exceedingly bold language about pulpits and laws and wicked magistrates. That is a sin which I hope will not die out. God grant we may inherit that also.

I should like to know very much how many there are in this hall to-day who were out in the street, as actual mobocrats, twenty years ago. I know there are some here who signed the various petitions to the City Government to prevent the meeting from being held; but it would be an interesting fact to know how many are here to-day, actually enlisted under the antislavery banner, who tore that sign to pieces. I wish we had those relics; the piece of that door which was long preserved, the door so coolly locked by Charles Burleigh, — it was a touching relic. We ought to have a portion of that sign which the Mayor threw down as a tub to the whale, hoping to save some semblance of his authority, — hoping the multitude would be satisfied with the sign, and spare the women in this hall, — forgetting that a mob is controlled only by its fears, not by pity or good manners.

But, Mr. President, it is a sad story to think of. Anti-slavery is a sad history to read, sad to look back upon. What a miserable refuse public opinion has been for the past twenty years! — what a wretched wreck of all that republican education ought to have secured! Take up that file of papers which Mr. Garrison showed you, and think, Republicanism, a Protestant pulpit, free schools, the model government, had existed in our city for sixty years, and this was the result! A picture, the very copy of that which Sir Robert Peel held up in the British Parliament, within a month after the mob, as proof that republicanism could never succeed. It is a sad picture to look back upon. The only light which redeems it is the heroism that consecrated this hall, and one house in Hollis Street, places which Boston will yet make pilgrimages to honor.

The only thing that Americans (for let us be Americans to-day, not simply Abolitionists), — the only thing for which Americans can rejoice, this day, is, that *everything* was not rotten. The *whole* head was not sick, nor the *whole* heart faint. There were *ten men*, even in Sodom! And when the Mayor forgot his duty, when the pulpit prostituted itself, and when the press became a pack of hounds, the women of Boston, and a score or two of men, remembered Hancock and Adams, and did their duty. And if there are young people who hear me to-day, let us hope that when this special cause of antislavery effort is past and gone, when another generation shall have come upon the stage, and new topics of dispute have arisen, there will be no more such scenes. How shall we ever learn toleration for what we do not believe? The last lesson a man ever learns is, that liberty of thought and speech is the right for all mankind; that the man who denies every article of our creed is to be allowed to preach just as often and just as loud as we ourselves. We have learned this, — been taught it by persecution on the ques-

tion of slavery. No matter whose the lips that would speak, they must be free and ungagged. Let us always remember that he does not really believe his own opinions, who dares not give free scope to his opponent. Persecution is really want of faith in our creed. Let us see to it, my friends, Abolitionists, that we learn the lesson the whole circle round. Let us believe that the whole of truth can never do harm to the whole of virtue. Trust it. And remember, that, in order to get the whole of truth, you must allow every man, right or wrong, freely to utter his conscience, and protect him in so doing.

The same question was wrought out here twenty years ago, as was wrought in the protest of fifty or a hundred Abolitionists, when an infidel (Abner Kneeland) was sent to Boston jail for preaching his sentiments. I hope that we shall all go out of this hall, remembering the highest lesson of this day and place, that every man's conscience is sacred. No matter how good our motives are in trying to gag him! Mayor Lyman had some good motives that day, had he only known what his office meant, and stayed at home, if he felt himself not able to fill it. It is not motives. Entire, unshackled freedom for every man's lips, no matter what his doctrine; — the safety of free discussion, no matter how wide its range; — no check on the peaceful assemblage of thoughtful men! Let us consecrate our labors for twenty years to come in doing better than those who went before us, and widening the circle of their principle into the full growth of its actual and proper significance.

Let me thank the women who came here twenty years ago, some of whom are met here to-day, for the good they have done me. I thank them for all they have taught me. I had read Greek and Roman and English history; I had by heart the classic eulogies of brave old men and martyrs; I dreamed, in my folly, that I heard the same tone in my youth from the cuckoo lips of Edward Everett; — these women taught me my mistake. They taught me that down in those hearts which loved a principle for itself, asked no man's leave to think or speak, true to their convictions, no matter at what hazard, flowed the real blood of '76, of 1640, of the hemlock-drinker of Athens, and of the martyr-saints of Jerusalem. I thank them for it! My eyes were sealed, so that, although I knew the Adamses and Otises of 1776, and the Mary Dyers and Ann Hutchinsons of older times, I could not recognize the Adamses and Otises, the Dyers and Hutchinsons, whom I met in the streets of '35. These women opened my eyes, and I thank them and you [turning to Mrs. Southwick and Miss Henrietta Sargent, who sat upon the platform] for that anointing. May our next twenty years prove us all apt scholars of such brave instruction!

THE PILGRIMS.*

MR. PRESIDENT: History tells us that the Pilgrims at this season of the year 1622 were very hungry, almost starving; but certainly their descendants must be far more insatiable than they then were, if, after all the noble things they have heard to-day, they can ask for more. It seems to me we are in the condition of that man whom Oliver Wendell Holmes describes in one of his lectures. You remember he says the lyceum-lecturers held a meeting, and found, as a matter of universal experience, that at a certain period in every lecture a man went out, and each one assigned a different reason for it. One thought it was business, another the heat, and a third fancied it was some offensive sentiment uttered by the speaker. But Holmes, being a physician, performed an autopsy, and found the man's brain was *full.* [Loud laughter and applause.] Now, Sir, I certainly think I may claim that reason for sitting down. After that eloquent and profound oration, and all we have listened to since, surely our brains must be full.

Why, who can do anything but repeat what we have heard? Do you not remember, Sir, when we were little boys, and followed the martial music, our steps keeping

* Speech at the dinner of the Pilgrim Society, in Plymouth, December 21, 1855, in response to the following toast: —

"*The Pilgrim Fathers,* — Their fidelity, amid hardships and perils, to truth and duty, has secured to their descendants prosperity and peace."

time, street after street, till we came to some broad way that our fears or our mothers forbade us to enter; and when the music turned away, our tiny feet kept time long afterwards? Can we get away from the spell which took possession of us in yonder church? I can only think in that channel. Who can get his mind away from the deep resounding march with which the speaker carried us from century to century, and held up the torch, and pointed out the significance of each age? All we can do is to utter some little reflection, — something suggested by that train of thought.

How true it is that the Puritans originated no new truth! How true it is, also, Mr. President, that it is not truth which agitates the world! Plato in the groves of the Academy sounded on and on to the utmost depth of philosophy, but Athens was quiet. Calling around him the choicest minds of Greece, he pointed out the worthlessness of their altars and the sham of public life, but Athens was quiet, — it was all *speculation*. When Socrates walked the streets of Athens, and, questioning everyday life, struck the altar till the faith of the passer-by faltered, it came close to *action*, and immediately they gave him hemlock, for the city was turned upside down. I might find a better illustration in the streets of Jerusalem. What the Puritans gave the world was not thought, but ACTION. Europe had ideas, but she was letting '*I dare not* wait upon *I would*,' like the cat in the adage. The Puritans, with native pluck, launched out into the deep sea. Men, who called themselves thinkers, had been creeping along the Mediterranean, from headland to headland, in their timidity; the Pilgrims launched boldly out into the Atlantic, and trusted God. [Loud applause.] That is the claim they have upon posterity. It was ACTION that made them what they were.

No, they did not originate anything, but they planted;

and the answer to all criticism upon them is to be — THE OAK. [Cheers.] The Edinburgh Reviewer takes up that acorn, the good ship Mayflower, and says, "I do not see stalwart branches, I do not see a broad tree here." Mr. President, *we* are to show it to him. The glory of the fathers is the children. Mr. Winthrop says the pens of the Puritans are their best defence. No, the Winthrops of to-day are to be the best defence of the Winthrops of 1630; they are to write that defence in the broad, legible steps of a life whose polar star is Duty, whose goal is Liberty, and whose staff is Justice. [Enthusiastic applause.] The glory of men is often, not what they actually produce, so much as what they enable others to do. My Lord Bacon, as he takes his proud march down the centuries, may lay one hand on the telegraph and the other on the steamboat, and say, "These are mine, for I taught you to invent." And the Puritan, wherever he finds a free altar, free lips, ay, and a free family, may say, "These are mine!" No matter for the stain of bigotry which rests upon his memory, since he taught us these.

I think, Mr. President, that the error in judging of the Puritans has been that which the oration of to-day sets right. We are to regard them *in posse*, not *in esse*, — in the possibilities which were wrapped up in that day, 1620, not in what poor human bodies actually produced at that time. Men look back upon the Carvers and Bradfords of 1620, and seem to think, if they existed in 1855, they would be clad in the same garments, and walking in the same identical manner and round that they did in 1620. It is a mistake. The Pilgrims of 1620 would be, in 1855, not in Plymouth, but in Kansas. [Loud cheers.] Solomon's Temple, they tell us, had the best system of lightning-rods ever invented, — he anticipated Franklin. Do you suppose, if Solomon lived now, he would stop at lightning-conductors? No, he would have telegraphs without wires, able to send messages both ways at the same time, and where only he who sent and he who received should know what the messages were.

Do you suppose that, if Elder Brewster could come up from his grave to-day, he would be contented with the Congregational Church and the five points of Calvin? No, Sir; he would add to his creed the Maine Liquor Law, the Underground Railroad, and the thousand Sharpe's Rifles, addressed "Kansas," and labelled "Books." [Enthusiastic and long-continued applause.] My idea is, if he took his staff in his hand and went off to exchange pulpits, you might hear of him at the Music Hall of Boston [where Rev. THEODORE PARKER preaches] and the Plymouth Church at Brooklyn [Rev. HENRY WARD BEECHER'S]. [Renewed applause.]

We should bear in mind development when we criticise the Pilgrims, — where they would be to-day. Indeed, to be as good as our fathers, we must be better. Imitation is not discipleship. When some one sent a cracked plate to China to have a set made, every piece in the new set had a crack in it. The copies of 1620 and 1787 you commonly see have the *crack*, and very large, too. Thee and thou, a stationary hat, bad grammar and worse manners, with an ugly coat, are not George Fox in 1855. You will recognize him in any one who rises from the lap of artificial life, flings away its softness, and startles you with the sight of a MAN. Neither do I acknowledge, Sir, the right of Plymouth to the whole rock. No, the rock underlies all America; it only crops out here. [Cheers.] It has cropped out a great many times in our history. You may recognize it always. Old Putnam stood upon it at Bunker Hill, when he said to the Yankee boys, "Don't fire till you see the whites of their eyes." Ingraham had it for ballast when he put his little sloop between two Austrian frigates, and threatened to blow them out of the water, if they did not

respect the broad eagle of the United States, in the case of Koszta. Jefferson had it for a writing-desk when he drafted the Declaration of Independence and the "Statute of Religious Liberty" for Virginia. Lovejoy rested his musket upon it when they would not let him print at Alton, and he said, "Death or free speech!" I recognized the clink of it to-day, when the apostle of the "Higher Law" came to lay his garland of everlasting — none a better right than he — upon the monument of the Pilgrims. [Enthusiastic cheering.] He says he is not a descendant of the Pilgrims. That is a mistake. There is a pedigree of the body and a pedigree of the mind. [Applause.] He knows so much about the Mayflower, that, as they say in the West, I know he was "*thar.*" [Laughter and applause.] Ay, Sir, the rock cropped out again. Garrison had it for an imposing-stone when he looked in the faces of seventeen millions of angry men and printed his sublime pledge, "I will not retreat a single inch, and I will be heard." [Great cheering.]

Sir, you say you are going to raise a monument to the Pilgrims. I know where I would place it, if I had a vote. I should place one corner-stone on the rock, and the other on that level spot where fifty of the one hundred were buried before the winter was over. In that touching, eloquent, terrific picture of what the Pilgrims passed through, rather than submit to compromise, which the orator sketched for us to-day, he omitted to mention that one half of their number went down into the grave; but the remainder closed up shoulder to shoulder, as firm, unflinching, hopeful as ever. Yes, *death* rather than the compromise of Elizabeth. [Loud applause.] I would write on their monument two mottoes: one, "The Right is more than our country!" and over the graves of the fifty, "Death, rather than Compromise!" Mr. President, I detest that word. It is so dangerous, I would not have it even in matters of expediency. As the Irishman said in Jefferson's day, when the "true-blue" Democrats took him from the emigrant ship, naturalized him at once, then hurried to the ballot-box, urging him to vote the true Democratic, *government* ticket, "The *government!* I never knew a government which was not the devil. Give me the opposition!" [Laughter.] The very word is misleading, — out with it! I would never have a compromise for anything.

My friend, Governor Boutwell, says the Puritans had no taste in architecture. I remember the first vote passed after they landed; it was, that each man build his own house. [Cheers.] I am for having each man build his own mental house now, without having too much uniformity in the architecture, and, at any rate, keeping clear of compromises and smothering phrases, and all shams and delusions.

What did the Pilgrims do? Why, Sir, it was a great question at that day which course to take. Cromwell and Hampden stood on one side, Carver and Bradford on the other. Which would best reform the English government, staying at home or going away? History answers which effected the most. Which has struck the heaviest blows at the English aristocracy, the efforts of those who stood nearest, or the sight and example of America, as she loomed up in gigantic proportions? Mr. President, they say that Michael Angelo once entered a palace at Rome where Raphael was ornamenting the ceiling, and as Angelo walked round, he saw that all the figures were too small for the room. Stopping a moment, he sketched on one side an immense head proportioned to the chamber; and when his friends asked him why, his reply was, "I criticise by creation, not by finding fault." Carver and Bradford did so. They came across the water, created a great model state, and bade England take warning. The Edinburgh Reviewer may be seen running up and down the sides of the Pilgrims, and taking their measure, — where does he get his yardstick? He gets it from the very institutions they made for him. [Applause.] He would never have known how to criticise, if their creations had not taught him.

Mr. President, I have already detained you much longer than I would. Surely to-day the Puritans have received their fit interpreter. We know them. Their great principles we are to carry with us; that one idea, persistency, — that was their polar star, and it is the key to all their success. They never lost sight of it. They sometimes talked for Buncombe; they did it when they professed allegiance to Elizabeth. Our fathers did it when they professed allegiance to George III., — it was only for Buncombe! [Laughter.] But, concealed under the velvet phrase, there was the stern Puritan muscle, which held on to individual right.

The Puritans believed that institutions were made for man. Europe established a civilization, which, like that of Greece, made the state everything, the man nothing. The man was made for the institutions; the man was made for the clothes. The Puritans said, "No, let us go out and make clothes for the man; let us make institutions for men!" That is the radical principle, it seems to me, which runs through all their history. You could not beguile them with the voice of the charmer, "charm he never so wisely"; but down through all the weary years of colonial history to the period of the Revolution, the Puritan pulse beat in unquailing, never-faltering allegiance to this principle of the sacredness of man. Let *us* hold on to it; it is to be *our* salvation.

Mr. President, the toast to which you called upon me to respond says our fathers have secured prosperity and peace. Yes, "secured" it. It is not here; we have not yet got it, but we shall have it. It is all "secured," for they planted so wisely, it will come. They planted their oak or pine tree in the broad lines of New England, and gave it room to grow. Their great care was, that it should grow, no matter at what cost. Goethe says, that, if you plant an oak in a flower-vase, either the oak must wither or the vase crack: some men go for saving the vase. Too many now-a-days have that anxiety: the Puritans would have let it crack. So say I. If there is anything that cannot bear free thought, let it crack. There is a class among us so conservative, that they are afraid the roof will come down if you sweep off the cobwebs. As Douglass Jerrold says, "They can never fully relish the new moon, out of respect for that venerable institution, the old one." [Great merriment and applause.]

Why, Sir, the first constitution ever made was framed in the Mayflower. It was a very good constitution, parent of all that have been made since, — a goodly family, some bad and some good. The parent was laid aside on the shelf the moment the progress of things required it. I hope none of the children have grown so strong that they can prevent the same event befalling themselves when necessity requires. Hold on to that idea with true New England persistency, — the sacredness of individual man, — and everything else will evolve from it. The Phillipses, Mr. President, did not come from Plymouth; they made their longest stay at Andover. Let me tell you an Andover story. One day, a man went into a store there, and began telling about a fire. "There had never been such a fire," he said, "in the county of Essex. A man going by Deacon Pettingill's barn saw an owl on the ridge-pole. He fired at the owl, and the wadding some how or other, getting into the shingles, set the hay on fire, and it was all destroyed, — ten tons of hay, six head of cattle, the finest horse in the country," &c. The

Deacon was nearly crazed by it. The men in the store began exclaiming and commenting upon it. "What a loss!" says one. "Why, the Deacon will wellnigh break down under it," says another. And so they went on, speculating one after another, and the conversation drifted on in all sorts of conjectures. At last, a quiet man, who sat spitting in the fire, looked up, and asked, "Did he hit the owl?" [Tumultuous applause.] That man was made for the sturdy reformer, of one idea, whom Mr. Seward described.

No matter what the name of the thing be; no matter what the sounding phrase is, what tub be thrown to the whale, always ask the politician and the divine, "Did he hit that owl?" Is liberty safe? Is man sacred? They say, Sir, I am a fanatic, and so I am. But, Sir, none of us have yet risen high enough. Afar off, I see Carver and Bradford, and I mean to get up to them. [Loud cheers.]

LETTER

TO JUDGE SHAW AND PRESIDENT WALKER.*

To LEMUEL SHAW, *Chief Justice of Massachusetts, and*
JAMES WALKER, *President of Harvard University.*

GENTLEMEN: Now that the press has ceased its ridicule of your homage to Morphy at the Revere House, — a criticism of little importance, — I wish to present the scene to you in a different light.

You, Mr. Chief Justice, represent *the law* of the Commonwealth; to you, Mr. President, is committed the moral guardianship of the young men of her University. Yet I find you both at a table of revellers, under a roof whose chief support and profit come from the illegal sale of intoxicating drink, and which boasts itself the champion and head of an organized, flagrant, and avowed contempt of the laws of the Commonwealth. No one was surprised to see at your side a Mayor who owes his office to the votes of that disorderly band whose chief is the Revere House. Few wondered at the presence of a Professor placed by private munificence to watch over the piety and morals of your College, Mr. President; though a manly protest against fashionable vice might do something to re-

* The hotels of Boston, with the connivance of the City Government, refuse to obey the Maine Liquor Law of Massachusetts. The Revere House, the most fashionable of our hotels, was chosen to offer a public dinner to Morphy, at which were present Judge Shaw, President Walker, the Mayor, Professor Huntington, and other dignitaries.

deem the office from seeming only an eaves-dropping spy on the opinions and manners of young men.

But you, Mr. Chief Justice, know that three quarters, if not four fifths, of all crime result from habits of intoxication; that nine tenths, at least, of all the murderers you have sent to the gallows had never been murderers had they not first been drunkards. You can look round you, and back for fifty years, and see places at the bar and on the bench, once filled by genius and hope, now vacant, — their tenants in drunkards' graves. You know how fearful the peril which modern civilization, and especially popular institutions, encounter from the cheapness of liquor, and the habits of indulgence in all our great cities; you know the long and earnest labors of noble men, for fifty years, in both hemispheres, against this evil, and the momentous experiment they are trying of legal prohibition to arrest it, resulting here in a stringent law against the sale of intoxicating drinks. You know also that the Revere House is the insolent leader of that heartless and selfish faction which, defeated before the people, seeks, by unblushing defiance of law, to overbear opinion and statute.

And you, Mr. President, the moral guardian of the young men of our University, well know its venerable statutes and unceasing efforts to prevent the use of wine within its walls. You know how many, often the brightest, names on your catalogue, too early marked with the asterisk of death, owe their untimely end to wine. Both of you know that the presence of men holding such offices as yours goes as far as recreant office and reputation can to make a bad roof respectable.

Yet I find you both at a midnight revel, doing your utmost to give character to a haunt which boasts its open and constant defiance of the moral sense of the State, solemnly expressed in its statutes.

No one denies, Gentlemen, your right to indulge what

social habits you please in the privacy of your own dwellings; or, in travelling, to use the customary accommodations of an inn, even though intoxicating drink is sold on its premises. Few will care to criticise, if, choosing some decent roof, you join your fellows and mock the moral sentiment of the community by a public carousal. But while you hold these high offices, we, the citizens of a Commonwealth whose character you represent, emphatically deny your right to appear at illegal revels in a gilded grog-shop, which, but for the sanction of such as you, had long ago met the indictment it deserves. How can we expect the police to execute a law upon which the Chief Justice pours contempt by his example? How shall the grand jury indict the nuisance of which the Supreme Bench has, for an hour, made a part? We, the citizens, have a right to claim that, should public opinion, by our labors, reach the point of presenting these gorgeous grog-shops at the criminal bar, we shall not find their frequenters on the bench.

Again and again, Mr. Chief Justice, have I heard you, at critical moments, in a voice whose earnest emotion half checked its utterance, remind your audience of the sacred duty resting on each man to respect and obey the law; assuring us that the welfare of society was bound up in this individual submission to existing law. How shall the prisoner at the bar reconcile the grave sincerity of the *magistrate* with this heedless disregard by the *man* of most important laws? If, again, the times should call you to bid us smother justice and humanity at the command of statutes, we may remind you with what heartless indifference you treated the law you were sworn and paid to uphold, and one on which the hearts of the best men in the State were most strongly set. Was it not enough that you let History paint you bowing beneath a slave-hunter's chain to enter your own court-room? but must you also present yourself in public, lifting to your lips the wine-cup, which, by the laws of the State over whose courts you preside, it is an indictable offence and a nuisance tc sell you?

And let me remind you, Mr. President, that even your young men sometimes pause amid scenes of temptation, or in our streets, where every tenth door opens to vice, — pause at some chance thought of home or rising regard for the sentiment of the community. And, Sir, should such frail purpose of even one youth falter before the sight of his President in a circle of wine-bibbers, and that fall lead to an unhonored grave, you will be bound to remember that, in the check and example you promised and were expected and set to hold upon him, you wholly failed; that in the most impressible moments of his life he saw the virtue of the State struggling with its sensual indulgence, its lust of dishonorable gain, its base pandering to appetite, already too strong; and in that struggle he saw your weight ostentatiously thrown into the scale of open and contemptuous disregard of the moral sense of the State. I well remember when, from a pulpit constantly boasting that its new creed had thrown away a formal and hollow faith and brought in the wholesome doctrine of works, you painted, so vividly, how hard it is for young men to say "No." Is this, Sir, the method you choose to illustrate the practical value of the new faith, and this the help you extend to the faltering virtue of your pupils, giving the sanction of your character and office to the prince of rumsellers and law-breakers, and flinging insult on one of the noblest reforms of the age?

I admit the right and duty of minorities to disregard immoral or unconstitutional laws. But no one ever though the prohibitory law immoral, and you, Mr. Chief Justice, have affirmed its constitutionality. Neither do I now arraign you, Gentlemen, for your private habit of wine-drinking. I do not complain that a judge, who sees so much crime come from it, still gives it his countenance; that a clergyman — the chief apostle of whose faith declared he would eat no meat while the world stood, if so doing made his brother to offend — still throws that stumbling-block in the way of his pupils. But I arraign the Chief Justice of Massachusetts, and the President of Harvard University, because, when the rum interest of the State is marshalling its strength to beat down a good and constitutional law by gross, open, and avowed disobedience, they are found lending their names, character, and office to give respectability to the grog-shop whose wealth enables it to lead that dishonorable and disloyal effort. As a citizen, I claim that you disgraced your places, if not yourselves; and I hope the day will come when such insult by such high officers to any statute of the Commonwealth, much more to one representing its highest moral purpose, will be deemed cause enough to impeach the one and remove the other.

WENDELL PHILLIPS.

August 1, 1859.

IDOLS.*

MR. PRESIDENT AND LADIES AND GENTLEMEN: I feel half inclined to borrow a little wit from an article in a late number of the Atlantic Monthly, — "My Double, and how he undid me," — and say, "I agree entirely with the gentleman who has just taken his seat." [Laughter.] "So much has been said, and so well said, that I feel there is no need of my occupying your attention." [Renewed laughter.] But then I should lose the hearty satisfaction it gives me to say with what delight I stand upon this platform, and how sincerely I appreciate the honor you do me, Mr. Chairman, by allowing me to aid in opening this course of lectures. I know, Sir, that you hoped, as I did, that this post would be filled by our great Senator, who seeks health on a foreign soil. No one laments more sincerely than I do that he felt it impossible and inconsistent with his other duties to be here. It is not too much to say that the occasion was worthy of a word even from Charles Sumner. [Hearty applause.]

Appreciating the lyceum system as I do, looking upon it as one of the departments of the national school, truly American in its origin, and eminently republican in its character and end, I feel how eloquently his voice would have done it justice. For this is no common evening, Mr. President. The great boast of New England is liberal

* Fraternity Lecture delivered in Boston, October 4, 1859

culture and toleration. Easier to preach than to practise! Many lyceums have opened their doors to men of different shades of opinion, and some few have even granted a fair amount of liberty in the choice of subject, and the expression of individual opinion. None of us can forget, on such an occasion as this, the eminently catholic spirit and brilliant success of that course of Antislavery Lectures in the winter of 1854 and 1855, which we owed chiefly to the energy and to the brave and liberal spirit of Dr. James W. Stone. But you go, Gentlemen, an arrow's flight beyond all lyceums; for, recognizing the essential character of civilization, you place upon your platform the representatives of each sex and of both races. Yes, Ladies and Gentlemen, you will listen to consummate eloquence, never heard in Boston before from the lyceum platform, because "guilty of a skin not colored like our own." [Applause.] And you will listen, besides, to woman, gracefully standing on a platform which boasts itself the source of national education. For decent justice has not been done to woman, in regard to her influence, either upon literature or society; and I welcome with inexpressible delight the inauguration of a course of lectures national and American in the proper sense of the words.

There are men who prate about "nationality," and "the empire," and "manifest destiny," — using brave words, when their minds rise no higher than some petty mass of white States making money out of cotton and corn. My idea of American nationality makes it the last best growth of the thoughtful mind of the century, treading under foot sex and race, caste and condition, and collecting on the broad bosom of what deserves the name of an empire, under the shelter of noble, just, and equal laws, all races, all customs, all religions, all languages, all literature, and all ideas. I remember, a year or two ago, they told us of a mob at Milwaukie that forced a man to bring out the body of his wife, born in Asia, — which, according to the custom of her forefathers, he was about to burn, — and compelled him to submit to American funeral rites, which his soul abhorred. The sheriff led the mob, and the press of the State vindicated the act. This is not my idea of American civilization. They will show you at Rome the stately column of the Emperor Trajan. Carved on its outer surface is the triumphal march of the Emperor, when he came back to Rome, leading all nations, all tongues, all customs, all races, in the retinue of his conquest; and they traced it on the eternal marble, circling the pillar from base to capital. Just such is my idea of the empire, broad enough and brave enough to admit both sexes, all creeds, and all tongues in the triumphal procession of this great daughter of the west of the Atlantic. [Loud applause.] That is the reason why I hail this step in Boston, — the brain of the Union, — saying to the negro and to woman, "Take your place among the teachers of American Democracy." [Applause.]

I said justice had never been done to woman for her influence upon literature and society. Society is the natural outgrowth of the New Testament, and yet nothing deserving of the name ever existed in Europe until, two centuries ago, in France, woman called it into being. Society, — the only field where the sexes have ever met on terms of equality, the arena where character is formed and studied, the cradle and the realm of public opinion, the crucible of ideas, the world's university, at once a school and a theatre, the spur and the crown of ambition, the tribunal which unmasks pretension and stamps real merit, the power that gives government leave to be, and outruns the lazy Church in fixing the moral sense of the age, — who shall fitly describe the lofty place of this element in the history of the last two centuries? Who shall deny that, more than anything else, it deserves the name of the most controlling element in the history of the two centuries just finished? And yet this is the realm of woman, the throne which, like a first conqueror, she founded and then filled.

So with literature. The literature of three centuries ago is not decent to be read: we expurgate it. Within a hundred years, woman has become a reader, and for that reason, as much or more than anything else, literature has sprung to a higher level. No need now to expurgate all you read. Woman, too, is now an author; and I undertake to say that the literature of the next century will be richer than the classic epochs, for that cause. Truth is one forever, absolute; but opinion is truth filtered through the moods, the blood, the disposition, of the spectator. Man has looked at creation, and given us his impressions, in Greek literature and English, one-sided, half-way, all awry. Woman now takes the stand to give us her views of God's works and her own creation; and exactly in proportion as woman, though equal, is eternally different from man, just in that proportion will the literature of the next century be doubly rich, because we shall have both sides. You might as well plant yourself in the desert, under the changeless gray and blue, and assert that you have seen all the wonders of God's pencil, as maintain that a male literature, Latin, Greek, or Asiatic, can be anything but a half part, poor and one-sided; as well develop only muscle, shutting out sunshine and color, and starving the flesh from your angular limbs, and then advise men to scorn Titian's flesh and the Apollo, since you have exhausted manly beauty, as think to stir all the depths of music with only half the chords. [Applause.] The diapason of human thought was never struck till Christian culture summoned woman into the republic of letters; and experience as well as nature tells us, "what God hath joined, let not man put asunder." [Applause.]

I welcome woman, therefore, to the platform of the world's teachers, and I look upon the world, in a very important sense, as one great school. As Humboldt said, ten years ago, "Governments, religion, property, books, are nothing but the scaffolding to build a man. Earth holds up to her Master no fruit but the finished man." Education is the only interest worthy the deep, controlling anxiety of the thoughtful man. To change Bryant a little:

> "The hills,
> Rock-ribbed and ancient as the sun,
> The venerable woods, rivers that move
> In majesty, and the complaining brooks
> That make the meadows green, and, poured round all
> Old Ocean's gray and melancholy waste,
> Are but the solemn decorations all
> Of the great *school* of man."

It is in this light and for this value that I appreciate the lyceum. We have four sources of education in this country, — talk, literature, government, religion. The lyceum makes one and the most important element of each. It is a church, without a creed, and with a constant rotation of clergymen. [Applause.] It teaches closer ethics than the pulpit. Let lyceum committees debate whether they shall invite Theodore Parker, or theological papers scold because Beecher stands on your platform, and out of such debate the people will pick a lesson of toleration better, more real, and more impressive than Locke's Treatise or a dozen sermons could give them. Responsibility teaches as nothing else can. That is God's great motor power. When your horse cannot move his load, throw a sack of grain on his back and he draws easily on. He draws by weight, not by muscle. Give the masses nothing to do, and they will topple down thrones and cut throats; give them the government, as here, and they will make pulpits useless and colleges an impertinence. It is the best part of literature, too, for it is the only part that is vital. I value letters. I thank God that I was taught for many years; enough to see inside the sham.

The upper tier of letters is mere amateur; does not understand its own business. William H. Prescott would have washed his hand twice, had Walker the filibuster grasped it unwittingly; but he sits down in his study and writes the history of filibusters, respectable only because they died three hundred years ago! He did not know that he was the mere annalist of the Walkers and Jefferson Davises of that age. [Applause.]

[In this connection, Mr. Phillips referred to Bunyan and to Shakespeare, by way of illustrating his point that the literature which is of use is the literature that is not honored as such when it is written.]

So it is with government. Government arrogates to itself that it alone forms men. As well might the man down here in the court-house, who registers the birth of children, imagine that he was the father of all the children he registers. [Loud laughter.] Everybody knows that government never began anything. It is the whole world that thinks and governs. Books, churches, governments, are what we make them. France is Catholic, and has a pope; but she is the most tolerant country in the world in matters of religion. New England is Protestant, and has toleration written all over her statute-book; but she has a pope in every village, and the first thing that tests a boy's courage is to dare to differ from his father. [Applause.] Popes! why, we have got two as signal popes as they had in Europe three centuries ago, — there is *Bellows* at Avignon and *Adams* at Rome. [Great merriment, followed by loud applause.] So with government. Some think government forms men. Let us take an example.

Take Sir Robert Peel and Webster as measures and examples; two great men, remarkably alike. Neither of them ever had an original idea. [Laughter.] Neither kept long any idea he borrowed. Both borrowed from any quarter, high or low, north or south, friend or enemy. Both were weathercocks, not winds; creatures, not creators. Yet Peel died England's idol, — the unquestioned head of the statesmen of the age; Webster the disgraced and bankrupt chief of a broken and ruined party. Why? Examine the difference. Webster borrowed free trade of Calhoun, and tariff of Clay; took his constitutional principles from Marshall, his constitutional learning from Story, and his doctrine of treason from Mr. George Ticknor Curtis [laughter]; and he followed Channing and Garrison a little way, then turned doughface in the wake of Douglas and Davis [applause and a few hisses]; at first, with Algernon Sidney (my blood boils yet as I think how I used to declaim it), he declared the best legacy he could leave his children was free speech and the example of using it; then of Preston S. Brooks and Legree he took lessons in smothering discussion and hunting slaves. In 1820, when the world was asleep, he rebuked the slave-trade; in 1850, when the battle was hottest, he let Everett omit from his works all the best antislavery utterances!

Sir Robert Peel was just like him. He "changed every opinion, violated" (so says one of the Reviews) "every pledge, broke up every party, and deserted every colleague he ever had," yet his sun went down in glory. Why? Because his step was ever onward; he lived to learn. Every change was a sacrifice, and he could truly use, in 1829, the glorious Latin Webster borrowed of him, "*Vera pro gratis*," — "I tell you unwelcome *truth*." But Webster's steps, crab-like, were backwards. [Applause and hisses.] Hisses! well, "Because thou art virtuous, shall there be no more cakes and ale?" Because you have your prejudices, shall there be no history written?

Our task is unlike that of some recent meetings, — *History*, not flattery. [Applause.] Webster moved by compulsion or calculation, not by conviction. He sunk from free trade to a tariff; from Chief Justice Marshall to Mr. George Ticknor Curtis; from Garrison to Douglas; from Algernon Sidney to the slave overseers. I read in this one of the dangers of our form of government. As Tocqueville says so wisely, "The weakness of a Democracy is that, unless guarded, it merges in despotism." Such a life is the first step, and half a dozen are the Niagara carrying us over.

But both "builded better than they knew." Both forced the outward world to think for itself, and become statesmen. No man, says D'Israeli, ever weakened government so much as Peel. Thank Heaven for that! — so much gained. Changing every day, their admirers were forced to learn to think for themselves. In the country once I lived with a Democrat who never had an opinion on the day's news till he had read the Boston Post. [Laughter.] Such close imitation is a little too hard. Webster's retainers fell off into the easier track of doing their own thinking. A German, once sketching a Middlesex County landscape, took a cow for his fixed point of perspective; she moved, and his whole picture was a muddle. Following Peel and Webster was a muddle; hence came the era of outside agitation, — and those too lazy to think for themselves at least took a fixed point for their political perspective, — Garrison or Charles Sumner, for instance.

[Mr. Phillips continued by remarking that all the people had ever asked of government was, not to take a step ahead, not to originate anything, but only to UNDO *its mistakes*, to take its foot from off its victim, take away its custom-houses, abolish its absurd and wicked legislation and free the slave. He then proceeded to urge upon his hearers the importance of free individual thought, — the questioning of whatever came before us, with an honest desire and effort to reach truth.] He said: —

We shall have enough to do if we do our duty. The world is awake, — some wholly, and some only half. Men who gather their garments scornfully and close about them when their fellows offer to express sympathy for the bravest scholar and most Christian minister the liberal New England sects know, — these timid little souls make daily uproar in the market-place, crying for a *Broad* Church, a BROAD Church, — and one who lives by venturing a bold theory to-day, and spending to-morrow in taking it back, finding that he has been

> "Dropping buckets into empty wells,
> And growing old in drawing nothing out,"

assures you that it is not cowardice, but lack of candles and of a liturgy, that makes him useless; and, kind-souled man, he apologizes, and begs us not to be startled with his strange new views, having lived so long in the thin air of his own vanity that he does not know we have had a broad Church for fifteen years, — broad enough for all races and colors, all sects, creeds, and parties, for heads and hearts too; broad enough to help the poor, teach the ignorant, shield the weak, raise the fallen, and lift the high higher, to honor God and earn the hate of bad men, — ministered to by one whose broad diocese is bounded on the north by the limits of habitable land, runs west with civilization, and east with the English language, and on the south stretches to the line where men stop thinking and live only to breathe and to steal. [Loud applause.]

This Broad-Church reformer knows his place so little, that he sneers at spiritualism and socialism, as "vices entitled to no terms." One, an honest effort, however mistaken, to make all men wholly and really brothers in life, property, and thought; and the other, that reaching into the land of spirit which has stirred the heart and roused the brain of the best men of all ages, and given to literature its soul. Does he give no heed to that profound maxim of Coleridge,— "There are errors which no wise man will treat with rudeness while there is a probability that they may be the refraction of some great truth still below the horizon"?

Yes, this "Broad Church"! — humanity would weep if it ever came, for one of its doctrines is, that the statute-book is more binding than the Sermon on the Mount, and that the rights of private judgment are a curse. Save us from a Church not broad enough to cover woman and the slave, all the room being kept for the grog-shop and the theatre, — provided the one will keep sober enough to make the responses, and the other will lend its embroidered rags for this new baby-house. [Laughter and applause.]

The honors we grant mark how high we stand, and they educate the future. The men we honor, and the maxims we lay down in measuring our favorites, show the level and morals of the time. Two names have been in every one's mouth of late, and men have exhausted language in trying to express their admiration and their respect. The courts have covered the grave of Mr. Choate with eulogy. Let us see what is their idea of a great lawyer. We are told that "he worked hard," "he never neglected his client," "he flung over the discussions of the forum the grace of a rare scholarship," "no pressure or emergency ever stirred him to an unkind word." A ripe scholar, a profound lawyer, a faithful servant of his client, a gentleman. This is a good record surely. May he sleep in peace! What he earned, God grant he may have! But the bar that seeks to claim for such a one a place among great jurists must itself be weak indeed; for this is only to make him out the one-eyed monarch of the blind. Not one high moral trait specified; not one patriotic act mentioned; not one patriotic service even claimed. Look at Mr. Webster's idea of what a lawyer should be in order to be called great, in the sketch he drew of Jeremiah Mason, and notice what stress he lays on the religious and moral elevation, and the glorious and high purposes which crowned his life! Nothing of this now! I forget. Mr. Hallett did testify for Mr. Choate's religion [laughter and applause]; but the law maxim is, that a witness should be trusted only in matters he understands, and that evidence, therefore, amounts to nothing. [Merriment.] Incessant eulogy; but not a word of one effort to lift the yoke of cruel or unequal legislation from the neck of its victim; not one attempt to make the code of his country wiser, purer, better; not one effort to bless his times or breathe a higher moral purpose into the community; not one blow struck for right or for liberty, while the battle of the giants was going on about him; not one patriotic act to stir the hearts of his idolaters; not one public act of any kind whatever about whose merit friend or foe could even quarrel, unless when he scouted our great charter as a "glittering generality," or jeered at the philanthropy which tried to practise the Sermon on the Mount! When Cordus, the Roman Senator, whom Tiberius murdered, was addressing his fellows, he began: "Fathers, they accuse me of illegal words; plain proof that there are no illegal deeds with which to charge me." So with these eulogies, — words, nothing but words; plain proof that there were no deeds to praise.

The divine can tell us nothing but that he handed a chair or a dish as nobody else could [laughter]; in politics, we are assured he did not wish to sail outside of Daniel Webster; and the Cambridge Professor tells his pupils, for their special instruction, that he did not dare to think in religion, for fear he should differ from South-side Adams! [Loud laughter and applause.] The Professor strains his ethics to prove that a good man may defend a bad man. Useless waste of labor! In Egypt, travellers tell us that the women, wholly naked, are very careful to veil their faces. So the Professor strains his ethics to cover this one fault. Useless, Sir, while the whole head is sick and the whole heart faint.

Yet this is the model which Massachusetts offers to the Pantheon of the great jurists of the world!

Suppose we stood in that lofty temple of jurisprudence, — on either side of us the statues of the great lawyers of every age and clime, — and let us see what part New England — Puritan, educated, free New England — would bear in the pageant. Rome points to a colossal figure and says, "That is Papinian, who, when the Emperor Caracalla murdered his own brother, and ordered the lawyer to defend the deed, went cheerfully to death, rather than sully his lips with the atrocious plea; and that is Ulpian, who, aiding his prince to put the army below the law, was massacred at the foot of a weak, but virtuous throne."

And France stretches forth her grateful hands, crying, "That is D'Aguesseau, worthy, when he went to face an enraged king, of the farewell his wife addressed him, — 'Go! forget that you have a wife and children to ruin, and remember only that you have France to save.'"

England says, "That is Coke, who flung the laurels of eighty years in the face of the first Stuart, in defence of the people. This is Selden, on every book of whose library you saw written the motto of which he lived worthy, 'Before everything, *Liberty!*' That is Mansfield, silver-tongued, who proclaimed,

> 'Slaves cannot breathe in England; if their lungs
> Receive our air, that moment they are free.'

This is Romilly, who spent life trying to make law synonymous with justice, and succeeded in making life and property safer in every city of the empire. And that is Erskine, whose eloquence, spite of Lord Eldon and George III., made it safe to speak and to print."

Then New England shouts, "This is Choate, who made it safe to murder; and of whose health thieves asked before they began to steal."

Boston had a lawyer once, worthy to stand in that Pantheon; one whose untiring energy held up the right arm of Horace Mann, and made this age and all coming ones his debtors; one whose clarion voice and life of consistent example waked the faltering pulpit to its duty in the cause of temperance, laying on that altar the hopes of his young ambition; one whose humane and incessant efforts to make the penal code worthy of our faith and our age ranked his name with McIntosh and Romilly, with Bentham, Beccaria, and Livingston. Best of all, one who had some claim to say, with Selden, "Above all things, *Liberty*," for in the slave's battle his voice was of the bravest, — Robert Rantoul. [Prolonged and hearty plaudits.] He died crowned with the laurels both of the Forum and Senate-house. The Suffolk Bar took no note of his death. No tongue stirred the air of the courts to do him honor. "When vice is useful, it is a crime to be virtuous," says the Roman proverb. Of that crime, Beacon Street, State Street, and Andover had judged Rantoul guilty.

The State, for the second time in her history, offers a pedestal for the statue of a citizen. Such a step deserves thought. On this let us dare to think. Always think twice when saints and sinners, honest men and editors, agree in a eulogy. [Laughter.] All wonders deserve investigation, specially when men dread it.

No man criticises when private friendship moulds the loved form in

> "Stone that breathes and struggles,
> Or brass that seems to speak."

Let Mr. Webster's friends crowd their own halls and grounds with his bust and statue. That is no concern of ours. But when they ask the State to join in doing him honor, we are natives of Massachusetts, and claim the right to express an opinion.

It is a grave thing when a State puts a man among her jewels, — especially one whose friends frown on discussion, — the glitter of whose fame makes doubtful acts look heroic. One paper, a tea-table critic, warns a speaker not born in the State to cease his criticism of the Webster statue. I do not know why Massachusetts may not import critics as well as heroes; for, let us be thankful, Webster was no Boston boy. But be sure you exercise your right to think NOW.

His eulogy has tasked the ripest genius and the heartiest zeal. Some men say his eulogist has no heart. That is a mistake and cruel injustice! As the French wit said of Fontenelle, he "has as good a heart as can be made out of brains." [Laughter.] No matter what act Webster did, no matter how foul the path he trod, he never lacked some one to gild it with a Greek anecdote, or hide it in a blaze of declamation! I do not say the deed was always whitened, but surely it was something that the eulogist shared the stain. They say in England that when Charles X., an exile in England, hunted there, others floundered through mud and water as they could, but the exiled king was followed by a valet who flung himself down in his path and Charles walked over him as indifferently as if he had really been a plank. How clean the king kept, I do not know. The valet got very muddy. A striking picture of Webster and his eulogists!

His bronze figure stands on the State-House Green. Standing there, it reminds me of some lines, written in an album by Webster, when asked to place his name under that of John Adams: —

"If by his name I write my own,
'T will take me where I am not known;
The cold salute will meet my ear, —
'Pray, stranger, how did you come here?'"

In the printed speech of Mr. Everett, you will find three feet, — exactly one yard, — by newspaper measurement, about the Northeastern Boundary map *with a red line on it!* but not a line, or hardly one, relating to the great treason of the 7th of March, 1850. The words he dared to speak, his friends dare not repeat; the life he dared to live, his friends dare not describe, at the foot of his statue! To mention now what he thought his great achievement will be deemed unkind!

Mr. Everett's silence was wise. He could not blame; nature denied him the courage. He was too wary to praise, for he recollected the French proverb, "Some compliments are curses." So he obeyed the English statesman's rule, "When you have nothing to say, be sure and say nothing."

But that is the printed speech. It seems some meddlesome fellow stood within reach of the speaker, and actually circulated, it is said, petitions for the removal of the statue from the public grounds. Then the orator forgot his caution, and interpolated a few unpremeditated sentences, "very forcible and eloquent," says the press, specially intended for this critic; terming this impudent meddler "Mr. Immaculate," and quoting for his special benefit the parable of the Pharisee and Publican, — "God be merciful to me a sinner!" Singular eulogy, to make out his idol a miserable "sinner"! [Laughter.] Is this the usual method, Mr. Chairman, of proving one's right to a statue? The Publican repented, and was forgiven; but is a statue, ten feet high, cast in bronze, a usual element of forgiveness? And, mark, the Publican *repented.* When did Mr. Webster repent, either in person or by the proxy of Mr. Edward Everett? We have no such record. The sin is confessed, acknowledged, as a mistake at least; but there 's no repentance!

Let us look a little into this doctrine of statues for sinners. Take Aaron Burr. Tell of his daring in Canada, his watch on the Hudson, of submissive juries, of his touching farewell to the Senate. "But then there was that indiscretion as to Hamilton." Well, Mr. Immaculate, remember "the Publican." Or suppose we take Benedict Arnold, — brave in Connecticut, gallant at Quebec, recklessly daring before Burgoyne! "But that little peccadillo at West Point!" Think of "the Publican," Mr. Immaculate. Why, on this principle, one might claim a statue for Milton's Satan. He was brave, faithful to his party, eloquent, shrewd about many a map "with a red line on it"! There 's only that trifle of the apple to forgive and forget in these generous and charitable days! No, if he wants an illustration, with due humility, I can give the orator a great deal better one. Sidney Smith had a brother as witty as himself, and a great hater of O'Connell. "Bobus Smith" (for so they called him) had one day marshalled O'Connell's faults at a dinner-talk, when his opponent flung back a glowing record of the great Irishman's virtues. Smith looked down a moment. "Well, such a man, — such a mixture; the only way would be to hang him first, and then erect a statue to him under the gallows." A disputed statue rising out of a sea of angry contempt, half-hearted admiration, and apologetic eulogy, reminds me of the Frenchman tottering up, at eighty years old, to vote for Louis Bonaparte. "Why, he is a scoundrel," said Victor Hugo. "True, — very true, — but he is a *necessary* scoundrel."

Ah, as the Greek said, "many men know how to flatter, few men know how to praise." These Cambridge Professors and fair-weather eulogists have no ability to measure Webster, — either his capacity or his faults. They were dazzled blind by the splendor of his endowments, they were lost in the tumult of his vices. Theodore Parker's estimate is the truest ever made. History will adopt it as her verdict. His head and heart were the only ones large enough to grasp the subject, and brave enough to paint it truly. [Enthusiastic applause.] The real admirer of Webster turns from these French daubs to find there the cool, truthful tone of Raphael, and feels that the statesman has met there his kindest critic, and the man his most appreciating judge. Accuse us not if we award him blame as well as praise. As I said just now, our task is history, not flattery. I know well that every statesman must compromise; but, as Macaulay says, "A public man is often under the necessity of consenting to measures he dislikes, to save others he thinks important. But the historian is under no such necessity. On the contrary, it is one of his most sacred duties to *point out* CLEARLY the errors of those whose general conduct he approves." If this be true of "*errors*," how still more sacred this duty when the question is one of treachery to Liberty herself!

Blame me not that I again open the record, Mr. Chairman. His injudicious friends will not let him die. Indeed, the heavy yoke he laid on innocent and friendless victims frets and curses them yet too keenly to allow him to be forgotten. He reaps only what he sowed. In the Talmud, the Jews have a story that Og, King of Bashan, lifted once a great rock, to hurl it on the armies of Judah. God hollowed it in the middle, letting it slip over the giant's neck, there to rest while he lived. This man lifted the Fugitive-Slave Bill to hurl it, as at Syracuse, on the trembling and hunted slave, and God has hung it like a millstone about his neck forevermore. [Applause.] While the echoes of Everett's periods still lingered in our streets, as I stood with the fresh-printed sheet of his eulogy in my hand, there came to me a man, successful after eight attempts, in flying from bondage. Week after week he had been in the woods, half starved, seeking in vain a shelter. For months he had pined in dungeons, waiting the sullen step of his master. At last God blessed his eighth effort, and he stood in Boston, on his glad way from the vulture of the States to the safe refuge of English law. He showed me his broad bosom scarred all over with the branding-iron, his back one mass of record how often the lash had tortured him for his noble efforts to get free. As I looked at him, the empty and lying eulogy dropped from my nerveless hand, and I thanked God that statue and eulogy both were only a horrid nightmare, and that there were still roofs in Boston, safe shelter for these heroic children of God's right hand. [Prolonged cheering.]

But you and I, Mr. Chairman, were born in Massachusetts, and we cannot but remember that the character of the State is shown by the character of those it crowns. A brave old Englishman tells us the Greeks "had officers who did pluck down statues if they exceeded due symmetry and proportion. We need such now," he adds, "to order monuments according to men's merits." Indeed we do! Daniel Webster said, on Bunker Hill, in one of his most glorious bursts of eloquence: "That motionless shaft will be the most powerful of speakers. Its speech will be of civil and religious liberty. It will speak of patriotism and of courage. It will speak of the moral improvement and elevation of mankind. Decrepit age will lean against its base, and ingenuous youth gather round it, speak to each other of the glorious events with which it is connected, and exclaim, 'Thank God I also am an American!'" It is a glorious lesson, and the noble old shaft tells it daily.

But when ingenuous youth stand at his pedestal, what shall they say? "Consummate jurist! Alas that your latest effort was to sneer at a 'higher law'! Most able and eloquent advocate! could you find no other cause to plead than that of our lowest instincts against our highest and holiest sentiments? Alas that your last and ablest argument was the duty of hunting slaves! Sagacious statesmen! Fated to die not very old, and yet live long enough to see all the plans of your manhood become obsolete ideas, except just those you had abandoned! Surely you were a great party leader! for you found the Whig party strong, spent life in its service, and died prophesying its annihilation; found it decent, at least in profession, left it despicable in utter shamelessness; found it the natural ally of free labor and free speech, stirred it to a contest with its rival in servile bidding for Southern fellowship, and left it despicable for the attempt, and still more despicable and ridiculous for its failure! The curses of the poor have blighted your laurels. You were mourned in ceiled houses and the marts of trade; but the dwellers in slave-huts and fugitives along the highways thanked God, when you died, that they had one enemy the less. Wherever that terrible face turned, it carried gloom to the bondman. On how many a humble hearth did it cost the loftiest Christian principle to forbear calling down curses on your head!

"And yet your flatterers tell us this was the 'grandest growth of our soil and institutions!' this the noblest heart Massachusetts can offer to the world for a place beside the Phocions and the Hampdens, the Jays and the Fayettes! Thank God, then, we are not Massachusetts men!"

When I think of the long term and wide reach of his influence, and look at the subjects of his speeches, — the mere shells of history, drum-and-trumpet declamation, dry law, or selfish bickerings about trade, — when I think of his bartering the hopes of four million of bondmen for the chances of his private ambition, I recall the criticism on Lord Eldon, — "No man ever *did* his race so much good as Eldon *prevented*." Again, when I remember the close of his life spent in ridiculing the antislavery movement as useless abstraction, moonshine, "mere rub-a-dub agitation," because it did not minister to trade and gain, methinks I seem to see written all over his statue Tocqueville's conclusion from his survey of French and American Democracy, — "*The man who seeks freedom for anything but freedom's self, is made to be a slave!*"

Monuments, anniversaries, statues, are schools, Mr. Webster tells us, whose lessons sink deep. Is this man's life a lesson which the State can commend to her sons? Professor Felton, as usual, embalmed his idol in a Greek anecdote. It is a good storehouse. Let us open it. In that great argument which gave us the two most consummate orations of antiquity, the question was whether Athens should grant Demosthenes a crown. He had fled from battle, and his counsels, though heroic, brought the city to ruin. His speech is the masterpiece of all eloquence. Of the accusation by Æschines, it is praise enough to say that it stands second only to that. In it Æschines warns the Athenians that in granting crowns they judged themselves, and were forming the characters of their children. His noble burst —

Τὸ δὲ μέγιστον, ἐὰν ἐπερωτῶσιν ὑμᾶς οἱ νεώτεροι πρὸς ποῖον χρὴ παοάδειγμα, &c. —

is worth translating: —

"Most of all, fellow-citizens, if your sons ask whose example they shall imitate, what will you say? For you know well it is not music, nor the gymnasium, nor the schools that mould young men; it is much more the public proclamations, the public example. If you take one whose life has no high purpose, one who mocks at morals, and crown him in the theatre, every boy who sees it is corrupted. When a bad man suffers his deserts, the people learn, — on the contrary, when a man *votes against what is noble and just*, [how exactly he describes this case!] and then comes home to teach his son, the boy will very properly say, 'Your lesson is impertinent and a bore.' Beware, therefore, Athenians, remembering posterity will rejudge your judgment, and that the character of a city is determined by the character of the men it crowns."

I recommend this page of Æschines to Mr. Felton.

Has the State, then, no worthier sons, that she needs import such poor material? Within her bosom rests the dust of Horace Mann, whose name hundreds of thousands of children on Western prairies, looking up to Massachusetts teachers, learn to bless. He bears the sceptre of Massachusetts influence to the shores of the Pacific. When at the head of our Normal School, a colored girl was admitted, and the narrow prejudice of Newton closed every door against her, "Come to my table; let my roof, then, be your home," said Mr. Mann. [Hearty applause.] Antioch College staggered under $60,000 debt. One, bearing the form of a man, came to its President, and said, "I will pay one sixth, if you will promise me no negro shall enter its halls." "Let it perish first," was Horace Mann's reply. [Renewed and enthusiastic applause.] The Legislature are asked to put his statue opposite Webster's. O no. When the Emperor makes his horse a consul, honest men decline a share in the consulship. While that ill-used iron stands there, our State is in bad odor to offer statues to anybody.

At Reval, one of the Hanse towns, they will show you, in their treasury, the sword which, two hundred years ago, beheaded a lawless Baron for daring to carry off his fugitive slave from the shelter of the city walls. Our great slave-hunter is beyond the reach of man's sword; but if any noble soul in the State will stir our mother Massachusetts to behead his image, we will cherish the name of that true Massachusetts boy as sacredly as they keep the brave old sword at Reval. [Loud and prolonged applause.]

HARPER'S FERRY.*

LADIES AND GENTLEMEN: Of course I do not expect — speaking from this platform, and to you — to say anything on the vital question of the hour which you have not already heard. But, when a great question divides the community, all men are called upon to vote, and I feel to-night that I am simply giving my vote. I am only saying "ditto" to what you hear from this platform day after day. And I would willingly have avoided, Ladies and Gentlemen, even at this last moment, borrowing this hour from you. I tried to do better by you. Like the Irishman in the story, I offered to hold the hat of Hon. Thomas Corwin of Ohio, [enthusiastic applause,] if he would only make a speech, and, I am sorry to say, he declines, most unaccountably, this generous offer. [Laughter.] So I must fulfil my appointment, and deliver my lecture myself.

"The Lesson of the Hour?" I think the lesson of the hour is insurrection. [Sensation.] Insurrection of thought always precedes the insurrection of arms. The last twenty years have been an insurrection of thought. We seem to be entering on a new phase of this great American struggle. It seems to me that we have never

* A Lecture delivered at Brooklyn, N. Y., Tuesday Evening, November 1, 1859. Mr. Phillips was advertised to speak on "The Lesson of the Hour," in Henry Ward Beecher's Church. Hon. Thomas Corwin, with others, was on the platform.

accepted, — as Americans, we have never accepted our own civilization. We have held back from the inference which we ought to have drawn from the admitted principles which underlie our life. We have all the timidity of the Old World, when we think of the people; we shrink back, trying to save ourselves from the inevitable might of the thoughts of the millions. The idea on the other side of the water seems to be, that man is created to be taken care of by somebody else. God did not leave him fit to go alone; he is in everlasting pupilage to the wealthy and the educated. The religious or the comfortable classes are an ever-present probate court to take care of him. The Old World, therefore, has always distrusted the average conscience, — the common sense of the millions.

It seems to me the idea of our civilization, underlying all American life, is, that men do not need any guardian. We need no safeguard. Not only the inevitable, but the best power this side of the ocean, is the unfettered average common sense of the masses. Institutions, as we are accustomed to call them, are but pasteboard, and intended to be, against the thought of the street. Statutes are mere milestones, telling how far yesterday's thought had travelled; and the talk of the sidewalk to-day is the law of the land. You may regret this; but the fact stands; and if our fathers foresaw the full effect of their principles, they must have planned and expected it. With us, Law is nothing unless close behind it stands a warm, living public opinion. Let that die or grow indifferent, and statutes are waste paper, lack all executive force. You may frame them strong as language can make; but once change public feeling, and through them or over them rides the real wish of the people. The good sense and conscience of the masses are our only title-deeds and police force. The Temperance cause, the antislavery movement, and your Barnburner party prove this. You may sigh for a strong government, anchored in the convictions of past centuries, and able to protect the minority against the majority, — able to defy the ignorance, the mistake, or the passion, as well as the high purpose, of the present hour; you may prefer the unchanging *terra firma* of despotism; but still the fact remains, that we are launched on the ocean of an unchained democracy, with no safety but in those laws of gravity which bind the ocean in its bed, — the instinctive love of right in the popular heart, — the divine sheet-anchor, that the race gravitates towards right, and that the right is always safe and best.

Somewhat briefly stated, such is the idea of American civilization; uncompromising faith — in the average selfishness, if you choose — of all classes, neutralizing each other, and tending towards that fair play which Saxons love. But it seems to me that, on all questions, we dread thought; we shrink behind something; we acknowledge ourselves unequal to the sublime faith of our fathers; and the exhibition of the last twenty years and of the present state of public affairs is, that Americans dread to look their real position in the face.

They say in Ireland that every Irishman thinks he was born sixty days too late, [laughter,] and that the world owes him sixty days. The consequence is, when a trader says such a thing is so much for cash, the Irishman thinks cash means to him a bill for sixty days. [Laughter.] So it is with Americans. They have no idea of absolute right. They were born since 1787, and absolute right means the truth diluted by a strong decoction of the Constitution of '89. They breathe that atmosphere; they do not want to sail outside of it; they do not attempt to reason outside of it. Poisoned with printer's-ink, or choked with cotton-dust, they stare at absolute right as the dream of madmen. For the last twenty years there has been going on, more or less heeded and understood in different States, an insurrection of ideas against this limited, cribbed, cabined, isolated American civilization, an insurrection to restore absolute right. If you said to an American, for instance, anything in regard to temperance, slavery, or anything else, in the course of the last twenty years, — anything about a principle, — he ran back instantly to the safety of such a principle, to the possibility of its existing with a particular sect, with a church, with a party, with a constitution, with a law. He had not yet raised himself to the level of daring to trust justice, which is the preliminary consideration to trusting the people; for whether native depravity be true or not, it is a truth, attested by all history, that the race gravitates towards justice, and that, making fair allowance for differences of opinion, there is an inherent, essential tendency to the great English principle of fair play at the bottom of our natures. [Loud applause.] The Emperor Nicholas, it is said, ordered his engineers to lay down for him a railway from St. Petersburg to Moscow, and presently the engineers brought him a large piece of card-paper, on which was laid down, like a snake, the designed path for the iron locomotive between the two capitals. "What 's that?" said Nicholas. "That 's the best road," was the reply. "What do you make it crooked for?" "Why, we turn this way to touch this great city, and to the left to reach that immense mass of people, and to the right again to suit the business of that district." "Yes." The Emperor turned the card over, made a new dot for Moscow, and another for St. Petersburg, took a ruler, made a straight line, and said, "Build me that road." [Laughter.]

"But what will become of this depot of trade? of that town?" "I don't know; they must look out for themselves." [Cheers.] And intelligent democracy says of slavery, or of a church, "This is justice, and that iniquity; the track of God's thunderbolt is a straight line from one to the other, and the church or state that cannot stand it must get out of the way." [Cheers.] Now our object for twenty years has been to educate the mass of the American people up to that level of moral life which shall recognize that free speech carried to this extent is God's normal school, educating the American mind, throwing upon it the grave responsibility of deciding a great question, and by means of that responsibility lifting it to a higher level of intellectual and moral life. Responsibility educates, and politics is but another name for God's way of teaching the masses ethics, under the responsibility of great present interest. To educate man is God's ultimate end and purpose in all creation. Trust the people with the gravest questions, and in the long run you educate the race; while, in the process, you secure, not perfect, but the best possible institutions. Now scholarship stands on one side, and, like your Brooklyn *Eagle*, says, "This is madness!" Well, poor man, he thinks so! [Laughter.] The very difficulty of the whole matter is, that he does think so, and this normal school that we open is for him. His seat is on the lowest end of the lowest bench. [Laughter and applause.] But he only represents that very chronic distrust which pervades all that class, specially the timid educated mind of these Northern States. Anacharsis went into the forum at Athens, and heard a case argued by the great minds of the day, and saw the vote. He walked out into the streets, and somebody said to him, "What think you of Athenian liberty?" "I think," said he, "wise men argue causes, and fools decide them." Just what the timid scholar two thousand years ago said in the streets of Athens, that which calls itself the scholarship of the United States says to-day of popular agitation, that it lets wise men argue questions, and fools decide them. But that unruly Athens, where fools decided the gravest questions of polity and right and wrong, where it was not safe to be just, and where property, which you had garnered up by the thrift and industry of to-day, might be wrung from you by the caprices of the mob to-morrow, — that very Athens probably secured the greatest human happiness and nobleness of its era, invented art, and sounded for us the depths of philosophy: God lent to it the noblest intellects, and it flashes to-day the torch that gilds yet the mountain-peaks of the Old World; while Egypt, the hunker conservative of antiquity, where nobody dared to differ from the priest, or to be wiser than his grandfather, — where men pretended to be alive, though swaddled in the grave-clothes of creed and custom as close as their mummies in linen, — is hid in the tomb it inhabited; and the intellect which Athens has created for us digs to-day those ashes to find out what hunkerism knew and did. [Cheers.] Now my idea of American civilization is, that it is a second part, a repetition of that same sublime confidence in the public conscience and the public thought which made the groundwork of Grecian Democracy.

We have been carrying on this insurrection of thought for thirty years. There have been various evidences of growth in education: I will tell you of one. The first evidence that a sinner, convicted of sin, and too blind or too lazy to reform, the first evidence he gives that his nature has been touched, is, that he becomes a hypocrite; he has the grace to pretend to be something. Now the first evidence the American people gave of that commencing grace of hypocrisy was this: in 1831, when we commenced the antislavery agitation, the papers talked about slavery, bondage, American slavery, boldly, frankly, and bluntly. In a few years it sounded hard; it had a grating effect; the toughest throat of the hardest Democrat felt it as it came out. So they spoke of the "patriarchal institution," [laughter,] then of the "domestic institution," [continued laughter,] and then of the "peculiar institution," [laughter,] and in a year or two it got beyond that. Mississippi published a report from her Senate, in which she went a stride further, and described it as "economic subordination," and baptized it by statute "warranteeism." [Renewed laughter.] A Southern Methodist bishop was taken to task for holding slaves in reality, but his Methodist brethren were not courageous enough to say "slaves" right out in meeting, and so they advised the bishop to get rid of his "impediment" [loud laughter]; and the late Mr. Rufus Choate, in the last Democratic canvass of my own State, undertaking and obliged to refer to the institutions of the South, and unwilling that his old New England lips, which had spoken so many glorious free truths, should foul their last days with the hated word, phrased it "a different type of industry." Now, hypocrisy — why, "it is the homage that Vice renders to Virtue." When men begin to weary of capital punishment, they banish the gallows inside the jail-yard, and let nobody see it without a special card of invitation from the sheriff. And so they have banished slavery into pet phrases and fancy flash-words. If, one hundred years hence, you should dig our Egyptian Hunkerism up from the grave into which it is rapidly sinking, we should need a commentator of the true German blood to find out what all these queer, odd, peculiar imaginative paraphrases meant in this middle of the nineteenth century. This is one evidence of progress.

I believe in moral suasion. The age of bullets is over. The age of ideas is come. I think that is the rule of our age. The old Hindoo dreamed, you know, that he saw the human race led out to its varied fortune. First, he saw men bitted and curbed, and the reins went back to an iron hand. But his dream changed on and on, until at last he saw men led by reins that came from the brain, and went back into an unseen hand. It was the type of governments; the first despotism, palpable, iron; and the last our government, a government of brains, a government of ideas. I believe in it, — in public opinion.

Yet, let me say, in passing, I think you can make a better use of iron than forging it into chains. If you must have the metal, put it into Sharpe's rifles. It is a great deal better used that way than in fetters; types are better than bullets, but bullets a thousand times rather than a clumsy statue of a mock great man, for hypocrites to kneel down and worship in a State-House yard. [Loud and renewed cheers, and great hissing.] I am so unused to hisses lately, that I have forgotten what I had to say. [Laughter and hisses.] I only know I meant what I did say.

My idea is, public opinion, literature, education, as governing elements.

Some men seem to think that our institutions are necessarily safe, because we have free schools and cheap books, and a public opinion that controls. But that is no evidence of safety. India and China had schools for fifteen hundred years. And books, it is said, were once as cheap in Central and Northern Asia as they are in New York. But they have not secured liberty, nor a controlling public opinion to either nation. Spain for three centuries had municipalities and town governments, as independent and self-supporting, and as representative of thought, as New England or New York has. But that did not save Spain. Tocqueville says that, fifty years before the great revolution, public opinion was as omnipotent in France as it is to-day, but it did not make France free. You cannot save men by machinery. What India and France and Spain wanted was live men, and that is what we want to-day; men who are willing to look their own destiny, and their own responsibilities, in the face. "Grant me to see, and Ajax asks no more," was the prayer the great poet put into the lips of his hero in the darkness which overspread the Grecian camp. All we want of American citizens is the opening of their own eyes, and seeing things as they are. The intelligent, thoughtful, and determined gaze of twenty millions of Christian people there is nothing, — no institution wicked and powerful enough to be capable of standing against it. In Keats's beautiful poem of "Lamia," a young man had been led captive by a phantom girl, and was the slave of her beauty, until the old teacher came in and fixed his thoughtful eye upon the figure, and it vanished.

You see the great Commonwealth of Virginia fitly represented by a pyramid standing upon its apex. A Connecticut-born man entered at one corner of her dominions, and fixed his cold gray eye upon the government of Virginia, and it almost vanished in his very gaze. For it seems that Virginia, for a week, asked leave "to be" of John Brown at Harper's Ferry. [Cheers and applause.] Connecticut has sent out many a schoolmaster to the other thirty States; but never before so grand a teacher as that Litchfield-born schoolmaster at Harper's Ferry, writing as it were upon the Natural Bridge, in the face of nations, his simple copy, — "Resistance to tyrants is obedience to God." [Loud cheers.]

I said that the lesson of the hour was insurrection. I ought not to apply that word to John Brown of Osawatomie, for there was no insurrection in his case. It is a great mistake to call him an insurgent. This principle that I have endeavored so briefly to open to you, of absolute right and wrong, states what? Just this: "Commonwealth of Virginia!" There is no such thing. Lawless, brutal force is no basis of a government, in the true sense of that word. *Quæ est enim civitas?* asks Cicero. *Omnis ne conventus etiam ferorum et immanium? Omnis ne etiam, fugitivorum ac latronum congregata unum in locum multitudo?* CERTE NEGABIS. No civil society, no government, can exist except on the basis of the willing submission of all its citizens, and by the performance of the duty of rendering equal justice between man and man.

Whatever calls itself a government, and refuses that duty, or has not that assent, is no government. It is only a pirate ship. Virginia, the Commonwealth of Virginia! She is only a chronic insurrection. I mean exactly what I say. I am weighing my words now. She is a pirate ship, and John Brown sails the sea a Lord High Admiral of the Almighty, with his commission to sink every pirate he meets on God's ocean of the nineteenth century. [Cheers and applause.] I mean literally and exactly what I say. In God's world there are no majorities, no minorities; one, on God's side, is a majority. You have often heard here, doubtless, and I need not tell you, the ground of morals. The rights of that one man are as sacred as those of the miscalled Commonwealth of Virginia. Virginia is only another Algiers. The barbarous horde who gag each other, imprison women for teaching children to read, prohibit the Bible, sell men on the auction-block, abolish marriage, condemn half their women to prostitution, and devote themselves to the breeding of human beings for sale, is only a larger and blacker Algiers. The only prayer of a true man for such is, "Gracious Heaven! unless they repent, send soon their Exmouth and Decatur." John Brown has twice as much right to hang Governor Wise, as Governor Wise has to hang him. [Cheers and hisses.] You see I am talking of that absolute essence of things which lives in the sight of the Eternal and the Infinite; not as men judge it in the rotten morals of the nineteenth century, among a herd of States that calls itself an empire, because it raises cotton and sells slaves. What I say is this: Harper's Ferry was the only government in that vicinity. Look at the trial. Virginia, true to herself, has shown exactly the same haste that the pirate does when he tries a man on deck, and runs him up to the yard-arm. Unconsciously she is consistent. Now you do not think this to-day, some of you, perhaps. But I tell you what absolute History shall judge of these forms and phantoms of ours. John Brown began his life, his public life, in Kansas. The South planted that seed; it reaps the first fruit now. Twelve years ago, the great men in Washington, the Websters and the Clays, planted the Mexican war; and they reaped their appropriate fruit in General Taylor and General Pierce pushing them from their statesmen's stools. The South planted the seeds of violence in Kansas, and taught peaceful Northern men familiarity with the bowie-knife and revolver. They planted nine hundred and ninety nine seeds, and this is the first one that has flowered; this is the first drop of the coming shower. People do me the honor to say, in some of the Western papers, that this is traceable to some teachings of mine. It is too much honor to such as me. Gladly, if it were not fulsome vanity, would I clutch this laurel of having any share in the great resolute daring of that man who flung himself against an empire in behalf of justice and liberty. They were not the bravest men who fought at Saratoga and Yorktown, in the war of 1776. O no! it was rather those who flung themselves at Lexington, few and feeble, against the embattled ranks of an empire, till then thought irresistible. Elderly men, in powdered wigs and red velvet, smoothed their ruffles, and cried, "Madmen!" Full-fed custom-house clerks said, "A pistol-shot against Gibraltar!" But Captain Ingraham, under the stars and stripes, dictating terms to the fleet of the Cæsars, was only the echo of that Lexington

18

gun. Harper's Ferry is the Lexington of to-day. Up to this moment, Brown's life has been one unmixed success. Prudence, skill, courage, thrift, knowledge of his time, knowledge of his opponents, undaunted daring, — he had all these. He was the man who could leave Kansas, and go into Missouri, and take eleven men, give them liberty, and bring them off on the horses which he carried with him, and two which he took as tribute from their masters in order to facilitate escape. Then, when he had passed his human *protégés* from the vulture of the United States to the safe shelter of the English lion, this is the brave, frank, and sublime truster in God's right and absolute justice, who entered his name in the city of Cleveland, "John Brown, of Kansas," advertised there two horses for sale, and stood in front of the auctioneer's stand, notifying all bidders of — what some would think — the defect in the title. [Laughter.] But he added, with nonchalance, when he told me the story, "They brought a very excellent price." [Laughter.] This is the man who, in the face of the nation, avowing his right, and laboring with what strength he had in behalf of the wronged, goes down to Harper's Ferry to follow up his work. Well, men say he failed. Every man has his Moscow. Suppose he did fail, every man meets his Waterloo at last. There are two kinds of defeat. Whether in chains or in laurels, LIBERTY knows nothing but victories. Soldiers call Bunker Hill a defeat; but Liberty dates from it, though Warren lay dead on the field. Men say the attempt did not succeed. No man can command success. Whether it was well planned, and *deserved* to succeed, we shall be able to decide when Brown is free to tell us all he knows. Suppose he did fail, in one sense, he has done a great deal still. Why, this is a decent country to live in now. [Laughter and cheers.] Actually, in this Sodom of ours, twenty-two men have been found ready to die for an idea.

God be thanked for John Brown, that he has discovered or created them! [Cheers.] I should feel some pride, if I was in Europe now, in confessing that I was an American. [Applause.] We have redeemed the long infamy of sixty years of subservience. But look back a bit. Is there anything new about this? Nothing at all. It is the natural result of antislavery teaching. For one, I accept it; I hoped for it. I cannot say that I prayed for it; I cannot say that I expected it. But at the same time, no sane man has looked upon this matter for twenty years, and supposed that we could go through this great moral convulsion, the great classes of society crashing and jostling against each other like frigates in a storm, and that there would not come such scenes as these.

In 1835 it was the other way. Then it was my bull that gored your ox. Then ideas came in conflict, and men of violence, men who trusted in their own right hands, men who believed in bowie-knives, — such sacked the city of Philadelphia; such made New York to be governed by a mob; Boston saw its mayor suppliant and kneeling to the chief of a broadcloth mob in broad daylight. It was all on that side. The natural result, the first result of this starting of ideas, is like people who get half awaked, and use the first weapons that lie at hand. The first show and unfolding of national life were the mobs of 1835. People said it served us right; we had no right to the luxury of speaking our own minds; it was too expensive; these lavish, prodigal, luxurious persons walking about here, and actually saying what they think. Why it was like speaking loud in the midst of the avalanches. To say "Liberty" in a loud tone, the Constitution of 1789 might come down, — it would not do. But now things have changed. We have been talking thirty years. Twenty years we have talked everywhere, under all circumstances; we have been mobbed out of great cities, and pelted out of little ones; we have been abused by great men and by little papers. [Laughter and applause.] What is the result? The tables have been turned; it is your bull that has gored my ox now. And men who still believe in violence, the five points of whose faith are the fist, the bowie-knife, fire, poison, and the pistol, are ranged on the side of Liberty, and, unwilling to wait for the slow but sure steps of thought, lay on God's altar the best they have. You cannot expect to put a real Puritan Presbyterian, as John Brown is, — a regular Cromwellian dug up from two centuries, — in the midst of our New England civilization, that dares not say its soul is its own, nor proclaim that it is wrong to sell a man at auction, and not have him show himself as he is. Put a hound in the presence of a deer, and he springs at his throat if he is a true bloodhound. Put a Christian in the presence of a sin, and he will spring at its throat if he is a true Christian. Into an acid we may throw white matter, but unless it is chalk, it will not produce agitation. So if in a world of sinners you were to put American Christianity, it would be calm as oil. But put one Christian, like John Brown of Osawatomie, and he makes the whole crystallize into right and wrong, and marshal themselves on one side or the other. God makes him the text, and all he asks of our comparatively cowardly lips is to preach the sermon, and say to the American people that, whether that old man succeeded in a worldly sense or not, he stood a representative of law, of government, of right, of justice, of religion, and they were a mob of murderers who gathered about him, and sought to wreak vengeance by taking his life. The banks of the Potomac, doubly dear now to history and to man! The dust of Washington rests there; and history will see forever on that river-side the brave old man on his pallet, whose dust, when God calls him hence, the Father of his Country would be proud to make room for beside his own. But if Virginia tyrants dare hang him, after this mockery of a trial, it will take two more Washingtons at least to make the name of the State anything but abominable in time to come. [Applause and hisses.] Well, I say what I really think. [Cheers, and cries of "Good! good!"] George Washington was a great man. Yet I say what I really think. And I know, Ladies and Gentlemen, that, educated as you have been by the experience of the last ten years here, you would have thought me the silliest as well as the most cowardly man in the world, if I should have come, with my twenty years behind me, and talked about anything else to-night except that great example which one man has set us on the banks of the Potomac. You expected, of course, that I should tell you my real opinion of it.

I value this element that Brown has introduced into American politics. The South is a great power, — no cowards in Virginia. [Laughter.] It was not cowardice. [Laughter.] Now, I try to speak very plain, but you will misunderstand me. There is no cowardice in Virginia. The South are not cowards. The lunatics in the Gospel were not cowards when they said, "Art thou come to torment us before the time?" [Laughter.] They were brave enough, but they saw afar off. They saw the tremendous power which was entering into that charmed circle; they knew its inevitable victory. Virginia did not tremble at an old gray-headed man at Harper's Ferry; they trembled at a John Brown in every man's own conscience. He had been there many years, and, like that terrific scene which Beckford has drawn for us in his *Hall of Eblis*, where the crowd runs around, each man with an incurable wound in his bosom, and agrees not to speak of it; so the South has been running up and down its political and social life, and every man keeps his right hand pressed on the secret and incurable sore, with an understood agreement, in church and state, that it never shall be mentioned, for fear the great ghastly fabric should come to pieces at the talismanic word. Brown uttered it; cried, "Slavery is sin! come, all true men, help pull it down," and the whole machinery trembled to its very base.

I value this movement for another reason. Did you ever see a blacksmith shoe a restless horse? If you have, you have seen him take a small cord and tie the upper lip. Ask him what he does it for, he will tell you to give the beast something to think of. [Laughter.] Now, the South has extensive schemes. She grasps with one hand a Mexico, and with the other she dictates terms to the Church, she imposes conditions on the state, she buys up Webster with a little or a promise, and Everett with nothing. [Great laughter and applause.] John Brown has given her something else to think of. He has turned her attention inwardly. He has taught her that there has been created a new element in this Northern mind; that it is not merely the thinker, that it is not merely the editor, that it is not merely the moral reformer, but the idea has pervaded all classes of society. Call them madmen if you will. Hard to tell who 's mad. The world says one man is mad. John Brown said the same of the Governor. You remember the madman in Edinburgh. A friend asked him what he was there for. "Well," cried he, "they said at home that I was mad; and I said I was not; but they had the majority." [Laughter.] Just so it is in regard to John Brown. The nation says he is mad. I appeal from Philip drunk to Philip sober; I appeal from the American people, drunk with cotton, and the New York Observer, [loud and long laughter,] to the American people fifty years hence, when the light of civilization has had more time to penetrate, when self-interest has been rebuked by the world rising and giving its verdict on these great questions, when it is not a small band of Abolitionists, but the civilization of the twentieth century, in all its varied forms, interests, and elements, which undertakes to enter the arena, and discuss this last great reform. When that day comes, what will be thought of these first martyrs, who teach us how to live and how to die?

Has the slave a right to resist his master? I will not argue that question to a people hoarse with shouting ever since July 4, 1776, that all men are created equal, that the right to liberty is inalienable, and that "resistance to tyrants is obedience to God." But may he resist to blood — with rifles? What need of proving that to a people who load down Bunker Hill with granite, and crowd their public squares with images of Washington; ay, worship the sword so blindly that, leaving their oldest statesmen idle, they go down to the bloodiest battle-field in Mexico to drag out a President? But may one help the slave resist, as Brown did? Ask Byron on his death-bed in the marshes of Missolonghi. Ask the Hudson as its waters kiss your shore, what answer they bring from the grave of Kosciusko. I hide the Connecticut Puritan behind Lafayette, bleeding at Brandywine, in behalf of a nation his rightful king forbade him to visit.

But John Brown violated the law. Yes. On yonder desk lie the inspired words of men who died violent deaths for breaking the laws of Rome. Why do you listen to them so reverently? Huss and Wickliffe violated laws; why honor them? George Washington, had he been caught before 1783, would have died on the gibbet, for breaking the laws of his sovereign. Yet I have heard that man praised within six months. Yes, you say, but these men broke *bad* laws. Just so. It is honorable, then, to break *bad* laws, and such law-breaking history loves and God blesses! Who says, then, that slave laws are not ten thousand times worse than any those men resisted? Whatever argument *excuses* them, makes John Brown a saint.

Suppose John Brown had not stayed at Harper's Ferry. Suppose on that momentous Monday night, when the excited imaginations of two thousand Charlestown people had enlarged him and his little band into four hundred white men and two hundred blacks, he had vanished, and when the gallant troops arrived there, two thousand strong, they had found nobody! The mountains would have been peopled with enemies; the Alleghanies would have heaved with insurrection! You never would have convinced Virginia that all Pennsylvania was not armed and on the hills. Suppose Massachusetts, free Massachusetts, had not given the world the telegraph, to flash news like sunlight over half the globe. Then Tuesday would have rolled away, while slow spreading through dazed Virginia crawled the news of this event. Meanwhile, a hundred men having rallied to Brown's side, he might have marched across the quaking State to Richmond and pardoned Governor Wise. Nat Turner's success, in 1831, shows this would have been possible. Free thought, mother of invention, not Virginia, baffled Brown. But free thought, in the long run, strangles tyrants. Virginia has not slept sound since Nat Turner led an insurrection in 1831, and she bids fair never to have a nap now. [Laughter.] For this is not an insurrection; this is the penetration of a different element. Mark you, it is not the oppressed race rising. Recollect history. There never was a race held in actual chains that vindicated its own liberty but one. There never was a serf nor a slave whose own sword cut off his own chain but one. Blue-eyed, light-haired Anglo-Saxon, it was not our race. We were serfs for three centuries, and we waited till commerce and Christianity and a different law had melted our fetters. We were crowded down into a villanage which crushed out our manhood so thoroughly that we had not vigor enough left to redeem ourselves. Neither France nor Spain, neither the Northern nor the Southern races of Europe have that bright spot on their escutcheon, that they put an end to their own slavery. Blue-eyed, haughty, contemptuous Anglo-Saxons, it was the black, — the only race in the record of history that ever, after a century of oppression, retained the vigor to write the charter of its emancipation with its own hand in the blood of the dominant race. Despised, calumniated, slandered San Domingo is the only instance in history where a race, with indestructible love of liberty, after bearing a hundred years of oppression, rose up under their own leader, and with their own hands wrested chains from their own limbs. Wait, garrulous, ignorant, boasting Saxon, till you have done half as much, before you talk of the cowardice of the black race!

The slaves of our country have not risen, but, as in most other cases, redemption will come from the interference of a wiser, higher, more advanced civilization on its exterior. It is the almost universal record of history, and ours is a repetition of the same drama. We have awakened at last the enthusiasm of both classes, — those that act from impulse and those that act from calculation. It is a libel on the Yankee to think that it includes the whole race, when you say that if you put a dollar on the other side of hell, the Yankee will spring for it at any risk [laughter]; for there is an element even in the Yankee blood which obeys ideas; there is an impulsive, enthusiastic aspiration, something left to us from the old Puritan stock; that which made England what she was two centuries ago; that which is fated to give the closest grapple with the Slave Power to-day. This is an invasion by outside power. Civilization in 1600 crept along our shores, now planting her foot, and then retreating; now gaining a foothold, and then receding before barbarism, till at last came Jamestown and Plymouth, and then thirty States. Harper's Ferry is perhaps one of Raleigh's or Gosnold's colonies, vanishing and to be swept away; by and by will come the immortal one hundred, and Plymouth Rock, with "MANIFEST DESTINY" written by God's hand on their banner, and the right of unlimited "ANNEXATION" granted by Heaven itself.

It is the lesson of the age. The first cropping out of it is in such a man as John Brown. Grant that he did not measure his means; that he was not thrifty as to his method; he did not calculate closely enough, and he was defeated. What is defeat? Nothing but education,—nothing but the first step to something better. All that is wanted is, that our public opinion shall not creep round like a servile, coward, corrupt, disordered, insane public opinion, and proclaim that Governor Wise, because he *says* he is a governor, *is* a governor; that Virginia is a State, because she says she is so.

Thank God, I am not a citizen. You will remember, all of you, citizens of the United States, that there was not a Virginia gun fired at John Brown. Hundreds of well-armed Maryland and Virginia troops rushed to Harper's Ferry, and—went away! *You* shot him! Sixteen marines, to whom you pay eight dollars a month,—your own representatives. When the disturbed State could not stand on her own legs for trembling, you went there and strengthened the feeble knees, and held up the palsied hands. Sixteen men, with the vulture of the Union above them, [sensation,] your representatives! It was the covenant with death and agreement with hell, which you call the Union of thirty States, that took the old man by the throat with a pirate hand; and it will be the disgrace of our civilization if a gallows is ever erected in Virginia that bears his body. "The most resolute man I ever saw," says Governor Wise, "the most daring, the coolest. I would trust his truth about any question. The sincerest!" Sincerity, courage, resolute daring, beating in a heart that feared God, and dared all to help his brother to liberty, — Virginia has nothing, nothing for those qualities but a scaffold! [Applause.] In her broad dominion she can only afford him six feet for a grave! God help the Commonwealth which bids such welcome to the noblest qualities that can grace poor human nature! Yet that is the acknowledgment of Governor Wise himself! I will not dignify such a horde with the name of a *despotism;* since despotism is sometimes magnanimous. Witness Russia, covering Schamyl with generous protection. Compare that with mad Virginia, hurrying forward this ghastly trial.

They say it cost the officers and persons in responsible positions more effort to keep hundreds of startled soldiers from shooting the five prisoners sixteen marines had made, than it cost those marines to take the armory itself. Soldiers and civilians, — both alike, — only a mob fancying itself a government! And mark you, I have said they were not a government. They not only are not a government, but they have not even the remotest idea of what a government is. [Laughter.] They do not begin to have the faintest conception of what a civilized government is. Here is a man arraigned before a jury, or about to be. The State of Virginia, as she calls herself, is about to try him. The first step in that trial is a jury; the second is a judge; and at the head stands the Chief Executive of the State, who holds the power to pardon murder; and yet that very Executive, who, according to the principles of the sublimest chapter in Algernon Sidney's immortal book, is bound by the very responsibility which rests on him to keep his mind impartial as to the guilt of any person arraigned, hastens down to Richmond, hurries to the platform, and proclaims to the assembled Commonwealth of

Virginia, "The man is a murderer, and ought to be hung." Almost every lip in the State might have said it except that single lip of its Governor; and the moment he had uttered these words, in the theory of the English law, it was not possible to impanel an impartial jury in the Commonwealth of Virginia; it was not possible to get the materials and the machinery to try him, according to even the ugliest pattern of English jurisprudence. And yet the Governor does not know that he has written himself down *non compos*, and the Commonwealth that he governs supposes itself still a Christian polity. They have not the faintest conception of what goes to make up a government. The worst Jeffries that ever, in his most drunken hour, climbed up a lamp-post in the streets of London, would not have tried a man who could not stand on his feet. There is no such record in the blackest roll of tyranny. If Jeffries could speak, he would thank God that at last his name might be taken down from the gibbet of History, since the Virginia bench has made his worst act white, set against the blackness of this modern infamy. [Applause.] And yet the New York press daily prints the accounts of the *trial*. Trial! In the names of Holt and Somers, of Hale and Erskine, of Parsons, Marshall, and Jay, I protest against the name. *Trial* for life, in Anglo-Saxon dialect, has a proud, historic meaning. It includes indictment by impartial peers; a copy of such indictment and a list of witnesses furnished the prisoner, with ample time to scrutinize both; liberty to choose, and time to get counsel; a sound body and a sound mind to arrange one's defence; I need not add, a judge and jury impartial as the lot of humanity will admit; honored bulwarks and safeguards, each one the trophy and result of a century's struggle. Wounded, fevered, lying half unconscious on his pallet, unable to stand on his feet, the trial half finished before his first request for aid had reached his friends, —

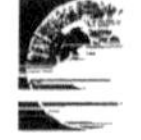

no list of witnesses or knowledge of them till the crier, calling the name of some assassin of his comrades, wakes him to consciousness; the judge a tool, and the prosecutor seeking popularity by pandering to the mob; no decent form observed, and the essence of a fair trial wholly wanting, our history and law alike protest against degrading the honored name of *Jury Trial* by lending it to such an outrage as this. The Inquisition used to break every other bone in a man's body, and then lay him on a pallet, giving him neither counsel nor opportunity to consult one, and wring from his tortured mouth something like a confession, and call it a trial. But it was heaven-robed innocence compared with the trial, or what the New York press call so, that has been going on in crazed and maddened Charlestown.

I wish I could say anything worthy of the great deed which has taken place in our day, — the opening of the sixth seal, the pouring out of the last vial but one on a corrupt and giant institution. I know that many men will deem me a fanatic for uttering this wholesale vituperation, as it will be called, upon a State, and this indorsement of a madman. I can only say that I have spoken on this antislavery question before the American people thirty years; that I have seen the day when this same phase of popular feeling — rifles and force — was on the other side. You remember the first time I was ever privileged to stand on this platform by the magnanimous generosity of your clergyman, when New York was about to bully and crush out the freedom of speech at the dictation of Captain Rynders. From that day to this, the same braving of public thought has been going on from here to Kansas, until it bloomed in the events of the last three years. It has changed the whole face of the sentiment in these Northern States. You meet with the evidence of it everywhere. When the first news from Harper's Ferry came to Massachusetts, if you were riding in the cars, if you were walking in the streets, if you met a Democrat or a Whig or a Republican, no matter what his politics, it was a singular circumstance that he did not speak of the guilt of Brown, of the atrocity of the deed, as you might have expected. The first impulsive expression, the first outbreak of every man's words was, "What a pity he did not succeed! [Laughter.] What a fool he was for not going off Monday, when he had all he wanted! How strange that he did not take his victory, and march away with it!" It indicated the unconscious leavening of a sympathy with the attempt. Days followed on; they commenced what they called their trial; you met the same classes again; no man said he ought to be hung; no man said he was guilty; no man predicated anything of his moral position; every man voluntarily and inevitably seemed to give vent to his indignation at the farce of a trial, indicative again of that unheeded, potent, unconscious, but wide-spread sympathy on the side of Brown.

Do you suppose that these things mean nothing? What the tender and poetic youth, as Emerson says, dreams to-day, and conjures up with inarticulate speech, is to-morrow the vociferated result of public opinion, and the day after is the charter of nations. The American people have begun to feel. The mute eloquence of the fugitive slave has gone up and down the highways and byways of the country; it will annex itself to the great American heart of the North, even in the most fossil state of its hunkerism, as a latent sympathy with its right side. This blow, like the first gun at Lexington, "heard around the world," — this blow at Harper's Ferry reveals men. Watch those about you, and you will see more of the temper and unconscious purpose and real moral position of men than you would imagine. This is the way nations are to be judged. Be not in a hurry; action will come soon enough from this sentiment. We stereotype feeling into intellect, and then into statutes, and finally into national character. We have now the first stage of growth. Nature s live growths crowd out and rive dead matter. Ideas strangle statutes. Pulse-beats wear down granite, whether piled in jails or capitols. The people's hearts are the only title-deeds, after all. Your Barnburners said, "Patroon titles are unrighteous." Judges replied, "Such is the law." Wealth shrieked, "Vested rights!" Parties talked of Constitutions; still, the people said, "Sin." They shot a sheriff. A parrot press cried, "Anarchy!" Lawyers growled, "Murder!" — still, nobody was hung, if I recollect aright. To-day, the *heart* of the Barnburner beats in the statute-book of your State. John Brown's movement against slavery is exactly the same. Wait awhile, and you 'll all agree with me. What is fanaticism to-day is the fashionable creed to-morrow, and trite as the multiplication table a week after.

John Brown has stirred those omnipotent pulses, — Lydia Maria Child's is one. She says, "That dungeon is the place for me," and writes a letter in magnanimous appeal to the better nature of Governor Wise. She says in it: "John Brown is a hero; he has done a noble deed. I think he was all right; but he is sick; he is wounded; he wants a woman's nursing. I am an Abolitionist; I have been so thirty years. I think slavery is a sin, and John Brown a saint; but I want to come and nurse him; and I pledge my word that if you will open his prison door, I will use the privilege, under sacred honor, only to nurse him. I enclose you a message to Brown; be sure and deliver it." And the message was, "Old man, God bless you! You have struck a noble blow; you have done a mighty work; God was with you; your heart was in the right place. I send you across five hundred miles the pulse of a woman's gratitude." And Governor Wise has opened the door, and announced to the world that she may go in. John Brown has conquered the pirate. [Applause.] Hope! there is hope everywhere. It is only the universal history:—

> "Right forever on the scaffold, Wrong forever on the throne;
> But that scaffold sways the future, and behind the dim unknown
> Standeth God within the shadow, keeping watch above his own."

BURIAL OF JOHN BROWN.*

HOW feeble words seem here! How can I hope to utter what your hearts are full of? I fear to disturb the harmony which his life breathes round this home. One and another of you, his neighbors, say, "I have known him five years," "I have known him ten years." It seems to me as if we had none of us known him. How our admiring, loving wonder has grown, day by day, as he has unfolded trait after trait of earnest, brave, tender, Christian life! We see him walking with radiant, serene face to the scaffold, and think what an iron heart, what devoted faith! We take up his letters, beginning "My dear wife and children, every one," — see him stoop on his way to the scaffold and kiss that negro child, — and this iron heart seems all tenderness. Marvellous old man! We have hardly said it when the loved forms of his sons, in the bloom of young devotion, encircle him, and we remember he is not alone, only the majestic centre of a group. Your neighbor farmer went, surrounded by his household, to tell the slaves there were still hearts and right arms ready and nerved for their service. From this roof four, from a neighboring roof two, to make up that score of heroes. How resolute each looked into the face of Virginia, how loyally each stood at his forlorn post, meeting death cheerfully, till that master-voice said, "It is

* Delivered at the grave of John Brown, at North Elba, December 8, 1859.

enough." And these weeping children and widow seem so lifted up and consecrated by long, single-hearted devotion to his great purpose, that we dare, even at this moment, to remind them how blessed they are in the privilege of thinking that in the last throbs of those brave young hearts, which lie buried on the banks of the Shenandoah, thoughts of them mingled with love to God and hope for the slave.

He has abolished slavery in Virginia. You may say this is too much. Our neighbors are the last men we know. The hours that pass us are the ones we appreciate the least. Men walked Boston streets, when night fell on Bunker's Hill, and pitied Warren, saying, "Foolish man! Thrown away his life! Why did n't he measure his means better?" Now we see him standing colossal on that blood-stained sod, and severing that day the tie which bound Boston to Great Britain. That night George III. ceased to rule in New England. History will date Virginia Emancipation from Harper's Ferry. True, the slave is still there. So, when the tempest uproots a pine on your hills, it looks green for months, — a year or two. Still, it is timber, not a tree. John Brown has loosened the roots of the slave system; it only breathes, — it does not live, — hereafter.

Men say, "How coolly brave!" But matchless courage seems the least of his merits. How gentleness graced it! When the frightened town wished to bear off the body of the Mayor, a man said, "I will go, Miss Fowke, under their rifles, if you will stand between them and me." He knew he could trust their gentle respect for woman. He was right. He went in the thick of the fight and bore off the body in safety. That same girl flung herself between Virginia rifles and your brave young Thompson. They had no pity. The pitiless bullet reached him, spite of woman's prayers, though the fight had long been over.

How God has blessed him! How truly he may say, "I have fought a good fight, I have *finished* my course." Truly he has *finished*, — done his work. God granted him the privilege to look on his work accomplished. He said, "I will show the South that twenty men can take possession of a town, hold it twenty-four hours, and carry away all the slaves who wish to escape." Did he not do it? On Monday night he stood master of Harper's Ferry, — could have left unchecked with a score or a hundred slaves. The wide sympathy and secret approval are shown by the eager, quivering lips of lovers of slavery, asking, "O, why did he not take his victory and go away?" Who checked him at last? Not startled Virginia. Her he had conquered. The Union crushed, — seemed to crush him. In reality God said, "That work is done; you have proved that a Slave State is only fear in the mask of despotism; come up higher, and baptize by your martyrdom a million hearts into holier life." Surely such a life is no failure. How vast the change in men's hearts! Insurrection was a harsh, horrid word to millions a month ago. John Brown went a whole generation beyond it, claiming the right for white men to help the slave to freedom by arms. And now men run up and down, not disputing his principle, but trying to frame excuses for Virginia's hanging of so pure, honest, high-hearted, and heroic a man. Virginia stands at the bar of the civilized world on trial. Round her victim crowd the apostles and martyrs, all the brave, high souls who have said, "God is God," and trodden wicked laws under their feet. As I stood looking at his grandfather's gravestone, brought here from Connecticut, telling, as it does, of his death in the Revolution, I thought I could hear our hero-saint saying, "My fathers gave their swords to the oppressor, — the slave still sinks before the pledged force of this nation. I give my sword to the slave my fathers forgot." If any swords ever reflected the smile of Heaven, surely it was those drawn at Harper's Ferry. If our God is ever the Lord of Hosts, making one man chase a thousand, surely that little band might claim him for their captain. Harper's Ferry was no single hour, standing alone, — taken out from a common life, — it was the flowering out of fifty years of single-hearted devotion. He must have lived wholly for one great idea, when these who owe their being to him, and these whom love has joined to the circle, group so harmoniously around him, each accepting serenely his and her part.

I feel honored to stand under such a roof. Hereafter you will tell children standing at your knees, "I saw John Brown buried, — I sat under his roof." Thank God for such a master. Could we have asked a nobler representative of the Christian North putting her foot on the accursed system of slavery? As time passes, and these hours float back into history, men will see against the clear December sky that gallows, and round it thousands of armed men guarding Virginia from her slaves. On the other side, the serene brow of that calm old man, as he stoops to kiss the child of a forlorn race. Thank God for our emblem. May he soon bring Virginia to blot out hers in repentant shame, and cover that hateful gallows and soldiery with thousands of broken fetters.

What lesson shall those lips teach us? Before that still, calm brow let us take a new baptism. How can we stand here without a fresh and utter consecration? These tears! how shall we dare even to offer consolation? Only lips fresh from such a vow have the right to mingle their words with your tears. We envy you your nearer place to these martyred children of God. I do not believe slavery will go down in blood. Ours is the age of thought. Hearts are stronger than swords. That last fortnight! How sublime its lesson! the Christian one of conscience,

— of truth. Virginia is weak, because each man's heart said amen to John Brown. His words, — they are stronger even than his rifles. These crushed a State. Those have changed the thoughts of millions, and will yet crush slavery. Men said, "Would he had died in arms!" God ordered better, and granted to him and the slave those noble prison hours, — that single hour of death; granted him a higher than the soldier's place, that of teacher; the echoes of his rifles have died away in the hills, — a million hearts guard his words. God bless this roof, — make it bless us. We dare not say bless you, children of this home! you stand nearer to one whose lips God touched, and we rather bend for your blessing. God make us all worthier of him whose dust we lay among these hills he loved. Here he girded himself and went forth to battle. Fuller success than his heart ever dreamed God granted him. He sleeps in the blessings of the crushed and the poor, and men believe more firmly in virtue, now that such a man has lived. Standing here, let us thank God for a firmer faith and fuller hope.

LINCOLN'S ELECTION.*

LADIES AND GENTLEMEN: If the telegraph speaks truth, for the first time in our history the *slave* has chosen a President of the United States. [Cheers.] We have passed the Rubicon, for Mr. Lincoln rules to-day as much as he will after the 4th of March. It is the moral effect of this victory, not anything which his administration can or will probably do, that gives value to this success. Not an Abolitionist, hardly an antislavery man, Mr. Lincoln consents to represent an antislavery idea. A pawn on the political chessboard, his value is in his position; with fair effort, we may soon change him for knight, bishop, or queen, and sweep the board. [Applause.] This position he owes to no merit of his own, but to lives that have roused the nation's conscience, and deeds that have ploughed deep into its heart. Our childish eyes gazed with wonder at Maelzel's chess-player, and the pulse almost stopped when, with the pulling of wires and creaking of wheels, he moved a pawn, and said, "Check!" Our wiser fathers saw a man in the box. There was great noise at Chicago, much pulling of wires and creaking of wheels, then forth steps Abraham Lincoln. But John Brown was behind the curtain, and the cannon of March 4th will only echo the rifles at Harper's Ferry. Last year, we stood looking

* Fraternity Lecture, delivered in Tremont Temple, Boston, November 7, 1860.

sadly at that gibbet against the Virginia sky. One turn of the kaleidoscope, — it is Lincoln in the balcony of the Cap'tol, and a million of hearts beating welcome below. [Cheers.]

Mr. Seward said, in 1850: "You may slay the Wilmot Proviso in the Senate-Chamber, and bury it beneath the Capitol, to-day; the dead corse, in complete steel, will haunt your legislative halls to-morrow." They slew the martyr-chief on the banks of the Potomac; we buried his dust beneath the snows of North Elba; and the statesman Senator of New York wrote for his epitaph, "Justly hung," while party chiefs cried, "Amen!" but one of those dead hands smote to ruin the Babylon which that Senator's ambition had builded, and the other lifts into the Capitol the President of 1861. [Applause.]

The battle has been a curious one, mixed and tossed in endless confusion. The combatants, in the chaos, caught up often the weapons of their opponents, and dealt the deadliest blows at their own ranks.

The Democratic party, agitating fiercely to put down agitation, break at last into a general quarrel in their effort to keep the peace! [Laughter.] They remind one of that sleepy crier of a New Hampshire court, who was ever dreaming, in his dog-naps, that the voice of judge or lawyer was a noisy interruption, and always woke shouting, "Silence!" Judge Livermore said once, "Mr. Crier, you are the noisiest man in court, with your everlasting shout of 'Silence'!" [Laughter.] The Abolitionists ought to be very sorry to lose Mr. Douglas from the national arena. [Applause.]

But the Bell-Everett party have been the comfort of the canvass, the sweet-oil, the safety-valve, the locomotive buffer, which, when collision threatened, broke the blow, and the storm exploded in a laugh. [Great merriment.] They played Sancho Panza to Douglas's Don Quixote.

[Renewed laughter.] We can afford to thank them. It is but fair, however, to confess that they differ from that illustrious Spaniard. His chief anxiety was about his dinner; their distress rose higher than loaves and fishes, — they trembled for our glorious Union. [Laughter.] The passions of men were all on fire, — the volcano in full activity. They confessed they did not know what to do; but they determined not to do they knew not what. Theirs was the *stand-still* policy, the cautious *statu quo* of the old law.

Now, Whately says there are two ways of being burned. The rash moth hurries into the flame, and is gone. The cautious, conservative horse, when his stable is on fire, stands stock-still, and is burnt up all the same. The Everett party chose the horse policy when their stable took fire. [Applause.] Don't you hear the horse's address: "In this stall my father stood in 1789. Methinks I hear his farewell neigh. How *agitated* the crowds seem outside there! I'll have no platform but that my father had in '89," — and so he dies. Yet the noble animal risked only his own harm. His mistakes drag none else to ruin. Four millions of human beings saw their fate hanging on this do-nothing, keep-silent, let-evil-alone party. Then their appeals to us to keep silent, to cease criticising chains and slave-auctions, hangings and burnings of men for free speech; their kindly assurances that, if *we* would only be still, no harm would come, — the whole trouble was our noise; they implored us not to cherish this dislike to these constitutional and necessary measures! Like the viper-pedler in Spain, who exhibited his stock to the inn guests all the evening, descanting on their life and vigor, and when at night, in the utter dark, one traveller felt something cold crawling on his face, cried out: "It is only my vipers, they are all loose; but if you'll only lie perfectly still and quiet, they won't hurt you the least." [Applause.]

But Republicanism has triumphed. [Loud applause.] The Democrat may forget his quarrels, and prepare to die with decency. For the Bell-Everett party, one egg has given a chicken. Mr. Appleton is elected. Beacon Street and Ann Street have fused. [Merriment.] As his constituents could not be admitted to Mr. Appleton's house, — there not being police enough to watch them, [great merriment,] — the speeches were made outside, and we got all the secrets. Mr. Stevenson thinks the election of Mr. Appleton "the most important that has taken place since the adoption of the Constitution." I observed, last summer, in the country, that the geese always bowed when they entered a barn, for fear of hitting their heads. [Laughter.] Mr. Burlingame needs no praise of mine. He stood, like Hancock and Adams, the representative of an idea, and the city that rejected him disgraced only herself. [Applause.] As an old English judge said of a sentence he blushed to declare, "In this I seem to pronounce sentence not on the prisoner, but on the law itself." It is Boston, not Burlingame, that has cause to blush today. [Cheers.] I do not envy Mr. Appleton his seat. You remember Webster painted Washington leaning one great arm on Massachusetts, and the other on South Carolina. Methinks I see our merchant prince entering Congress. One hand rests familiarly on the shoulder of Beacon Street, the other on a cambric handkerchief, twice doubled, to save the possibility of his touching the shoulder of Ann Street. [Laughter and applause.] What is his first act when seated, — he, the representative of the fag-ends of half a dozen parties, — the broken meat of the political charity-basket? He speak the voice of Boston, the home of Sam Adams, in this glorious hour! What will it be? When Sherman is named for Speaker, he says "No," while the heart of Boston says "Yes." And what is his second and last act? To gather round his table Davis and Mason, — men who gloried in the blow which exiled Sumner from the Senate for four years, and made Christendom tremble for his life, — men who come for his wine, and not for his wit, — and Boston, in his person, sinks to be their associate, — no, their lackey. I affirm, he does not represent Boston. [Cheers.] Look at its Lincoln vote! I appeal from Philip drunk to Philip sober, from Ann Street, cozened by old fogies, to Ann Street under guidance of her native instincts. [Loud applause.] Mr. Appleton represents neither the merchants of Boston nor its grog-shops, though his friends boast of having carried him by their aid. They are both too good for him.

But the Bell-Everett party cannot say, with Francis I. at Pavia, when he addressed the first lady by position in the State, "Madam, we have lost all but honor," since the soreness of expected defeat led them to insult an invited guest, a lady, and that lady, like the mother of Francis, the first by position in the State. [Loud applause.] Of the first Governor of Massachusetts (unless we count Endicott, and then call Winthrop our *second* Governor), the last historian writes: "The qualities that denote the gentleman were eminently his. Cordial and ready to every expression of respect and courtesy, he gave all their due, whether in great or little things." Good and bad qualities, they tell us, are inherited, — pass down with the blood. To be sure, now and then they lie latent for one generation. Can ours be the generation of eclipse? It must be so, for surely the ignorance of good manners which offers an insult is trivial, compared with the silence of those who know better than their lackeys, are as responsible for the act, and refuse acknowledgment or protest. [Applause.]

Well, the battle is ended. What have we gained? Let us, Ladies and Gentlemen, who care nothing for men or for offices, whose only interest is justice and the great future of the Republic, look round and weigh the spoils.

Everybody speculates, the pulpit affirms, the merchant guesses, and the oracular press lays down the law. Why should not the lyceum be in the fashion? To begin, then, at home. For the first time within my memory we have got a man for Governor of Massachusetts, a frank, true, whole-souled, honest MAN. [Cheering.] That gain alone is worth all the labor. But the office is not the most important in the Commonwealth; only now and then it becomes commanding; in a sad Burns week, for instance, when Mr. Washburn was masquerading as Governor, and when, as Emerson said, "if we had a man, and not a cockade, in the chair, something might be done"; or, later, when the present Chief Magistrate pushed Judge Loring, on false pretences, from his stool. Such occasions remind us we have a Governor. But in common times, the Chief Justiceship is far more commanding, — is the real Gibraltar of our State contests. John A. Andrew should have been Chief Justice. [Applause.] You remember they made the first William Pitt Earl of Chatham, and he went into eclipse in the House of Lords. Some one asked Chesterfield what had become of Pitt. "He has had a fall up-stairs," was the answer. Governor Andrew or Judge Andrew sounds equally well. But I like the right man in the right place. The chief justiceship belongs to the party of progress. Their Sparta can point to many sons worthy of the place, — Sewall, Hoar, Dana, or we might have offered another laurel for the brow of our great Senator, were it only to show him that the profession he once honored still remembers her truant son. [Great applause.] The outgoing administration, which entailed that office on talents, however respectable, that belong to the party of resistance, placed itself by the side of Arnold selling West Point to the British.

Such an appointment was the Parthian arrow of a traitor and a snob.

Then we have Lincoln for President [applause], — a Whig, — a Revolutionary Whig, —a freedom-loving Whig, — a Whig in the sense that Jefferson, Hamilton, and Washington were Whigs. How much is that worth? I said we had passed the Rubicon. Cæsar crossed the Rubicon, borne in the arms of a people trodden into poverty and chains by an oligarchy of slaveholders; but that oligarchy proved too strong even for Cæsar and his legions. Judged by its immediate success, Cæsar's life was a failure as much as John Brown's; the Empire rotted into the grave which slavery digs for all its victims. What better right have we to hope? Let us examine. The Republican party says now what Mr. Sumner said in 1852, that it "knows no better aim, under the Constitution, than to bring back the government" to where it stood in 1789. That is done. The echo of cannon from ocean shore to the Rocky Mountains proclaims it accomplished.

How much is such success worth? I suppose you will not claim that Mr. Lincoln is better than Washington. As only Abolition telescopes have dared to discover any spots on that sun, certainly, while Mr. Everett lives and the Ledger is printed, no one will presume to say there can be a better President than Washington. Indeed, Mr. Seward asks in great contempt of any man who undertakes to improve the Constitution, "Are you more just than Washington, wiser than Hamilton, more humane than Jefferson?" Well, then, Washington, pursuing the very policy which Mr. Lincoln proposes to follow, launched the ship of state on seas white with the fervor of the Revolutionary love of liberty, and made shipwreck. Every administration grew worse than its predecessor, and at last slavery, having wound its slimy way to the top of the Capitol,

"Hangs hissing at the nobler man below."

The whole argument of the canvass has been, that the experiment of self-government under this Constitution, began by the best of men, has been a failure. "The country is wrecked; take us for pilots, or you are lost," — has been the cry of the Republicans. Mr. Sumner has drawn the sad picture so well and so often that I need not attempt it. Our Presidents tools of the Slave Power, our army used to force slavery on our own Territories and neighbor-nations, free speech punished with death in one half the Union, and met with insult and starvation in the other, the slave-trade reopened, and our most distinguished scholar telegraphing apologies when his son sits at school beside a colored boy, and explaining his own indiscreet freedom of speech as the sad result of anodynes. [Applause.] Surely Mr. Seward, seeing all this, was right in confessing, at Rochester, in 1858, "Thus far our course has not been according to the humane hopes and expectations of our fathers." And, in 1860, "Not over the face of the whole world is there to be found one representative of our country who is not an apologist of the extension of slavery." And again, in Kansas, a month ago, "Our fathers thought slavery would cease before now; but the people became demoralized; the war went back, *back*, BACK, until 1854, until all guaranties of freedom in every part of the United States were abandoned, ... and the flag of the United States was made the harbinger, not of freedom, but of human bondage."

At Rochester, he went on to paint the picture of our national wreck so darkly, that his own feelings led him, in conclusion, to declare, that, if the final battle goes against him, he will leave America, shake the dust off his feet, and find "a more congenial home; for where Liberty dwells, there is my country."

But Mr. Seward closes that speech in hope, — hope grounded on this, that the Republican party has arisen.

"It is a party of one idea; an idea that fills and expands all generous souls; the idea of equality, — the equality of all men before human tribunals, as they are all equal before the Divine tribunal and laws."

That is his rainbow of hope. It is a noble idea, — equality before the law, — a mark which an old Greek declared, two thousand years ago, distinguished freedom from barbarism. Mark it, and let us question Mr. Lincoln about it.

Do you believe, Mr. Abraham Lincoln, that the negro is your political and social equal, or ought to be? Not a bit of it.

Do you believe he should sit on juries? Never.

Do you think he should vote? Certainly not.

Should he be considered a citizen? I tell you frankly, no.

Do you think that, when the Declaration of Independence says, "All men are created equal," it intends the political equality of blacks and whites? No, sir.

If this "idea that fills all generous minds" be equality, surely Mr. Lincoln's mind is as yet empty. If this is the only hope of our being able to achieve what our fathers failed to do, mount those Arab horses, Mr. Seward, and fly to the desert! But you can't fly with me, as the song goes; first, because, if we are defeated, I mean to die in the last ditch [applause]; and, secondly, notwithstanding the emptiness of Mr. Lincoln's mind, I think we shall yet succeed in making this a decent land to live in. [Cheers.] May I tell you why? Place yourselves at the door of the Chicago Convention. Do you see Mr. Lincoln? He believes a negro may walk where he wishes, eat what he earns, read what he can, and associate with any other who is exactly of the same shade of black he is. That is all he can grant. Well, on the other side is Mr. Seward. He believes the free negro should sit on juries, vote, be eligible to office, — that 's all. So much he thinks he can grant without hurting the Union.

Now raise your eyes up! In the blue sky above, you will see Mr. Garrison and John Brown! [Prolonged cheering.] They believe the negro, bond or free, has the same right to fight that a white man has, — the same claim on us to fight for him; and as for the consequences to the Union, who cares? Liberty first, and the Union afterwards, is their motto. [Cheers.] Liberty first, and, as the Scotch say, "Let them care who come ahind."

That Convention selected Lincoln for their standard-bearer. Enough gain for once. "First the blade, then the ear, then the full corn in the ear." [Loud cheers.] Dr. Windship began with a dumb-bell of ten pounds; after four years, he raises two hundred and fifty pounds in each hand. The elephants, when crossing a river, send the smallest first. Don't mount those Arab steeds yet, Mr. Seward! "Wait a little longer." Who knows whether that Liberator, whose printing-office Mayor Otis could not find in 1835, may not be issued from the eastern room of the White House in 1873, and Mr. Seward himself, instead of saying that John Brown was "justly hung," may dare then to declaim, as Charles O'Connor does now, in the Supreme Court at Albany: —

"A man who knows that the law under which he lives violates the first principles of natural justice . . . . . is bound to strive, by all honorable means, to break down and defeat that law. Among these honorable means is the right of armed resistance, — the sacred right of revolution. . . . . . This is the higher law which sanctified the revolt of George Washington against the constituted authorities then existing in this country. . . . . . The laurel-wreath of victory surrounds the name of Washington. Ill-success, defeat, overthrow, and death, in an ignominious form, might have been his fate. Such was the fate of many who, in this respect, perhaps, were as pure and virtuous as he. We revere the name of Emmett; we revere the name of Wallace, ... of every virtuous man who has perished in unsuccessful attempts to achieve the independence of his country. . . . . .

"And therefore, if negro slavery be a thing so unjust and so wicked as my friends and their associates esteem it, I must admit that we cannot consistently refuse the same tribute to the recent abolition martyr, John Brown. He fell! So have many illustrious champions of justice. He failed! So did Emmett, and so did Wallace. His means were inadequate! So were theirs: the event proved it. He struggled indeed for the liberty of a distant people, who were not his kinsmen, who were not of his color, who had few claims upon his sympathy, and none upon his affections. That may be an argument against him with those who think that heroism and virtue should never be disinterested; but it has no real weight.

"We have not been in the habit of withholding our meed of praise from Kosciusko, Pulaski, De Kalb, or Lafayette, all of whom fought, and two of whom perished for us. We withheld not our tribute of admiration from Lafayette when, in his old age, he visited our country. No one asserted that he should have stayed at home, instead of coming in aid of a remote and distant people, and imperilling his life for their emancipation. No! we received him as the people's guest, and the whole American nation, from one end of our republic to the other, bowed down in heartfelt homage to his virtue.

"How can my learned friends, with their avowed principles, withhold from John Brown the tribute of their admiration, or from his deeds the sanction of their approval?"

That is the opinion of Charles O'Connor, the head of the New York Bar, the new-fledged orator of Democracy, and the counsel for Virginia in the Lemmon case.

I expect to live to hear that sentence quoted in 1872, under the very dome of the Capitol, by some Senator anxious for a Presidential nomination! [Applause.] Do you doubt it? Why, it is not impossible that Virginia herself, clothed and in her right mind, may yet beg of

New York the dust of John Brown for some mausoleum at Richmond, as repentant Florence, robed in sackcloth, begged of Ravenna the dust of that outlawed Dante, whom a century before she ordered to be burned alive. [Great cheering.] You think me a fanatic, perhaps? Well, I have been thought so once or twice before. [Laughter.] May I tell you the reason of the faith that is in me? It does not hang on President Lincoln or any other President. Certainly not while he is checkmated by both House and Senate. I think little of the direct influence of governments. I think, with Guizot, that "it is a gross delusion to believe in the sovereign power of political machinery." To hear some men talk of the government, you would suppose that Congress was the law of gravitation, and kept the planets in their places. Mr. Webster sneered at the antislavery and kindred movements as "rub-a-dub agitations." Judge Story plumes himself on our government abolishing the slave-trade in 1808, as if in that it was not the servant of Clarkson and Wilberforce, Benezet and Woolman!

I never take up a paper full of Congress squabbles, reported as if sunrise depended upon them, without thinking of that idle English nobleman at Florence, whose brother, just arrived from London, happening to mention the House of Commons, he languidly asked, "Ah! is that thing going still?" [Great merriment.] Did you ever see on Broadway — you may in Naples — a black figure grinding chocolate in the windows? He seems to turn the wheel, but in truth the wheel turns him. [Laughter.] Now such is the President of the United States. He seems to govern; he only reigns. As Lord Brougham said in a similar case, — Lincoln is in *place*, Garrison in *power*. [Applause.] "Rub-a-dub agitation," forsooth! as if Mr. Webster could have a Whig party, or anything else, in these reading days, without that agitation which calls into being and sustains the press, which melts and moulds the popular will and heart. What would the Tribune be without the antislavery movement? Let progressive men be mum, and the Tribune would starve. We could better do without it, than it without us. This talk of politicians about quieting agitation, and yet expecting progress, or even life, is like the present Shah of Persia, (not one of whose subjects in fifty thousand can read, and not one in a hundred thousand can write,) exclaiming, when Sir Gore Ousely told him of the large revenue from the British post-office, "I 'll have a post-office to-morrow." [Loud applause.] You might as well have jury trials in Timbuctoo. [Laughter.] It is worse than making bricks without straw; it is making bricks without clay.

Observe, I do not depreciate statesmanship. It requires great ability to found states and governments, but only common talent to carry them on. It took Fulton and Watt to create the steam-engine; but a very ordinary man can engineer a train from Boston to Albany.

Some critics sneer at old histories for recording only what government did. They should remember how much, in old times, governments covered the whole field of human life, — trade, letters, religion, and industry. The annals of a dynasty were then, to a great extent, the history of the times. We call for different histories, because the times have so much changed. At present, it is not cabinets, but art, science, literature, opinion, fashion, and trade that mould national character and purpose. These, the London Times confessed, a dozen years ago, were infinitely more than statutes or parties. The late canvass was worth a dozen Lincolns. The agitation was a yeomanly service to liberty. It educated the people. One such canvass makes amends for the cowardice of our scholars, and consoles us under the infliction of Harvard College. [Laughter and applause.] Indeed, government is only a necessary evil, like other go-carts and crutches. Our need of it shows exactly how far we are still children. All governing over-much kills the self-help and energy of the governed. Compare the last century with this, or the European with the Yankee. Every narrowing of the sphere of government proves growth in the people, and is the seed of further growth.

Civilization dwarfs political machinery. Without doubt, the age of Fox and Pitt was one in which the prejudices of courts and the machinery of cabinets had large sway. But how absurd to say even of Pitt and Fox that they shaped the fate of England. The inventions of Watt and Arkwright set free millions of men for the ranks of Wellington; the wealth they created clothed and fed those hosts; the trade they established necessitated the war, if it was at all or ever necessary. Berlin and Milan decrees would have smothered every man in England. The very goods they manufactured, shut out from the continent, would have crowded the inhabitants off their little island. It was land monopoly that declared war with France, and trade fought the battle. Napoleon was struck down by no eloquence of the House of Commons, by no sword of Wellington. He was crushed and ground to powder in the steam-engines of James Watt.

Cobden and O'Connell, out of the House of Commons, were giants; in it, dwarfs. Sir Robert Peel, the cotton-spinner, was as much a power as Sir Robert Peel, the Prime Minister. We went to stare at the Lord Chancellor, not for his seals and velvet bag, but because he was Harry Brougham of the Edinburgh Review. Rowland Hill and Adam Smith, Granville Sharpe and Pilgrim's Progress, the London Times and the Stock Exchange, outweigh a century of Cannings and Palmerstons, Gladstones, Liverpools, and Earls Grey.

Weighed against the New England Primer, Lyman

Beecher, and Franklin, against the New York Tribune and Herald, all our thirteen Presidents kick the beam. The pulpit and the steamboat are of infinitely more moment than the Constitution. The South owes the existence of slavery to-day to the cunning of a Massachusetts Yankee, Eli Whitney; and Fulton did more to perpetuate the Union than a Senate-Chamber of Websters. I will not say that Mr. Banks, at the head of the Illinois Railway (if he ever gets there), will be a more influential man than while Governor of this State, but I will say that the founders and presidents of our railways are a much more influential body than the Senate of the Union.

Still, though I think little of political machinery, I value the success of the Republican party; not so much as an instrument, but as a milestone. It shows how far we have got. Let me explain. [Laughter.] You know that geologists tell us that away back there, before Moses [laughter], the earth hung a lurid mass of granite, hot, floating in thick carbonic acid gas for an atmosphere,— poison, thick gas. Gradually the granite and choke-damp, as miners call it, united and made limestone; then more choke-damp was absorbed, and sandstone came; more still, and coal appeared. By this time, the air had parted with all its poison, and was pure enough to breathe. Then came man! Just such has been our progress. Our government hung a lurid, floating mass in the poisonous atmosphere of New York Observers and Heralds, Tract Societies, pro-slavery pulpits, Union meetings, Calhouns, Everetts, Websters, and Halletts, slave-hunters, Curtises. The chemical process began. They were partially absorbed. We had Whig parties, anti-Texas meetings, and Free-soil factions. The change went on, and finally we have a party that dares to say slavery is a sin — *in some* places! The air begins to grow almost pure enough to breathe. [Applause.]

Scientific men think that electricity did much to hasten the coming of limestone and coal, and the disappearance of poison gas. In our case, too, electricity, — by which I mean the Garrison party [loud laughter and applause], — flashing through and through and all over the lazy heavens, quickened our change also. But the growth will be a great deal quicker in time to come. [Loud applause.] One great evil of politics — one that almost outweighs the help it indirectly gives to education — is the chains it puts on able men. Those chains are much loosened now. Listen to Mr. Seward on the prairies! Notice how free and eloquent he has been since the Chicago Convention! And this change is not due to age. You know, I am apt to say, among other impertinent things, that you can always get the truth from an American statesman after he has turned seventy, or given up all hope of the Presidency. [Applause.] I should like a law that one third of our able men should be ineligible to that office; then every third man would tell us the truth. The last ten years of John Quincy Adams were the frankest of his life. In them, he poured out before the people the treason and indignation which formerly he had only written in his diary. And Josiah Quincy, the venerable, God bless him! has told us more truth since he was eighty, than he ever did before. [Applause.] They tell us that until this year they have not been able to survey Mount Washington; its iron centre warped the compass. Just so with our statesmen before they reach seventy, their survey of the state is ever false. That great central magnet at Washington deranges all their instruments.

Let me take the speeches of Mr. Seward as an illustration of American statesmen. I take him, because he is a live man, and a worthy sample. [Applause.] I agree with the doctors' rule, — *Medicamenta non agunt in cadaver*, — "Dead bodies are no test of drugs." But he is a fair test, — a real live statesman; not one of those petty politicians who hang on agitation for what they can pick up, as I have seen birds, in summer, watch round a horse's feet for the insects his tread disturbs. No, he is a statesman.

In 1848, at Cleveland, Mr. Seward said: "We of New York are guilty of slavery still by withholding the right of suffrage from the race we have emancipated. You of Ohio are guilty in the same way by a system of black laws still more aristocratic and odious. . . . . . It is written in the Constitution of the United States, *in violation of the Divine law*, that we shall surrender the fugitive slave who takes refuge at our fireside from his relentless pursuers."

Mark the confession! the Constitution he stands sworn to support *violates the Divine law!* Does he advise his hearers to obey it? O no! He goes on: "Extend a cordial welcome to the fugitive who lays his weary limbs at your door, and defend him as you would your paternal gods." This is one of his methods of "an effective aggression on slavery." That sounds well. No twaddle about non-extension. No wonder Senator Mason summoned such a bloody fanatic before the Harper's Ferry Committee!

Well, in the Senate, in 1850, he declares that "the law of nature, written on the hearts and consciences of freemen, repudiates the fugitive slave clause"; that "we cannot be either true Christians or true freemen, if we impose on another a chain that we defy all human power to fasten on ourselves"; and he "thinks it wrong to hold men in bondage, at any time, and under any circumstances." But yet, at the same time, having counselled Ohio to resist the slave clause, and denounced it as a "compact no Christian nation would ever make," he goes on to pledge himself to use only "constitutional and peaceful means" to resist slavery, all about the paternal gods to the contrary notwithstanding! You need not summon him, Mr. Mason! He won't do any harm! In 1860, just after Harper's Ferry, he tells the South, that, if their sovereignty is assailed, within or without, no matter on what pretext, or who the foe, he will defend it as he would his own! You see, peaceful measures *against* slavery; guns and bayonets *for* it!

Do these words mean that? O no! Go with me to Madison, in September, and stand before that beautiful Capitol between the three lakes, and you will hear these same lips saying: —

"It has been by a simple rule of interpretation I have studied the Constitution of my country. That rule has been simply this: that by no word, no act, no combination into which I might enter, should any one human being of all the generations to which I belong, much less any class of human beings of any nation, race, or kindred, be oppressed and kept down in the least degree in their efforts to rise to a higher state of liberty and happiness. Amid all the glosses of the times, amid all the essays and discussions to which the Constitution of the United States has been subjected, this has been the simple, plain, broad light in which I have read every article and every section of that great instrument. Whenever it requires of me that this hand shall keep down the humblest of the human race, then I will lay down power, place, position, fame, everything, rather than adopt such a construction or such a rule. If, therefore, in this land there are any who would rise, I say to them, in God's name, good speed! If there are in foreign lands people who would improve their condition by emigration, or if there be any here who would go abroad in search of happiness, in the improvement of their condition, or in their elevation toward a higher state of dignity and happiness, they have always had, and they always shall have, a cheering word, and such efforts as I can consistently make in their behalf." [Cheers.]

That is good! It sounds like Kossuth! Now, then, we understand him fully. He will never help a slaveholder, and believe all races equal. Not quite. Is he in favor of complete equality, social and all? Is the country as open to the black man as the white? O no! In February last, he declared that the man who said so libelled the Republican party! And at St. Paul, in September, he bade them remember this was the country of the white man! and lets them understand that the Republican party opposes only the *extension* of slavery. In 1850, he declared "this violation of the Divine law," which he calls "the Constitution," — this "compact which no Christian state would ever make," and no Christian man could ever obey, — "the only just and equal government that ever existed! no other government ever could be so wise, just, free, and equal!" And he affirms that no time or change could ever produce one more beneficent! Last Friday, in New York, he said that whoever doubts that this Constitution ("this violation of the Divine law") will "last forever, has no faith in reason, no faith in justice, no faith in truth, no faith in virtue"! If this be so, then "*violations* of the Divine law" seem about as eternal as the Divine law itself; and the Italian who prayed, "Good Lord, good Devil," was a sensible man, and was only laying a very prudent and necessary anchor to the windward! [Laughter and applause.]

At Washington, in February, he thought John Brown "was misguided and desperate," and "justly hung." He talks of "social horrors" and "disunion," and irons his face out to portentous length and sadness. [Laughter.] But at Chicago, in September, John Brown, he says, "was the only one man [when the Missouri Compromise was repealed] who hoped against the prevailing demoralization, and cheered and sustained me [Mr. Seward] through it!" And at St. Paul, he snaps his fingers at disunion, and, amid shouts of derisive laughter, cries out, "Who 's afraid?"

They exhibited at the Crystal Palace, in 1851, a Damascus blade, so flexible that it could be placed in a sheath, coiled like a snake. Something like it seems Mr. Seward's conscience, only the blade boasted it could *bend*. Seward, after coiling in and out, insists on our believing that he never bent a whit!

But hear him now, since the nomination at Chicago! See the lion toss his free limbs on the prairie! Standing in Kansas, with the spirit of John Brown hovering over him, his name written on every hill-top, hear the old Governor proclaim, "All men shall have the ballot or none; all men shall have the bullet or none." Crossing into Missouri, he says, the principle that every man should own the soil he tills, and the head and hands he works with, "is going through; it is bound to go through"; when a by-stander said, "Not here," he retorted, "Yes, *here*. As it is has gone through eighteen States of the Union, it is bound to go through the other fifteen. It is bound to go through all of the thirty three States of the Union, for the simple reason that it is going through the world." [Prolonged applause.]

That smacks of good old-fashioned John Brown and Garrison Abolition, — not non-extension! I know Mr. Everett will deem such words very indiscreet. [Laughter.] I knew an old lady to whom a friend had given a nice silk umbrella. She had kept it standing in a corner twenty years, when one day her grandson seized it to go out. "You 're not going to take that out in the wet!" she exclaimed. "Never, while I live!" This is just like Mr. Everett's free speech, always laid up in cotton! [Laughter and applause.]

They say, if you stand on the prairie of an August night at full moon, you can hear the corn grow, so quick are nature's processes out there. Had you been by Governor Seward that day, you might have heard him grow. [Loud applause.]

And as Seward grows, so grow millions of others, and so the world moves. "The sword," says Victor Hugo, "is but a hideous flash in the darkness, — Right is an eternal ray." Wait! Be patient! In 1760, what Boston rebel boys felt, James Otis spoke, George Washington achieved, and Everett praises to-day. The same routine will go on. What fanatics feel, Garrison prints, some future Seward will achieve, and, at the safe distance of half a century, some courtly Everett will embalm in matchless panegyrics. [Cheers.]

You see exactly what my hopes rest upon. Growth! The Republican party have undertaken a problem, the solution of which will force them to our position. Not Mr. Seward's "Union and Liberty," which he stole and poisoned from Webster's "Liberty and Union." No; their motto will soon be, "Liberty first," a long pause, then "Union afterwards." [Applause and a solitary hiss.]

In 1842, Lindley had finished the railway at Hamburg, and was to open it, when the great fire broke out. The self-satisfied citizens called the Englishman to see how well their six-penny squirts and old pails could put out the fire. But it raged on, till one quarter of the city was in ruins. "Mynherr Lindley, what shall we do?" cried the frightened Senators of Hamburg. "Let me blow up a couple of streets," he answered. "Never, never, never." Another day of flames. "Mynherr Lindley, blow up the streets and welcome, only save us." "Too late," replied the engineer. "To do that, I must blow up the Senate-House itself." They debated an hour, and then said, "Mynherr Lindley, save us in your own way." In one hour, the Senate-House was in ruins, and the fire ceased. "Be quiet, Mr. Garrison," said 1830. "Don't you see our six-penny Colonization Society, and our old-fashioned pails of church resolves, nicely copied and laid away in vestries? See how we 'll put out this fire of slavery." But it burned on fiercer, fiercer. "What shall we do now?" asked startled Whiggery. "Keep the new States free, abolish slavery in the District, shut the door against Texas." "Too much," said Whiggery; "we are busy now making Webster President, and proving that Mr. Everett never had an antislavery idea." But the flames roll on. Republicanism proposes to blow up a street or two. No, no; nothing but to blow up the Senate-House will do; and soon frightened Hamburg will cry, "Mynherr Garrison, Mynherr Garrison, save us on your own terms!" [Loud applause.]

You perceive my hope of freedom rests on these rocks: 1st, mechanical progress. First man walked, dug the earth with his hands, ate what he could pick up; then he subdues the horse, invents the plough, and makes the water float him down stream; next come sails, wind-mills, and water-power; then sewing-machines lift woman out of torture, steam marries the continents, and the telegraph flashes news like sunlight over the globe. Every step made hands worth less, and brains worth more; and that is the death of slavery. You can make apples grow one half pippin and the other half russet. They say that the Romans could roast one half of a boar, and boil the other side. [Laughter.] But I am sure you cannot make a nation with one half steamboats, sewing-machines, and Bibles, and the other half slaves. Then another rock of my hope is these Presidential canvasses, — the saturnalia of American life, — when slaves like Seward are unchained from the Senate-House, as of old in Rome, and let loose on the prairies, to fling all manner of insult on their masters. He may veil it all hereafter in dignified explanations, but the prairies give back an hundred-fold for all seed dropped there. [Applause.] Then the ghost of John Brown makes Virginia quick to calculate the profit and loss of slavery. Beside this, honest men, few, but the salt of the times, and school-houses and pulpits, and now and then a stray prince, who, looking down South, declines to venture among a barbarous people, lest, unlike St. Paul's case, they show him very little kindness. So, with trade, art, letters, conscience, fashion, now and then a college redeemed from old fogies, now and then a saint, and now and then a hero lent us by heaven, we may come at last to be as wise as Napoleon, and believe "there is no power without justice"; we may grow to be as good Christians as Cicero, and hold that "baseness can never be expedient"; we may be as good Protestants as Tocqueville, and declare that "whoever loves freedom for anything but freedom's self, is made to be a slave."

It is indeed cheering to notice the general tone of speaking in this canvass; — the much nobler tone of Mr. Seward, for instance, in speaking of the Union on the prairies, than it used to be. I recollect a striking picture he drew in 1850 of the value of the Union, and every line was *dollars!* "Amplitude of territory," increase of population, "fields, workshops, ships, mines, the plough, loom, anvil, canals, railways, steamboats," and the "navy," — all earthborn. Now he cries, Whoever says trade is the cement of the Union, libels the idea of American civilization. That is good! [Applause.]

The saddest thing in the Union meetings of last year was the constant presence, in all of them, of the clink of coin, — the whir of spindles, — the dust of trade. You would have imagined it was an insurrection of pedlers against honest men. [Laughter.] Mr. Everett at Faneuil Hall, when he sought for the value of the Union, could only bewail the loss of our "commercial intercourse," the certainty of "hostile tariffs," and danger to the "navy"! And this is literally all the merits of the

Union which he catalogues! No; I do him injustice. He does ask, trembling, in case of disunion, "Where, O where, will be the flag of the United States?" Well, I think the Historical Society had better take it for their Museum. [Laughter and applause.]

Mr. O'Connor, too, who gave the key-note to the New York meeting. The only argument he has for the Union is his assurance that, if we dissolve, there 'll be no more "marble store fronts" on Broadway, and no brown-stone palaces in the Fifth Avenue! Believe me, this is literally all he named, except one which Mr. Everett must have been under the influence of an anodyne to have forgotten, but which, perhaps, it is better, on the whole, for Mr. O'Connor, *being an Irishman*, to recollect. It is this: in case of dissolving, we shall no longer own the grave of Washington, which, Mr. Everett having paid for, the New York peddling orator finds it hard to lose! And so it strikes me!

But I must confess, those pictures of the mere industrial value of the Union made me profoundly sad. I look, as, beneath the skilful pencil, trait after trait leaps to glowing life, and ask at last, Is this all? Where are the nobler elements of national purpose and life? Is this the whole fruit of ages of toil, sacrifice, and thought, — those cunning fingers, the overflowing lap, labor vocal on every hillside, and commerce whitening every sea, — all the dower of one haughty, overbearing race? The zeal of the Puritan, the faith of the Quaker, a century of Colonial health, and then this large civilization, does it result only in a workshop, — fops melted in baths and perfumes, and men grim with toil? Raze out, then, the Eagle from our banner, and paint instead Niagara used as a cotton-mill!

O no! not such the picture my glad heart sees when I look forward. Once plant deep in the nation's heart the love of right, let there grow out of it the firm purpose of duty, and then from the higher plane of Christian manhood we can put aside on the right hand and the left these narrow, childish, and mercenary considerations.

> "Leave to the soft Campanian
> His baths and his perfumes;
> Leave to the sordid race of Tyre
> Their dyeing-vats and looms;
> Leave to the sons of Carthage
> The rudder and the oar;
> Leave to the Greek his marble nymphs,
> And scrolls of wordy lore"; —

but for us, the children of a purer civilization, the pioneers of a Christian future, it is for us to found a Capitol whose corner-stone is Justice, and whose top-stone is Liberty; within the sacred precincts of whose Holy of Holies dwelleth One who is no respecter of persons, but hath made of one blood all nations of the earth to serve him. Crowding to the shelter of its stately arches, I see old and young, learned and ignorant, rich and poor, native and foreign, Pagan, Christian, and Jew, black and white, in one glad, harmonious, triumphant procession!

> "Blest and thrice blest the Roman
> Who sees Rome's brightest day;
> Who sees that long victorious pomp
> Wind down the sacred way,
> And through the bellowing Forum,
> And round the suppliant's Grove,
> Up to the everlasting gates
> Of Capitolian Jove!"

MOBS AND EDUCATION.

"On Sunday forenoon," says the Liberator of December 21, 1860, "the Twenty-Eighth Congregational Society (Theodore Parker's Fraternity) held their usual Sunday meeting in Music Hall. It having been rumored for several days previous, that Mr. Phillips was likely to be mobbed and assaulted, a large detachment of police was in attendance at the hall, at an early hour. Before the services commenced, large numbers of the police were stationed in two small rooms adjoining the platform. Others were stationed in various parts of the hall, and building. Members of the detective police force were also present. . . . . .

"The regular religious exercises of the day were conducted in the usual manner."

I WAS present here last Sunday, and noticed that some of the friends of the speaker expressed their sympathy with his sentiments by applause. You will allow me to request that to-day, at least, we preserve the usual decorum of this place and this hour, and listen — even if you should like anything particularly — in silence.

About a fortnight ago, — on the 3d of this month, — certain men, supported by the Mayor, broke up an anti-slavery meeting. I propose to consider that morning, as illustrating American education. Some of you may think that everybody talks, now, of slavery, free speech, and the negro. That is true; and I am not certain that the longest liver of you all will ever see the day when it will not be so. The negro for fifty, or thirty, years has been the basis of our commerce, the root of our politics, the pivot of our pulpit, the inspiration of almost all that is destined to live in our literature. For a hundred years, at least, our history will probably be a record of the struggles of a proud and selfish race to do justice to one that circumstances have thrown into its power. The effects of slavery will not vanish in one generation, or even in two. It were a very slight evil, if they could be done away with more quickly.

Fredrika Bremer said, the fate of the negro is the romance of our history. It will probably be a long while, a very long while, before the needle of our politics will float free from this disturbance, before trade will cease to feel the shock of this agitation, before the pulpit can throw off vassalage to this prejudice and property, before letters take heart and dare to speak the truth. A bitter prejudice must be soothed, a bloody code repealed, a huckstering Constitution amended or made way with, social and industrial life rearranged, and ministers allowed to take the Bible, instead of the Stock List, as the basis of their sermons. Meanwhile, you must expect that every shock and oscillation of the stormy elements will stir up the dregs of society, lewd fellows of the baser sort, to deeds of anger and outrage; and meanwhile every honest and earnest man will speak, and every such man will be glad to hear, as occasion calls, of this the great duty that Providence has placed in our hands.

I bate no jot of trust that this noble trial of self-government will succeed. Heirs of a glorious past, we have manhood enough to be the benefactors of the future, and to hand down this hard-earned fabric, freed from its greatest, perhaps its only, danger.

The planting of these states always amazed the casual observer, and has been a subject of the deepest interest to

thoughtful men "The wildest theories of the human reason were reduced to practice by a community so humble that no statesman condescended to notice it, and a legislation without precedent was produced off-hand by the instincts of the people." The profoundest scholar of that day said, "No man is wiser for his learning," — a sentiment which Edmund Burke almost echoed; and it seems as if our comparatively unlettered fathers proved it. They framed a government which, after two hundred years, is still the wonder and the study of statesmen. It was only another proof that governments are not made, they grow, that the heart is the best logician, that character, which is but cousin to instinct, is a better guide than philosophy. Wordsworth said, of a similar awakening:

> "A few strong instincts, and a few plain rules,
> Among the herdsmen of the Alps, have wrought
> More for mankind, at this unhappy day,
> Than all the pride of intellect and thought."

That sunrise has colored the whole morning of our history. It is the cardinal principle of our national life, that God has given every man sense enough to manage his own affairs. Out of that, by a short process, come universal suffrage and the eligibility of every man to office. The majority rules, and law rests on numbers, not on intellect or virtue. A sound rule, and, if not the only one consistent with freedom and progress, at least the one that best serves these. But the harm is, that, while theoretically holding that no vote of the majority can authorize injustice, we practically consider public opinion the real test of what is true and what is false; and hence, as a result, the fact which Tocqueville has noticed, that practically our institutions protect, not the interests of the whole community, but the interests of the majority. Every man knows best how to manage his own affairs. Simple statement, perfectly sound; but we mix it up somehow with that other rule, that every man is eligible to office, and then we hurry on to the habit of considering every man competent for everything. Does a man achieve success in some particular point, we hail him a universal Crichton, and endow him with a genius for all work. A mechanic invents a new stitch in a carpet-web; straightway he is named for Congress. Does a man edit a Respectable Daily to bankruptcy, we put him on a commission to choose for us water not fit to drink, or let him carry a railroad half-way to ruin, by paying dividends that were never earned. That militia colonel survived a Western brawl, — call it a battle and a victory, and choose him President at once. This man is a brilliant historian, — send him Ambassador to England. Another has argued ably an india-rubber case, — send him to fade out in the Senate. Does a man fail utterly, — a bankrupt poet or office-seeker, — he edits a newspaper. We lack, entirely, discrimination. Because a man is entitled to draw upon us for fifty dollars, we put a thousand to his credit. That a man edits the Tribune so as to pay, — no very high order of talent, — is no proof that he knows better than other men who should be President of the United States. Bayard Taylor may be a genius and a traveller, without the least trace of patriotism or the least spark of a gentleman. A hundred years ago, you must have served an apprenticeship of seven years to make a shoe; now talk seven months on the right side, you may be Governor of a State.

I said that, in spite of the heedlessness and good nature of this mistake, the rule that every man should be eligible to office is the best rule you can have. Our large measure of national success, in spite of this heedlessness, shows how truly the Swede spoke when he said, *Quantula sapientia regitur mundus*, — "How little wit it takes to hold office!" But, though life be long and sunny, one fit of severe ill ness is a great evil. It is quite true, that routine incapacity stumbles along very well at common times; but there come hours when we need a pilot, and then we suffer. Such an hour we have just passed through.

Certain men, who seem utterly ignorant of the principle, that only by letting each man speak exactly what he sees fit, at the time he chooses, can the progress of truth be secured, attempted to put down certain other men, assembled to discuss the abolition of slavery. I want to look at that attempt as illustrating the ignorance of the actors, the ignorance of the press, and the incapacity of the city government. And I take this subject specially because it enables me to lay before you a correct account of the course of events that morning, which no journal of the city has bestirred itself to procure. And I seize this, the first opportunity given me, to do justice to both parties, — the assailants and the assailed.

Look first at the press. With the exception of The Atlas and Bee, no one of the daily papers has uttered one word of hearty, fitting rebuke of the mob. They have all serious objections to mobs in the abstract, but none at all to mobs in the street, none to this particular mob. This was not a case of virtuous men refusing to obey a bad law, of whom it has been well said, "They do not dispute the right of the majority to command, they only appeal from the sovereignty of the nation to the sovereignty of mankind." But this was a blow at the right of free speech, a right which no sane man in our age and land denies. Yet you have still to read the first word of fitting, fearless, hearty rebuke, from the Boston daily press, of a mob, well dressed, met to crush free speech. I have known Boston for thirty years. I have seen many mobs. With one exception, I have yet to see the first word of honest rebuke, from the daily press, of a well-dressed mob met to crush honest men; and that exception was the Boston

Daily Advocate of Mr. Hallett, in 1835 and 1837. Let me say, in passing, that it is a singular result of our institutions, that we have never had in Boston any but well-dressed mobs. Still they are dangerous precedents, — well-dressed men hire hungry mechanics to mob free speech. Beware! such men may "better the instruction." The "flour mobs" followed close on the pro-slavery mobs in New York. But such a press, — what a tool, what a despicable tool!

The press will think me unjustifiable, perhaps, for they affect to have discovered that there was no mob, only the majority taking rightful possession of a public meeting. We will consider that by and by.

The press says the mob was composed of "Boston gentlemen." A very natural mistake for a press which does not know a mob when it sees it. But can we let that description stand? Broadcloth and fine linen do not make a gentleman! Ill manners and ignorance do not make one. Earning a right to twelve months in the House of Correction does not make one. [Laughter.] Resisting the laws to help the stock market does not. Running, before you are sent, with volunteer haste, to do the dirty work of base men, does not make one. And yet these are the only colors by which men before unseen made themselves visible that day on the surface of affairs. One must be born again into the Kingdom of Mammon, before he thinks such men gentlemen. And as the ringleaders were not born in Boston, let us save the dear old town from the disgrace of having them called *Boston gentlemen*. The gossip of the street says they were excusable on account of pecuniary losses, — they were men out of employ. The ringleader said he came there to save his property. Let us examine of what material the mob was really made. We have a right to inquire, it is important we should know, who make up this Chamber of Inquisitors, this new

Star-Chamber, which undertakes to tell us, as Archbishop Laud and Charles Stuart told our fathers, what creed we shall hold, and what public meetings we shall attend. Who were they?

Weak sons of moderate fathers, dandled into effeminacy, of course wholly unfit for business. But overflowing trade sometimes laps up such, as it does all obtainable instruments. Instead of fire-engines, we take pails and dippers, in times of sore need. But such the first frost nips into idleness. Narrow men, ambitious of office, fancying that the inheritance of a million entitles them to political advancement. Bloated distillers, some rich, some without wit enough to keep the money they stole. Old families run to seed in respectable dulness, — *fruges consumere nati*, — born only to eat. Trading families, in the third generation, playing at stock-jobbing to lose in State Street what their fathers made by smuggling in India. Sweep in a hundred young rogues, the grief of mothers and the disgrace of their names, good as naughts to fill up a place in what is called "society," and entitled as such to shrink from notice, — but the motes we do not usually see get looked at when they trouble our eyes. Snobbish sons of fathers lately rich, anxious to show themselves rotten before they are ripe. [Hitherto there had been no demonstrations from the hearers, except occasional suppressed laughter at the speaker's sarcasms. The laughter here was received with hisses by a portion of the audience.] These, taking courage from the presence of bolder rogues, some from jail and others whom technical skill saved therefrom, — the whole led by a third-rate lawyer broken down to a cotton-clerk [hisses], borrowing consequence from married wealth, — not one who ever added a dollar, much less an idea, to the wealth of the city, not one able to give a reason or an excuse for the prejudice that is in him, — these are the men, this is the house of nobles, whose leave we are to ask before we speak and hold meetings. These are the men who tell *us*, the children of the Pilgrims, the representatives of Endicott and Winthrop, of Sewall and Quincy, of Hancock and Adams and Otis, what opinions we shall express, and what meetings we shall hold! These are the men who, the press tells us, being a majority, took rightful possession of the meeting of the 3d of December, [applause and cries of "Good,"] and, "without violating the right of free speech," organized it, and spoke the sober sense of Boston!

I propose to examine the events of that morning, in order to see what idea our enlightened press entertain of the way in which "gentlemen" take possession of a meeting, and the fitness of *those* "gentlemen" to take possession of a meeting.

On the 3d of December, certain gentlemen — Rev. J. Sella Martin, James Redpath, Mr. Eldridge, Mr. O'Connor, Mr. Le Barnes — hired the Temple for a Convention to assemble at their request. The circular which they issued a month before, in November, invited the "leaders and representatives of all the antislavery bodies, and those who have done honor to their own souls by the advocacy of human freedom," to meet them in convention. Certainly the fops and the clerks of Boston could not come under that description. The notice published the day before proclaimed that the convention "was not met for debate, that each speaker should confine himself to giving, briefly, his views on the question, 'How shall American slavery be abolished?'" Does Mr. Fay, or any one of his associates, dare to say, in the presence of the citizens of Boston, that he entered that hall to join in good faith in any such investigation? The temper and quality of the meeting was shown by the statement of that notice, that it chose the anniversary of the "martyrdom" of John Brown as the day for its meeting, and mentioning his death as "too glorious to need defence or eulogy." If any one of Mr. Fay's associates entered that hall with written resolutions in their pockets, denouncing John Brown and expressing "horror for his piratical, bloody, and nefarious attempt," by what claim, as gentlemen, do they justify their presence there?

But waive that, and grant that they were rightfully present. When a convention assembles at the call of a committee of gentlemen, it is a well-recognized and settled right and custom of the callers to organize that convention through a committee, or otherwise to appoint officers for the body. If the committee report a list, it is sometimes put to vote, and sometimes not. When a vote is taken, it is mere form; for all well-disposed men, if they contest a convention, uniformly leave it the right to organize itself, and meet it, if anywhere, on the passage of its resolutions. In conformity with this custom, the Rev. J. Sella Martin took the floor as temporary Chairman. He appointed a committee to appoint officers. That committee reported a list, with Mr. Sanborn of Concord as Chairman. Mr. Martin announced him, as he had an entire, well-recognized right to do, for the Chairman of that meeting.

But suppose the Convention chose to insist on its strict right, and to organize itself without regard to its callers. Then it was perfectly in order for any member to address the temporary chair, and make a motion to that effect. Did any one do it? No. On the contrary, one person, who seems to shrink from having his name known, nominated Mr. Richard S. Fay as chairman ["Good!" cheers and hisses], and put the motion. This anonymous skulker does not seem to know parliamentary law enough to remember that he should address the chair, or that he should wait to have his motion seconded; but without that, and without any call for the nays, Mr. Fay assumes to be Chairman. There having been, then, in the eye of strict parliamentary law, no motion, — for all the books lay it down that "no motion can be made without addressing the chair," — there having been no motion, no seconding, no call for the nays, there being no announcement of the vote, either by the Chairman or by Mr. Anonymous, when Mr. Richard S. Fay walked to that platform and assumed to be Chairman, he announced himself the ringleader of a mob [applause, and one cry of "No!"] by the strictest letter of parliamentary law. Journals which undertake to know, style him the rightful Chairman. And when Mr. Douglass, in common courtesy, handed him a glass of water, Mr. Fay says, "This acknowledges me as Chairman!" Profound logician, this Mr. Fay! A glass of water is his title to office, and Mr. Frederick Douglass is authorized to confer it.

And then commences an exhibition of his wonderful powers as a presiding officer. The moment a chairman takes his seat, the first duty is the call for the appointment of secretary and other officers. This wonderful meeting had no officer, except its equally wonderful Chairman. Unburdening himself of his coat, he was not self-possessed enough to find in his pocket the scroll of resolutions which every one saw protruding from it, — whereupon he said, "I thought I had got among honest men." Some bystanders thought this insolence. I am rather inclined to believe it possible, that, having escaped from the mob to our platform, he was congratulating himself upon having gotten for once among honest men. [Much laughter.] He then undertakes to read the resolutions, and offer them to the Convention, ignorant again — ignorant again — that there was just one man in that meeting, and only one, who had no right to offer a resolution, and that was himself, on his own theory; for every boy knows, except this young cotton-clerk, that no presiding officer is entitled to offer a resolution.

Following, then, the example of Mr. Anonymous, who nominated him, he does not wait to have the resolutions seconded, he does not call for the nays, but he declares them carried. This could not have been fright, for although he was observed to tremble and grow pale when hundreds cried out "Shame!" at the reading of his third and fourth resolves, yet some one saying, "Don't be frightened, we won't hurt you," had considerably reassured him. [Laughter.] Then somebody makes a motion to adjourn. Mr. Fay puts it. While he is doing so, Mr. Frederick Douglass addresses him. He turns, introduces Mr. Douglass to the audience, and gives him the floor, ignorant again — ignorant again — that a motion to adjourn is not debatable. Some one in the audience, while Mr. Douglass is speaking, reminds him there is a motion before the house. This vigilant Chairman waves the speaker aside, puts the motion to adjourn, declares it carried, and then introduces Mr. Douglass again to this adjourned Convention, and bids him remember the rule of the call, to speak briefly, and to the point! [Great laughter.] And then this adjourned Chairman of a dead Convention sits and listens half an hour to a speech from Mr. Douglass. Whereafter, another man makes a motion to adjourn; he puts it, declares it carried, and then, — on the poet's principle, "twice he slew the slain," — recognizing, I suppose, that even his mob, twice adjourned, is done with, takes his hat and vanishes, — this orderly Chairman!

Common chairmen, before quitting their conventions, appoint a committee of finance, to see that the expenses are paid; but this opulent and magnanimous, Union-loving Chairman, [cheers and some hisses,] having announced that he came to the hall to save his property, does it by leaving his victims to pay the expenses. [Laughter.] And when Mr. Hayes reminded him, during the pendency of the motion to adjourn, that he must not do so until he had arranged for the payment for the hall, this representative of State Street defied Mr. Hayes to compel him to pay for the hall he had used. I blush, even for State Street, under such a fact. And the gallant men who followed him — O shame even to Boston dandies! — were heard encouraging each other with cries of "The police are with us, — the other side pay for them, and we use them!"

Some men assert that Mr. Fay really came to that hall to put down free speech by violence. As it was said that no man was ever so wise as Lord Thurlow looked, so these citizens think no honest man was ever so ignorant as Mr. Fay appeared. I am inclined to believe that he came there designing to crush that Convention in a parliamentary way, but did not know how to do it. Like the captain of the Maine schooner caught in our harbor narrows [here a youth in the gallery raised the mob cry, "All up," which failed, however, to produce any sensation], who, when some one asked, "Who captains this schooner?" called back, "I undertook to captain her, but find it rather too much for me"; — so Mr. Fay undertook to *captain a parliamentary mob*, but found it rather too much for him. Being fully determined, however, to crush the Convention, and finding the quiet and trained friends of it able to outwit and outgeneral him, he took refuge in violence. He challenged his opponent to a duel, then knocked him over the head with the but of his pistol while his back was turned. Lord George Bentinck leaped from the sporting-field and the race-course to the leadership of the House of Commons. Perhaps Mr. Fay thought he could do as much.

After the kid-gloved mobocrat had left the hall, Mr. Sanborn, quietly requesting the real friends of order to remain seated while the mob followed its leader, showed them that all their labor had been in vain. Then Mr. J. Murray Howe, without any flimsy veil of parliamentary pretext, a bully girdled by bullies, failing to excite any violent resistance, urged or incited the police to arrest all whom his followers struck, on the ground of removing the cause of the disturbance. And the shameless Mayor closed the scene [hisses], — the plot unmasked by the quiet discipline of the friends of order was disclosed, and the City Government succored its defeated accomplices by clearing the hall in the prostituted names of law and order. [Loud cheers and some hisses.]

I have named only the leaders of this mob, and described the pitiful quality of their followers. You will ask me, How did such a mass influence the Mayor? I am sorry to say, that among that crowd were men influential by wealth and position, men seldom seen in an antislavery meeting, whose presence there at that unusual hour, — ten o'clock in the morning, — sitting in silence, was an encouragement to their personal friends, the mob. You may see, still looking down on Washington Street, the gilded names of Lawrence and Dickinson, and, side by side, the proud motto, "The Union, the Constitution, the Enforcement of the Laws." [Cheers.] One of those names, which the city has hitherto loved to honor, was present in that crowd, in a class of meetings where he is seldom seen, — never at ten o'clock in the morning, — while his personal friends resisted, with the encouragement of his unusual presence, the enforcement of the most sacred of all laws, that of free speech. Need I explain any otherwise the servility of the Mayor?

Some men say that free speech was really crushed out on that occasion. No. On that same day, that same meeting held a session, addressed by the most hated of its speakers, expressing their opinions on slavery and the scene of the morning. The exact, literal truth is, that

Mr. Richard S. Fay *stole* the Tremont Temple from those who had hired it. Let us hope he will pay his debts without going through court. Those men whom he fought can say they were never sued yet for any hall they had used; he cannot say as much to-day. Doubtless they intended to crush free speech; but do not let us dignify Jack Sheppard and Dickens's Fagin into Cromwells and Bonapartes. These mobocrats intended to be Cromwells. So did the two tailors who undertook to tear down the throne of George III., and issued the famous proclamation, "We, the people of England." History does not record that they succeeded; neither did their imitators on the 3d of December. Still, these angry and misguided men incurred very grave responsibility. Stealing a hall is not very bad in men who hardly know what they are about. Violating the rights of your neighbors may be forgiven, when the parties offending will soon repent, and those rights are no more affected than the sun by the cloud that passes over him. But when Mr. Fay had housed himself in luxury and quiet, at night, that lawless and coward spirit which he had stirred up and let loose broke into the houses of our hated and friendless colored people, pursued any one of them it dared follow, finding him alone, cruelly beat, almost to death, several, and ill-treated many of them. If any one of those mangled men had died of his wounds, Richard S. Fay, in the sight of God and all honest men, if not of the law also, had been a murderer. The atonement he owes to our city which he has disgraced, is a public acknowledgment of his crime. The compensation he owes to those men pillaged and beaten by his followers, is to see that, so far as gold can, their sufferings are alleviated. Let us hope that the wealth and the influence which countenanced his wrong will move to aid him in his repentance.

The picture is one of men undertaking work for which

their education never fitted them, — a common mistake of American life. There are thousands among us engaged in mechanical routine whose souls have large grasp, and take in the universe. Critical hours unveil the lustre of such spirits. Our self-made men are the glory of our institutions. But this is a case of men undertaking to join in public debate and preside over public meetings, whose souls are actually absorbed in pricing calico and adding up columns of figures. It is a singular sight. White men, having enjoyed the best book education, to see them struggling with two colored men, whose only education was oppression and the antislavery enterprise! But in that contest of parliamentary skill, the two colored men never made a mistake, while every step of their opponents was folly upon folly. Of course, upon the great question of moral right, there is no comparison. History gives us no closer parallel than the French Convention of Lafayette and Mirabeau assailed by the fish-women of the streets.

Let us turn now to the part of the City Government. Every man eligible to office, — but with a race like ours, fired with the love of material wealth, with a continent given us by God to subdue and crowd it with cities, to unite the oceans with rails, — in such an age and with such a race, trade must absorb all the keenest energies of each generation. The consequence is, that politics takes up with small men, men without grasp enough for large business; with leisure, therefore, on their hands; men popular because they have no positive opinions, — these are the men of politics. The result is, as Tocqueville has hinted, that our magistrates never have more education than we give to the mass, that they have no personal experience of their own. Such men do very well for ordinary occasions, when there is nothing to do. Common times only try common men. In a calm sea all boats alike show mastership in floating. On the

3d day of the month, we might have supposed every man to know that a meeting was to be protected against a mob, that the duty of the police was not to settle disputed questions and motions, but only to see that they were argued out without violence, — that they were there to arrest any man who committed an assault. The absurdity of turning the Convention out of doors to quiet its tumult, is the method of a quack who stabs his patient in order to cure the disease.

But our Mayor, poor as he is, did know all this. He was awed out of his duty by the social position of the mobocrats. The individual policemen were respectable and orderly, evidently disposed to enforce order, had they been allowed. No complaint can be made of them. But we know neither them nor their chief. For us, the Mayor represents the City Government. I hold him, single and alone, responsible for the success of the mob. [Slight hissing.] Abolitionists are the best judges; they have been through many such a scene. They assert that, if they could have been left alone, they could have quelled that mob, unaided. [Derisive laughter.] Mr. Hayes, of the Temple, the most competent witness in the city, offered the Mayor, on the spot, to keep order within the building if he could be allowed six men; and he has publicly avowed his belief, that, had the chief simply announced, from the platform, his purpose to keep order impartially, order would have reigned; but the mob knew that the police, in spite of their individual feelings, must obey orders, and were therefore, of course, on the mob side. The rioters were constantly boasting, "The police are all right," "They are with us," "Three cheers for the police!" [Cheers and hisses.]

To the courtesy and forbearance of the Abolitionists the Chief of Police has borne public witness. They were the only persons assaulted, yet they were the only persons arrested. They were the only persons knocked down, and they were the only persons carried from the hall by the police. The chief says that individual Abolitionists were removed by mistake. Singular that this mistake should never have happened to those who were using their canes and their fists, and should have taken place only in regard to persons conspicuous for their courtesy and forbearance!

The friends of the Mayor urge that the mob was too strong for the whole force of the government. Let him show that he spoke one word, that he lifted one finger, that he remonstrated with one rioter, and we will grant him that excuse. But the pilot who says the storm is too strong for him must show that he put his hand once, at least, upon the helm, to see whether it would obey the hold.

Our present Mayor is not singular; he does not stand alone. We have not had a decent Mayor for ten years. [Sensation, and vehement hisses.] Vassals of the grog-shop, and mortgaged to State Street, what could you expect from them? Of course Smith and Bigelow are beneath notice, — mere hounds of the slave-hunt, a hand's-breadth ahead of the pack. But these other degenerate magistrates find here and there a predecessor to keep them in countenance; indeed, all the Mayors on the Atlantic coast are their models, with one or two noble exceptions. That mob which Messrs. Fay and Howe inaugurated spent the night among our colored citizens' dwellings, beating, kicking, and stabbing all whom they met. The police were on special duty in those streets in the night. The morning opened, the courts assembled, the magistrate took his seat. The only person arrested for that night's disorder is one black boy, fourteen years old, who had defended himself against bullies!

I do not remember precisely the mob against the Irish

in Broad Street, but I am told that the same is true of that riot, that none but those assaulted were arrested. I have known three cases of magistrates quelling mobs. One was Neal Dow, in Portland, — not necessary, some thought, to fire. But let us grant Portland her fame, — she has quelled a mob. Providence, also, under a magistrate whose name I wish I could remember, (Governor Arnold, I am told,) quelled her mob with bullets; and last year, Mayor Henry, of Philadelphia, — a name that ought to be written in letters of gold, — taught purse-proud ignorance and brutality to obey the laws. The wealth of Philadelphia petitioned him not to allow Mr. Curtis to lecture. One of the petitioners waited on him and said, "Sir, do you know the treasonable sentiments of Mr. Curtis?" "No, sir," was the answer; "I know only that it is my duty to protect him." "Do you know, sir, that the wealthiest houses have petitioned you to stop the meeting?" "Yes, sir." "What shall you do if they appear, and put a stop to the lecture?" "Send them to the watch-house." [Applause.] Mr. Curtis lectured, and Mayor Henry was re-elected. While such men live, I am opposed to rotation in office. [Laughter.]

It is a long while since we have had such a Mayor. Your magistrates have always needed twenty-four hours, and closetings with indignant citizens, before they learned their duties. In 1835, Mayor Lyman, — a lawyer, a scholar, a gentleman, — instead of protecting Mr. Garrison, or dying in front of him, spent the critical hour of the mob's existence in vain intercessions with his personal friends, in pitiful appeals to drunken broadcloth, [slight hissing,] and went home to realize the noble opportunity he had lost of endearing his memory to law, liberty, and the good name of the city, to realize the grave duty he had failed to meet, and to spend his after life in bitter and unavailing regret over that disgraceful and wicked hour of his magistracy. But he lived, — he lived to repent; and later services did endear his name to the Commonwealth. There is no evidence that our more recent Mayors know even enough to be ashamed.

The men of that day lived to beg pardon of the very persons they had mobbed. All Boston glorified them, that month; they walked State Street in pride. But you would think me cruel, to-day, if I gibbeted their names. The hour is near, it knocks at yonder door, when whoever reminds an audience that Richard S. Fay and Mayor Lincoln broke up an antislavery meeting will be considered, even by State Street and the Courier, bitter and uncharitable, [hisses,] as eminently unchristian, in reminding the disgraced and the forgotten of their sins.

What was the meeting thus assailed? It was a meeting met to discuss slavery, — a topic which makes the republic tremble, the settlement of which is identical with the surviving of our government, — a topic upon which every press, every legislature, every magistrate, south of Mason and Dixon's line, flings defiance at the Union, amid the plaudits of Mr. Fay and his friends. What day was it? The anniversary of the martyrdom of the only man whose name stirs the pulses of Europe in this generation. [Derisive laughter.] English statesmen confess never to have read a line of Webster. You may name Seward in Munich and Vienna, in Pesth or in Naples, and vacant eyes will ask you, "Who is he?" But all Europe, the leaders and the masses, spoke by the lips of Victor Hugo, when he said, "The death of Brown is more than Cain killing Abel; it is Washington slaying Spartacus." [Laughter from some parts of the hall, and from others applause.]

What was the time of this meeting? An hour when our Senators and Representatives were vindicating the free speech of Massachusetts in Washington, in the face of armed men. Are we to surrender it in the streets at home, to the hucksters and fops of the Exchange? This day on which I speak, a year ago, those brave young hearts which held up John Brown's hands faced death without a murmur, for the slave's sake. In the light of their example, God forbid we should give up free speech!

Whom is it proposed to silence? Men who for thirty years, from the ocean to Kansas, sacrificing reputation, wealth, position, seeing their houses pillaged, their friends mobbed in the streets, have forced this question on reluctant senates and statesmen, until at last, all other issues driven out of the arena, God chains this age to the redemption of the slave. Victors in such a fight, after such a field, after having taught this nation, at such woful cost, the sacredness of free discussion, who are these traders that weigh their gold against our rights? Who is this boaster parading his two hundred thousand dollars, and telling us he will spend every one of them to "put down this agitation"? He "put down this agitation"! That attempt was announced before, from the steps of the Revere House. The unhappy statesman, defeated, heart-broken, sleeps by the solemn waves of the Atlantic. "*Contempsi Catilinæ gladios, non tuos pertimescam.*" The half omnipotence of Webster we defied; who heeds this pedler's empty wind?

How shall we prevent such insolent attempts for the future? Educate the future Fays more thoroughly. Teach them the distinction between duties and dollars. Plant deep in the heart of the masses the conviction of the utter sacredness of the right of free speech. Our fathers made their sons hate the Pope so thoroughly, that hatred of Popery is no longer an intellectual conviction, but has become a constituent element of Yankee blood and bone. Put the sacredness of free speech into the same condition. Carve in letters of gold in every school-house this letter of our loved Governor elect, — the best word a Massachusetts Governor has said since the first Winthrop gave his fine definition of civil liberty. Mr. Andrew says: —

"'The right to think, to know, and to utter,' as John Milton said, is the dearest of all liberties. Without this right, there can be no liberty to any people; with it, there can be no slavery."

And Mr. Andrew goes on: —

'I care not for the truth or error of the opinions held or uttered, nor for the wisdom of the words or time of their attempted expression, when I consider this great question of fundamental significance, this great right which must first be secure before free society can be said to stand on any foundation, but only on temporary or capricious props.

"Rich or poor, white or black, great or small, wise or foolish, in season or out of season, in the right or in the wrong, whosoever will speak, let him speak, and whosoever will hear, let him hear. And let no one pretend to the prerogative of judging another man's liberty. In this respect there is, and there can be, no superiority of persons or privileges, nor the slightest pretext for any."

Thank God for such a Governor to come! [Applause.] Make that Massachusetts, and then we may stop a boy in the streets and make him Mayor, sure that, without need of thought or consultation, he will gird himself to protect unpopular free speech, and put down fashionable riot, instead of lazily protecting fashionable riot, and putting down unpopular free speech.

I have used strong words. But I was born in Boston, and the good name of the old town is bound up with every fibre of my heart. I dare not trust myself to describe the insolence of men who undertake to dictate to you and me what we shall say in these grand old streets. But who can adequately tell the sacredness and the value of free speech? Who can fitly describe the enormity of the crime of its violation? Free speech, at once the instrument and the guaranty and the bright consummate flower of all liberty. Free speech in these streets, once trod by Henry Vane, its apostle and champion. Free speech, in that language which holds the dying words of Algernon Sidney, its martyr. As Everett said, near forty years ago: —

"I seem to hear a voice from the tombs of departed ages, from the sepulchres of nations that died before the sight. They exhort us, they adjure us, to be faithful to our trust. They implore us, by the long trials of struggling humanity, by the awful secrets of the prison-house where the sons of Freedom have been immured, by the noble heads which have been brought to the block, by the eloquent ruins of nations, they conjure us not to quench the light that is rising on the world. Greece cries to us by the convulsed lips of her poisoned, dying Demosthenes, and Rome pleads with us in the mute persuasion of her mangled Tully."

Let us listen to the grave and weighty words of the nephew of Charles James Fox, Lord Holland, in his protest when British Tories tried to stop the discussion of Catholic Emancipation, — words of which Macaulay says, "They state a chief article of the political creed of the Whigs with singular clearness, brevity, and force."

"We are," Lord Holland says, "well aware that the privileges of the people, the rights of free discussion, and the spirit and letter of our popular institutions, must render — *and they are intended to render* — the continuance of an extensive grievance, and of the dissatisfaction consequent thereupon, dangerous to the tranquillity of the country, and ultimately subversive of the authority of the state. Experience and theory alike forbid us to deny that effect of a free constitution: a sense of justice and a love of liberty equally deter us from lamenting it. But we have always been taught to look for the remedy of such disorders in the redress of the grievances which justify them, and in the removal of the dissatisfaction from which they flow; not in restraints on ancient privileges, not *in inroads on the right of public discussion, nor in violations of the principles of a free government.*"

Governments exist to protect the rights of minorities. The loved and the rich need no protection, — they have many friends and few enemies. We have praised our Union for seventy years. This is the first time it is tested. Has it educated men who know their rights, and dare to maintain them? Can it bear the discussion of a great national sin, anchored deep in the prejudices and interests of millions? If so, it deserves to live. If not, the sooner it vanishes out of the way the better.

The time to assert rights is when they are denied; the men to assert them are those to whom they are denied. The community which dares not protect its humblest and most hated member in the free utterance of his opinions, no matter how false or hateful, is only a gang of slaves.

"At the conclusion of the exercises, Mr. Phillips's friends flocked upon the platform to congratulate him. After a while, Mr. Phillips left the platform, accompanied by several friends, who were joined, in the lower entry, by some twenty in number. As the party emerged from the building to the avenue leading from the hall to Winter Street, a large crowd was found collected there, who set up various cries, such as 'There he is!' 'Crush him out!' 'Down with the Abolitionists!' 'Bite his head off!' 'All up!' &c., and surged toward Mr. Phillips, with the manifest purpose of preventing his egress. In this, however, they were balked by the resolute front of his friends and the energy of the police, who forced the crowd to give way.

"On entering Winter Street, the mob, which almost blockaded the street, yelled and hissed, and gave vent to their impotent rage by such cries as those given above; but the party proceeded down the street, and up Washington Street, surrounded by a strong detachment of police, and followed by an immense throng of people, many of them, however, friends of Mr. Phillips, and determined to protect him from injury. No demonstrations of violence, happily, were made. The singular procession excited the attention of people living on the route largely, and the windows looking on the street were crowded with faces expressing wonder and curiosity. Arrived at his house in Essex Street, Mr. Phillips entered, with a few of his friends, when three cheers were given by some of those present, which were answered by hisses from the other side. Deputy-Chief Ham then requested the crowd to disperse, which they did, though somewhat slowly, and with manifest reluctance. So ended the disgraceful scene." — *Liberator*.

DISUNION.*

THE office of the pulpit is to teach men their duty. Wherever men's thoughts influence their laws, it is the duty of the pulpit to preach politics. If it were possible to conceive of a community whose opinions had no influence on their government, there the pulpit would have no occasion to talk of government. I never heard or knew of such a community. Though sheltered by Roman despotism, Herod and the chief priests abstained from this and that because they "feared the people." The Sultan dared to murder his Janizaries only when the streets came to hate them as much as he did. The Czar, at the head of a government whose constitution knows no check but poison and the dagger, yet feels the pressure of public opinion. Certainly, where pews are full of voters, no question but the sermon should be full of politics.

"The Lord reigneth; let the earth rejoice." "The covenant with death" is annulled; "the agreement with hell" is broken to pieces. The chain which has held the slave system since 1787 is parted. Thirty years ago, Southern leaders, sixteen years ago, Northern Abolitionists, announced their purpose to seek the dissolution of the American Union. Who dreamed that success would come so soon? South Carolina, bankrupt, alone, with a

* Lecture delivered in the Music Hall, January 20, 1861, — a large part of the Hall and the avenues to it occupied by the mob.

hundred thousand more slaves than whites, four blacks to three whites, within her borders, flings her gauntlet at the feet of twenty-five millions of people in defence of an idea, to maintain what she thinks her right. I would New England could count one State as fearless among her six! Call it not the madness of an engineer who stands in front of his cannon at the moment of discharge; call it rather the forlorn hope of the mariner, seizing plank or spar in the fury of the storm. The mistake of South Carolina is, she fancies there is more chance of saving slavery outside of the Union than inside. Three States have followed her example. Probably the rest of the Slave States, or many of them, will find themselves unable to resist the infection, and then the whole merciless conspiracy of 1787 is ended, and timid men will dare to hate slavery without trembling for bread or life.

Let us look at the country, — the North, the South, and the government. The South divided into three sections: — 1st. Those who hold slaves exactly as they do bank-stock or land, — and of course love the Union, which enables them to treat man as property, — timid wealth shrinking from change, but so timid as to stand dumb. 2d. Those who have ruled the nation sixty years, monopolizing Presidents' chairs and Embassies; defeated now, these plan, in earnest sincerity, for another nation with Presidencies and Embassies all to themselves. 3d. A class made up from these two, who cling to the Union in their hearts, but threaten loudly, well knowing the loudest threats get the best bargain.

The object of the South is a separate confederacy, hoping they can stand long enough for the North to ask for annexation on their terms.

Then comes the government, so called, — in reality a conspiracy against justice and honest men; some of its members pilferers and some traitors, the rest pilferers and traitors too. Like all outgoing administrations, they have no wish to lessen the troubles of their successors by curing the nation's hurt, — rather aggravate it. They have done all the mischief in their power, and long now only to hear the clock strike twelve on the fourth day of March.

Then look at the North, divided into three sections: — 1st. The defeated minority, glad of anything that troubles their conquerors. 2d. The class of Republicans led by Seward, offering to surrender anything to save the Union. [Applause.] Their gospel is the Constitution [applause], and the slave clause is their Sermon on the Mount. [Laughter and applause.] They think that, at the judgment-day, the blacker the sins they have committed to save the Union, the clearer will be their title to heaven. 3d. The rest of the Republicans, led by the Tribune — all honor to the Tribune, faithful and true! — who consider their honor pledged to fulfil in office the promises made in the canvass. Their motto is: "The Chicago platform, every inch of it; not a hair's-breadth of the Territories shall be surrendered to slavery." [Applause.] But they, too, claim the cannon's mouth to protect forts, defend the flag, and save the Union. At the head of this section, we have every reason to believe, stands Mr. Abraham Lincoln.

All these are the actors on the stage. But the foundation on which all stand divides only into two parts: those who like slavery, and mean it shall last; those who hate it, and mean it shall die. In the boiling gulf goes on the perpetual conflict of acid and alkali; all these classes are but bubbles on the surface. The upper millstone is *right*, and the lower *wrong*. Between them, governments and parchments, parties and compromises, are being slowly ground to powder.

Broadly stated, the South plans a Southern Confederacy to uphold slavery, — the North clings to the Union to uphold trade and secure growth. Without the Union, Mr. Seward tells us we can neither be safe, rich, strong, nor happy. We used to think justice was before thrift, and nobleness better than happiness. I place no great reliance on that prudent patriotism which is the child of interest. The Tribune, unusually frank, pre-eminently honorable and lofty as has been its tone of late, still says, "Be it the business of the people everywhere to forget the negro, and remember only the country." [Applause.]

After drifting, a dreary night of thirty years, before the hurricane, our ship of state is going to pieces on the lee shore of slavery. Every one confesses that the poison of our body politic is slavery. European critics, in view of it, have pronounced the existence of the Union hitherto a "fortunate accident." Orators floated into fame on one inspired phrase, "irrepressible conflict." Jefferson died foreseeing that this was the rock on which we should split. Even Mr. Webster, speaking with bated breath, in the cold chill of 1850, still dared to be a statesman, and offered to meet the South on this question, suggesting a broad plan for the cure of our dread disease. But now, with the Union dropping asunder, with every brain and tongue active, we have yet to hear the first statesman-word, the first proposal to consider the fountain and origin of all our ills. We look in vain through Mr. Seward's speech for one hint or suggestion as to any method of dealing with our terrible hurt. Indeed, one of his terrors of disunion is, that it will give room for "an European, an uncompromising hostility to slavery." Such an hostility — the irrepressible conflict of right and wrong — William H. Seward, in 1861, pronounces "fearful"! To describe the great conflict of the age, the first of American statesmen, in the year of Garibaldi and Italy, can find no epithet but "fearful."

The servile silence of the 7th of March, 1850, is outdone, and to New York Massachusetts yields the post of infamy which her great Senator has hitherto filled. Yes, of all the doctors bending over the patient, not one dares to name his disease, except the Tribune, which advises him to forget it! Throughout half of the great cities of the North, every one who touches on it is mobbed into silence! This is, indeed, the saddest feature of our times.

Let us, then, who, unlike Mr. Seward, are not afraid to tell, even now, all and just what we wish, — let us look at the real nature of the crisis in which we stand. The Tribune says we should "forget the negro." It seems to me that all our past, all our present, and all our future command us at this moment to think of nothing but the negro. [Slight laughter derisively.]

Let me tell you why. Mr. Seward says, "The first object of every human society is safety"; I think the first duty of society is JUSTICE. Alexander Hamilton said, "Justice is the end of government. It is the end of civil society." If any other basis of safety or gain were honest, it would be impossible. "A prosperous iniquity," says Jeremy Taylor, "is the most unprofitable condition in the world." The nation which, in moments when great moral questions disturb its peace, consults first for its own *safety*, is atheist and coward, and there are three chances out of four that it will end by being knave. We were not sent into the world to plant cities, to make Unions or save them. Seeing that all men are born equal, our first civil duty is to see that our laws treat them so. The convulsion of this hour is the effort of the nation to do this, its duty, while politicians and parties strive to balk it of its purpose. The nation agonizes this hour to recognize man as man, forgetting color, condition, sex, and creed.

Our Revolution earned us only *independence*. Whatever our fathers meant, the chief lesson of that hour was that America belongs to Americans. That generation learned it thoroughly; the second inherited it as a prejudice; we, the third, have our bones and blood made of it. When thought passes through purpose into character, it becomes the unchangeable basis of national life. That Revolutionary lesson need never be learned again, and will never die out. Let a British fleet, with admirals of the blue and red, cover our Atlantic coast, and in ten days Massachusetts and Carolina will stand shoulder to shoulder; the only rivalry, who shall die nearest the foe. [Loud applause, with cries of "Good."]

That principle is all our Revolution directly taught us. Massachusetts was hide-bound in the aristocracy of classes for years after. The bar and the orthodox pulpit were our House of Lords. A Baptist clergyman was little better than a negro. The five points of Massachusetts decency were, to trace your lineage to the Mayflower, graduate at Harvard College, be a good lawyer or a member of an orthodox church,—either would answer [laughter],—pay your debts, and frighten your child to sleep by saying "Thomas Jefferson." Our theological aristocracy went down before the stalwart blows of Baptist, Unitarian, and Freethinker, — before Channing and Abner Kneeland. Virginia slaveholders, making theoretical democracy their passion, conquered the Federal Government, and emancipated the working-classes of New England. Bitter was the cup to honest Federalism and the Essex Junto. To-day, Massachusetts only holds to the lips of Carolina a beaker of the same beverage I know no man who has analyzed this passage in our history so well as Richard Hildreth. The last thirty years have been the flowering out of this lesson. The Democratic principle, crumbling classes into men, has been working down from pulpits and judges' seats, through shop-boards and shoe-benches, to Irish hodmen, and reached the negro at last. The long

toil of a century cries out, *Eureka!* — "I have found it!" — the diamond of an immortal soul and an equal manhood under a black skin as truly as under a white one. For this, Leggett labored and Lovejoy died. For this, the bravest soul of the century went up to God from a Virginia scaffold. [Hisses and applause.] For this, young men gave up their May of youth, and old men the honors and ease of age. It went through the land writing history afresh, setting up and pulling down parties, riving sects, mowing down colossal reputations, making us veil our faces in shame at the baseness of our youth's idols, sending bankrupt statesmen to dishonored graves.

We stand to-day just as Hancock and Adams and Jefferson stood when stamp-act and tea-tax, Patrick Henry's eloquence and the massacre of March 5th, Otis's blood and Bunker Hill, had borne them to July, 1776. Suppose at that moment John Adams had cried out, "Now let the people everywhere forget Independence, and remember only 'God save the King'!" [Laughter.] The toil of a whole generation — thirty years — has been spent in examining this question of the rights and place of the negro; the whole earnest thought of the nation given to it; old parties have been wrecked against it, new ones grown out of it; it stifles all other questions; the great interests of the nation necessarily suffer, men refusing to think of anything else but this; it struggles up through all compromises, asserting its right to be heard; no green withes of eloquence or cunning, trade, pulpit, Congress, or college, succeed in binding this Samson; the business of the seaboard begs it may be settled, no matter how; the whole South is determined to have it met, proclaiming that she does not secede because of personal liberty laws or a Republican President, but because of the state of *Northern feeling* of which these are *signs*. It is not Northern laws or officers they fear, but Northern *conscience*. Why, then, should not the North accept the issue, and try to settle the question forever? You may run the Missouri line to the Pacific, but Garrison still lives; and while he does, South Carolina hates and fears Massachusetts. [Applause.] No Congressional resolves can still our brains or stifle our hearts; till you do, the slaveholder feels that New England is his natural foe. There can therefore be no real peace till we settle the slave question. If thirty years of debate have not fitted us to meet it, when shall we be able?

But the most honest Republicans say a State has no right to secede; we will show first that we have a government, and then, not before, settle disputed questions. Suppose a State has no right to secede, of what consequence is that? A Union is made up of willing States, not of conquered provinces. There are some rights, quite perfect, yet wholly incapable of being enforced. A husband or wife who can only keep the other partner within the bond by locking the doors and standing armed before them, had better submit to peaceable separation. [Applause.] A firm where one partner refuses to act has a full right to his services, but how compel them? South Carolina may be punished for her fault in going out of the Union, but that does not keep her in it. Why not recognize soberly the nature and necessity of our position? Why not, like statesmen, remember that homogeneous nations like France tend to centralization; confederacies like ours tend inevitably to dismemberment? France is the slow, still deposit of ages on central granite; only the globe's convulsion can rive it! We are the rich mud of the Mississippi; every flood shifts it from one side to the other of the channel. Nations like Austria, victim states, held under the lock and key of despotism, — or like ourselves, a herd of States, hunting for their food together, — must expect that any quarrel may lead to disunion. Beside, *Inter arma, silent leges*, — armies care nothing for constables. This is not a case at law, but revolution.

Let us not, however, too anxiously grieve over the Union of 1787. Real Unions are not made, they grow. This was made, like an artificial waterfall or a Connecticut nutmeg. It was not an oak which to-day a tempest shatters. It was a wall hastily built, in hard times, of round boulders ; the cement has crumbled, and the smooth stones, obeying the law of gravity, tumble here and there. Why should we seek to stop them, merely to show that we have a right and can ? That were only a waste of means and temper. Let us build, like the Pyramids, a fabric which every natural law guarantees ; or, better still, *plant* a Union whose life survives the ages, and quietly gives birth to its successor.

Mr. Seward's last speech, which he confesses does not express his real convictions, denies every principle but one that he proclaimed in his campaign addresses ; that one — which, at Lansing, he expressly said "he was ashamed to confess" — that one is this : Everything is to be sacrificed to save the Union. I am not aware that, on any public occasion, varied and wide as have been his discussions and topics, he has ever named the truth or the virtue which he would not sacrifice to save the Union. For thirty years, there has been stormy and searching discussion of profound moral questions ; one, whom his friends call our only statesman, has spoken often on all ; yet he has never named the sin which he does not think would be a virtue, if it contributed to save the Union.

Remembering this element of his statesmanship, let us listen to the key-note of his late speech : "The first object of every human society is safety or security, for which, if need be, they will and they must sacrifice every other."

I will not stop to say that, even with his explanation,

his principle is equivocal, and, if unlimited, false; that, unqualified, it justifies every crime, and would have prevented every glory of history; that by it, James II. and Bonaparte were saints; under one sense, the Pilgrims were madmen, and under another, the Puritans did right to hang Quakers. But grant it. Suppose the Union means wealth, culture, happiness, and safety, man has no right to buy either by crime.

Many years ago, on the floor of Congress, Kentucky and Tennessee both confessed that "the dissolution of the Union was the dissolution of slavery." Last month, Senator Johnson of Tennessee said: "If I were an Abolitionist, and wanted to accomplish the abolition of slavery in the Southern States, the first step I would take would be to break the bonds of this Union. I believe the continuance of slavery depends on the preservation of this Union, and a compliance with all the guaranties of the Constitution." In September last (at La Crosse), Mr. Seward himself said, "What are they [the Southern States] in for but to have slavery saved for them by the Federal Union? Why would they go out, for they could not maintain and defend themselves against their own slaves?" In this last speech, he tells us it is the Union which restricts the opposition to slavery within narrow limits, and prevents it from being, like that of Europe, a "direct and uncompromising" demand for abolition.

Now, if the Union created for us a fresh Golconda every month, if it made every citizen wise as Solomon, blameless as St. John, and safe as an angel in the courts of Heaven, to cling to it would still be a damnable crime, hateful to God, while its cement was the blood of the negro, — while it, and it alone, made the crime of slaveholding possible in fifteen States.

Mr. Seward is a power in the state. It is worth while to understand his course. It cannot be caprice. His position decides that of millions. The instinct which leads him to take it shows his guess (and he rarely errs) what the majority intend. I reconcile thus the utter difference and opposition of his campaign speeches, and his last one. I think he went West, sore at the loss of the nomination, but with too much good sense, perhaps magnanimity, to act over again Webster's sullen part when Taylor stole his rights.

Still, Mr. Seward, though philosophic, though keen to analyze and unfold the theory of our politics, is not cunning in plans. He is only the hand and tongue; his brain lives in private life on the Hudson River side. Acting under that guidance, he thought Mr. Lincoln not likely to go beyond, even if he were able to keep, the whole Chicago platform. Accordingly, he said: "I will give free rein to my natural feelings and real convictions, till these Abolitionists of the Republican ranks shall cry, 'O what a mistake! We ought to have nominated Seward; another time we will not be balked.'" Hence the hot eloquence and fearless tone of those prairie speeches. He returns to Washington, finds Mr. Lincoln sturdily insisting that his honor is pledged to keep in office every promise made in the platform. Then Mr. Seward shifts his course, saying: "Since my abolitionism cannot take the wind from my rival's sails, I 'll get credit as a Conservative. Accepting the premiership, I will forestall public opinion, and do all possible to bind the coming administration to a policy which I originate." He offers to postpone the whole Chicago platform, in order to save the Union, — though last October, at Chicago, he told us postponement never settles anything, whether it is a lawsuit or a national question; better be beat and try again than postpone.

This speech of Mr. Seward I regard as a declaration of war against the avowed policy of the incoming President. If Lincoln were an Andrew Jackson, as his friends aver, he would dismiss Mr. Seward from his Cabinet. The incoming administration, if honest and firm, has two enemies to fight, — Mr. Seward and the South.

His power is large. Already he has swept our Adams into the vortex, making him offer to sacrifice the whole Republican platform, though, as events have turned, he has sacrificed only his own personal honor. Fifteen years ago, John Quincy Adams prophesied that the Union would not last twenty years. He little thought that disunion, when it came, would swallow his son's honor in its gulf.*

At such hours, New England Senators and Representatives have, from the very idea of their ultraism, little or no direct weight in Congress. But while New England is the brain of the Union, and therefore foreshadows what will be public opinion in the plastic West five years hence, it is of momentous consequence that the people here should make their real feelings known; that the pulpit and press should sound the bugle-note of utter defiance to slavery itself, — Union or no Union, Constitution or no Constitution, freedom for every man between the oceans, and from the hot Gulf to the frozen pole! You may as well dam up Niagara with bulrushes as bind our antislavery purpose with Congressional compromise. The South knows it. While she holds out her hand for Seward's offer, she keeps her eye fixed on us, to see what we think. Let her see that we laugh it to scorn. Sacrifice anything to keep the slaveholding States in the Union? God forbid! we will rather build a bridge of gold, and pay their toll over it, — accompany them out with glad noise of trumpets, and "speed the parting guest." Let them not "stand on the order of their going, but go at once"! Let them take the forts, empty our arsenals and

* Since this was said, Mr. Adams has had his reward, — winning high office by treachery to his party, as his father did before, and as his grandfather tried to do and failed.

sub-treasuries, and we will lend them, beside, jewels of gold and jewels of silver, and Egypt be glad when they are departed. [Laughter and applause.]

But let the world distinctly understand why they go, — to save slavery; and why we rejoice in their departure, — because we know their declaration of independence is the jubilee of the slave. The eyes of the world are fixed on us as the great example of self-government. When this Union goes to pieces, it is a shock to the hopes of the struggling millions of Europe. All lies bear bitter fruit. To-day is the inevitable fruit of our fathers' faithless compromise in 1787. For the sake of the future, in freedom's name, let thinking Europe understand clearly why we sever. They saw Mr. Seward paint, at Chicago, our utter demoralization, Church and State, government and people, all classes, educated and uneducated, — all brought by the Slave Power, he said, to think slavery a blessing, and do anything to save it. So utter did he consider this demoralization, that he despaired of native Americans, and trusted to the hunted patriots and the refuse of Europe, which the emigrant-trains bore by his house, for the salvation of the valley of the Mississippi. To-day, they see that very man kneeling to that Slave Power, and begging her to take all, but only consent to grant him such a Union, — Union with such a power! How, then, shall Kossuth answer, when Austria laughs him to scorn? Shall Europe see the slaveholder kick the reluctant and kneeling North out of such a Union? How, then, shall Garibaldi dare look in the face of Napoleon? If, therefore, it were only to honor self-government, to prove that it educates men, not pedlers and cowards, let us proclaim our faith that honest labor can stand alone; its own right hand amply able to earn its bread and defend its rights [applause]; and, if it were not so, our readiness at any cost to welcome disunion when it comes bringing freedom to four million of hapless slaves! [Applause.] What a sad comment on free institutions, that they have produced a South of tyrants, and a North of cowards; a South, ready to face any peril to save slavery, and a North unwilling to risk a dollar to serve freedom?

Why do I set so little value on the Union? Because I consider it a failure; certainly, so far as slavery is concerned, it is a failure. If you doubt me, look at the picture of its effects which Mr. Seward painted at Chicago.

Look at our history. Under it, 700,000 slaves have increased to 4,000,000. We have paid $800,000,000 directly to the support of slavery. This secession will cost the Union and business $200,000,000 more. The loss which this disturbing force has brought to our trade and industry, within sixty years, it would be safe to call $500,000,000. Is the Union a pecuniary success? Under it, Slavery has been strong enough to rule the nation for sixty years, and now breaks it to pieces because she can rule no longer. Under it, public morals have been so lowered, that while, at its outset, nine men out of ten were proud to be called Abolitionists, now nine out of ten would deem it not only an insult, but a pecuniary injury, to be charged with being so. Ever since it existed, its friends have confessed that, to save the Union, it was necessary and proper to crush free speech. Witness John Adams's sedition laws. Witness mobs of well-dressed merchants in every Northern city now. Witness one half of the Republican party lamenting free speech, this hour, throughout the North.

Mr. Seward confessed, at Chicago, that neither free speech nor free suffrage existed in one half of the States. No Northern man can trade, live, or talk there. For twenty years, men have been mobbed, robbed, lynched, hung, and burned there, solely for loving liberty; and while the Federal Government never lifted a finger to prevent or punish it, the very States whose citizens have been outraged have been too indifferent even to remonstrate. Massachusetts, who once remonstrated, saw her own agent mobbed out of Charleston with her full consent.

Before the Union existed, Washington and Jefferson uttered the boldest antislavery opinions ; to-day they would be lynched in their own homes ; and their sentiments have been mobbed this very year in every great city of the North. The Fugitive Slave Bill could never have been passed nor executed in the days of Jay. Now no man who hopes for office dares to insist that it is unconstitutional. Slavery has turned our churches of Christ to churches of commerce.

John Quincy Adams, the child of our earlier civilization, said the Union was worthless, weighed against that liberty it was meant to secure. Mr. Seward, the child of the Union, says there are few men, and there ought to be few, who would not prefer saving the Union to securing freedom ; and standing to-day at the head of nineteen millions of freemen, he confesses he does not deem it prudent to express his "most cherished convictions" on this subject,* while every honest man fears, and three fourths of Mr. Seward's followers hope, that the North, in this conflict of right and wrong, will, spite of Horace Greeley's warning, "Love liberty less than profit, dethrone conscience, and set up commerce in its stead." You know it. A Union

* Mr. Seward said, at St. Paul, last September : "I do not believe there has been one day, since 1787, until now, when slavery had any power in this government, except what it derived from buying up men of weak virtue, no principle, and great cupidity, and terrifying men of weak nerve, in the Free States. . . . . . Fellow-citizens, either in one way or the other, whether you agree with me in attributing it to the interposition of Divine Providence or not, this battle has been fought, this victory has been won. Slavery to-day is, for the first time, not only powerless, but without influence in the American republic. . . . . . For the first time in the history of the republic, the

whose despotism is so cruel and searching that one half our lawyers and one half our merchants stifle conscience for bread, — in the name of Martin Luther and John Milton, of Algernon Sidney and Henry Vane, of John Jay and Samuel Adams, I declare such a Union a failure.

It is for the chance of saving such a Union that Mr. Seward and Mr. Adams break in Washington all the promises of the canvass, and countenance measures which stifle the conscience and confuse the moral sense of the North. Say not that my criticism is harsh. I know their pretence. It is, we must conciliate, compromise, postpone, practise finesse, make promises or break them, do anything, to gain time and concentrate the North against slavery. Our fathers tried that policy in 1787. That they miserably failed is proved by a Capitol filled with knaves and traitors, yet able to awe and ruin honest men. It was tried in 1821, and failed. It was tried in 1850, and failed. Who is audacious enough to ask another trial? The Republicans say: "Conciliate, use soft language, organize — behind the door — bands of volunteers; and when we have saved Washington, we may dare speak out." That is good policy for midnight conspirators. But if we are a government, if we are a nation, we should say: "Tell the truth! If coercion is our policy, tell the truth. Call for volunteers in every State, and vindicate the honor of the nation in the light of the sun!" [Applause.]

Slave Power has not even the power to terrify or alarm the freeman so as to make him submit, and scheme, and coincide, and compromise. It rails now with a feeble voice, as it thundered in our ears for twenty or thirty years past. With a feeble and muttering voice, they cry out that they will tear the Union to pieces. Who's afraid? They complain that, if we will not surrender our principles, and our system, and our right — being a majority — to rule, and if we will not accept their system and such rules as they will give us, they will go out of the Union. Who's afraid? Nobody's afraid nobody can be bought." (Yet now Mr. Seward himself trembles!)

The cunning which equivocates to-day, in order to secure a peaceful inauguration on the 4th of March, will yield up all its principles before the 1st of July. Beside, when opiate speeches have dulled the Northern conscience, and kneeling speeches have let down its courage, who can be sure that even Seward's voice, if he retain the wish, can conjure up again such a North as stands face to face with Southern arrogance to-day?

The Union, then, is a failure. What harm can come from disunion, and what good?

The seceding States will form a Southern Confederacy. We may judge of its future from the history of Mexico. The Gulf States intend to reopen the slave-trade. If Kentucky and Tennessee, Virginia, Maryland, and North Carolina secede, the opening of that trade will ruin them, and they will gravitate to us, free. Louisiana cannot secede, except on paper; the omnipotent West needs her territory, as the mouth of its river. She must stay with us as a State or a conquered province, and may have her choice. [Laughter.] Beside, she stands on sugar, and free-trade bankrupts her. Consider the rest of the Slave States as one power, how can it harm us? Let us see the ground of Mr. Seward's fears. Will it increase our expenses or lessen our receipts? No; every one of those States costs the Union more than it contributes to it. Can it harm us by attacks? States without commerce or manufactures, and with an army of four millions of natural enemies encamped among them, have given bonds to keep the peace. Will they leave us so small and weak by going that we cannot stand alone? Let us see. There is no reason to suppose that the Free States, except California, will not cling together. *Idem velle, idem nolle*, — to like and dislike the same things, says the Latin proverb, is friendship. When a great number of persons agree in a great number of things, that insures a union; that is not the case with the North and South, therefore we separate; that is the case with the whole North, therefore we shall remain united. How strong shall we be? Our territory will be twice as large as Austria, three times as large as France, four times as large as Spain, six times as large as Italy, seven times as large as Great Britain. Those nations have proved, for a considerable period, that they had sufficient land to stand on. Our population will be about nineteen millions, — more than the Union had in 1840. I do not think we were much afraid of anybody in 1840. Our blood is largely Yankee, a race that saved Carolina from her own Tories, in the Revolution. [Laughter.] Without that hinderance, we could fight now, certainly, as well as we did then; and then, with three million men only, we measured swords with the ablest nation of Europe, and conquered. I think, therefore, we have no reason to be very nervously anxious now. Indeed, Mr. Seward's picture of the desolation and military weakness of the divided States, if intended for the North, is the emptiest lie in his speech. I said *lie;* I meant it. I will tell you why. Because one William H. Seward said, last fall, at Lansing: "We are maintaining a standing army at the heavy cost of one thousand dollars per man, and a standing navy, — for what? to protect Michigan or Massachusetts, New York or Ohio? *No; there is not a nation on the face of the earth which would dare to attack these Free States, or any of them, if they were even disunited.* We are doing it in order that slaves may not escape from Slave States into the Free, and to secure those States from domestic insurrection; and because, if we provoke a foreign foe, slavery cries out that it is in danger." Surely the speaker of those words has no right to deny that our expenses and danger will be less, and our power to meet both greater, when the Slave States are gone.

Indeed, everybody knows this. And this trembling

dread of losing the Union, which so frightens the people that, in view of it, Mr. Seward, as a practical man, dares not now tell, as he says, what he really thinks and wishes, is the child of his and Webster's insincere idolatry of the Union. To serve party and personal ambition, they made a god of the Union; and to-day their invention returns to plague the inventors. They made the people slaves to a falsehood; and that same deluded people have turned their fetters into gags for Mr. Seward's lips. Thank God for the retribution!

But the Union created commerce; disunion will kill it.

The Union the mother of commerce? I doubt it. I question whether the genius and energy of the Yankee race are not the parent of commerce and the fountain of wealth, much more than the Union. That race, in Holland, first created a country, and then, standing on piles, called modern commerce into being. That race, in England, with territory just wide enough to keep its eastern and western harbors apart, monopolized, for centuries, the trade of the world, and annexed continents only as coffers wherein to garner its wealth. Who shall say that the same blood, with only New England for its anchorage, could not drag the wealth of the West into its harbors? Who shall say that the fertile lands of Virginia and the Mississippi enrich us because they will to do so, and not because they are compelled? As long as New England is made of granite, and the nerves of her sons of steel, she will be, as she always has been, the brain of North America, united or disunited; and harnessing the elements, steam and lightning, to her car of conquest, she will double the worth of every prairie acre by her skill, cover ocean with her canvas, and gather the wealth of the Western hemisphere into her harbors.

Despite, then, of Seward's foreboding, our confederacy will be strong, safe, and rich. Honest it will be, and

therefore happy. Its nobleness will be, that, laughing at prophets, and scorning chances, it has taken the prop from the slave system, and in one night the whole fabric will tumble to pieces. Disunion is abolition! That is all the value disunion has for me. I care little for forms of government or extent of territory; whether ten States or thirty make up the Union. No foreign state dare touch us, united or disunited. It matters not to me whether Massachusetts is worth one thousand millions, as now, or two thousand millions, as she might be, if she had no Carolina to feed, protect, and carry the mails for. The music of disunion to me is, that at its touch the slave breaks into voice, shouting his jubilee.

What supports slavery? Northern bayonets, calming the masters' fears. Mr. Seward's words, which I have just quoted, tell you what he thinks the sole use of our army and navy. Disunion leaves God's natural laws to work their good results. God gives every animal means of self-protection. Under God's law, insurrection is the tyrant's check. Let us stand out of the path, and allow the Divine law to have free course.

Next, Northern opinion is the opiate of Southern conscience. Disunion changes that. Public opinion forms governments, and again governments react to mould opinion. Here is a government just as much permeated by slavery as China or Japan is with idolatry.

The Republican party take possession of this government. How are they to undermine the Slave Power? That power is composed, 1st, of the inevitable influence of wealth, $2,000,000,000, — the worth of the slaves in the Union, — so much capital drawing to it the sympathy of all other capital; 2d, of the artificial aristocracy created by the three-fifths slave basis of the Constitution; 3d, by the potent and baleful prejudice of color.

The aristocracy of the Constitution! Where have you

seen an aristocracy with half its power? You may take a small town here in New England, with a busy, active population of 2,500, and three or four such men as Governor Aikin, of South Carolina, riding leisurely to the polls, and throwing in their visiting-cards for ballots, will blot out the entire influence of that New England town in the Federal Government. That is your Republicanism! Then, when you add to that the element of prejudice, which is concentrated in the epithet that spells negro with two "gg's," you make the three-strand cable of the Slave Power, — the prejudice of race, the omnipotence of money, and the almost irresistible power of aristocracy. That is the Slave Power.

How is Mr. Lincoln to undermine it while in the Union? Certainly, by turning every atom of patronage and pecuniary profit in the keeping of the Federal Government to the support of freedom. You know the contrary policy has been always acted upon ever since Washington, and been openly avowed ever since Fillmore. No man was to receive any office who was not sound on the slavery question. You remember the debate in the Senate, when that was distinctly avowed to be the policy of Mr. Fillmore. You remember Mr. Clay letting it drop out accidentally, in debate, that the slaveholders had always closely watched the Cabinet, and kept a majority there, in order to preserve the ascendency of slavery. This is the policy which, in the course of fifty years, has built up the Slave Power. Now, how is the Republican party ever to beat that power down? By reversing that policy, in favor of freedom. Cassius Clay said to me, five years ago: "If you will allow me to have the patronage of this government five years, and exercise it remorselessly, down to New Orleans; never permit any one but an avowed Abolitionist to hold office under the Federal Government, I will revolutionize the Slave States themselves in two administrations." That is a scheme of efficient politics. But the Republican party has never yet professed any such policy.

Mr. Greeley, on the contrary, avowed, in the Tribune, that he had often voted for a slaveholder willingly, and he never expected the time would come when he should lay down the principle of refusing to vote for a slaveholder to office; and that sentiment has not only been reiterated by others of the Republican party, but has never been disavowed by any one. But suppose you could develop politics up to this idea, that the whole patronage of the government should be turned in favor of abolition; it would take two or three generations to overthrow what the Slave Power has done in sixty years, with the strength of aristocracy and the strength of prejudice on its side. With only the patronage of the government in its control, the Republican party must work slowly to regenerate the government against those two elements in opposition, when, with them in its favor, the Slave Power has been some sixty years in bringing about such a result as we see around us. To reverse this, and work only with the patronage of the government, it would take you long to effect the cure. In my soul, I believe that a dissolution of the Union, sure to result speedily in the abolition of slavery, would be a lesser evil than the slow, faltering, diseased, gradual dying-out of slavery, constantly poisoning us with the festering remains of this corrupt political, social, and literary state. I believe a sudden, conclusive, definite disunion, resulting in the abolition of slavery, in the disruption of the Northern mind from all connection with it, all vassalage to it, *immediately*, would be a better, healthier, and more wholesome cure, than to let the Republican party exert this gradual influence through the power of the government for thirty or sixty years.

We are seeking the best way to get rid of a great

national evil. Mr. Seward's way is to take the Union as a "fixed fact," and then educate politics up to a certain level. In that way we have to live, like Sinbad, with Cushing and Hillard and Hallett and O'Connor and Douglas, and men like them, on our shoulders, for the next thirty or forty years; with the Deweys and President Lords, and all that class of men, — and all this timid servility of the press, all this lack of virtue and manhood, all this corruption of the pulpit, all this fossil hunkerism, all this selling of the soul for a mess of pottage, is to linger, working in the body politic for thirty or forty years, and we are gradually to eliminate the disease! What an awful future! What a miserable chronic disease! What a wreck of a noble nation the American Republic is to be for fifty years!

And why? Only to save a piece of parchment that Elbridge Gerry had instinct enough to think did not deserve saving, as long ago as 1789! Mr. Seward would leave New York united to New Orleans, with the hope (sure to be balked) of getting freer and freer from year to year. I want to place her, at once, in the same relation towards New Orleans that she bears to Liverpool. You can do it, the moment you break the political tie. What will that do? I will tell you. The New York pulpit is to-day one end of a magnetic telegraph, of which the New Orleans cotton-market is the other. The New York stock-market is one end of the magnetic telegraph, and the Charleston Mercury is the other. New York statesmanship! Why, even in the lips of Seward, it is sealed, or half sealed, by considerations which take their rise in the canebrakes and cotton-fields of fifteen States. Break up this Union, and the ideas of South Carolina will have no more influence on Seward than those of Palmerston. The wishes of New Orleans would have no more influence on Chief Justice Bigelow than the wishes of London. The threats of Davis, Toombs, and Keitt will have no more influence on the Tribune than the thunders of the London Times or the hopes of the Chartists. Our Bancrofts will no longer write history with one eye fixed on Democratic success, nor our Websters invent "laws of God" to please Mr. Senator Douglas. We shall have as close connection, as much commerce; we shall still have a common language, a common faith, and common race, the same common social life; we shall intermarry just the same; we shall have steamers running just as often and just as rapidly as now. But what cares Dr. Dewey for the opinion of Liverpool? Nothing! What cares he for the opinion of Washington? Everything! Break the link, and New York springs up like the fountain relieved from a mountain load, and assumes her place among decent cities. I mean no special praise of the English courts, pulpit, or press by these comparisons; my only wish is to show that, however close the commercial relations might continue to be between North and South, and in spite of that common faith and common tongue and common history, which would continue to hold these thirty States together, still, as in the case of this country and England, wedded still by those ties, the mere sundering of a political union would leave each half free, as the disunion of 1776 did, from a large share of the corrupt influence of the other.

That is what I mean by disunion. I mean to take Massachusetts, and leave her exactly as she is, commercially. She shall manufacture for the South just as Lancashire does. I know what an influence the South has on the manufacturers and clergy of England;—that is inevitable, in the nature of things. We have only human nature to work with, and we cannot raise it up to the level of angels. We shall never get beyond the sphere of human selfishness, but we can lift this human nature up to a higher level, if we can but remove the weight of that political relation which now rests upon it. What I would do with Massachusetts is this: I would make her, in relation to South Carolina, just what England is. I would that I could float her off, and anchor her in mid-ocean!

Severed from us, South Carolina must have a government. You see now a reign of terror, — threats to raise means. That can only last a day. Some system must give support to a government. It is an expensive luxury. You must lay taxes to support it. Where will you levy your taxes? They must rest on productions. Productions are the result of skilled labor. You must educate your laborer, if you would have the means for carrying on a government. Despotisms are cheap; free governments are a dear luxury, — the machinery is complicated and expensive. If the South wants a theoretical republic, she must pay for it, — she must have a basis for taxation. How will she pay for it? Why, Massachusetts, with a million workmen, — men, women, and children, — the little feet that can just toddle bringing chips from the wood-pile, — Massachusetts only pays her own board and lodging, and lays by about four per cent a year. And South Carolina, with one half idlers, and the other half slaves, — a slave doing only half the work of a freeman, — only one quarter of the population actually at work, — how much do you suppose she lays up? Lays up a loss! By all the laws of political economy, she lays up bankruptcy; of course she does! Put her out, and let her see how sheltered she has been from the laws of trade by the Union! The free labor of the North pays her plantation patrol; we pay for her government, we pay for her postage, and for everything else. Launch her out, and let her see if she can make the year's ends meet! And when she tries, she must educate her labor in order to get the basis for taxation. Educate slaves! Make a locomotive with its furnaces of open wire-work, fill them with anthracite coal, and when you have raised it to white heat, mount and drive it through a powder-magazine, and you are safe, compared with a slaveholding community educating its slaves. But South Carolina must do it, in order to get the basis for taxation to support an independent government. The moment she does it, she removes the safeguard of slavery. What is the contest in Virginia now? Between the men who want to make their slaves mechanics, for the increased wages it will secure, and the men who oppose, for fear of the influence it will have on the general security of slave property and white throats. Just that dispute will go on, wherever the Union is dissolved. Slavery comes to an end by the laws of trade. Hang up your Sharpe's rifle, my valorous friend! The slave does not ask the help of your musket. He only says, like old Diogenes to Alexander, "Stand out of my light!" Just take your awkward proportions, you Yankee Democrat and Republican, out of the light and heat of God's laws of political economy, and they will melt the slave's chains away!

Indeed, I much doubt whether the South can maintain her cotton culture at all, as a separate, slaveholding government. Cotton is only an annual in the United States. In St. Domingo and the tropics it is a tree lasting from five to twenty years. Within the Union it is, then, strictly speaking, a forced product; or at least it touches the highest northern belt of possible culture, only possible there under very favorable circumstances. We all know how hard and keen is the competition of this generation; men clutching bread only by restless hands and brains. Expose now our cotton to the full competition of India, Africa, and the tropics; burden it by taxes with the full cost of a slaveholding government, necessarily an expensive one, — a tax it has never yet felt, having shirked it on to the North; quicken other cotton-fields into greater activity by the unwillingness of France and England to trust their supply to States convulsed by political quarrels; — and then see if, in such circumstances, the price of cotton in the markets of the world will not rule so low, that to raise it by slovenly slave-culture will not be utter loss, — so utter as to drive it wholly from our States, at least while they remain Slave States.

Indeed, the Gulf States are essentially in a feudal condition, an aristocracy resting on slaves, — no middle class. To sustain government on the costly model of our age necessitates a middle class of trading, manufacturing energy. The merchant of the nineteenth century spurns to be a subordinate. The introduction of such a class will create in the Gulf States that very irrepressible conflict which they leave us to avoid, — which, alive now in the Border States, makes these unwilling to secede, — which once created will soon undermine the aristocracy of the Gulf States and bring them back to us free.

Take your distorted Union, your nightmare monster, out of the light and range of these laws of trade and competition; then, without any sacrifice on your part, slavery will go to pieces! God made it a law of his universe, that villany should always be loss; and if you will only not attempt, with your puny efforts, to stand betwixt the inevitable laws of God's kingdom, as you are doing to-day, and have done for sixty years, by the vigor that the industry of sixteen States has been able to infuse into the sluggish veins of the South, slavery will drop to pieces by the very influence of the competition of the nineteenth century. That is what we mean by Disunion!

That is my *coercion!* Northern pulpits cannonading the Southern conscience; Northern competition emptying its pockets; educated slaves awaking its fears; civilization and Christianity beckoning the South into their sisterhood. Soon every breeze that sweeps over Carolina will bring to our ears the music of repentance, and even she will carve on her Palmetto, "We hold this truth to be self-evident, — that all men are created equal."

All hail, then, Disunion! "Beautiful on the mountains are the feet of Him that bringeth good tidings, that publisheth peace, that saith unto Zion, Thy God reigneth." The sods of Bunker Hill shall be greener, now that their great purpose is accomplished. Sleep in peace, martyr of Harper's Ferry! — your life was not given in vain. Rejoice, spirits of Fayette and Kosciusko! — the only stain upon your swords is passing away. Soon, throughout all America, there shall be neither power nor wish to hold a slave.

PROGRESS.*

"And Jacob said unto Pharaoh, The days of the years of my pilgrimage are an hundred and thirty years: few and evil have the days of the years of my life been, and have not attained unto the days of the years of the life of my fathers in the days of their pilgrimage."

THUS spoke a prince who had won from his elder brother both birthright and blessing; who had seen "the angels of God ascending and descending"; was able to say, "With my staff I passed over this Jordan, and now I am become two bands"; who had seen God face to face, and still lived; to whom was pledged the Divine promise, "I will make of thee a great nation, in thy seed shall all the families of the earth be blessed"; whose ears had just drunk in the glad tidings of his favorite son, "Joseph is yet alive; he is governor over all the land of Egypt." Thus timid and disconsolate gray hairs bewail their own times. To most men, the golden age is one long past.

But Nature is ever growing. Science tells us every change is improvement. This globe, once a mass of molten granite, now blooms almost a paradise. So in man's life and history. One may not see it in his own short day. You must stand afar off to judge St. Peter's. The shadow on the dial seems motionless, but it touches

* Address delivered before the Twenty-eighth Congregational Society in Music Hall, Boston, Sunday forenoon, February 17, 1861: the mob, as before, filling many parts of the Hall and the avenues leading to it.

noon at last. Place the ages side by side, and see how they differ. Three quarters of the early kings of France died poor and in prison, by the dagger or poison of their rivals. The Bonapartes stole large fortunes and half the thrones of Europe, yet all died natural deaths in their beds, and though discrowned, kept their enormous wealth.

When the English marched from Boston to Concord, they fired into half the Whig dwellings they passed. When Lane crossed Kansas, pursuing Missouri ruffians, he sent men ahead to put a guard at every border-ruffian's door, to save inmate and goods from harm. When Goldsmith reminded England that "a heart buried in a dungeon is as precious as that seated on a throne," there were one hundred and sixty-nine crimes punished with death. Now not only England, but every land governed by the English race, is marked by the mildness of its penal code, only one, two, or three classes of offenders being now murdered by law.

It is not yet fifteen years since the first Woman's Rights Convention was held. The first call for one in Massachusetts, a dozen years ago, bore a name heard often in manful protest against popular sins, — that of Waldo Emerson. But in that short fifteen years, a dozen States have changed their laws. One New York statute, a year old, securing to married women control of their wages, will do more to save New York City from being grog-shop and brothel than a thousand pulpits could do. When Kansas went to Topeka to frame a Constitution, one third of the Convention were in favor of giving women the right to vote. Truly, the day breaks. If time served, I could find a score of familiar instances. It is enough to state the general principle, that civilization produces wants. Wants awaken intellect. To gratify them disciplines intellect. The keener the want, the lustier the growth. The power to use new truths in science, new ideas in morals or art, obliterates rank, and makes the lowest man useful or necessary to the state. Popes and kings no longer mark the ages; but Luther and Raphael, Fulton and Faust, Howard and Rousseau. A Massachusetts mechanic, Eli Whitney, made cotton king; a Massachusetts printer, William Lloyd Garrison, has undermined its throne. Thus civilization insures equality. Types are the fathers of democrats.

It is not always, however, ideas or moral principles that push the world forward. Selfish interests play a large part in the work. Our Revolution of 1776 succeeded because trade and wealth joined hands with principle and enthusiasm, — a union rare in the history of revolutions. Northern merchants fretted at England's refusal to allow them direct trade with Holland and the West Indies. Virginia planters, heavily mortgaged, welcomed anything which would postpone payment of their debts, — a motive that doubtless avails largely among Secessionists now. So merchant and planter joined heartily with hot-headed Sam Adams, and reckless Joseph Warren, penniless John Adams, that brilliant adventurer Alexander Hamilton, and that young scapegrace Aaron Burr, to get independence. [Laughter.] To merchant, independence meant only direct trade, — to planter, cheating his creditors.

Present conflict of interests is another instrument of progress. Religious persecution planted these States; commercial persecution brought about the Revolution; John Bull's perseverance in a seven-years war fused us into one nation; his narrow and ill-tempered effort to govern us by stealth, even after the peace of 1783, drove us to the Constitution of 1789.

I think it was Coleridge who said, if he were a clergyman in Cornwall, he should preach fifty-two sermons a year against wreckers. In the same spirit, I shall find the best illustration of our progress in the history of the slave question.

Some men sit sad and trembling for the future, because the knell of this Union has sounded. But the heavens are almost all bright; and if some sable clouds linger on the horizon, they have turned their silver linings almost wholly to our sight. Every man who possesses his soul in patience sees that disunion is gain, disunion is *peace*, disunion is virtue.

Thomas Jefferson said: "It is unfortunate that the efforts of mankind to recover the freedom of which they have been deprived should be accompanied with violence, with errors, and even with crime. But while we weep over the means, we must pray for the end."

We may see our future in the glass of our past history. The whole connection of Massachusetts Colony with England was as much disgrace as honor to both sides. On the part of England, it was an attempt to stretch principles which were common sense and justice applied to an island, but absurd and tyrannical applied across the ocean. It was power without right, masked in form. On the side of the Colony, it was petty shifts, quibbles, equivocations, cunning dodges, white lies, ever the resource of weakness. While England was bulldog, Massachusetts was fox. Whoever cannot take his right openly by force, steals what he can by fraud. The Greek slave was a liar, as all slaves are. Tocqueville says, "Men are not corrupted by the exercise of power, nor debased by submission; but by the exercise of power they think illegal, and submission to a rule they consider oppressive." That sentence is a key to our whole colonial history. When we grew strong enough to dare to be frank, we broke with England. Timid men wept; but now we see how such disunion was gain, peace, and virtue. Indeed, seeming disunion was real union. We were then two snarling hounds, leashed together; we are now one in a true marriage, one in blood, trade, thought, religion, history, in mutual love and

respect; where one then filched silver from the other, each now pours gold into the other's lap; our only rivalry, which shall do most honor to the blood of Shakespeare and Milton, of Franklin and Kane.

In that glass we see the story of North and South since 1787, and I doubt not for all coming time. The people of the States between the Gulf and the great Lakes, yes, between the Gulf and the Pole, are essentially one. We are one in blood, trade, thought, religion, history; nothing can long divide us. If we had let our Constitution grow, as the English did, as oaks do, we had never passed through such scenes as the present. The only thing that divides us now, is the artificial attempt in 1787, to force us into an unripe union. Some lawyers got together and wrote out a constitution. The people and great interests of the land, wealth, thought, fashion, and creed, immediately laid it upon the shelf, and proceeded to *grow* one for themselves. The treaty power sufficed to annex a continent, and change the whole nature of the government. The war power builds railroads to the Pacific. Right to regulate commerce builds observatories and dredges out lakes. Right to tax protects manufactures; and had we wanted a king, some ingenious Yankee would have found the right to have one clearly stated in the provision for a well-regulated militia. [Laughter.] All that is valuable in the United States Constitution is a thousand years old. What is good is not new, and what is new is not good. That vaunted statesmanship which concocts constitutions never has amounted to anything. The English Constitution, always found equal to any crisis, is an old mansion, often repaired, with quaint additions, and seven gables, each of different pattern. Our Constitution is a new clapboard house, so square and sharp it almost cuts you to look at it, staring with white paint and green blinds, as if dropped in the landscape, or come out to spend an afternoon. [Laughter.]

The trouble now is, that, in regard to the most turbulent question of the age, our politicians and a knot of privileged slaveholders are trying to keep the people inside of this parchment band. Like Lycurgus, they would mould the people to fit the Constitution, instead of cutting the Constitution to fit the people. Goethe said, "If you plant an oak in a flower-vase, one of two things will happen, — the oak will die, or the vase break." Our acorn swelled; the tiny leaves showed themselves under the calm eye of Washington, and he laid down in hope. By and by the roots enlarged, and men trembled. Of late, Webster and Clay, Everett and Botts, Seward and Adams, have been anxiously clasping the vase, but the roots have burst abroad at last, and the porcelain is in pieces. [Sensation.] All ye who love oaks, thank God for so much! That Union of 1787 was one of fear; we were driven into it by poverty and the commercial hostility of England. As cold masses up all things, — sticks, earth, stones, and water into dirty ice, — heat first makes separation, and then unites those of the same nature. The heat of sixty years' agitation has severed the heterogeneous mass; wait awhile, it will fuse together all that is really one.

Let me show you why I think the present so bright, and why I believe that disunion is gain, peace, and honor.

Why is the present hour sunshine? Because, for the first time in our history, we have a North. That event which Mr. Webster anticipated and prophesied has come to pass. In a real, true sense, we have a North. By which I do not mean that the North rules; though, politically speaking, the crowned and sceptred North does, indeed, take her seat in that council where she has thus far been only a tool. But I mean that freemen, honest labor, makes itself heard in our State. The North ceases to be fox or spaniel, and puts on the lion. She asserts and claims. She no longer begs, cheats, or buys.

Understand me. In 1787, slave property, worth, perhaps, two hundred million of dollars, strengthened by the sympathy of all other capital, was a mighty power. It was the Rothschild of the state. The Constitution, by its *three-fifths slave basis*, made slaveholders an order of nobles. It was the house of Hapsburg joining hands with the house of Rothschild. Prejudice of race was the third strand of the cable, bitter and potent as Catholic ever bore Huguenot, or Hungary ever spit on Moslem. This fearful trinity won to its side that mysterious omnipotence called *Fashion*, — a power which, without concerted action, without either thought, law, or religion on its side, seems stronger than all of them, and fears no foe but wealth. Such was slavery. In its presence the North always knelt and whispered. When slavery could not bully, it bubbled its victim. In the convention that framed the Constitution, Massachusetts men said, as Charles Francis Adams says now, "What matters a pitiful three-fifths slave basis, and guaranty against insurrection, to an institution on its death-bed, — gasping for its last breath? It may *conciliate*, — is only a shadow, — nothing more, — why stand on words? So they shut their eyes, as he does, on realities, and chopped excellent logic on forms.

But at that moment, the Devil hovered over Charleston, with a handful of cotton-seed. [Applause.] Dropped into sea-island soil, and touched by the magic of Massachusetts brains, it poisoned the atmosphere of thirty States. That cotton fibre was a rod of empire such as Cæsar never wielded. It fattened into obedience pulpit and rostrum, court, market-place, and college, and leashed New York and Chicago to its chair of state. Beware, Mr. Adams, "he needs a long spoon who sups with the Devil." In the kaleidoscope of the future, no statesman eye can foresee the forms. God gives manhood but one clew to success, — utter and exact justice: that he guarantees shall be always expediency. Deviate one hair's-breadth, — grant but a dozen slaves, — only the tiniest seed of concession, — you know not how "many and tall branches of mischief shall grow therefrom." That handful of cotton-seed has perpetuated a system which, as Emerson says, "impoverishes the soil, depopulates the country, demoralizes the master, curses the victim, enrages the bystander, poisons the atmosphere, and hinders civilization."

I need not go over the subsequent compromises in detail. They are always of the same kind: mere words, Northern men assured us, — barren concessions. "Physical geography and Asiatic scenery" hindered any harm. But the South was always specially anxious to have these barren "words," and marvellously glad when she got them. Northern politicians, in each case, were either bullied or cheated, or feigned to be bullied, as they are about to do now. And the people were glad to have it so. I do not know that the politicians *are* a whit better now than then. I should not be willing to assert that Seward and Adams are any more honest than Webster and Winthrop, and certainly they have just as much spaniel in their make.

But the gain to-day is, we have a *people*. Under their vigilant eyes, mindful of their sturdy purpose, sustained by their determination, many of our politicians *act* much better. And out of this popular heart is *growing* a Constitution which will wholly supersede that of 1787.

A few years ago, while Pierce was President, the Republican party dared to refuse the appropriations for support of government, — the most daring act ever ventured in a land that holds Bunker Hill and Brandywine. They dared to persevere some twenty or thirty days. It seems a trifle; but it is a very significant straw. Then for weeks when Banks was elected, and a year ago, again, the whole government was checked till the Republicans put their Speaker in the chair. Now the North elects her President, the South secedes. I suppose we shall be bargained away into compromise. I know the strength and virtue of the farming West. It is one of the bright spots that our sceptre tends there, rather than to the seaboard. Four or eight years hence, when this earthquake will repeat itself, the West may be omnipotent, and we shall see brave things. It is not the opinion of the absolute majority which rules, but that amount of public opinion which can be brought to bear on a particular point at a given time. Therefore the compact, energetic, organized Seaboard, with the press in its hand, rules, spite of the wide-spread, inert, unorganized West. While the agricultural frigate is getting its broadside ready, the commercial clipper has half finished its slave voyage.

In spite of Lincoln's wishes, therefore, I fear he will never be able to stand against Seward, Adams, half the Republican wire-pullers, and the Seaboard. But even now, if Seward and the rest had stood firm, as Lincoln, Sumner, Chase, Wade, and Lovejoy, and the Tribune have hitherto done, I believe you might have polled the North, and had a response, three to one : "Let the Union go to pieces, rather than yield one inch." I know no sublimer hour in history. The sight of these two months is compensation for a life of toil. Never let Europe taunt us again that our blood is wholly cankered by gold. Our people stood, willing their idolized government should go to pieces for an idea. True, other nations have done so. England in 1640, — France in 1791, — our colonies in 1775. Those were proud moments. But to-day touches a nobler height. Their idea was their own freedom. To-day, the idea, loyal to which our people willingly see their Union wrecked, is largely the hope of justice to a dependent, helpless, hated race. Revolutions never go backward. The live force of a human pulse-beat can rive the dead lumber of government to pieces. Chain the Hellespont, Mr. Xerxes-Seward, before you dream of balking the Northern heart of its purpose, — freedom to the slave! The old sea never laughed at Persian chains more haughtily than we do at Congress promises.

I reverently thank God that he has given me to see such a day as this. Remember the measureless love of the North for the Union, — its undoubting faith that disunion is ruin, — and then value as you ought this last three months. If Wilberforce could say on his death-bed, after fifty years' toil, "Thank God, I have lived to see the day that England is willing to give twenty million sterling for the abolition of slavery," what ought our gratitude to be for such a sight as this? Twenty millions of people willing, would only their leaders permit, to barter their govment for the hope of justice to the negro! And this result has come in defiance of the pulpit, spite of the half omnipotence of commerce, with all the so-called leaders of public opinion against us, — literature, fashion, prejudice of race, and present interest. It is the uprising of common sense, the protest of common conscience, the untaught, instinctive loyalty of the people to justice and right.

But you will tell me of dark clouds, mobs in every Northern city. Grant it, and more. When Lovejoy was shot at Alton, Illinois, while defending his press, and his friends were refused the use of Faneuil Hall, William Ellery Channing, William Sturgis, and George Bond, the saints and merchants of Boston, rallied to the defence of free speech. Now we hold meetings only when and how the Mayor permits [hisses and great applause], yet no merchant prince, no pulpit hero, rallies to our side. But raise your eyes from the disgraced pavements of Boston, and look out broader. That same soil which drank the blood of Lovejoy now sends his brother to lead Congress in its fiercest hour; that same prairie lifts his soul's son to crush the Union as he steps into the Presidential chair. Sleep in peace, martyr of Alton, good has come out of Nazareth! The shot which turned back our Star of the West from the waters of Charleston, and tolled the knell of the Union, was the rebound of the bullet that pierced your heart.

When Lovejoy died, men used to ask, tauntingly, what good has the antislavery cause done? what changes has it wrought? As well stand over the cradle, and ask what use is a baby? He will be a man some time, — the antislavery cause is now twenty-one years old.

This hour is bright from another cause. Since 1800, our government has been only a tool of the Slave Power. The stronghold of antislavery has been the sentiment of the people. We have always prophesied that our government would be found too weak to bear so radical an agitation as this of slavery. It has proved so; the government is a wreck. But the people have shown themselves able to deal with it, — able to shake this sin from their lap as easily as the lion does dew-drops from his mane.

Mark another thing. No Northern man will allow you to charge him with a willingness to extend slavery. No matter what his plan, he is anxious to show you it is not a compromise! and will not extend slavery one inch! Mr. Dana is eloquent on this point, Mr. Adams positive, Mr. Seward cunning, Thurlow Weed indignant. [Laughter.] Virtue is not wholly discrowned, while hypocrisy is the homage laid at her feet. With such progress, why should we compromise?

Everybody allows — North and South — that any compromise will only be temporary relief. The South knows it is a lie, meant to tide over a shallow spot. The North knows it, too. The startled North, in fact, now says

"Yes, I'll continue to serve you till my hair be grown, then I'll bring down the very temple itself." That is what a compromise really means. The progress is seen in this. The South always has said: "Yes, give me so much; I will not keep my part of the bargain, but hold you to yours, and get more the moment I can." Hitherto, the North has said yes, and her courage consisted in skulking. Seward would *swear* to support the Constitution, but not keep the oath. I use his name to illustrate my idea. But it is always with the extremest reluctance I bring myself to see a spot on the fame of that man, who, at his own cost, by severe toil, braving fierce odium, saved our civilization from the murder of the idiot Freeman.

But you may also ask, if compromise be even a temporary relief, why not make it?

1st. Because it is wrong.

2d. Because it is suicidal. Secession, appeased by compromise, is only emboldened to secede again to-morrow, and thus get larger concessions. The cowardice that yields to threats invites them.

3d. Because it delays emancipation. To-day, England, horror-struck that her five million operatives who live on cotton should depend on States rushing into anarchy, is ransacking the world for a supply. Leave her to toil under that lash, and in five years, South Carolina will be starved into virtue. One thousand slaves are born each day. Hurry emancipation three years, and you raise a million human beings into freeborn men.

4th. Compromise demoralizes both parties. Mark! the North, notwithstanding all its progress, does not now quit the South. In the great religious bodies and the state, it is the sinners who kick the virtuous out of the covenant with death! Mr. Dana, in his recent speech, does not secede because unwilling to commit the three constitutional sins. The South secedes from him because he will not commit one more.

5th. Compromise risks insurrection, the worst door at which freedom can enter. Let universal suffrage have free sway, and the ballot supersedes the bullet. But let an arrogant and besotted minority curb the majority by tricks like these, and when you have compromised away Lincoln, you revive John Brown. On this point of insurrection, let me say a word.

Strictly speaking, I repudiate the term "insurrection." The slaves are not a herd of vassals. They are a nation, four millions strong; having the same right of revolution that Hungary and Florence have. I acknowledge the right of two million and a half of white people in the seven seceding States to organize their government as they choose. Just as freely I acknowledge the right of four million of black people to organize *their* government, and to vindicate that right by arms.

Men talk of the peace of the South under our present government. It is no real peace. With the whites, it is only that bastard peace which the lazy Roman loved, — *ut se apricaret*, that he might sun himself. It is only safe idleness, sure breeder of mischief. With the slave, it is only war in disguise. Under that mask is hid a war keener in its pains, and deadlier in its effects, than any open fight. As the Latin adage runs, — *mars gravior sub pace latet*, — war bitterer for its disguise.

Thirty years devoted to earnest use of moral means show how sincere our wish that this question should have a peaceful solution. If your idols — your Websters, Clays, Calhouns, Sewards, Adamses — had done their duty, so it would have been. Not ours the guilt of this storm, or of the future, however bloody. But I hesitate not to say, that I prefer an insurrection which frees the slave in ten years to slavery for a century. A slave I pity. A rebellious slave I respect. I say now, as I said ten years ago, I do not shrink from the toast with which

Dr. Johnson flavored his Oxford Port, "Success to the first insurrection of the blacks in Jamaica!" I do not shrink from the sentiment of Southey, in a letter to Duppa: "There are scenes of tremendous horror which I could smile at by Mercy's side. An insurrection which should make the negroes masters of the West Indies is one." I believe both these sentiments are dictated by the highest humanity. I know what anarchy is. I know what civil war is. I can imagine the scenes of blood through which a rebellious slave population must march to their rights. They are dreadful. And yet, I do not know, that, to an enlightened mind, a scene of civil war is any more sickening than the thought of a hundred and fifty years of slavery. Take the broken hearts; the bereaved mothers; the infant, wrung from the hands of its parents; the husband and wife torn asunder; every right trodden under foot; the blighted hopes, the imbruted souls, the darkened and degraded millions, sunk below the level of intellectual life, melted in sensuality, herded with beasts, who have walked over the burning marl of Southern slavery to their graves; and where is the battle-field, however ghastly, that is not white, — white as an angel's wing, — compared with the blackness of that darkness which has brooded over the Carolinas for two hundred years? Do you love mercy? Weigh out the fifty thousand hearts that have beaten their last pulse amid agonies of thought and suffering fancy faints to think of; and the fifty thousand mothers, who, with sickening senses, watch for footsteps which are not wont to tarry long in their coming, and soon find themselves left to tread the pathway of life alone; add all the horrors of cities sacked and lands laid waste, — that is war; weigh it now against some trembling young girl sent to the auction-block, some man, like that taken from our court-house and carried back into Georgia; multiply this individual agony into four miltions; multiply that into centuries; and that into all the relations of father and child, husband and wife; heap on all the deep, moral degradation, both of the oppressor and the oppressed, and tell me if Waterloo or Thermopylæ can claim one tear from the eye even of the tenderest spirit of mercy, compared with this daily system of hell amid the most civilized and Christian people on the face of the earth! *

No, I confess I am not a non-resistant. The reason why I have advised the slave to be guided by a policy of peace is because he has had, hitherto, no chance. If he had one, if he had as good a chance as those who went up to Lexington years ago, I should call him the basest recreant that ever deserted wife and child, if he did not vindicate his liberty by his own right hand.

Mr. Richard H. Dana, Jr., says, in such a contest his sympathies would be with his own race.† Mine would be

* Since I said this, ten years ago, I find that Macaulay makes the same comparison between a short civil war and long despotism, — putting into Milton's mouth the following: "For civil war, that it is an evil I dispute not. But that it is the greatest of evils, that I stoutly deny. It doth indeed appear to the misjudging to be a worse calamity than bad government, because its miseries are collected together within a short space and time, and may easily, at one view, be taken in and perceived. But the misfortunes of nations ruled by tyrants, being distributed over many centuries and many places, as they are of greater weight and number, so they are of less display."

† The following is the paragraph in Mr. Dana's address referred to by Mr. Phillips: —

"An appeal to arms is a war of the races. They meet on the equality of the battle-field, and the victory goes to the strongest; and I confess that, when I consider what the white race is, and what the black race is, what civilization is, and what the white race is and always has been, and what the black race is and always has been, — and this doctrine of the races has impressed itself on my mind much more than before, from what I have seen of all races during the last year and a half, — I confess that, in a contest like that, my duty and my sympathies would go with my own race. I know it is a contest for freedom, but it is a contest for life and for freedom on both with the right. "The Almighty has no attribute which can take sides with us in such a contest," says Jefferson, speaking of a struggle in which the black race "is to go up," and his own, the white race, is "to go down." Let me advise Mr. Dana to learn Christianity of this infidel, and Justice of this slaveholder. I feel bound to add my doubt whether a slave insurrection would be a bloody one. In all revolutions, except the French, the people have always shown themselves merciful. Witness Switzerland, St. Domingo, Hungary, Italy. Tyranny sours more than suffering. The Conservative hates the Abolitionist more than we do him. The South hates the North. The master speaks ten bitter words of the slave, where the slave speaks five of the master. Refuse, then, all compromise, — send the Slave States out to face the danger of which they are fully aware, — announce frankly that we welcome the black race to liberty, won in battle, as cordially as we have done Kossuth and Garibaldi, and probably there will never be an insurrection. Prudent and masterly statesmanship will avert it by just concession. Thus Disunion is Peace, as well as Liberty and Justice.

But I was speaking of compromise. Compromise degrades us, and puts back freedom in Europe. If the North manfully accepts the Potomac for her barrier, avows her gladness to get rid of tyrants, her willingness and her ability to stand alone, she can borrow as much money in Europe as before, and will be more respected. Free institutions are then proved breeders of men. If, instead of this, the North belittles herself by confessing her fears, her weakness, her preference for peace at any

sides, because *slavery is to end when war begins.* One race is to go up, and one to go down. It is a question of extermination, or banishment, or subjugation, or all three. And I have not arrived at that degree of philanthropy, that I desire to see the black race controlling all that vast country, and our own white civilized race driven out, subjugated, or exterminated."

price, what capitalist will trust a rope of sand, — a people which the conspiracy of Buchanan's Cabinet could not disgust, nor the guns of Carolina arouse?

Will compromise eliminate all our Puritan blood, — make the census add up against us, and in favor of the South, — write a new Bible, — blot John Brown from history, — make Connecticut suck its idle thumbs like a baby, and South Carolina invent and save like a Yankee? If it will, it will succeed. If it will not, Carolina don't want it, any more than Jerrold's duck wants you to hold an umbrella over him in a hard shower. Carolina wants separation, — wants, like the jealous son, her portion, and must waste it in riotous madness before she return a repentant prodigal.

Why do I think disunion gain, peace, and virtue?

The Union, even if it be advantageous to all the States, is surely indispensable only to the South.

Let us rise to the height of our position. This is revolution, not rebellion.

Suppose we welcome disunion, manfully avow our real sentiment, "liberty and equality," and draw the line at the Potomac. We do not want the Border States. Let them go, be welcome to the forts, take the Capital with them. [Applause and hisses.] What to us is a hot-house city, empty streets, and useless marble? Where Macgregor sits is the head of the table. Active brains, free lips, and cunning hands make empires. Paper capitals are vain. Of course, we must assume a right to buy out Maryland and Delaware. Then, by running our line at the Potomac, we close the irrepressible conflict, and have homogeneous institutions. Then we part friends. The Union thus ended, the South no longer hates the North. Cuba she cannot have. France, England, and ourselves forbid. If she spread over Central America, that will bring no cause of war to a Northern confederacy. We

are no filibusters. Her nearness to us there cannot harm us. Let Kansas witness that while Union fettered her, and our national banner clung to the flagstaff heavy with blood, we still made good George Canning's boast, "Where that banner is planted, foreign dominion shall not come." With a government heartily on his side, and that flag floating in the blessings of twenty million of freemen, the loneliest settler in the shadow of the Rocky Mountains will sleep fearless.

Why, then, should there not be peace between two such confederacies? There must be. Let me show you why: —

1st. The laws of trade will bind us together, as they now do all other lands. This side of the ocean, at least, we are not living in feudal times, when princes make war for ambition. We live in days when men of common sense go about their daily business, while frightened kings are flying along the highways. Leave neighborhood and trade alone to work their usual results, and we shall be at peace. Observe, only Northerners are lynched at the South now. Spaniards, French, Scotch are safe. When English Captain Vaughan is tarred and feathered, the Mayor offers a reward, and the grand jury indict. After a fair, sensible disunion, such as I have described, a Boston man will be as well off as Captain Vaughan. Fair treaties are better security than sham constitutions.

At any rate, disunion could not make the two sections any more at war than they are now. Any change in this respect would be an improvement. If the North and Mexico had touched boundaries, would they ever have quarrelled? Nothing but Southern filibusterism, which can never point North, ever embroiled us with Mexico. To us in future the South will be another Mexico; we shall not wish to attack her; she will be too weak, too intent on her own broils, to attack us.

Even if the Border States do not secede, let us, for the slave's sake, welcome the schism between them and the Gulf States, which that very difference of conduct will be sure to cause. A house divided against itself cannot stand. Only twenty-three out of every hundred inhabitants are slaves in the Border States, — twenty-three slaves to seventy-seven freemen. A worn-out soil, fear of loss by fugitives, dread of danger to a hated institution, thus weak in proportion to Northern enemies, will urge slaveholders to push their slaves southward. Another census may find the Border States with only ten or fifteen slaves out of one hundred inhabitants, — ten slaves to ninety freemen. Reduced to such compass, slavery is manageable; we shall soon see plans of emancipation, compensation, and freedom. On the contrary, the Gulf States now have forty-six slaves in every hundred inhabitants, — forty-six slaves to fifty-four freemen. Strengthened by this tendency of the slave population southward, and the opening of the slave trade, we may soon see the black race a majority, and either as a nation of mixed races, or as black republics, the Gulf States will gravitate back to us *free.*

The South cannot make war on any one. Suppose the fifteen States hang together a year, — which is almost an impossibility, —

1st. They have given bonds in two thousand millions of dollars — the value of their slaves — to keep the peace.

2d. They will have enough to do to attend to the irrepressible conflict at home. Virginia, Kentucky, Missouri, will be their Massachusetts; Winter Davis, Blair, and Cassius Clay, their Seward and Garrison.

3d. The Gulf States will monopolize all the offices. A man must have Gulf principles to belong to a healthy party. Under such a lead, disfranchised Virginia, in opposition, will not have much heart to attack Pennsylvania.

4th. The census shows that the Border States are pushing their slaves South. Fear of their free Northern neighbors will quicken the process, and so widen the breach between Gulf and Border States by making one constantly more and the other less Slave States. Free trade in sugar bankrupts Louisiana. Free trade in men bankrupts Virginia. Free trade generally lets two thirds of the direct taxation rest on the numerous, richer, and more comfortable whites of the Border States; hence further conflict. Such a despotism, with every third man black and a foe, will make no wars.

Why should it attack us? We are not a cannon thundering at its gates. We are not an avalanche overhanging its sunny vales. Our influence, that of freedom, is only the air, penetrating everywhere; like heat, permeating all space. The South cannot stand isolated on a glass cricket. The sun will heat her, and electricity convulse. She must outwit ideas before she can get rid of them. A fevered child in July might as well strike at the sun, as the South attack us for that, the only annoyance we can give her, — the sight and influence of our nobler civilization.

Disunion is gain. I venture the assertion, in the face of State Street, that of any five Northern men engaged in Southern trade, exclusively, four will end in bankruptcy. If disunion sifts such commerce, the North will lose nothing.

I venture the assertion, that seven at least of the Southern States receive from the government more than they contribute to it. So far, their place will be more profitable than their company.

The whole matter of the Southern trade has been grossly exaggerated, as well as the importance of the Mississippi River. Freedom makes her own rivers of iron. Facts show that for one dollar the West sends or brings by the river, she sends and brings four to and from the East by wagon and rail.

If, then, Mississippi and Louisiana bar the river with forts, they will graciously be allowed to pay for them, while Northern railroads grow rich carrying behind steam that portion of wheat, bacon, silk, or tea, which would otherwise float lazily up and down that yellow stream.

The Cincinnati *Press*, which has treated the subject with rare ability, asserts that, excepting provisions which the South must, in any event, buy of the West, the trade of Cincinnati with Southern Indiana alone is thrice her trade with the whole South. As our benevolent societies get about one dollar in seven south of Mason and Dixon's line, so our traders sell there only about one dollar in five. Such trade, if cut off, would ruin nobody. In fact, the South buys little of us, and pays only for about half she buys. [Laughter and hisses.]

Now we build Southern roads, pay Southern patrol, carry Southern letters, support, out of the nation's treasures, an army of Southern office-holders, waste more money at Norfolk in building ships which will not float, than is spent in protecting the five Great Lakes, which bear up millions of commerce. These vast pensions come back to us in shape of Southern traders, paying on the average one half their debts. Dissolve the Union, and we shall save this outgo, and probably not sell without a prospect of being paid. While the laws of trade guarantee that even if there be two nations, we shall have their carrying-trade and manufacture for them just so long as we carry and manufacture cheaper than other men.

Southern trade is a lottery, to which the Union gives all the prizes. Put it on a sound basis by disunion, and the North gains. If we part without anger, the South buys, as every one does, of the cheapest seller. We get her honest business, without being called to fill up the gap of bankruptcy which the wasteful system of slave-labor must occasion. In this generation, no Slave State in the Union has made the year's ends meet. In counting the wealth of the Union, such States are a *minus* quantity. Should the Gulf States, however, return, I have no doubt the United States treasury will be called on to pay all these secession debts.

Disunion is honor. I will not point to the equivocating hypocrisy of all our Northern leaders. I will not count up all the bankrupt statesmen, — blighted names, — skeletons marking the sad path of the caravan over our desert of seventy years, — they are too familiar. As years roll on, history metes out justice. But take the last instance, — take Mr. Richard H. Dana, Jr., as example, a name historic for generations, a scholar of world-wide fame. He finds in the Constitution the duty of returning fugitive slaves, all alike, "the old and the ignorant, the young and the beautiful," to be surrendered to the master, whether he be man or brute. Mr. Dana avows his full readiness to perform this legal duty. All honor at least to the shameless effrontery with which he avows his willingness. Most of our public men, like the English Tories of 1689, are "ashamed to name what they are not ashamed to do." He paints the hell of slavery in words that make the blood cold, and then boasts, this Massachusetts scholar, — gentleman, his friends would call him, — boasts that no man can charge him with having ever said one word against the surrender of fugitive slaves! Counsel in all the Boston slave-cases, he "never suffered himself to utter one word which any poor fugitive negro, or any friend of his, could construe into an assertion that a fugitive slave should not be restored"!

He unblushingly claims merit for himself and Massachusetts, — I doubt if, in the scornful South, he will have "his claim allowed," — that he and Massachusetts have constantly executed laws which "offended their sense of honor, and ran counter to their moral sentiments," which he considers a "painful *duty*." To be sure, Mr. Dana has discovered, in his wide travels and extensive voyages, a "peculiar" class of people, narrow-minded, very little read in Greek, who think, poor simpletons, that this slave-hunting is a sin. But then, Aristotle did not look at things in this light. He took broader views, and proves conclusively that three virtues and one sin exactly make a saint, and Mr. Dana is too good a churchman to dispute with Aristotle. He sees no reason why, notwithstanding this clause, as to forcing our fellow-men back into hell, "a conscientious man" should not swear to obey the Constitution, and actually obey it. Now Mr. Seward and Mr. Joel Parker, who both believe in the fugitive-slave clause, and willingly *swear* to enforce it, have each given public notice they will not enforce it. Mr. Dana will swear, and perform too. They will swear, but not perform. Their guilt is perjury; his is man-stealing. On the whole, I should rather be Seward than Dana; for perjury is the more gentlemanly vice, to my thinking. Perjury only filches your neighbor's rights. Man-stealing takes rights and neighbor too.

After all this, Mr. Dana objects to the Crittenden compromise. Something short of that he can allow, because he does not call these other offers, Adams's and such like, "compromises"! It seems he objects more to the word than the thing. But the Crittenden proposal he is set against, for a reason which may strike you singular in a man willing to return slaves; but then we are bundles of inconsistencies, all of us. But this slave-hunter cannot abide Crittenden, because, listen! because he thinks "an investment in dishonor is a bad investment! An investment in infidelity to the principles of liberty is a bad investment!" Hunt slaves? Yes, it is a duty. Give some territory to slavery, and peril the Republican party?

Never, it is a "bad investment"! De Quincey says: "If once a man indulges in murder, very soon he comes to think little of robbing; from robbing he comes next to drinking, and from that to ill manners and procrastination. Once enter this downward path, and you know not where you 'll stop." Mr. Dana has, however, taken warning, and stops at man-stealing.

Some of you will call this personality. I will tell you some time, when the hour serves, why I use personality. Enough now to remind you his clients are wealth, culture, power, and white blood. Mine are four million of human beings, standing dumb suppliants on the threshold of Christianity and civilization, and hundreds of fugitives trembling at every motion of the door-latch. Whoever perils their safety, or holds back the day of their redemption by ingenious sophistry, base word, or base act, shall always find in me a critic. Let no man call me harsh; I only *repeat* with emphasis words such men are not ashamed to *speak*. Southern Legrees can plead, if not an excuse, yet some extenuation. But when a Massachusetts Republican, a Massachusetts lawyer, a Massachusetts scholar, avows such sentiments, he puts himself below the Legrees. Blame not this plainness of speech. I have a hundred friends, as brave souls as God ever made, whose hearths are not as safe after honored men make such speeches.

Faneuil Hall, too, kneels patient for its burden, and by its President that meeting says to the South,—Only name your terms, that is all we will trouble you to do. Like Luther's priest, who, when Catholics told him to pray one way and Protestants another, ended by repeating the alphabet, and begging God to frame a prayer agreeable to himself, so our Boston orator offers the South *carte blanche*, the whole bundle of compromises,—Will she only condescend to indicate her preference?

Mr. Dana is a man above the temptations of politics. The President of the Faneuil Hall meeting has no political aspirations, an independent merchant. Such speeches show how wide the gangrene of the Union spreads. Mr. Dana's speech was made, he says, in the shadow of Bunker's Hill, in sight of the spot where Washington first drew his sword. The other speech was borne to the roof of Faneuil Hall by the plaudits of a thousand merchants. Surely, such were not the messagės Cambridge and our old Hall used to exchange! Can you not hear Warren and Otis crying to their recreant representatives: "Sons, scorn to be slaves! Believe, for our sakes, we did not fight for such a government. Trample it under foot. You cannot be poorer than we were. It cannot cost you more than our seven years of war. Do it, if only to show that we have not lived in vain"?

UNDER THE FLAG.*

"Therefore thus saith the Lord: Ye have not hearkened unto me in proclaiming liberty every one to his brother, and every man to his neighbor: behold, I proclaim a liberty for you, saith the Lord, to the sword, to the pestilence, and to the famine." — JER. xxxiv. 17.

MANY times this winter, here and elsewhere, I have counselled peace, — urged, as well as I knew how, the expediency of acknowledging a Southern Confederacy, and the peaceful separation of these thirty-four States. One of the journals announces to you that I come here this morning to retract those opinions. No, not one of them! [Applause.] I need them all, — every word I have spoken this winter, — every act of twenty-five years of my life, to make the welcome I give this war hearty and hot. Civil war is a momentous evil. It needs the soundest, most solemn justification. I rejoice before God to-day for every word that I have spoken counselling peace; but I rejoice also with an especially profound gratitude, that now, the first time in my antislavery life, I speak under the stars and stripes, and welcome the tread of Massachusetts men marshalled for war. [Enthusiastic cheering.] No matter what the past has been or said; to-day the slave asks God for a sight of this banner, and counts it the pledge of his redemption. [Applause.] Hitherto it may have meant what you thought, or what I

* A Discourse delivered in the Music Hall, Boston, April 21, 1861, before the Twenty-eighth Congregational Society, the platform profusely decorated with the Stars and Stripes.

did; to-day it represents sovereignty and justice. [Renewed applause.] The only mistake that I have made, was in supposing Massachusetts wholly choked with cotton-dust and cankered with gold. [Loud cheering.] The South thought her patience and generous willingness for peace were cowardice; to-day shows the mistake. She has been sleeping on her arms since '83, and the first cannon-shot brings her to her feet with the war-cry of the Revolution on her lips. [Loud cheers.] Any man who loves either liberty or manhood must rejoice at such an hour. [Applause.]

Let me tell you the path by which I at least have trod my way up to this conclusion. I do not acknowledge the motto, in its full significance, "Our country, right or wrong." If you let it trespass on the domain of morals, it is knavish. But there is a full, broad sphere for loyalty; and no war-cry ever stirred a generous people that had not in it much of truth and right. It is sublime, this rally of a great people to the defence of what they think their national honor! A "noble and puissant nation rousing herself like a strong man from sleep, and shaking her invincible locks." Just now, we saw her "reposing, peaceful and motionless; but at the call of patriotism, she ruffles, as it were, her swelling plumage, collects her scattered elements of strength, and awakens her dormant thunders."

But how do we justify this last appeal to the God of battles? Let me tell you how I do. I have always believed in the sincerity of Abraham Lincoln. You have heard me express my confidence in it every time I have spoken from this desk. I only doubted sometimes whether he were really the head of the government. To-day he is at any rate Commander-in-chief.

The delay in the action of government has doubtless been necessity, but policy also. Traitors within and without made it hesitate to move till it had tried the machine of government just given it. But delay was wise, as it matured a public opinion definite, decisive, and ready to keep step to the music of the government march. The very postponement of another session of Congress till July 4th plainly invites discussion, — evidently contemplates the ripening of public opinion in the interval. Fairly to examine public affairs, and prepare a community wise to co-operate with the government, is the duty of every pulpit and every press.

Plain words, therefore, now, before the nation goes mad with excitement, is every man's duty. Every public meeting in Athens was opened with a curse on any one who should not speak what he really thought. "I have never defiled my conscience from fear or favor to my superiors," was part of the oath every Egyptian soul was supposed to utter in the Judgment-Hall of Osiris, before admission to heaven. Let us show to-day a Christian spirit as sincere and fearless. No mobs in this hour of victory, to silence those whom events have not converted. We are strong enough to tolerate dissent. That flag which floats over press or mansion at the bidding of a mob, disgraces both victor and victim.

All winter long, I have acted with that party which cried for peace. The antislavery enterprise to which I belong started with peace written on its banner. We imagined that the age of bullets was over; that the age of ideas had come; that thirty millions of people were able to take a great question, and decide it by the conflict of opinions; that, without letting the ship of state founder, we could lift four millions of men into Liberty and Justice. We thought that if your statesmen would throw away personal ambition and party watchwords, and devote themselves to the great issue, this might be accomplished. To a certain extent it has been. The North has answered to the call. Year after year, event by event, has indicated the rising education of the people, — the readiness for a higher moral life, the calm, self-poised confidence in our own convictions that patiently waits — like master for a pupil — for a neighbor's conversion. The North has responded to the call of that peaceful, moral, intellectual agitation which the antislavery idea has initiated. Our mistake, if any, has been that we counted too much on the intelligence of the masses, on the honesty and wisdom of statesmen as a class. Perhaps we did not give weight enough to the fact we saw, that this nation is made up of different ages; not homogeneous, but a mixed mass of different centuries. The North *thinks*, — can appreciate argument, — is the nineteenth century, — hardly any struggle left in it but that between the working class and the money-kings. The South *dreams*, — it is the thirteenth and fourteenth century, — baron and serf, — noble and slave. Jack Cade and Wat Tyler loom over its horizon, and the serf, rising, calls for another Thierry to record his struggle. There the fagot still burns which the Doctors of the Sorbonne called, ages ago, "the best light to guide the erring." There men are tortured for opinions, the only punishment the Jesuits were willing their pupils should look on. This is, perhaps, too flattering a picture of the South. Better call her, as Sumner does, "the Barbarous States." Our struggle, therefore, is between barbarism and civilization. Such can only be settled by arms. [Prolonged cheering.] The government has waited until its best friends almost suspected its courage or its integrity; but the cannon shot against Fort Sumter has opened the only door out of this hour. There were but two. One was compromise; the other was battle. The integrity of the North closed the first; the generous forbearance of nineteen States closed the other. The South opened this with cannon-shot, and Lincoln

shows himself at the door. [Prolonged and enthusiastic cheering.] The war, then, is not aggressive, but in self-defence, and Washington has become the Thermopylæ of Liberty and Justice. [Applause.] Rather than surrender that Capital, cover every square foot of it with a living body [loud cheers]; crowd it with a million of men, and empty every bank vault at the North to pay the cost. [Renewed cheering.] Teach the world once for all, that North America belongs to the Stars and Stripes, and under them no man shall wear a chain. [Enthusiastic cheering.] In the whole of this conflict, I have looked only at Liberty, — only at the slave. Perry entered the battle of the Lakes with "DON'T GIVE UP THE SHIP!" floating from the masthead of the Lawrence. When with his fighting flag he left her crippled, heading north, and, mounting the deck of the Niagara, turned her bows due west, he did all for one and the same purpose, — to rake the decks of the foe. Steer north or west, acknowledge secession or cannonade it, I care not which; but "Proclaim liberty throughout all the land unto all the inhabitants thereof." [Loud cheers.]

I said, civil war needs momentous and solemn justification. Europe, the world, may claim of us, tnat, before we blot the nineteenth century by an appeal to arms, we shall exhaust every concession, try every means to keep the peace; otherwise, an appeal to the God of battles is an insult to the civilization of our age; it is a confession that our culture and our religion are superficial, if not a failure. I think that the history of the nation and of the government both is an ample justification to our own times and to history for this appeal to arms. I think the South is all wrong, and the administration is all right. [Prolonged cheering.] Let me tell you why. For thirty years the North has exhausted conciliation and compromise. They have tried every expedient, they have relinquished every right, they have sacrificed every interest, they have smothered keen sensibility to national honor, and Northern weight and supremacy in the Union; have forgotten they were the majority in numbers and in wealth, in education and strength; have left the helm of government and the dictation of policy to the Southern States. For all this, the conflict waxed closer and hotter. The administration which preceded this was full of traitors and thieves. It allowed the arms, ships, money, military stores of the North to be stolen with impunity. Mr. Lincoln took office, robbed of all the means to defend the Constitutional rights of the government. He offered to withdraw from the walls of Sumter everything but the flag. He allowed secession to surround it with the strongest forts which military science could build. The North offered to meet in convention her sister States, and arrange the terms of peaceful separation. Strength and right yielded everything, — they folded their hands, waited the returning reason of the mad insurgents. Week after week elapsed, month after month went by, waiting for the sober second-thought of two millions and a half of people. The world saw the sublime sight of nineteen millions of wealthy, powerful, united citizens, allowing their flag to be insulted, their rights assailed, their sovereignty defied and broken in pieces, and yet waiting, with patient, brotherly, magnanimous kindness, until insurrection, having spent its fury, should reach out its hand for a peaceful arrangement. Men began to call it cowardice, on the one hand; and we, who watched closely the crisis, feared that this effort to be magnanimous would demoralize the conscience and the courage of the North. We were afraid that, as the hour went by, the virtue of the people, white-heat as it stood on the fourth day of March, would be cooled by the temptations, by the suspense, by the want and suffering which it was feared would stalk from the Atlantic to the valley of the Mississippi. We were afraid the government would wait too long, and find at last, that, instead of a united people, they were deserted, and left alone to meet the foe.

All this time, the South knew, recognized, by her own knowledge of Constitutional questions, that the government could not advance one inch towards acknowledging secession; that when Abraham Lincoln swore to support the Constitution and laws of the United States, he was bound to die under the flag on Fort Sumter, if necessary. [Loud applause.] They knew, therefore, that the call on the administration to acknowledge the Commissioners of the Confederacy was a delusion and a swindle. I know the whole argument for secession. Up to a certain extent, I accede to it. But no administration that is not traitor can acknowledge secession until we are hopelessly beaten in fair fight. [Cheers.] The right of a State to secede, under the Constitution of the United States, — it is an absurdity; and Abraham Lincoln knows nothing, has a right to know nothing, but the Constitution of the United States. [Loud cheers.] The right of a State to secede, as a revolutionary right, is undeniable; but it is the nation which is to recognize that; and the nation offered, at the suggestion of Kentucky, to meet the question in full convention. The offer was declined. The government and the nation, therefore, are all right. [Applause.] They are right on constitutional law; they are right on the principles of the Declaration of Independence. [Cheers.]

Let me explain this more fully, for this reason; because — and I thank God for it, every American should be proud of it — you cannot maintain a war in the United States of America against a constitutional or a revolutionary right. The people of these States have too large brains and too many ideas to fight blindly, — to lock horns like a couple of beasts in the sight of the world. [Applause.] Cannon think in this nineteenth century; and you must put the North in the right, — wholly, undeniably, inside of the Constitution and out of it, — before you can justify her in the face of the world; before you can pour Massachusetts like an avalanche through the streets of Baltimore, [great cheering,] and carry Lexington on the 19th of April south of Mason and Dixon's line. [Renewed cheering.] Let us take an honest pride in the fact that our Sixth Regiment made a way for itself through Baltimore, and were the first to reach the threatened Capital. In this war Massachusetts has a right to be the first in the field.

I said I knew the whole argument for secession. Very briefly let me state the points. No government provides for its own death; therefore there can be no constitutional right to secede. But there is a revolutionary right. The Declaration of Independence establishes, what the heart of every American acknowledges, that the people — mark you, THE PEOPLE! — have always an inherent, paramount, inalienable right to change their governments, whenever they think — whenever *they* think — that it will minister to their happiness. That is a revolutionary right. Now, how did South Carolina and Massachusetts come into the Union? They came into it by a convention representing the people. South Carolina alleges that she has gone out by convention. So far, right. She says that when the *people* take the State rightfully out of the Union, the right to forts and national property goes with it. Granted. She says, also, that it is no matter that we bought Louisiana of France, and Florida of Spain. No bargain made, no money paid, betwixt us and France or Spain, could rob Florida or Louisiana of her right to remodel her government whenever the people found it would be for their happiness. So far, right. THE PEOPLE, — mark you! South Carolina presents herself to the administration at Washington, and says, "There is a vote of my convention, that I go out of the Union." "I cannot see you," says Abraham Lincoln. [Loud cheers.] "As President, I have no eyes but constitutional eyes; I cannot see you." [Renewed cheers.] He could only say, like Speaker Lenthal before Charles the First, "I have neither eyes to see nor tongue to speak but as the Constitution is pleased to direct me, whose servant I am." He was right. But Madison said, Hamilton said, the Fathers said, in 1789, "No man but an enemy of liberty will ever stand on technicalities and forms, when the essence is in question." Abraham Lincoln could not see the Commissioners of South Carolina, but the North could; the nation could; and the nation responded, "If you want a Constitutional secession, such as you claim, but which I repudiate, I will waive forms: let us meet in convention, and we will arrange it." [Applause.] Surely, while one claims a right within the Constitution, he may, without dishonor or inconsistency, meet in convention, even if finally refusing to be bound by it. To decline doing so is only evidence of intention to provoke war. Everything under that instrument is peace. Everything under that instrument may be changed by a national convention. The South says, "No!" She says, "If you don't allow me the Constitutional right, I claim the revolutionary right." The North responds, "When you have torn the Constitution into fragments, I recognize the right of THE PEOPLE of South Carolina to model their government. Yes, I recognize the right of the three hundred and eighty-four thousand white men, and four hundred and eighty-four thousand black men to model their Constitution. Show me one that they have adopted, and I will recognize the revolution. [Cheers.] But the moment you tread outside of the Constitution, the black man is not three fifths of a man, — he is a whole one." [Loud cheering.] Yes, the South has the right of revolution; the South has a right to model her government; and the moment she shows us four million of black votes thrown even against it, and balanced by five million of other votes, I will acknowledge the Declaration of Independence is complied with [loud applause], — that the PEOPLE south of Mason and Dixon's line have remodelled their government to suit themselves; and our function is only to recognize it.

Further than this, we should have the right to remind them, in the words of our Declaration of Independence, that "governments long established are not to be changed for light and transient causes," and that, so long as government fulfils the purposes for which it was made, — the liberty and happiness of the people, — no one section has the right capriciously to make changes which destroy joint interests, advantages bought by common toil and sacrifice, and which division necessarily destroys. Indeed, we should have the right to remind them that no faction, in what has been recognized as one nation, can claim, by any law, the right of revolution to set up or to preserve a system which the common conscience of mankind stamps as wicked and infamous. The law of nations is only another name for the common sense and average conscience of mankind. It does not allow itself, like a county court, to be hoodwinked by parchments or confused by technicalities. In its vocabulary, the right of revolution means the right of the people to protect themselves, not the privilege of tyrants to tread under foot good laws, and claim the world's sympathy in riveting weakened chains.

I say the North had a right to assume these positions. She did not. She had a right to ignore revolution until these conditions were complied with; but she did not. She waived it. In obedience to the advice of Madison, to the long history of her country's forbearance, to the magnanimity of nineteen States, she waited; she advised the government to wait. Mr. Lincoln, in his inaugural, indicated that this would be the wise course. Mr. Seward hinted it in his speech in New York. The London Times bade us remember the useless war of 1776, and take warning against resisting the principles of popular sovereignty. The Tribune, whose unflinching fidelity and matchless ability make it in this fight "the white plume of Navarre," has again and again avowed its readiness to waive forms and go into convention. We have waited. We said, "Anything for peace." We obeyed the magnanimous statesmanship of John Quincy Adams. Let me read you his advice, given at the "Jubilee of the Constitution," to the New York Historical Society, in the year 1839. He says, recognizing this right of the *people* of a State, — mark you, not a State: the Constitution in this matter knows no States; the right of revolution knows no States: it knows only THE PEOPLE. Mr. Adams says: —

"The PEOPLE of each State in the Union have a right to secede from the confederated Union itself.

"Thus stands the RIGHT. But the indissoluble link of union between the people of the several States of this confederated nation is, after all, not in the *right*, but in the *heart*.

"If the day should ever come (may Heaven avert it!) when the affections of the people of these States shall be alienated from each other, when the fraternal spirit shall give way to cold indifference, or collisions of interest shall fester into hatred, the bands of political association will not long hold together parties no longer attracted by the magnetism of conciliated interests and kindly sympathies; and far better will it be for the people of the disunited States to part in friendship from each other, than to be held together by constraint. Then will be the time for reverting to the precedents which occurred at the formation and adoption of the Constitution, to form again a more perfect union, by dissolving that which could no longer bind; and to leave the separated parts to be reunited by the law of political gravitation to the centre."

The North said "Amen" to every word of it. They waited. They begged the States to meet them. They were silent when the cannon-shot pierced the flag of the Star of the West. They said "Amen" when the government offered to let nothing but the bunting cover Fort Sumter. They said "Amen" when Lincoln stood alone, without arms, in a defenceless Capital, and trusted himself to the loyalty and forbearance of thirty-four States.

The South, if the truth be told, *cannot* wait. Like all usurpers, they dare not give time for the people to criticise their power. War and tumult must conceal the irregularity of their civil course, and smother discontent and criticism at the same time. Besides, bankruptcy at home can live out its short term of possible existence only by conquest on land and piracy at sea. And, further, only by war, by appeal to popular frenzy, can they hope to delude the Border States to join them. War is the breath of their life.

To-day, therefore, the question is, by the voice of the South, "Shall Washington or Montgomery own the continent?" And the North says, "From the Gulf to the Pole, the Stars and Stripes shall atone to four millions of negroes whom we have forgotten for seventy years; and, before you break the Union, we will see that justice is done to the slave." [Enthusiastic and long-continued cheers.]

There is only one thing those cannon-shot in the harbor of Charleston settled, — that there never can be a compromise. [Loud applause.] We Abolitionists have doubted whether this Union really meant justice and liberty. We have doubted the intention of nineteen millions of people. They have said, in answer to our criticism: "We believe that the Fathers meant to establish justice. We believe that there are hidden in the armory of the Constitution weapons strong enough to secure it. We are willing yet to try the experiment. Grant us time." We have doubted, derided the pretence, as we supposed. During these long and weary weeks we have waited to hear the Northern conscience assert its purpose. It comes at last. [An impressive pause.] Massachusetts blood has consecrated the pavements of Baltimore, and those stones are now too sacred to be trodden by slaves. [Loud cheers.]

You and I owe it to those young martyrs, you and I owe it, that their blood shall be the seed of no mere empty triumph, but that the negro shall teach his children to bless them for centuries to come. [Applause.] When Massachusetts goes down to that Carolina fort to put the Stars and Stripes again over its blackened walls [enthusiasm], she will sweep from its neighborhood every institution which hazards their ever bowing again to the palmetto. [Loud cheers.] All of you may not mean it now. Our fathers did not think in 1775 of the Declaration of Independence. The Long Parliament never thought of the scaffold of Charles the First, when they entered on the struggle; but having begun, they made thorough work. [Cheers.] It is an attribute of the Yankee blood, — slow to fight, and fight once. [Renewed cheers.] It was a holy war, that for Independence: this is a holier and the last, — that for LIBERTY. [Loud applause.]

I hear a great deal about Constitutional liberty. The mouths of Concord and Lexington guns have room only for one word, and that is LIBERTY. You might as well ask Niagara to chant the Chicago Platform, as to say how far war shall go. War and Niagara thunder to a music of their own. God alone can launch the lightnings, that they may go and say, Here we are. The thunderbolts of His throne always abase the proud, lift up the lowly, and execute justice between man and man.

Now let me turn one moment to another consideration. What should the government do? I said "thorough" should be its maxim. When we fight, we are fighting for justice and an idea. A short war and a rigid one is the maxim. Ten thousand men in Washington! it is only a bloody fight. Five hundred thousand men in Washington, and none dare come there but from the North. [Loud cheers.] Occupy St. Louis with the millions of the West, and say to Missouri, "You cannot go out!" [Applause.] Cover Maryland with a million of the friends of the administration, and say: "We must have our capital within reach. [Cheers.] If you need compensation for slaves taken from you in the convulsion of battle, here it is. [Cheers.] Government is engaged in the fearful struggle to show that '89 meant justice, and there is something better than life, holier than even real and just property, in such an hour as this." And again, we must remember another thing, — the complication of such a struggle as this. Bear with me a moment. We put five hundred thousand men on the banks of the Potomac. Virginia is held by two races, white and black. Suppose those black men flare in our faces the Declaration of Independence. What are we to say? Are we to send Northern bayonets to keep s[illegible] under the feet of Jefferson Davis? [Many voices, "[illegible]!" "Never!"] In 1842, Governor Wise of Virginia, the symbol of the South, entered into argument with Quincy Adams, who carried Plymouth Rock to Washington. [Applause.] It was when Joshua Giddings offered his resolution stating his constitutional doctrine that Congress had no right to interfere, in any event, in any way, with the slavery of the Southern States. Plymouth Rock refused to vote for it. Mr. Adams said (substantially): "If foreign war comes, if civil war comes, if insurrection comes, is this beleaguered capital, is this besieged government, to see millions of its subjects in arms, and have no right to break the fetters which they are forging into swords? No; the war power of the government can sweep this institution into the Gulf." [Cheers.] Ever since 1842, that statesman-like claim and warning of the North has been on record, spoken by the lips of her wisest son. [Applause.]

When the South cannonaded Fort Sumter the bones of Adams stirred in his coffin. [Cheers.] And you might have heard him, from that granite grave at Quincy, proclaim to the nation: "The hour has struck! Seize the thunderbolt God has forged for you, and annihilate the system which has troubled your peace for seventy years!" [Cheers.] Do not say this is a cold-blooded suggestion. I hardly ever knew slavery go down in any other circumstances. Only once, in the broad sweep of the world's history, was any nation lifted so high that she could stretch her imperial hand across the Atlantic, and lift by one peaceful word a million of slaves into liberty. God granted that glory only to our mother-land.

You heedlessly expected, and we Abolitionists hoped, that such would be our course. Sometimes it really seemed so, and we said confidently, the age of bullets is over. At others the sky lowered so darkly that we felt our only exodus would be one of blood; that, like other nations, our Bastile would fall only before revolution. Ten years ago I asked you, How did French slavery go down? How did the French slave-trade go down? When Napoleon came back from Elba, when his fate hung trembling in the balance, and he wished to gather around him the sympathies of the liberals of Europe, he no sooner set foot in the Tuileries than he signed the edict abolishing the slave-trade, against which the Abolitionists of England and France had protested for twenty years in vain. And the trade went down, because Napoleon felt he must do something to gild the darkening hour of his second attempt to clutch the sceptre of France. How did the slave system go down? When, in 1848, the Provisional Government found itself in the Hôtel de Ville, obliged to do something to draw to itself the sympathy and liberal feeling of the French nation, they signed an edict — it was the first from the rising republic — abolishing the death-penalty and slavery. The storm which rocked the vessel of state almost to foundering snapped forever the chain of the French slave. Look, too, at the history of Mexican and South American emancipation; you will find that it was in every instance, I think, the child of convulsion.

That hour has come to us. So stand we to-day. The Abolitionist who will not now cry, when the moment serves, "Up, boys, and at them!" is false to liberty. [Great cheering. A voice, "So is every other man."] Yes, to-day Abolitionist is merged in citizen, — in American. Say not it is a hard lesson. Let him who fully knows his own heart and strength, and feels, as he looks down into his child's cradle, that he could stand and see that little nestling borne to slavery, and submit, — let him cast the first stone. But all you, whose blood is wont to stir over Naseby and Bunker Hill, will hold your peace, unless you are ready to cry with me, — *Sic semper tyrannis!* "So may it ever be with tyrants!" [Loud applause.]

Why, Americans, I believe in the might of nineteen millions of people. Yes, I know that what sewing-machines and reaping-machines and ideas and types and school-houses cannot do, the muskets of Illinois and Massachusetts can finish up. [Cheers.] Blame me not that I make everything turn on liberty and the slave. I believe in Massachusetts. I know that free speech, free toil, school-houses, and ballot-boxes are a pyramid on its broadest base. Nothing that does not sunder the solid globe can disturb it. We defy the world to disturb us. [Cheers.] The little errors that dwell upon our surface, we have medicine in our institutions to cure them all. [Applause.]

Therefore there is nothing left for a New England man, nothing but that he shall wipe away the stain which hangs about the toleration of human bondage. As Webster said at Rochester, years and years ago: "If I thought that there was a stain upon the remotest hem of the garment of my country, I would devote my utmost labor to wipe it off." [Cheers.] To-day that call is made upon Massachusetts. That is the reason why I dwell so much on the slavery question. I said I believed in the power of the North to conquer; but where does she get it. I do not believe in the power of the North to subdue two millions and a half of Southern men, unless she summons justice, the negro, and God to her side [cheers]; and in that battle we are sure of this, — we are sure to rebuild the Union down to the Gulf. [Renewed cheering.] In that battle, with that watchword, with those allies, the thirteen States and their children will survive, — in the light of the world, a nation which has vindicated the sincerity of the Fathers of '87, that they bore children, and not pedlers, to represent them in the nineteenth century. [Repeated cheers.] But without that, — without that, I know also we shall conquer. Sumter annihilated compromise. Nothing but victory will blot from history that sight of the Stars and Stripes giving place to the palmetto. But without justice for inspiration, without God for our ally, we shall break the Union asunder; we shall be a confederacy, and so will they. This war means one of two things, — Emancipation or Disunion. [Cheers.] Out of the smoke of the conflict there comes that, — nothing else. It is impossible there should come anything else. Now, I believe in the future and permanent union of the races that cover this continent from the pole down to the Gulf. One in race, one in history, one in religion, one in industry, one in thought, we never can be permanently separated. Your path, if you forget the black race, will be over the gulf of Disunion, — years of unsettled, turbulent, Mexican and South American civilization, back through that desert of forty years to the Union which is sure to come.

But I believe in a deeper conscience, I believe in a North more educated than that. I divide you into four sections. The first is the ordinary mass, rushing from mere enthusiasm to

"A battle whose great aim and scope
They little care to know,
Content, like men-at-arms, to cope
Each with his fronting foe."

Behind that class stands another, whose only idea in this controversy is sovereignty and the flag. The seaboard, the wealth, the just-converted hunkerism of the country, fill that class. Next to it stands the third element, the people; the cordwainers of Lynn, the farmers of Worcester, the dwellers on the prairie, — Iowa and Wisconsin, Ohio and Maine, — the broad surface of the people who have no leisure for technicalities, who never studied law, who never had time to read any further into the Constitution than the first two lines, — "Establish *Justice* and secure *Liberty*." They have waited long enough; they have eaten dirt enough; they have apologized for bankrupt statesmen enough; they have quieted their consciences enough; they have split logic with their Abolition neighbors long enough; they are tired of trying to find a place between the forty-ninth and forty-eighth corner of a constitutional hair [laughter]; and now that they have got their hand on the neck of a rebellious aristocracy, in the name of the PEOPLE, they mean to strangle it. That I believe is the body of the people itself. Side by side with them stands a fourth class, — small, but active, — the Abolitionists, who thank God that he has let them see his salvation before they die. [Cheers.]

The noise and dust of the conflict may hide the real question at issue. Europe may think, some of us may, that we are fighting for forms and parchments, for sovereignty and a flag. But really the war is one of opinions: it is Civilization against Barbarism: it is Freedom against Slavery. The cannon-shot against Fort Sumter was the yell of pirates against the DECLARATION OF INDEPENDENCE; the war-cry of the North is the echo of that sublime pledge. The South, defying Christianity, clutches its victim. The North offers its wealth and blood in glad atonement for the selfishness of seventy years. The result is as sure as the throne of God. I believe in the possibility of justice, in the certainty of union. Years hence, when the smoke of this conflict clears away, the world will see under our banner all tongues, all creeds, all races, — one brotherhood, — and on the banks of the Potomac, the Genius of Liberty, robed in light, four and thirty stars for her diadem, broken chains under feet, and an olive-branch in her right hand. [Great applause.]

THE WAR FOR THE UNION.*

LADIES AND GENTLEMEN: It would be impossible for me fitly to thank you for this welcome; you will allow me, therefore, not to attempt it, but to avail myself of your patience to speak to you, as I have been invited to do, upon the war.

I know, Ladies and Gentlemen, that actions — deeds, not words — are the fitting duty of the hour. Yet, still, cannon think in this day of ours, and it is only by putting thought behind arms that we render them worthy, in any degree, of the civilization of the nineteenth century. [Applause.] Besides, the government has two thirds of a million of soldiers, and it has ships sufficient for its purpose. The only question seems to be, what the government is to do with these forces, — in what path, and how far it shall tread. You and I come here to-night, not to criticise, not to find fault with the Cabinet. We come here to recognize the fact, that in moments like these the statesmanship of the Cabinet is but a pine shingle upon the rapids of Niagara, borne which way the great popular heart and the national purpose direct. It is in vain now, with these scenes about us, in this crisis, to endeavor to create public opinion; too late now to educate twenty millions of people. Our object now is to concentrate and to manifest, to make evident and to make intense, the matured purpose of the nation. We are to show the world,

* Lecture delivered in New York and Boston, December, 1861.

if it be indeed so, that democratic institutions are strong enough for such an hour as this. Very terrible as is the conspiracy, momentous as is the peril, Democracy welcomes the struggle, confident that she stands like no delicately-poised throne in the Old World, but, like the Pyramid, on its broadest base, able to be patient with national evils, — generously patient with the long forbearance of three generations, — and strong enough when, after that they reveal themselves in their own inevitable and hideous proportions, to pronounce and execute the unanimous verdict, — Death!

Now, Gentlemen, it is in such a spirit, with such a purpose, that I come before you to-night to sustain this war. Whence came this war? You and I need not curiously investigate. While Mr. Everett on one side, and Mr. Sumner on the other, agree, you and I may take for granted the opinion of two such opposite statesmen, — the result of the common sense of this side of the water and the other, — that slavery is the root of this war. [Applause.] I know some men have loved to trace it to disappointed ambition, to the success of the Republican party, convincing three hundred thousand nobles at the South, who have hitherto furnished us the most of the presidents, generals, judges, and ambassadors we needed, that they would have leave to stay at home, and that twenty millions of Northerners would take their share in public affairs. I do not think that cause equal to the result. Other men before Jefferson Davis and Governor Wise have been disappointed of the Presidency. Henry Clay, Daniel Webster, and Stephen A. Douglas were more than once disappointed, and yet who believes that either of these great men could have armed the North to avenge his wrongs? Why, then, should these pigmies of the South be able to do what the giants I have named could never achieve? Simply because there is a radical difference between the two sections, and that difference is slavery. A party victory may have been the *occasion* of this outbreak. So a tea-chest was the occasion of the Revolution, and it went to the bottom of Boston harbor on the night of the 16th of December, 1773; but that tea-chest was not the cause of the Revolution, neither is Jefferson Davis the cause of the rebellion. If you will look upon the map, and notice that every Slave State has joined or tried to join the rebellion, and no Free State has done so, I think you will not doubt substantially the origin of this convulsion.

Now, Ladies and Gentlemen, you know me — those of you who know me at all — simply as an Abolitionist. I am proud and glad that you should have known me as such. In the twenty-five years that are gone, — I say it with no wish to offend any man before me, — but in the quarter of a century that has passed, I could find no place where an American could stand with decent self-respect, except in constant, uncontrollable, and loud protest against the sin of his native land. But, Ladies and Gentlemen, do not imagine that I come here to-night to speak simply and exclusively as an Abolitionist. My interest in this war, simply and exclusively as an Abolitionist, is about as much gone as yours in a novel where the hero has won the lady, and the marriage has been comfortably celebrated in the last chapter. I know the danger of political prophecy, — a kaleidoscope of which not even a Yankee can guess the next combination, — but for all that, I venture to offer my opinion, that on this continent the system of domestic slavery has received its death-blow. [Loud and long-continued applause.] Let me tell you why I think so. Leaving out of view war with England, which I do not expect, there are but three paths out of this war. One is, the North conquers; the other is, the South conquers; and the third is, a compromise. Now, if the North conquers, or there be a compromise, one or the other of two things

must come, — either the old Constitution or a new one. I believe that, so far as the slavery clauses of the Constitution of '89 are concerned, it is dead. It seems to me impossible that the thrifty and painstaking North, after keeping six hundred thousand men idle for two or three years, at a cost of two million dollars a day; after that flag lowered at Sumter; after Baker and Lyon and Ellsworth and Winthrop and Putnam and Wesselhœft have given their lives to quell the rebellion; after our Massachusetts boys, hurrying from ploughed field and workshop to save the capital, have been foully murdered on the pavements of Baltimore, — I cannot believe in a North so lost, so craven, as to put back slavery where it stood on the 4th of March last. [Cheers.] But if there be reconstruction without those slave clauses, then in a little while, longer or shorter, slavery dies, — indeed, on any other basis but the basis of '89, she has nothing else now to do but to die. On the contrary, if the South — no, I cannot say conquers — my lips will not form that word — but if she balks us of victory, the only way she can do it is to write Emancipation on her own banner, and thus bribe the friends of liberty in Europe to allow its aristocrats and traders to divide the majestic republic whose growth and trade they fear and envy. Either way, the slave goes free. Unless England flings her fleets along the coast, the South can never spring into separate existence, except from the basis of negro freedom; and I for one cannot yet believe that the North will consent again to share his chains. Exclusively as an Abolitionist, therefore, I have little more interest in this war than the frontiersman's wife had in his struggle with the bear, when she did n't care which whipped. But before I leave the Abolitionists, let me say one word. Some men say we are the cause of this war. Gentlemen, you do us too much honor! If it be so, we have reason to be proud of it; for in my heart, as an American, I believe this year the most glorious of the Republic since '76. The North, craven and contented until now, like Mammon, saw nothing even in heaven but the golden pavement; to-day she throws off her chains. We have a North, as Daniel Webster said. This is no epoch for nations to blush at. England might blush in 1620, when Englishmen trembled at a fool's frown, and were silent when James forbade them to think; but not in 1649, when an outraged people cut off his son's head. Massachusetts might have blushed a year or two ago, when an insolent Virginian, standing on Bunker Hill, insulted the Commonwealth, and then dragged her citizens to Washington to tell what they knew about John Brown; but she has no reason to blush to-day, when she holds that same impudent Senator an acknowledged felon in her prison-fort. In my view, the bloodiest war ever waged is infinitely better than the happiest slavery which ever fattened men into obedience. And yet I love peace. But it is real peace; not peace such as we have had; not peace that meant lynch-law in the Carolinas and mob-law in New York; not peace that meant chains around Boston Court-House, a gag on the lips of statesmen, and the slave sobbing himself to sleep in curses. No more such peace for me; no peace that is not born of justice, and does not recognize the rights of every race and every man.

Some men say they would view this war as white men. I condescend to no such narrowness. I view it as an American citizen, proud to be the citizen of an empire that knows neither black nor white, neither Saxon nor Indian, but holds an equal sceptre over all. [Loud cheers.] If I am to love my country, it must be lovable; if I am to honor it, it must be worthy of respect. What is the function God gives us, — what is the breadth of responsibility he lays upon us? An empire, the home of every race, every creed, every tongue, to whose citizens is committed, if not the only, then the grandest system of pure self-government. Tocqueville tells us that all nations and all ages tend with inevitable certainty to this result; but he points out, as history does, this land as the normal school of the nations, set by God to try the experiment of popular education and popular government, to remove the obstacles, point out the dangers, find the best way, encourage the timid, and hasten the world's progress. Let us see to it, that with such a crisis and such a past, neither the ignorance, nor the heedlessness, nor the cowardice of Americans forfeits this high honor, won for us by the toils of two generations, given to us by the blessing of Providence. It is as a citizen of the leading State of this Western continent, vast in territory, and yet its territory nothing when compared with the grandeur of its past and the majesty of its future, — it is as such a citizen that I wish, for one, to find out my duty, express as an individual my opinion, and aid thereby the Cabinet in doing its duty under such responsibility. It does not lie in one man to ruin us, nor in one man to save us, nor in a dozen. It lies in the twenty millions, in the thirty millions, of thirty-four States.

Now how do we stand? In a war, — not only that, but a terrific war, — not a war sprung from the caprice of a woman, the spite of a priest, the flickering ambition of a prince, as wars usually have; but a war inevitable; in one sense, nobody's fault; the inevitable result of past training, the conflict of ideas, millions of people grappling each other's throats, every soldier in each camp certain that he is fighting for an idea which holds the salvation of the world, — every drop of his blood in earnest. Such a war finds no parallel nearer than that of the Catholic and the Huguenot of France, or that of Aristocrat and Republican in 1790, or of Cromwell and the Irish, when victory meant extermination. Such is our war. I look upon it as the commencement of the great struggle between the disguised aristocracy and the democracy of America. You are to say to-day whether it shall last ten years or seventy, as it usually has done. It resembles closely that struggle between aristocrat and democrat which began in France in 1789, and continues still. While it lasts, it will have the same effect on the nation as that war between blind loyalty, represented by the Stuart family, and the free spirit of the English Constitution, which lasted from 1660 to 1760, and kept England a second-rate power almost all that century.

Such is the era on which you are entering. I will not speak of war in itself, — I have no time; I will not say, with Napoleon, that it is the practice of barbarians; I will not say that it is good. It is better than the past. A thing may be *better*, and yet not *good*. This war is better than the past, but there is not an element of good in it. I mean, there is nothing in it which we might not have gotten better, fuller, and more perfectly in other ways. And yet it is better than the craven past, infinitely better than a peace which had pride for its father and subserviency for its mother. Neither will I speak of the cost of war, although you know that we never shall get out of this one without a debt of at least two or three thousand millions of dollars. For if the prevalent theory prove correct, and the country comes together again on anything like the old basis, we pay Jeff Davis's debts as well as our own. Neither will I remind you that debt is the fatal disease of republics, the first thing and the mightiest to undermine government and corrupt the people. The great debt of England has kept her back in civil progress at least a hundred years. Neither will I remind you that, when we go out of this war, we go out with an immense disbanded army, an intense military spirit embodied in two thirds of a million of soldiers, the fruitful, the inevitable source of fresh debts and new wars. I pass by all that; yet lying within those causes are things enough to make the most sanguine friends of free institutions tremble for our future. I pass those by. But let me remind you of another tendency of the time. You know, for instance, that the writ of *habeas corpus*, by which government is bound to render a reason to the judiciary before it lays its hands upon a citizen, has been called the high-water mark of English liberty. Jefferson, in his calm moments, dreaded the power to suspend it in any emergency whatever, and wished to have it in "eternal and unremitting force." The present Napoleon, in his treatise on the English Constitution, calls it the gem of English institutions. Lieber says that *habeas corpus*, free meetings like this, and a free press, are the three elements which distinguish liberty from despotism. All that Saxon blood has gained in the battles and toils of two hundred years are these three things. But to-day, Mr. Chairman, every one of them — *habeas corpus*, the right of free meeting, and a free press — is annihilated in every square mile of the Republic. We live to-day, every one of us, under martial law. The Secretary of State puts into his bastile, with a warrant as irresponsible as that of Louis, any man whom he pleases. And you know that neither press nor lips may venture to arraign the government without being silenced. At this moment one thousand men, at least, are "bastiled" by an authority as despotic as that of Louis, — three times as many as Eldon and George III. seized when they trembled for his throne. Mark me, I am not complaining. I do not say it is not necessary. It is necessary to do anything to save the ship. [Applause.] It is necessary to throw everything overboard in order that we may float. It is a mere question whether you prefer the despotism of Washington or that of Richmond. I prefer that of Washington. [Loud applause.] But, nevertheless, I point out to you this tendency, because it is momentous in its significance. We are tending with rapid strides, you say *inevitably*, — I do not deny it; *necessarily*, — I do not question it; we are tending toward that strong government which frightened Jefferson; toward that unlimited debt, that endless army. We have already those alien and sedition laws which, in 1798, wrecked the Federal party, and summoned the Democratic into existence. For the first time on this continent we have passports, which even Louis Napoleon pronounces useless and odious. For the first time in our history government spies frequent our great cities. And this model of a strong government, if you reconstruct it on the old basis, is to be handed into the keeping of whom? If you compromise it by reconstruction, to whom are you to give these delicate and grave powers? To compromisers. Reconstruct this government, and for twenty years you can never elect a Republican. Presidents must be so wholly without character or principle, that two angry parties, each hopeless of success, contemptuously tolerate them as neutrals. Now I am not exaggerating the moment. I can parallel it entirely. It is the same position that England held in the times of Eldon and Fox, when Holcroft and Montgomery, the poet, Horne Tooke and Frost and Hardy, went into dungeons, under laws which Pitt executed and Burke praised,—times when Fox said he despaired of English liberty but for the power of insurrection, — times which Sidney Smith said he remembered, when no man was entitled to an opinion who had not £ 3,000 a year. Why! there is no right — do I exaggerate when I say that there is no single right?— which government is scrupulous and finds itself able to protect, except the pretended right of a man to his slaves! Every other right has fallen now before the necessities of the hour.

Understand me, I do not complain of this state of things; but it is momentous. I only ask you, that out of this peril you be sure to get something worthy of the crisis through which you have passed. No government of free make could stand three such trials as this. I only paint you the picture, in order, like Hotspur, to say: "Out of this nettle, danger, be you right eminently sure that you pluck the flower, safety." [Applause.] Standing in such a crisis, certainly it commands us that we should endeavor to find the root of the difficulty, and that now, once for all, we should put it beyond the possibility of troubling our peace again. We cannot afford, as Republicans, to run that risk. The vessel of state, — her timbers are strained beyond almost the possibility of surviving. The tempest is one which it demands the wariest pilot to outlive. We cannot afford, thus warned, to omit anything which can save this ship of state from a second danger of the kind.

What shall we do? The answer to that question comes partly from what we think has been the cause of this convulsion. Some men think — some of your editors think — many of ours, too — that this war is nothing but the disappointment of one or two thousand angered politicians, who have persuaded eight millions of Southerners, against their convictions, to take up arms and rush to the battle-field; — no great compliment to Southern sense! [Laughter.] They think that, if the Federal army could only appear in the midst of this demented mass, the eight millions will find out for the first time in their lives that they have got souls of their own, tell us so, and then we shall all be piloted back, float back, drift back into the good old times of Franklin Pierce and James Buchanan. [Laughter.] There is a measure of truth in that. I believe that if, a year ago, when the thing first showed itself, Jefferson Davis and Toombs and Keitt and Wise, and the rest, had been hung for traitors at Washington, and a couple of frigates anchored at Charleston, another couple in Savannah, and half a dozen in New Orleans, with orders to shell those cities on the first note of resistance, there never would have been this outbreak [applause], or it would have been postponed at least a dozen years; and if that interval had been used to get rid of slavery, we never should have heard of the convulsion. But you know we had nothing of the kind, and the consequence is, what? Why, the amazed North has been summoned by every defeat and every success, from its workshops and its factories, to gaze with wide-opened eyes at the lurid heavens, until at last, divided, bewildered, confounded, as this twenty millions were, we have all of us fused into one idea, that the Union meant justice, — shall mean justice, — owns down to the Gulf, and we will have it. [Applause.] What has taken place meanwhile at the South? Why, the same thing. The divided, bewildered South has been summoned also out of her divisions by every success and every defeat (and she has had more of the first than we have), and the consequence is, that she too is fused into a swelling sea of State pride, hate of the North, —

> "Unconquerable will,
> And study of revenge, immortal hate,
> And courage never to submit nor yield."

She is in earnest, every man, and she is as unanimous as the Colonies were in the Revolution. In fact, the South recognizes more intelligibly than we do the necessities of her position. I do not consider this a secession. It is no secession. I agree with Bishop-General Polk, — it is a conspiracy, not a secession. There is no wish, no intention to go peaceably and permanently off. It is a conspiracy to make the government do the will and accept the policy of the slaveholders. Its root is at the South, but it has many a branch in Wall Street and in State Street. [Cheers.] It is a conspiracy, and on the one side is every man who still thinks that he that steals his brother is a gentleman, and he that makes his living is not. [Applause.] It is the aristocratic element which survived the Constitution, which our fathers thought could be safely left under it, and the South to-day is forced into this war by the natural growth of the antagonistic principle. You may pledge whatever submission and patience of Southern institutions you please, it is not enough. South Carolina said to Massachusetts in 1835, when Edward Everett was Governor, "Abolish free speech, — it is a nuisance." She is right, — from her stand-point it is. [Laughter.] That is, it is not possible to preserve the quiet of South Carolina consistently with free speech ; but you know the story Sir Walter Scott told of the Scotch laird, who said to his old butler, "Jock, you and I can't live under this roof." "And where does your honor think of going?" So free speech says to South Carolina to-day. Now I say you may pledge, compromise, guarantee what you please. The South well knows that it is not your purpose, — it is your character she dreads. It is the nature of Northern institutions, the perilous freedom of discussion, the flavor of our ideas, the sight of our growth, the very neighborhood of such States, that constitutes the danger. It is like the two vases launched on the stormy sea. The iron said to the crockery, "I won't come near you." "Thank you," said the weaker vessel; "there is just as much danger in my coming near you." This the South feels; hence her determination ; hence, indeed, the imperious necessity that she should rule and shape our government, or of sailing out of it. I do not mean that she plans to take possession of the North, and choose our Northern Mayors; though she has done that in Boston for the last dozen years, and here till this fall. But she conspires and aims to control just so much of our policy, trade, offices, presses, pulpits, cities, as is sufficient to insure the undisturbed existence of slavery. She conspires with the full intent so to mould this government as to keep it what it has been for thirty years, according to John Quincy Adams, — a plot for the extension and perpetuation of slavery. As the world advances, fresh guaranties are demanded. The nineteenth century requires sterner gags than the eighteenth. Often as the peace of Virginia is in danger, you must be willing that a Virginia Mason shall drag your citizens to Washington, and imprison them at his pleasure. So long as Carolina needs it, you must submit that your ships be searched for dangerous passengers, and every Northern man lynched. No more Kansas rebellions. It is a conflict between the two powers, Aristocracy and Democracy, *which shall hold this belt of the continent.* You may live here, New York men, but it must be in submission to such rules as the quiet of Carolina requires. That is the meaning of the oft-repeated threat to call the roll of one's slaves on Bunker Hill, and dictate peace in Faneuil Hall. Now, in that fight, I go for the North, — for the Union.

In order to make out this theory of "irrepressible con flict," it is not necessary to suppose that every Southerner hates every Northerner (as the *Atlantic Monthly* urges). But this much is true: some three hundred thousand slaveholders at the South, holding two thousand millions of so-called property in their hands, controlling the blacks, and befooling the seven millions of poor whites into being their tools, — into believing that their interest is opposed to ours, — this order of nobles, this privileged class, has been able for forty years to keep the government in dread, dictate terms by threatening disunion, bring us to its verge at least twice, and now almost to break the Union in pieces. A power thus consolidated,. which has existed seventy years, setting up and pulling down parties, controlling the policy of the government, and changing our religion, and is emboldened by uniform success, will not burst like a bubble in an hour. For all practical purposes, it is safe to speak of it as the South; no other South exists, or will exist, till our policy develops it into being. This is what I mean. An aristocracy rooted in wealth, with its network spread over all social life, its poison penetrating every fibre of society, is the hardest possible evil to destroy. Its one influence, FASHION, is often able to mock at Religion, Trade, Literature, and Politics combined. One half the reason why Washington has been and is in peril, — why every move is revealed and checkmated, — is that your President is unfashionable, and Mrs. Jefferson Davis is not. Unseen chains are sometimes stronger than those of iron, and heavier than those of gold.

It is not in the plots, it is in the inevitable character of the Northern States, that the South sees her danger. And the struggle is between these two ideas. Our fathers, as I said, thought they could safely be left, one to outgrow the other. They took gunpowder and a lighted match, forced them into a stalwart cannon, screwed down the muzzle, and thought they could secure peace. But it has resulted differently; their cannon has exploded, and we stand among fragments.

Now some Republicans and some Democrats — not Butler and Bryant and Cochrane and Cameron, not Boutwell and Bancroft and Dickinson, and others — but the old set — the old set say to the Republicans, "Lay the pieces carefully together in their places; put the gunpowder and the match in again, say the Constitution backward instead of your prayers, and there will never be another rebellion!" I doubt it. It seems to me that like causes will produce like effects. If the reason of the war is because we are two nations, then the cure must be to make us one nation, to remove that cause which divides us, to make our institutions homogeneous. If it were possible to subjugate the South, and leave slavery just as it is, where is the security that we should not have another war in ten years? Indeed, such a course invites another war, whenever demagogues please. I believe the policy of reconstruction is impossible. And if it were possible, it would be the greatest mistake that Northern men could commit. [Cheers.] I will not stop to remind you that, standing as we do to-day, with the full constitutional right to abolish slavery, — a right Southern treason has just given us, — a right, the use of which is enjoined by the sternest necessity, — if, after that, the North goes back to the Constitution of '89, she assumes, a second time, afresh, unnecessarily, a criminal responsibility for slavery. Hereafter no old excuse will avail us. A second time, with open eyes, against our highest interest, we clasp bloody hands with tyrants to uphold an acknowledged sin, whose fell evil we have fully proved.

But that aside, peace with an unchanged Constitution would leave us to stand like Mexico. States married, not matched; chained together, not melted into one; foreign nations aware of our hostility, and interfering to embroil, rob, and control us. We should be what Greece was under the intrigues of Philip, and Germany when Louis XIV. was in fact her dictator. We may see our likeness in Austria, every fretful province an addition of weakness; in Italy, twenty years ago, a leash of angry hounds. A Union with unwilling and subjugated States, smarting with defeat, and yet holding the powerful and dangerous element of slavery in it, and an army disbanded into laborers, food for constant disturbance, would be a standing invitation to France and England to insult and dictate, to thwart our policy, demand changes in our laws, and trample on us continually.

Reconstruction is but another name for the submission of the North. It is her subjection under a mask. It is nothing but the confession of defeat. Every merchant, in such a case, puts everything he has at the bidding of Wigfall and Toombs in every cross-road bar-room at the South. For, you see, never till now did anybody but a few Abolitionists believe that this nation could be marshalled one section against the other in arms. But the secret is out. The weak point is discovered. Why does the London press lecture us like a schoolmaster his seven-year-old boy? Why does England use a tone such as she has not used for half a century to any power? Because she knows us as she knows Mexico, as all Europe knows Austria, — that we have the cancer concealed in our very vitals. Slavery, left where it is, after having created such a war as this, would leave our commerce and all our foreign relations at the mercy of any Keitt, Wigfall, Wise, or Toombs. Any demagogue has only to stir up a proslavery crusade, point back to the safe experiment of 1861, and lash the passions of the aristocrats, to cover the sea with privateers, put in jeopardy the trade of twenty States, plunge the country into millions of debt, send our stocks down fifty per cent, and cost thousands of lives. Reconstruction is but making chronic what now is transient. What that is, this week shows. What that is, we learn from the tone England dares to assume toward this divided republic. I do not believe reconstruction possible. I do not believe the Cabinet intend it. True, I should care little if they did, since I believe the administration can no more resist the progress of events, than a spear of grass can retard the step of an avalanche. But if they do, allow me to say, for one, that every dollar spent in this war is worse than wasted, every life lost is a public murder, and that any statesman who leads these States back to reconstruction will be damned to an infamy compared with which Arnold was a saint and James Buchanan a public benefactor. [Slight disturbance in the rear part of the hall; cries of "Put him out!" etc.] No, do not put him out; his is the very mind I wish to reach. I said reconstruction is not possible. I do not believe it is, for this reason; the moment these States begin to appear victorious, the moment our armies do anything that evinces final success, the wily statesmanship and unconquerable hate of the South will write "Emancipation" on her banner, and welcome the protectorate of a European power. And if you read the European papers of to-day, you need not doubt that she will have it. Intelligent men agree that the North stands better with Palmerston for minister, than she would with any minister likely to succeed him. And who is Palmerston? While he was Foreign Secretary, from 1848 to 1851, the British press ridiculed every effort of the French Republicans,—sneered at Cavaignac and Ledru Rollin, Lamartine and Hugo,—while they cheered Napoleon on to his usurpation; and Lord Normanby, then Minister at Paris, early in December, while Napoleon's hand was still wet with the best blood of France, congratulated the despot on his victory over the Reds, applying to the friends of Liberty the worst epithet that an Englishman knows. This last outrage lost Palmerston his place; but he rules to-day,—though rebuked, not changed.

The value of the English news this week is the indication of the nation's mind. No one doubts now, that, should the South emancipate, England would make haste to recognize and help her. In ordinary times, the government and aristocracy of England dread American example. They may well admire and envy the strength of our government, when, instead of England's impressment and pinched levies, patriotism marshals six hundred thousand *volunteers* in six months. The English merchant is jealous of our growth;

only the liberal middle classes really sympathize with us. When the two other classes are divided, this middle class rules. But now Herod and Pilate are agreed. The aristocrat, who usually despises a trader, whether of Manchester or Liverpool, as the South does a negro, now is Secessionist from sympathy, as the trader is from interest. Such a union no middle class can checkmate. The only danger of war with England is, that, as soon as England declared war with us, she would recognize the Southern Confederacy immediately, just as she stands, slavery and all, as a military measure. As such, in the heat of passion, in the smoke of war, the English people, all of them, would allow such a recognition even of a slaveholding empire. War with England insures disunion. When England declares war, she gives slavery a fresh lease of fifty years. Even if we have no war with England, let another eight or ten months be as little successful as the last, and Europe will acknowledge the Southern Confederacy, slavery and all, as a matter of course. Further, any approach toward victory on our part, without freeing the slave, gives him free to Davis. So far, the South is sure to succeed, either by victory or defeat, unless we anticipate her. Indeed, the only way, the only sure way, to break this Union, is to try to save it by protecting slavery. "Every moment lost," as Napoleon said, "is an opportunity for misfortune." Unless we emancipate the slave, we shall never conquer the South without her trying emancipation. Every Southerner, from Toombs up to Fremont, has acknowledged it. Do you suppose that Davis and Beauregard, and the rest, mean to be exiles, wandering contemned in every great city of Europe, in order that they may maintain slavery and the Constitution of '89? They, like ourselves, will throw everything overboard before they will submit to defeat, — defeat from Yankees. I do not believe, therefore, that reconciliation is possible, nor do I believe the

Cabinet have any such hopes. Indeed, I do not know where you will find the evidence of *any* purpose in the administration at Washington. [Hisses, cheers, and laughter.] If we look to the West, if we look to the Potomac, what is the policy? If, on the Potomac, with the aid of twenty Governors, you assemble an army, and do nothing but return fugitive slaves, that proves you competent and efficient. If, on the banks of the Mississippi, unaided, the magic of your presence summons an army into existence, and you drive your enemy before you a hundred miles farther than your second in command thought it possible for you to advance, that proves you incompetent, and entitles your second in command to succeed you. [Tremendous applause, and three cheers for Fremont.]

Looking in another direction, you see the government announcing a policy in South Carolina. What is it? Well, Mr. Secretary Cameron says to the general in command there: "You are to welcome into your camp all comers; you are to organize them into squads and companies; use them any way you please;—but there is to be no general arming." That is a very significant exception. The hint is broad enough for the dullest brain. In one of Charles Reade's novels, the heroine flies away to hide from the hero, announcing that she never shall see him again. Her letter says: "I will never see you again, David. You, of course, won't come to see me at my old nurse's dear little cottage [laughter], between eleven in the morning and four in the afternoon, because I sha'n't see you." [Laughter.] So Mr. Cameron says there is to be no general arming, but I suppose there is to be a very particular arming. [Laughter.] But he goes on to add: "This is no greater interference with the institutions of South Carolina than is necessary,—than the war will cure." Does he mean he will give the slaves back when the war is over? I don't know. All I know is, that the Port Royal expedition proved one thing, — it laid forever that ghost of an argument, that the blacks loved their masters, — it settled forever the question whether the blacks were with us or with the South. My opinion is, that the blacks are the key of our position. [A Voice, "That is it."] He that gets them wins, and he that loses them goes to the wall. [Applause.] Port Royal settled one thing, — the blacks are with us, and not with the South. At present they are the only Unionists. I know nothing more touching in history, nothing that art will immortalize and poetry dwell upon more fondly, — I know no tribute to the Stars and Stripes more impressive than that incident of the blacks coming to the water-side with their little bundles, in that simple faith which had endured through the long night of so many bitter years. They preferred to be shot rather than driven from the sight of that banner they had so long prayed to see. And if that was the result when nothing but General Sherman's equivocal proclamation was landed on the Carolinas, what should we have seen if there had been eighteen thousand veterans with Fremont, the statesman-soldier of this war, at their head [loud applause], and over them the Stars and Stripes, gorgeous with the motto, "Freedom for all! freedom forever!" If that had gone before them, in my opinion they would have marched across the Carolinas, and joined Brownlow in East Tennessee. [Applause.] The bulwark on each side of them would have been one hundred thousand grateful blacks; they would have cut this rebellion in halves, and while our fleets fired salutes across New Orleans, Beauregard would have been ground to powder between the upper millstone of McClellan and the lower of a quarter-million of blacks rising to greet the Stars and Stripes. [Great cheering.] McClellan may drill a better army, — more perfect soldiers. He will never marshal a stronger force than those grateful thousands. That is the way to save insurrection. He is an enemy to civil liberty, the worst enemy to his own land, who asks for such delay or perversion of government policy as is sure to result in insurrection. Our duty is to save these four millions of blacks from their own passions, from their own confusion, and eight millions of whites from the consequences of it. ["Hear, hear!"] And in order to do it, we nineteen millions of educated, Christian Americans are not to wait for the will or the wisdom of a single man, — we are not to wait for Fremont or McClellan: the government is our dictator. It might do for Rome, a herd of beggars and soldiers, kept quiet only by the weight of despotism, — it might do for Rome, in moments of danger, to hurl all responsibility into the hands of a dictator. But for us, educated, thoughtful men, with institutions modelled and matured by the experience of two hundred years, — it is not for us to evade responsibility by deferring to a single man. I demand of the government a policy. I demand of the government to show the doubting infidels of Europe that democracy is not only strong enough for the trial, but that she breeds men with brains large enough to comprehend the hour, and wills hot enough to fuse the purpose of nineteen millions of people into one decisive blow for safety and for Union. [Cheers.] You will ask me how it is to be done. I would have it done by Congress. We have the power.

When Congress declares war, says John Quincy Adams, Congress has all the powers incident to carrying on war.*

* "Sir, in the authority given to Congress by the Constitution of the United States to *declare war, all the powers incidental to war* are, by necessary implication, conferred upon the *government* of the United States. . . . . There are two classes of powers vested by the Constitution of the United States in their Congress and executive government: the powers to be executed in time of peace and the powers incident to war. That the powers of peace are limited by provisions within the body of the Constitution itself; but that the powers of war are limited and regulated only by the laws and

It is not an unconstitutional power, — it is a power conferred by the Constitution; but the moment it comes into play it rises beyond the limit of constitutional checks. I know it is a grave power, this trusting the government with despotism. But what is the use of government, except just to help us in critical times? All the checks and ingenuity of our institutions are arranged to secure for us men wise and able enough to be trusted with grave powers, — bold enough to use them when the times require. Lancets and knives are dangerous instruments. The use of surgeons is, that, when lancets are needed, somebody may know how to use them, and save life. One great merit of democratic institutions is, that, resting as they must on educated masses, the government may safely be trusted, in a great emergency, with despotic power, without fear of harm, or of wrecking the state. No other form of government can venture such confidence without

usages of nations, and are subject to no other limitation. . . . . . I do not admit that there is, *even among the peace powers of Congress*, no such authority; but *in war*, there are many ways by which *Congress not only have the authority, but are bound to interfere with the institution of slavery in the States.* . . . . . When the Southern States are the battle-field between Slavery and Emancipation, Congress may sustain the institution by war, or perhaps *abolish it by* treaties of peace; and they will not only possess the constitutional power so to interfere, but *they will be bound in duty to do it, by the express provisions of the Constitution itself.* From the instant the slaveholding States become the theatre of a war, *civil, servile, or foreign*, from that instant *the war powers of Congress extend to interference with the institution of slavery in every way by which it can be interfered with.* . . . . . With a call to keep down slaves, in an insurrection and a civil war, comes a full and plenary power *to this House* and *to the Senate* over the whole subject. It is a war power. Whether it be a war of invasion or a war of insurrection, Congress has power to carry on the war, and must carry it on, according to the laws of war: and by the laws of war an invaded country has all its laws and municipal institutions *swept by the board*, and martial law takes the place of them. This *power in Congress* has, perhaps, never been called into exercise under the present Constitution of the United States." — *Speeches of John Quincy Adams in the U. S. House of Representatives*, 1836 - 1842.

risk of national ruin. Doubtless the war power is a very grave power; so are some ordinary peace powers. I will not cite extreme cases, — Louisiana and Texas. We obtained the first by treaty, the second by joint resolutions; each case an exercise of power as grave and despotic as the abolition of slavery would be, and, unlike that, plainly unconstitutional, — one which nothing but stern necessity and subsequent acquiescence by the nation could make valid. Let me remind you that seventy years' practice has incorporated it as a principle in our constitutional law, that what the necessity of the hour demands, and the continued assent of the people ratifies, is law. Slavery has established that rule. We might surely use it in the cause of justice. But I will cite an unquestionable precedent. It was a grave power, in 1807, in time of peace, when Congress abolished commerce; when, by the embargo of Jefferson, no ship could quit New York or Boston, and Congress set no limit to the prohibition. It annihilated commerce. New England asked, "Is it constitutional?" The Supreme Court said, "Yes." New England sat down and starved. Her wharves were worthless, her ships rotted, her merchants beggared. She asked no compensation. The powers of Congress carried bankruptcy from New Haven to Portland; but the Supreme Court said, "It is legal," and New England bowed her head. We commend the same cup to the Carolinas to-day. We say to them that, in order to save the government, there resides somewhere despotism. It is in the war powers of Congress. That despotism can change the social arrangements of the Southern States, and has a right to do it. Every man of you who speaks of the emancipation of the negroes allows it would be decisive if it were used. You allow that, when it is a military necessity, we may use it. What I claim is, in honor of our institutions, that we are not put to wait for the wisdom or the courage of a general. Our fathers left us with no such miserable plan of government. They gave us a government with the power, in such times as these, of doing something that would save the helm of state in the hands of its citizens. [Cheers.] We could cede the Carolinas; I have sometimes wished we could shovel them into the Atlantic. [Applause and laughter.] We can cede a State. We can do anything for the time being; and no theory of government can deny its power to make the most unlimited change. The only alternative is this: Do you prefer the despotism of your own citizens or of foreigners? That is the only question in war. [Cheers.] In peace no man may be deprived of his life but "by the judgment of his peers, or the law of the land." To touch life, you must have a grand jury to present, a petit jury to indict, a judge to condemn, and a sheriff to execute. That is constitutional, the necessary and invaluable bulwark of liberty, in peace. But in war the government bids Sigel shoot Lee, and the German is at once grand jury, petit jury, judge, and executioner. That, too, is constitutional, necessary, and invaluable, protecting a nation's rights and life.

Now this government, which abolishes my right of *habeas corpus*, — which strikes down, because it is necessary, every Saxon bulwark of liberty, — which proclaims martial law, and holds every dollar and every man at the will of the Cabinet, — do you turn round and tell me that this same government has no rightful power to break the cobweb — it is but a cobweb — which binds a slave to his master, — to stretch its hands across the Potomac, and root up the evil which, for seventy years, has troubled its peace, and now culminates in rebellion? I maintain, therefore, the power of the government itself to inaugurate such a policy; and I say, in order to save the Union, do justice to the black. [Applause.]

I would claim of Congress — in the exact language of

Adams, of the "*government*" — a solemn act abolishing slavery throughout the Union, securing compensation to loyal slaveholders. As the Constitution forbids the States to make and allow nobles, I would now, by equal authority, forbid them to make slaves or allow slaveholders.

This has been the usual course at such times. Nations, convulsed and broken by too powerful elements or institutions, have used the first moment of assured power — the first moment that they clearly saw and fully appreciated the evil — to cut up the dangerous tree by the roots. So France expelled the Jesuits, and the Middle Ages the Templars. So England, in her great rebellion, abolished nobility and the Established Church; and the French Revolution did the same, and finally gave to each child an equal share in his deceased father's lands. For the same purpose, England, in 1745, abolished clanship in Scotland, the root of the Stuart faction; and we, in '76, abolished nobles and all tenure of estates savoring of privileged classes. Such a measure supplies the South just what she needs, — capital. That sum which the North gives the loyal slaveholder, not as acknowledging his property in the slave, but a measure of conciliation, — perhaps an acknowledgment of its share of the guilt, — will call mills, ships, agriculture, into being. The free negro will redeem to use lands never touched, whose fertility laughs Illinois to scorn, and finds no rival but Egypt. And remember, besides, as Montesquieu says, "The yield of land depends less on its fertility than on the freedom of its inhabitants." Such a measure binds the negro to us by the indissoluble tie of gratitude; the loyal slaveholder, by strong self-interest, — our bonds are all his property; the other whites, by prosperity, — they are lifted in the scale of civilization and activity, educated and enriched. Our institutions are then homogeneous. We grapple the Union together with hooks of steel, — make it as lasting as the granite which underlies the continent.

People may say this is a strange language for me, — a Disunionist. Well, I was a Disunionist, sincerely, for twenty years. I did hate the Union, when Union meant lies in the pulpit and mobs in the street, when Union meant making white men hypocrites and black men slaves. [Cheers.] I did prefer purity to peace, — I acknowledge it. The child of six generations of Puritans, knowing well the value of union, I did prefer disunion to being the accomplice of tyrants. But now, when I see what the Union must mean in order to last, when I see that you cannot have union without meaning justice, and when I see twenty millions of people, with a current as swift and as inevitable as Niagara, determined that this Union shall mean justice, why should I object to it? I endeavored honestly, and am not ashamed of it, to take nineteen States out of this Union, and consecrate them to liberty, and twenty millions of people answer me back, "We like your motto, only we mean to keep thirty-four States under it." Do you suppose I am not Yankee enough to buy union when I can have it at a fair price? I know the value of union; and the reason why I claim that Carolina has no right to secede is this: we are not a partnership, we are a marriage, and we have done a great many things since we were married in 1789 which render it unjust for a State to exercise the right of revolution on any ground now alleged. I admit the right. I acknowledge the great principles of the Declaration of Independence, that a state exists for the liberty and happiness of the people, that these are the ends of government, and that, when government ceases to promote those ends, the people have a right to remodel their institutions. I acknowledge the right of revolution in South Carolina, but at the same time I acknowledge that right of revolution only when government has ceased to promote those ends. Now we have been married for seventy years.

We have bought Florida. We rounded the Union to the Gulf. We bought the Mississippi for commercial purposes. We stole Texas for slave purposes. Great commercial interests, great interests of peace, have been subserved by rounding the Union into a perfect shape; and the money and sacrifices of two generations have been given for this purpose. To break up that Union now, is to defraud us of mutual advantages relating to peace, trade, national security, which cannot survive disunion. The right of revolution is not matter of caprice. "Governments long established," says our Declaration of Independence, "are not to be changed for light and transient causes." When so many important interests and benefits, in their nature indivisible and which disunion destroys, have been secured by common toils and cost, the South must vindicate her revolution by showing that our government has become destructive of its proper ends, else the right of revolution does not exist. Why did we steal Texas? Why have we helped the South to strengthen herself? Because she said that slavery within the girdle of the Constitution would die out through the influence of natural principles. She said: "We acknowledge it to be an evil; but at the same time it will end by the spread of free principles and the influence of free institutions." And the North said: "Yes; we will give you privileges on that account, and we will return your slaves for you." Every slave sent back from a Northern State is a fresh oath of the South that she would not secede. Our fathers trusted to the promise that this race should be left under the influence of the Union, until, in the maturity of time, the day should arrive when they would be lifted into the sunlight of God's equality. I claim it of South Carolina. By virtue of that pledge she took Boston and put a rope round her neck in that infamous compromise which consigned to slavery Anthony Burns. I demand the fulfilment on her part even of that infamous pledge. Until South Carolina allows me a the influence that nineteen millions of Yankee lips, asking infinite questions, have upon the welfare of those four millions of bondsmen, I deny her right to secede. [Applause.] Seventy years has the Union postponed the negro. For seventy years has he been beguiled with the promise, as she erected one bulwark after another around slavery, that he should have the influence of our common institutions. I claim it to-day. Never, with my consent, while the North thinks that the Union can or shall mean justice, shall those four hundred thousand South Carolina slaves go beyond the influence of Boston ideas. That is my strong reason for clinging to the Union. This is also one main reason why, unless upon most *imperative* and *manifest* grounds of need and right, South Carolina has no right of revolution; none till she fulfils her promise in this respect.

I know how we stand to-day, with the frowning cannon of the English fleet ready to be thrust out of the port-holes against us. But I can answer England with a better answer than William H. Seward can write. I can answer her with a more statesmanlike paper than Simon Cameron can indite. I would answer her with the Stars and Stripes floating over Charleston and New Orleans, and the itinerant Cabinet of Richmond packing up archives and wearing-apparel to ride back to Montgomery. There is one thing, and only one, which John Bull respects, and that is success. It is not for us to give counsel to the government on points of diplomatic propriety; but I suppose we may express our opinion; and my opinion is, that, if I were the President of these thirty-four States, while I was, I should want Mason and Slidell to stay with me. I say, then, first, as a matter of justice to the slave, we owe it to him; the day of his deliverance has come. The long promise of seventy years is to be fulfilled. The South draws back from the pledge. The North is bound, in honor of the memory of her fathers, to demand its exact fulfilment, and in order to save this Union, which now means justice and peace, to recognize the rights of four millions of its victims. This is the dictate of justice;—justice, which at this hour is craftier than Seward, more statesmanlike than Cameron; justice, which appeals from the cabinets of Europe to the people; justice, which abases the proud and lifts up the humble; justice, which disarms England, saves the slaves from insurrection, and sends home the Confederate army of the Potomac to guard its own hearths; justice, which gives us four millions of friends, spies, soldiers in the enemy's country, planted each one at their very hearth-sides; justice, which inscribes every cannon with "Holiness to the Lord!" and puts a Northern heart behind every musket; justice, which means victory now and peace forever. To all cry of demagogues asking for boldness, I respond with the cry of "Justice, immediate, absolute justice!" And if I dared to descend to a lower level, I should say to the merchants of this metropolis, Demand of the government a speedy settlement of this question. Every hour of delay is big with risk. Remember, as Governor Boutwell suggests, that our present financial prosperity comes because we have corn to export in place of cotton; and that another year, should Europe have a good harvest and we an ordinary one, while an inflated currency tempts extravagance and large imports, general bankruptcy stares us in the face. Do you love the Union? Do you really think that on the other side of the Potomac are the natural brothers and customers of the manufacturing ingenuity of the North? I tell you, certain as fate, God has written the safety of that relation in the same scroll with justice to the negro. The hour strikes. You may win him to your side; you may anticipate the South; you may save twelve millions of customers. Delay it, let God grant McClellan victory, let God grant the Stars and Stripes over New Orleans, and it is too late.

Jeff Davis will then summon that same element to his side, and twelve millions of customers are added to Lancashire and Lyons. Then commences a war of tariffs, embittered by that other war of angered nationalities, which are to hand this and the other Confederacy down for twenty-five or thirty years, divided, weakened, and bloody with intestine struggle. And what will be our character? I do not wholly agree with Edward Everett, in that very able and eloquent address which he delivered in Boston, in which, however, he said one thing pre-eminently true, — he, the compromiser, — that if, in 1830-31, nullification, under Jackson, had been hung instead of compromised, we never should have had Jeff Davis. [Loud applause.] I agree with him, and hope we shall make no second mistake of the kind. But I do not agree with him in the conclusion that these nineteen States, left alone, would be of necessity a second-rate power. No. I believe in brains; and I know these Northern men have more brains in their right hands than others have in their heads. [Laughter and cheers.] I know that we mix our soil with brains, and that, consequently, we are bound to conquer. Why, the waves of the ocean might as well rebel against our granite coast, or the wild bulls of the prairies against man, as either England or the South undertake to stop the march of the nineteen Free States of this continent. [Applause.]

It is not power that we should lose, but it is character. How should we stand when Jeff Davis had turned that corner upon us, — abolished slavery, won European sympathy, and established his Confederacy? Bankrupt in character, — outwitted in statesmanship. Our record would be, as we entered the sisterhood of nations, —

"Longed and struggled and begged to be admitted into the partnership of tyrants, and they were kicked out!" And the South would spring into the same arena, bearing on her brow, — "She flung away what she thought gainful and honest, in order to gain her independence!" A record better than the gold of California or all the brains of the Yankee.

Righteousness is preservation. You who are not Abolitionists do not come to this question as I did, — from an interest in these four millions of black men. I came on this platform from sympathy with the negro. I acknowledge it. You come to this question from an idolatrous regard for the Constitution of '89. But here we stand. On the other side of the ocean is England, holding out, not I think a threat of war, — I do not fear it, — but holding out to the South the intimation of a willingness, if she will but change her garments, and make herself decent, [laughter,] to take her in charge, and give her assistance and protection. There stands England, the most selfish and treacherous of modern governments. [Loud and long-continued cheers.] On the other side of the Potomac stands a statesmanship, urged by personal and selfish interests, which cannot be matched, and between them they have but one object, — it is in the end to divide the Union.

Hitherto the negro has been a hated question. The Union moved majestic on its path, and shut him out, eclipsing him from the sun of equality and happiness. He has changed his position to-day. He now stands between us and the sun of our safety and prosperity, and you and I are together on the same platform, — the same plank, — our object to save the institutions which our fathers planted. Save them in the service of justice, in the service of peace, in the service of liberty; and in that service demand of the government at Washington that they shall mature and announce a purpose. That flag lowered at Sumter, that flight at Bull Run, will rankle in the heart of the republic for centuries. Nothing will ever medicine that wound but the government announcing to the world that it knows well whence came its trouble, and is determined to effect its cure, and, consecrating the banner to liberty, to plant it on the shores of the Gulf. [Applause.] I say in the service of the negro; but I do not forget the white man, the eight millions of poor whites, thinking themselves our enemies, but who are really our friends. Their interests are identical with our own. An Alabama slaveholder, sitting with me a year or two ago, said: —

> "In our northern counties they are your friends. A man owns one slave or two slaves, and he eats with them, and sleeps in the same room (they have but one), as much as a hired man here eats with the farmer he serves. There is no difference. They are too poor to send their sons North for education. They have no newspapers, and they know nothing but what they are told by us. If you could get at them, they would be on your side, but we mean you never shall."

In Paris there are one hundred thousand men whom caricature or epigram can at any time raise to barricade the streets. Whose fault is it that such men exist? The government's; and the government under which such a mass of ignorance exists deserves to be barricaded. The government under which eight millions of people exist, so ignorant that two thousand politicians and a hundred thousand aristocrats can pervert them into rebellion, deserves to be rebelled against. In the service of those men I mean, for one, to try to fulfil the pledge my fathers made when they said, "We will guarantee to every State a republican form of government." [Applause.] A privileged class, grown strong by the help and forbearance of the North, plots the establishment of aristocratic government in form as well as essence, — conspires to rob the non-slaveholders of their civil rights. This is just the danger our national pledge was meant to meet. Our fathers' honor, national good faith, the cause of free institutions, the peace of the continent, bid us fulfil this pledge, — insist on using the right it gives us to preserve the Union.

I mean to fulfil the pledge that free institutions shall be preserved in the several States, and I demand it of the government. I would have them, therefore, announce to the world what they have never yet done. I do not wonder at the want of sympathy on the part of England with us. The South says, "I am fighting for slavery." The North says, "I am not fighting against it." Why should England interfere? The people have nothing on which to hang their sympathy.

I would have government announce to the world that we understand the evil which has troubled our peace for seventy years, thwarting the natural tendency of our institutions, sending ruin along our wharves and through our workshops every ten years, poisoning the national conscience. We know well its character. But Democracy, unlike other governments, is strong enough to let evils work out their own death, — strong enough to face them when they reveal their proportions. It was in this sublime consciousness of strength, not of weakness, that our fathers submitted to the well-known evil of slavery, and tolerated it until the viper we thought we could safely tread on, at the touch of disappointment, starts up a fiend whose stature reaches the sky. But our cheeks do not blanch. Democracy accepts the struggle. After this forbearance of three generations, confident that she has yet power to execute her will, she sends her proclamation down to the Gulf, — Freedom to every man beneath the Stars, and death to every institution that disturbs our peace or threatens the future of the republic.

THE CABINET.*

I QUITE agree with the view which my friend (Rev. M. D. Conway) takes of the present situation of the country, and of our future. I have no hope, as he has not, that the intelligent purpose of our government will ever find us a way out of this war. I think, if we find any way out of it, we are to stumble out of it by the gradual education of the people, making their own way on, a great mass, without leaders. I do not think that anything which we can call the *government* has any *purpose* to get rid of slavery. On the contrary, I think the present purpose of the government, so far as it has now a purpose, is to end the war and save slavery. I believe Mr. Lincoln is conducting this war, at present, with the purpose of saving slavery. That is his present line of policy, so far as trustworthy indications of any policy reach us. The Abolitionists are charged with a desire to make this a political war. All civil wars are necessarily political wars, — they can hardly be anything else. Mr. Lincoln is intentionally waging a *political* war. He knows as well as we do at this moment, as well as every man this side of a lunatic hospital knows, that, if he wants to save lives and money, the way to end this war is to strike at slavery. I do not believe that McClellan himself is mad or idiotic enough to have avoided that idea, even if he has tried to

* Speech at Abington, in the Grove, August 1, 1862.

do so. But General McClellan is waging a political war; so is Mr. Lincoln. When General Butler ordered the women and children to be turned out of the camps at New Orleans, and one of the colonels of the Northwest remonstrated, and hid himself in his tent, rather than witness the misery which the order occasioned, — when the slaveholders came to receive the women and children who were to be turned out of the camps, and the troops actually charged upon them with bayonets to keep them out of the line, — General Butler knew what he was doing. It was not to save rations, it was not to get rid of individuals; it was to conciliate New Orleans. It was a political move. When Mr. Lincoln, by an equivocal declaration, nullifies General Hunter, he does not do it because he doubts either the justice or the efficiency of Hunter's proclamation; he does it because he is afraid of Kentucky on the right hand, and the Daily Advertiser on the left. [Laughter.] He has not taken one step since he entered the Presidency that has been a purely military step, and he could not. A civil war can hardly be anything but a political war. That is, all civil wars are a struggle between opposite ideas, and armies are but the tools. If Mr. Lincoln believed in the North and in Liberty, he would let our army act on the principles of Liberty. He does not. He believes in the South as the most efficient and vital instrumentality at the present moment, therefore defers to it. I had a friend who went to Port Royal, went among the negro huts, and saw the pines that were growing between them shattered with shells and cannon-balls. He said to the negroes, "When those balls came, were you here?" "Yes." "Did n't you run?" "No, massa, we knew they were not meant for us." It was a sublime, childlike faith in the justice, the providence, of the Almighty. Every Southern traitor on the other side of the Potomac can say of McClellan's cannon-ball, if he ever fires one, "We know it is not meant for us." For they know he is fighting a political war, as all of us must; the only question is, In the service of which political idea shall the war be waged, — in the service of saving the Union as it was, or the Union as it ought to be? Mr. Lincoln dare not choose between these two phrases. He is waging a war which he dare not describe, in the service of a political idea that he dare not shape into words. He is not fighting vigorously and heartily enough even to get good terms in case of a treaty, — not to talk of victory. All savages call clemency cowardice; they respect nothing but force. The Southern barbarians mistake clemency for cowardice; and every act of Lincoln, which he thinks is conciliation, they take for evidence of his cowardice, or his distrust. I do not say that McClellan is a traitor, but I say this, that if he had been a traitor from the crown of his head to the sole of his foot, he could not have served the South better than he has done since he was commander-in-chief [applause]; he could not have carried on the war in more exact deference to the politics of that side of the Union. And almost the same thing may be said of Mr. Lincoln, — that if he had been a traitor, he could not have worked better to strengthen one side, and hazard the success of the other. There is more danger to-day that Washington will be taken than Richmond. Washington is besieged more truly than Richmond is. After fifteen months of war, such is the position of the strongest nation on the globe; for the nineteen Northern States, led by a government which serves their ideas, are the strongest nation on the face of the globe. Now, I think, and if I were in the Senate I should have said to the government, that every man who under the present policy loses his life in the swamps of the South, and every dollar sent there to be wasted, only prolongs a murderous and wasteful war, waged for no purpose whatever. This is my meaning. In this war, mere victory on a battle-field amounts to nothing, contributes little or nothing toward ending the war. If our present policy led to decisive victories, therefore, (which it does not,) it would be worth little. The war can only be ended by annihilating that oligarchy which formed and rules the South and makes the war, — by annihilating a state of society. No social state is really annihilated, except when it is replaced by another. Our present policy neither aims to annihilate that state of things we call "the South," made up of pride, idleness, ignorance, barbarism, theft, and murder, nor to replace it with a substitute. Such an aimless war I call wasteful and murderous. Better that that South should go to-day, than that we should prolong such a war. To keep 500,000 men in the field, we must have 560,000 men on the rolls, for there are 58,000 or 60,000 men necessarily invalid in an army of half a million; and to keep that 560,000 good, you must have a fresh recruiting every year of 123,000 men. This nation is to give, year by year, while this war lasts, 123,000 men to the army, and that number are to fall out of the ranks, according to the experience of the last sixteen months, by death either from disease or the sword; or, if not death, then wounds so serious as to make a man's life only a burden to himself and the community. A hundred and twenty-three thousand men a year, and, I suppose, a million of dollars a day, and a government without a purpose!

You say, "Why not end the war?" We cannot. Jefferson said of slavery, "We have got the wolf by the ears; we can neither hold him nor let him go." That was his figure We have now got the South — this wolf — by the ears; we *must* hold her; we cannot let her go. There is to be no peace on this continent, as I believe, until these thirty States are united. You and I may live to be seventy years old; we shall never see peace on this continent until we see one flag from the Lakes to the Gulf, and we shall never see it until slavery is eliminated from the institutions of these States. Let the South go to-morrow, and you have not got peace. Intestine wai here, border war along the line, aggression and intrigue on the part of the South! She has lived with us for seventy years, and kept us constantly in turmoil. Exasperated by suffering, grown haughty by success, the moment she goes off, is such a neighbor likely to treat us any better, with our imaginary line between us, than she has treated us for seventy years while she held the sceptre? The moment we ask for terms, she counts it victory, and the war in another shape goes on. You and I are never to see peace, we are never to see the possibility of putting the army of this nation, whether it be made up of nineteen or thirty-four States, on a peace footing, until slavery is destroyed. A large army, immense expenses, a foreign party encamped among us, a despotic government, using necessarily despotic war powers, — that is the future until slavery is destroyed. As long as you keep a tortoise at the head of the government, you are digging a pit with one hand and filling it with the other. The war means digging a pit with your two hands, and filling it up with the lives of your sons and the accumulations of your fathers. Now, therefore, until this nation announces, in some form or other, that this is a war, not against Jefferson Davis, but against the system; until the whole nation indorses the resolution of the New York Chamber of Commerce, "Better every rebel die than one loyal soldier," [applause,] and begs of the government, demands of the government, to speak that word which is victory and peace, — until we do that, we shall have no prospect of peace.

I do not believe in the government. I agree entirely with Mr. Conway. I do not believe this government has got either vigor or a purpose. It drifts with events. If Jefferson Davis is a sane man, if he is a sagacious man, and has the power to control his army, he will never let it take Washington; for he knows as well as we do, that shelling the dome of that Capitol to ashes, that the Capitol in flames or surmounted with the rebel flag, would be the fiery cross to melt the North into unity, and to demand emancipation. [Applause.] We are paying a million of dollars a day for soldiers to dig ditches in the Chickahominy swamps, but the best expense we could be put to would be to lose the marble Capitol under the shells of Beauregard; for the very telegraph that flashed the news North and West would go back laden with the demand that if, in the providence of God, Lincoln had survived the bombardment of Washington, and Hamlin was not President, — which I wish he were, — he should proclaim emancipation. Possibly that would make even him over into an Abolitionist. I do not believe that Jefferson Davis, while he is able to control his forces, will ever allow them to take Washington. He wants time. If we float on until the 4th of March, 1863, England could hardly be blamed if she did acknowledge the South. A very fair argument could be urged, on principles of international law, that she ought to do it. The South will have gone far to prove her right to be acknowledged. She will have maintained herself two full years against such efforts as no nation ever made. Davis wants to tide over to that time, without rousing the North. He does not wish any greater successes than will just keep us where we are, and allow Europe to see the South strong, vigorous, and the North only her equal. One such move as that on Washington, and the South would kick the beam. He knows it. If any man has light enough on the future to pray God to do any particular thing, I advise him to pray for an attack on Washington and its capture, for nothing less than that seems likely, within a few months, to wake up these Northern States to the present emergency. But for these considerations, I see not why Jefferson Davis should not throw all his troops upon Washington, first informing General McClellan of the proposed attack, and demanding of him enough Federal troops to protect the rebel property at Richmond during Beauregard's absence.

The President, judged by both proclamations that have followed the late confiscation act of Congress, has no mind whatever. He has not uttered a word which gives even a twilight glimpse of any antislavery purpose. He may be honest, — nobody cares whether the tortoise is honest or not; he has neither insight, nor prevision, nor decision. It is said in Washington streets that he long ago wrote a proclamation abolishing slavery in the State of Virginia, but McClellan bullied him out of it. It is said, too, — what is extremely probable, — that he has more than once made up his mind to remove McClellan, and Kentucky bullied him out of it. The man who has been beaten to that pulp in sixteen months, what hope can we have of him? None. There is no ground for any expectations from this government. We are to pray for such blows as will arouse the mass of the people into systematic, matured, intelligent interference in the action of the government. When I was here a year ago, I said I thought the President needed the advice of great bodies of prominent men. That has taken a year. The New York Chamber of Commerce, the Common Council, and the Defence Committee, have just led the way. Some of the Western Councils have followed, it is said. Let us hope that they may have decisive effect at Washington; but I do not believe they will. I do not believe there is in that Cabinet — Seward, Chase, Stanton, Wells, or the President of the country — enough to make a leader. If

McClellan should capitulate in his swamp, if Johnston should take Washington, if Butler should be driven out of New Orleans, if those ten fabulous iron ships from England at Mobile could be turned into realities, and Palmerston acknowledge the Confederacy, I should have hope; for I do not believe these nineteen millions of people mean to be beaten; and if they do, I do not believe they can afford to be beaten. I think, when we begin to yield, the South will demand such terms as even the Boston Courier cannot get low enough to satisfy them. [Laughter and applause.] You do not know the sublime impudence and haughtiness of the tyrants of the South. You have not yet measured the terms which Jefferson Davis will impose upon the North, when, if ever, it proposes accommodation. The return of fugitives, the suppression of antislavery discussion, monopoly of the Mississippi, surrender of some Border States, — a thousand things that would make the yoke too heavy to be borne. I never did believe in the capacity of Abraham Lincoln, but I do believe in the pride of Davis, in the vanity of the South, in the desperate determination of those fourteen States; and I believe in a sunny future, because God has driven them mad; and their madness is our safety. They will never consent to anything that the North can grant; and you must whip them, because, unless you do, they will grind you to powder.

This war is to go on. There will be drafting in three months or six. The hunker, when he is obliged to go to war, will be like the man of whom Mr. Conway told us, who was willing to sit by a negro in the cars rather than stand all night, — he will be willing that the negro shall fight, with him or without him. That is a part of the logic of events which will be very effective; but even that will not make Lincoln declare for emancipation. We shall wait one year or two, if we wait for him, before we get it. In the mean time what an expense of blood and treasure each day! It is a terrible expense that democracy pays for its mode of government. If we lived in England now, if we lived in France now, a hundred men, convinced of the exigency of the moment, would carry the nation here or there. It is the royal road, short, sharp, and stern, like the 2d of December, with Napoleon's cannon enfilading every street in Paris. Democracy, when it moves, has to carry the whole people with it. The minds of nineteen millions of people are to be changed and educated. Ministers and politicians have been preaching to them that the negro will not fight, that he is a nuisance, that slavery is an ordination of God, that the North ought to bar him out with statutes. The North wakes up, its heart poisoned, its hands paralyzed with these ideas, and says to its tortoise President, "Save us, but not through the negro!" You do not yet believe in the negro. The papers are accumulating statistics to prove that the negro will work, and asking whether he will fight. If he will not fight, we are gone, that is all! If he will not work without the lash, the Union is over. If the hunker theory is correct, there can be no peace nor union on this continent, except under the heel of a slaveholding despotism. It is not the South we have to conquer; it is the Egypt of the Southern half of Illinois; it is the Devil in the editor's chair of the Boston Courier [merriment]; it is the lump of unbaked dough, with no vitality except hatred of Charles Sumner, which sits in the editorial chair of the Daily Advertiser [applause]; it is the man who goes down to Virginia with the army, and thinks he goes there to watch the house of General Lee, and make the slaves work for him, while the master has gone to Corinth or to Richmond. These are the real enemies of the republic; and if Lincoln could be painted, as Vanity Fair once painted him, like Sinbad with the Old Man of the Sea on his shoulders, it should be these conservative elements weighing down the heart and the purpose of your President that the limner should present. If we go to the bottom, it will be because we have, in the providence of God, richly deserved it. It is the pro-slavery North that is her own greatest enemy. Lincoln would act, if he believed the North wanted him to. The North, by an overwhelming majority, is ready to have him act, will indorse and support anything he does, yes, hopes he will go forward. True, it is not yet ripe enough to demand; but it is fully willing, indeed waits, for action. With chronic Whig distrust and ignorance of the people, Lincoln halts and fears. Our friend Conway has fairly painted him. He is not a genius; he is not a man like Fremont, to stamp the lava mass of the nation with an idea; he is not a man like Hunter, to coin his experience into ideas. I will tell you what he is. He is a first-rate *second-rate* man. [Laughter.] He is one of the best specimens of a second-rate man, and he is honestly waiting, like any other servant, for the people to come and send him on any errand they wish. In ordinary times, when the seas are calm, you can sail without a pilot,—almost any one can avoid a sunken ledge that the sun shows him on his right hand, and the reef that juts out on his left; but it is when the waves smite heaven, and the thunder-cloud makes the waters ink, that you need a pilot; and to-day the nation's bark scuds, under the tempest, lee-shore and maelstrom on each side, needing no holiday captain, but a pilot, to weather the storm. Mr. Conway thinks we are to ride on a couple of years, and get one. I doubt it. Democracy is poisoning its fangs. It is making its way among the ballot-boxes of the nation. I doubt whether our next Congress will be as good as the last. That is not saying much. I doubt whether there will be such a weight of decided Republicanism in it as there was in the last Congress. I should be afraid to commit to the nation to-day the choice of a President. What we want is some stunning misfortune; what we want is a baptism of blood, to make the aching and bereaved hearts of the people cry out for Fremont, for an idea, at the head of the armies. [Applause.] Meanwhile, we must wander on in the desert, wasteful murderers. Every life lost in that swamp is murder by the Cabinet at Washington. Every dollar spent is stolen from the honest toil of the North, to pamper the conceited pride of the South in her own institution. Whose fault? Largely ours, — not wholly Lincoln's. He is as good as the average North, but not a leader, which is what we need. In yonder grove, July after July, in years just past, the Whigs of this Commonwealth lavished their money to fire guns once every minute to smother the speeches that were made on our platform. You remember it. The sons of those men are dying in the South because their fathers smothered the message which, heeded, might have saved this terrible lesson to the nation. [Sensation.] Who shall say that God is not holding to their lips the cup which they poisoned? That Massachusetts is to be made over again, and, under competent leaders, hurled as a thunderbolt against the rebellion. We are not to shrink from the idea that this is a political war: it must be. But its politics is a profound faith in God and the people, in justice and liberty, as the eternal safety of nations as well as of men. [Applause.] It is of that Lincoln should make his politics, planting the corner-stone of the new Union in the equality of every man before the law, and justice to all races. [Renewed applause.] If military necessity did not call for a million of blacks in the army, civil necessity would dictate it. Slavery, instead of being a dreaded perplexity, something we are to wail over, is a God-given weapon, a glorious opportunity, a sword rough-ground by God, and ready every moment for our use. The nation,

the most stupid in it, — all but the traitors, — know and confess that to abolish it would end the rebellion. Thus, therefore, God gives us *knowledge*, keeps for us the weapon; all we need ask for is courage to use it. I say, therefore, as Mr. Conway did, cease believing in the Cabinet; there is nothing there for you. Pray God that, before he abandons this nation, he will deign to humble it by one blow that shall make it spring to its feet, and use the strength it has. Beseech him to put despair into the hearts of the Cabinet. If we are ever called to see another President of the United States on horseback flying from his Capital, waste no tears! He will return to that Capital on the arms of a million of adult negroes, the sure basis of a Union which will never be broken. [Applause.]

I like some of the signs of the times. I like the resolutions of the New York Chamber of Commerce. I like the article from Wilkes's Spirit of the Times, bidding us criticise McClellan, and no longer believe that Napoleons are made of mud. [Laughter.] I think the two poles of popular influence have been struck; the young men, the sporting men, the fast men, the dissipated men, the New York Herald's constituency, and the commercial class, the merchants and bankers of the great metropolis. The thirty thousand copies of Wilkes which are circulated every week have a mighty influence. When its readers begin to believe that McClellan is made of mud, it is a bright sign. Do not look to the Capital. We did think there was something in Stanton; there may be; but he is overslaughed, he is eclipsed, he has gone into retirement behind Seward. The policy which prevails at Washington is to do nothing, and wait for events. I asked the lawyers of Illinois, who had practised law with Mr. Lincoln for twenty years, "Is he a man of decision, is he a man who can say no?" They all said: "If you had gone to the Illinois bar, and selected the man least capable of saying no, it would have been

Abraham Lincoln. He has no stiffness in him." I said to the bankers and the directors of railroads in Chicago, "Is McClellan a man who can say no?" and they said: "Banks we had only a few months; we don't think much of him; but to every question you asked, he would say yes or no in sixty minutes. McClellan never answered a question while he was here. If there was one to be decided, he floated until events decided it. He was here months, and never decided a single question that came up in the management of the Illinois Central." These are the men we have put at the head of the Union, and for fourteen months they have been unable to say yes or no. But that is the fault of the nation. We should have been five hundred millions of dollars richer, and sixty-three thousand lives more populous, if even Banks had been Commander-in-Chief instead of McClellan. [Applause.] I do not believe that Banks knows how to handle an army, as we all know he has no ideas, but I believe he would have pressed that army on and against something, and that is all it needed. I had a private letter from a captain in McClellan's army in the Peninsula, in which he said: "We have had five chances to enter Richmond; we might have done it after Yorktown, after Williamsburg, and after Seven Pines, just as well as not; no troops in front of us, we ourselves in full condition for an advance. Instead of that, we sat down and dug."

The most serious charge I have against the President, the only thing that makes a film upon his honesty, — for I believe him as honest as the measure of his intellect and circumstances of his life allow, — is this: that, while I do not believe that in his heart he trusts McClellan a whit more than I do, from fear of the Border States and Northern conservatism he keeps him at the head of the army, which loses two thousand men by disease every week, and spends from sixty to seventy thousand dollars a day; and if, twenty years hence, he renders up an account of his stewardship to his country, you that live, mark me! will see him confess that this whole winter he never believed in McClellan's ability. That is the sore spot in the character of an otherwise honest officer, and that is where this fear of conservatism sends him. Mr. Wickliffe of Kentucky and Mr. Davis of Kentucky put their feet down and say, "Do this, and the Border States leave you." There is not a Republican at the North who will be allowed to say it. Governor Andrew lisped it once, in his letter to Secretary Stanton, and how few, except the Abolitionists, dared to stand by him, even in Massachusetts! There is no public opinion that would support Mr. Sumner, with a loyal Commonwealth behind him, in making such a speech, once in the winter, as Garrett Davis made every day, with a Commonwealth behind him which has to be held in the Union by the fear of Northern bayonets. It is because Conservatism is bold and Republicanism is coward ["Hear!"] that Abraham Lincoln has to stand where he does to-day. There will be no mystery if this nation goes to pieces. It will be God punishing it according to the measure of its sins. Ten years ago the Whig party could have educated it, and so postponed or averted this convulsion. It was left to pass on in its career, and the South finds it divided in sentiment, servile in purpose; our soldiers the servants of rebels; our officers, with shoulder-straps, on the soil of a rebellious State like Virginia, more sycophantic to the slaveholder who comes to their camp, than Webster was in the Senate when Clay threatened him with the lash of Southern insolence, fifteen years ago. If this rebellion cannot shake the North out of her servility, God will keep her in constant agitation until he does shake us into a self-respecting, courageous people, fit to govern ourselves. [Applause.] This war will last just long enough to make us over into men, and when it has done this, we shall conquer with as much ease as the lion takes the tiniest animal in his gripe. If Mr. Lincoln could only be wakened to the idea which Mr. Conway has expressed, that God gives him the thunderbolt of slavery with which to crush the rebellion; that there was never a rebellion arranged by Providence to be put down so easily, so completely, so beneficially as this; that, unlike the aristocracy of France and England, rooting itself underneath the whole surface of society, slavery almost makes good the prayer of the Roman tyrant, "Would that the people had one neck, and I could cut it!"—if Mr. Lincoln could only understand this, victory would be easy. God has massed up slavery into three hundred thousand hands. He has marked it by the black color, so that the most ignorant cannot err, so that the blindest shall see enough to strike at this central figure which holds the life-blood of the rebellion. [Applause.] Let us do our duty, and feel, however long the war, however fatal and disastrous the experience, that we have left no stone unturned, no word unspoken, which can save a mighty nation from the greatest sufferings God ever inflicted on an age.

My friend says he would say to the tyrants of the Old World, "Come on!" That is a fearful taunt. The collision of two such nations as the England of this side the Atlantic, and the England of the other, would shake the globe. No such war has been known since Christ. Half of all the old wars massed into one would not equal it. We should sweep the commerce of the mightiest commercial nation from the ocean. We should send starvation into Lancashire and Lyons, and she would make our coast a desolation, and send anguish into millions of homes. The ingenuity of one race divided into two nations, which has reached an almost superhuman acuteness, would be all poured into the channel of the bloodiest war; and behind it would be the Saxon determination, which, like that of the bull-dog, its type, will die in the death-grapple before it yields. Old national hate, fresh-edged and perpetuated, — untold wealth destroyed, — millions of lives lost, lives of the most cultivated nations, — the progress of the race stopped, — chaos come again over the fairest portion of Christendom, — fifty millions of people, dealing such death-blows across the Atlantic in the nineteenth century, — it is a burden which we are to pray God he will not call upon us to bear, — a curse from which he will graciously save civilization and the race. On the contrary, let us hope that Southern success may be so rapid and abundant, that a blow like that which stuns the drunkard into sobriety may stun our Cabinet into vigor, and that nineteen millions of people, putting forth their real strength in the right direction, may keep peace outside our borders until we make peace within. [Loud applause.]

LETTER TO THE TRIBUNE.

To the Editor of the New York Tribune:—

SIR: You misrepresent me when you say that I dis courage enlistments in the Union armies; though, for aught I know, the garbled extracts and lying versions of New York papers may make me do that and many other things I never thought of. You know, by experience, that the American press, in general, neither tries nor means to speak truth about Abolitionists of any type. I have never discouraged enlistments. In the Union army are my kindred and some of my dearest friends. Others rest in fresh and honorable graves. No one of these ever heard a word from me to discourage his enlisting. I had the honor, last March, to address the Fourteenth Massachusetts at Fort Albany, and, this very week, the Thirty-third Massachusetts at Camp Cameron. No man in either regiment heard anything from my lips to discourage his whole-souled service of the Union.

Allow me to state my own position. From 1843 to 1861, I was a Disunionist, and sought to break this Union, convinced that disunion was the only righteous path, and the best one for the white man and the black. I sought disunion, not through conspiracy and violence, but by means which the Constitution itself warranted and protected. I rejoice in those efforts. They were wise and useful. Sumter changed the whole question. After that, peace and justice both forbade disunion. I now believe three things: —

1. The destruction of slavery is inevitable, whichever section conquers in this struggle.

2. There never can be peace or union till slavery is destroyed.

3. There never can be peace till one government rules from the Gulf to the Lakes; and having wronged the negro for two centuries, we owe him the preservation of the Union to guard his transition from slavery to freedom, and make it short, easy, and perfect.

Believing these three things, I accept Webster's sentiment, "Liberty and Union, now and forever, one and inseparable." Gladly would I serve that Union, — giving it musket, sword, voice, pen, — the best I have. But the Union which has for twenty-five years barred me from its highest privileges by demanding an oath to a pro-slavery Constitution, still shuts that door in my face; and this administration still clings to a policy which, I think, makes every life now lost in Virginia, and every dollar now spent there, utter waste. I cannot conscientiously support such a Union and administration. But there is room for honest difference of opinion. Others can support it. To such I say, Go; give to the Union your best blood, your heartiest support.

Is there, then, no place left for me? Yes. I believe in the Union. But government and the Union are one thing. This *administration* is quite another. Whether the administration will ever pilot us through our troubles, I have serious doubts: that it never will, unless it changes its present policy, I am quite certain. Where, then, is my place under a republican government which only reflects and executes public opinion? I believe in getting through this war by the machinery of regular government, not by any Cromwell stalking into the Senate-Chamber or the

White House. Where, then, is my post, especially under an administration that avowedly sits waiting, begging to be told what to do? I must educate, arouse, and mature a public opinion which shall compel the administration to adopt and support it in pursuing the policy I can aid. This I do by frankly and candidly criticising its present policy, civil and military. However "inapt and objectionable" you may think my "means," they are exactly described in your own words: "The good citizen may owe his government counsel, entreaty, admonition, to abandon a mistaken policy, as well as force to sustain it in the discharge of its great responsibilities." No administration can demand of a citizen to sacrifice his *conscience*, and the limits within which he is bound to sacrifice his *opinion* are soon reached. If the press had not systematically eulogized a general, whom none knew, and few really trusted, we should have saved twelve months, five hundred millions of dollars, and a hundred thousand lives. In my opinion, had the Tribune continued, last August, to do its duty and demand vigor of the government, you would have changed or controlled the Cabinet in another month, and saved us millions of dollars, thousands of lives, and untold disgrace. Such criticism is always every thinking man's duty. War excuses no man from this duty: least of all now, when a change of public sentiment, to lead the administration to and support it in a new policy, is our only hope of saving the Union. The Union belongs to me as much as to Abraham Lincoln. What right has he or any official — our servants — to claim that I shall cease criticising his mistakes, when they are dragging the Union to ruin? I find grave faults in President Lincoln; but I do not believe he makes any such claim.

I said on the 1st of August, that, had I been in the Senate, I should have refused the administration a dollar or a man until it adopted a right policy. That I repeat.

Had I been, in that way, a part of the government, I should have tried so to control its action. You were bound as a journalist, I think, to have impressed that duty on the Republican party which holds the administration. Such a course is right and proper under free governments. But when Congress has decided, and under its authority, or by his own, the President demands soldiers, the hour for such effort or protest is gone. We have no right now to "discourage enlistments," as a means to change public opinion, or to influence the administration. Our remedy is different. If we cannot actively aid, we must submit to the penalty, and strive meanwhile to change that public thought which alone can alter the action of government.

That duty I try to do in my measure. My criticism is not, like that of the traitor presses, meant to paralyze the administration, but to goad it to more activity and vigor, or to change the Cabinet. I claim of you, as a journalist of broad influence, that you resume the post which I think you deserted last summer, and hasten the ripening of that necessary public purpose by constant and fearless criticism of the whole policy of the administration, civil and military, in order to avert years of war, to save thousands of lives, to guard the industry of the future from grinding taxes, to secure speedy and complete justice for the negro, and to put the Union beyond hazard.

Respectfully yours,

WENDELL PHILLIPS.

August 16, 1862.

TOUSSAINT L'OUVERTURE.*

LADIES AND GENTLEMEN: I have been requested to offer you a sketch made some years since, of one of the most remarkable men of the last generation, — the great St. Domingo chief, Toussaint l'Ouverture, an unmixed negro, with no drop of white blood in his veins. My sketch is at once a biography and an argument, — a biography, of course very brief, of a negro soldier and statesman, which I offer you as an argument in behalf of the race from which he sprung. I am about to compare and weigh races; indeed, I am engaged to-night in what you will think the absurd effort to convince you that the negro race, instead of being that object of pity or contempt which we usually consider it, is entitled, judged by the facts of history, to a place close by the side of the Saxon. Now races love to be judged in two ways, — by the great men they produce, and by the average merit of the mass of the race. We Saxons are proud of Bacon, Shakespeare, Hampden, Washington, Franklin, the stars we have lent to the galaxy of history; and then we turn with equal pride to the average merit of Saxon blood, since it streamed from its German home. So, again, there are three tests by which races love to be tried. The first, the basis of all, is courage, — the element which says, here and to-day, "This continent is

* Lecture delivered in New York and Boston, December, 1861.

mine, from the Lakes to the Gulf: let him beware who seeks to divide it!" [Cheers.] And the second is the recognition that force is doubled by purpose; liberty regulated by law is the secret of Saxon progress. And the third element is persistency, endurance; first a purpose, then death or success. Of these three elements is made that Saxon pluck which has placed our race in the van of modern civilization.

In the hour you lend me to-night, I attempt the Quixotic effort to convince you that the negro blood, instead of standing at the bottom of the list, is entitled, if judged either by its great men or its masses, either by its courage, its purpose, or its endurance, to a place as near ours as any other blood known in history. And, for the purpose of my argument, I take an island, St. Domingo, about the size of South Carolina, the third spot in America upon which Columbus placed his foot. Charmed by the magnificence of its scenery and fertility of its soil, he gave it the fondest of all names, Hispaniola, Little Spain. His successor, more pious, rebaptized it from St. Dominic, St. Domingo; and when the blacks, in 1803, drove our white blood from its surface, they drove our names with us, and began the year 1804 under the old name, Hayti, the land of mountains. It was originally tenanted by filibusters, French and Spanish, of the early commercial epochs, the pirates of that day as of ours. The Spanish took the eastern two thirds, the French the western third of the island, and they gradually settled into colonies. The French, to whom my story belongs, became the pet colony of the mother land. Guarded by peculiar privileges, enriched by the scions of wealthy houses, aided by the unmatched fertility of the soil, it soon was the richest gem in the Bourbon crown; and at the period to which I call your attention, about the era of our Constitution, 1789, its wealth was almost incredible. The effeminacy of the white race rivalled that of the Sybarite of antiquity, while the splendor of their private life outshone Versailles, and their luxury found no mate but in the mad prodigality of the Cæsars. At this time the island held about thirty thousand whites, twenty or thirty thousand mulattoes, and five hundred thousand slaves. The slave-trade was active. About twenty-five thousand slaves were imported annually; and this only sufficed to fill the gap which the murderous culture of sugar annually produced. The mulattoes, as with us, were children of the slaveholders, but, unlike us, the French slaveholder never forgot his child by a bondwoman. He gave him everything but his name, — wealth, rich plantations, gangs of slaves; sent him to Paris for his education, summoned the best culture of France for the instruction of his daughters, so that in 1790 the mulatto race held one third of the real estate and one quarter of the personal estate of the island. But though educated and rich, he bowed under the same yoke as with us. Subjected to special taxes, he could hold no public office, and, if convicted of any crime, was punished with double severity. His son might not sit on the same seat at school with a white boy; he might not enter a church where a white man was worshipping; if he reached a town on horseback, he must dismount and lead his horse by the bridle; and when he died, even his dust could not rest in the same soil with a white body. Such was the white race and the mulatto, — the thin film of a civilization beneath which surged the dark mass of five hundred thousand slaves.

It was over such a population, — the white man melted in sensuality; the mulatto feeling all the more keenly his degradation from the very wealth and culture he enjoyed; the slave, sullen and indifferent, heeding not the quarrels or the changes of the upper air, — it was over this population that there burst, in 1789, the thunder-storm of the French Revolution. The first words which reached the island were the motto of the Jacobin Club, — "Liberty, Equality." The white man heard them aghast. He had read of the streets of Paris running blood. The slave heard them with indifference; it was a quarrel in the upper air, between other races, which did not concern him. The mulatto heard them with a welcome which no dread of other classes could quell. Hastily gathered into conventions, they sent to Paris a committee of the whole body, laid at the feet of the National Convention the free gift of six millions of francs, pledged one fifth of their annual rental toward the payment of the national debt, and only asked in return that this yoke of civil and social contempt should be lifted from their shoulders.

You may easily imagine the temper in which Mirabeau and Lafayette welcomed this munificent gift of the free mulattoes of the West Indies, and in which the petition for equal civil rights was received by a body which had just resolved that all men were equal. The Convention hastened to express its gratitude, and issued a decree which commences thus: "All freeborn French citizens are equal before the law." Ogé was selected — the friend of Lafayette, a lieutenant-colonel in the Dutch service, the son of a wealthy mulatto woman, educated in Paris, the comrade of all the leading French Republicans — to carry the decree and the message of French Democracy to the island. He landed. The decree of the National Convention was laid on the table of the General Assembly of the island. One old planter seized it, tore it in fragments, and trampled it under his feet, swearing by all the saints in the calendar that the island might sink before they would share their rights with bastards. They took an old mulatto, worth a million, who had simply asked for his rights under that decree, and hung him. A white lawyer of seventy, who drafted the petition, they hung at his side. They took Ogé, broke him on the wheel, ordered him to be drawn and quartered, and one quarter of his body to be hung up in each of the four principal cities of the island; and then they adjourned.

You can conceive better than I can describe the mood in which Mirabeau and Danton received the news that their decree had been torn in pieces and trampled under foot by the petty legislature of an island colony, and their comrade drawn and quartered by the orders of its Governor. Robespierre rushed to the tribune and shouted, "Perish the colonies rather than sacrifice one iota of our principles!" The Convention reaffirmed their decree, and sent it out a second time to be executed.

But it was not then as now, when steam has married the continents. It took months to communicate; and while this news of the death of Ogé and the defiance of the National Convention was going to France, and the answer returning, great events had taken place in the island itself. The Spanish or the eastern section, perceiving these divisions, invaded the towns of the western, and conquered many of its cities. One half of the slaveholders were Republicans, in love with the new constellation which had just gone up in our Northern sky, seeking to be admitted a State in this Republic, plotting for annexation. The other half were loyalists, anxious, deserted as they supposed themselves by the Bourbons, to make alliance with George III. They sent to Jamaica, and entreated its Governor to assist them in their intrigue. At first, he lent them only a few hundred soldiers. Some time later, General Howe and Admiral Parker were sent with several thousand men, and finally, the English government entering more seriously into the plot, General Maitland landed with four thousand Englishmen on the north side of the island, and gained many successes. The mulattoes were in the mountains, awaiting events. They distrusted the government, which a few years before they had assisted to put down an insurrection of the whites, and which had forfeited its promise to grant them civil privileges. Deserted by both sections, Blanchelande, the Governor, had left the capital, and fled for refuge to a neighboring city.

In this state of affairs, the second decree reached the island. The whites forgot their quarrel, sought out Blanchelande, and obliged him to promise that he never would publish the decree. Affrighted, the Governor consented to that course, and they left him. He then began to reflect that in reality he was deposed, that the Bourbons had lost the sceptre of the island. He remembered his successful appeal to the mulattoes, five years before, to put down an insurrection. Deserted now by the whites and by the mulattoes, only one force was left him in the island, — that was the blacks: they had always remembered with gratitude the *code noir*, black code, of Louis XIV., the first interference of any power in their behalf. To the blacks Blanchelande appealed. He sent a deputation to the slaves. He was aided by the agents of Count d'Artois, afterward Charles X., who was seeking to do in St. Domingo what Charles II. did in Virginia, (whence its name of Old Dominion,) institute a reaction against the rebellion at home. The two joined forces, and sent first to Toussaint. Nature made him a Metternich, a diplomatist. He probably wished to avail himself of this offer, foreseeing advantage to his race, but to avail himself of it so cautiously as to provide against failure, risking as little as possible till the intentions of the other party had been tested, and so managing as to be able to go on or withdraw as the best interest of his race demanded. He had practised well the Greek rule, "Know thyself," and thoroughly studied his own part. Later in life, when criticising his great mulatto rival, Rigaud, he showed how well he knew himself. "I know Rigaud," he said; "he drops the bridle when he gallops, he shows his arm when he strikes. For me, I gallop also, but know where to stop: when I strike I am felt, not seen. Rigaud works only by blood and massacre. I know how to put the people in movement: but when I appear, all must be calm."

He said, therefore, to the envoys, "Where are your credentials?" "We have none." "I will have nothing to do with you." They then sought François and Biassou, two other slaves of strong passions, considerable intellect, and great influence over their fellow-slaves, and said, "Arm, assist the government, put down the English on the one hand, and the Spanish on the other"; and on the 21st of August, 1791, fifteen thousand blacks, led by François and Biassou, supplied with arms from the arsenal of the government, appeared in the midst of the colony. It is believed that Toussaint, unwilling himself to head the movement, was still desirous that it should go forward, trusting, as proved the case, that it would result in benefit to his race. He is supposed to have advised François in his course, — saving himself for a more momentous hour.

This is what Edward Everett calls the Insurrection of St. Domingo. It bore for its motto on one side of its banner, "Long live the King"; and on the other, "We claim the Old Laws." Singular mottoes for a rebellion! In fact, it was the *posse comitatus;* it was the only French army on the island; it was the only force that had a right to bear arms; and what it undertook, it achieved. It put Blanchelande in his seat; it put the island beneath his rule. When it was done, the blacks said to the Governor they had created, "Now, grant us one day in seven; give us one day's labor; we will buy another, and with the two buy a third," — the favorite method of emancipation at that time. Like the Blanchelande of five years before, he refused. He said, "Disarm! Disperse!" and the blacks answered, "The right hand that has saved you, the right hand that has saved the island for the Bourbons, may perchance clutch some of our own rights"; and they stood still. [Cheering.] This is the first insurrection, if any such there were in St. Domingo, — the first determined purpose on the part of the negro, having saved the government, to save himself.

Now let me stop a moment to remind you of one thing. I am about to open to you a chapter of bloody history, — no doubt of it. Who set the example? Who dug up from its grave of a hundred years the hideous punishment of the wheel, and broke Ogé, every bone, a living man? Who flared in the face of indignant and astonished Europe the forgotten barbarity of quartering the yet palpitating body? Our race. And if the black man learned the lesson but too well, it does not lie in our lips to complain. During this whole struggle, the record is, — written, mark you, by the white man, — the whole picture from the pencil of the white race, — that for one life the negro took in battle, in hot and bloody fight, the white race took, in the cool malignity of revenge, three to answer for it. Notice, also, that up to this moment the slave had taken no part in the struggle, except at the bidding of the government; and even then, not for himself, but only to sustain the laws.

At this moment, then, the island stands thus: The Spaniard is on the east triumphant; the Englishman is on the northwest intrenched; the mulattoes are in the mountains waiting; the blacks are in the valleys victorious; one half the French slaveholding element is republican, the other half royalist; the white race against the mulatto and the black; the black against both; the Frenchman against the English and Spaniard; the Spaniard against both. It is a war of races and a war of nations. At such a moment Toussaint l'Ouverture appeared.

He had been born a slave on a plantation in the north of the island, — an unmixed negro, — his father stolen from Africa. If anything, therefore, that I say of him to-night moves your admiration, remember, the black race claims it all, — we have no part nor lot in it. He was fifty years old at this time. An old negro had taught him to read. His favorite books were Epictetus, Raynal, Military Memoirs, Plutarch. In the woods, he learned some of the qualities of herbs, and was village doctor. On the estate, the highest place he ever reached was that of coachman. At fifty, he joined the army as physician. Before he went, he placed his master and mistress on shipboard, freighted the vessel with a cargo of sugar and coffee, and sent them to Baltimore, and never afterward did he forget to send them, year by year, ample means of support. And I might add, that, of all the leading negro generals, each one saved the man under whose roof he was born, and protected the family. [Cheering.]

Let me add another thing. If I stood here to-night to tell the story of Napoleon, I should take it from the lips of Frenchmen, who find no language rich enough to paint the great captain of the nineteenth century. Were I here to tell you the story of Washington, I should take it from your hearts, — you, who think no marble white enough on which to carve the name of the Father of his Country. [Applause.] I am about to tell you the story of a negro who has left hardly one written line. I am to glean it from the reluctant testimony of Britons, Frenchmen, Spaniards, — men who despised him as a negro and a slave, and hated him because he had beaten them in many a battle. All the materials for his biography are from the lips of his enemies.

The second story told of him is this. About the time he reached the camp, the army had been subjected to two insults. First, their commissioners, summoned to meet the French Committee, were ignominiously and insultingly dismissed; and when, afterward, François, their general, was summoned to a second conference, and went to it on horseback, accompanied by two officers, a young lieutenant, who had known him as a slave, angered at seeing him in the uniform of an officer, raised his riding-whip and struck him over the shoulders. If he had been the savage which the negro is painted to us, he had only to breathe the insult to his twenty-five thousand soldiers, and they would have trodden out the Frenchmen in blood. But the indignant chief rode back in silence to his tent, and it was twenty-four hours before his troops heard of this insult to their general. Then the word went forth, "Death to every white man!" They had fifteen hundred prisoners. Ranged in front of the camp, they were about to be shot. Toussaint, who had a vein of religious fanaticism, like most great leaders, — like Mohammed, like Napoleon, like Cromwell, like John Brown [cheers], — he could preach as well as fight, — mounting a hillock, and getting the ear of the crowd, exclaimed: "Brothers, this blood will not wipe out the insult to our chief; only the blood in yonder French camp can wipe it out. To shed that is courage; to shed this is cowardice and cruelty beside"; — and he saved fifteen hundred lives. [Applause.]

I cannot stop to give in detail every one of his efforts. This was in 1793. Leap with me over seven years; come to 1800; what has he achieved? He has driven the Spaniard back into his own cities, conquered him there, and put the French banner over every Spanish town; and for the first time, and almost the last, the island obeys one law. He has put the mulatto under his feet. He has attacked Maitland, defeated him in pitched battles, and permitted him to retreat to Jamaica; and when the French army rose upon Laveaux, their general, and put him in chains, Toussaint defeated them, took Laveaux out of prison, and put him at the head of his own troops. The grateful French in return named him General-in-Chief. *Cet homme fait l'ouverture partout*, said one, — "This man makes an opening everywhere," — hence his soldiers named him L'Ouverture, *the opening*.

This was the work of seven years. Let us pause a moment, and find something to measure him by. You remember Macaulay says, comparing Cromwell with Napoleon, that Cromwell showed the greater military genius, if we consider that he never saw an army till he was forty; while Napoleon was educated from a boy in the best military schools in Europe. Cromwell manufactured his own army; Napoleon at the age of twenty-seven was placed at the head of the best troops Europe ever saw. They were both successful; but, says Macaulay, with such disadvantages, the Englishman showed the greater genius. Whether you allow the inference or not, you will at least grant that it is a fair mode of measurement. Apply it to Toussaint. Cromwell never saw an army till he was forty; this man never saw a soldier till he was fifty. Cromwell manufactured his own army — out of what? Englishmen, — the best blood in Europe. Out of the middle class of Englishmen, — the best blood of the island. And with it he conquered what? Englishmen, — their equals. This man manufactured his army out of what? Out of what you call the despicable race of negroes, debased, demoralized by two hundred years of slavery, one hundred thousand of them imported into the island within four years, unable to speak a dialect intelligible even to each other. Yet out of this mixed, and, as you say, despicable mass, he forged a thunderbolt and hurled it at what? At the proudest blood in Europe, the Spaniard, and sent him home conquered [cheers]; at the most warlike blood in Europe, the French, and put them under his feet; at the pluckiest blood in Europe, the English, and they skulked home to Jamaica. [Applause.] Now if Cromwell was a general, at least this man was a soldier. I know it was a small territory; it was not as large as the continent; but it was as large as that Attica, which, with Athens for a capital, has filled the earth with its fame for two thousand years. We measure genius by quality, not by quantity.

Further, — Cromwell was only a soldier; his fame stops there. Not one line in the statute-book of Britain can be traced to Cromwell; not one step in the social life of England finds its motive power in his brain. The state he founded went down with him to his grave. But this man no sooner put his hand on the helm of state, than the ship steadied with an upright keel, and he began to evince a statesmanship as marvellous as his military genius. History says that the most statesmanlike act of Napoleon was his proclamation of 1802, at the peace of Amiens, when, believing that the indelible loyalty of a native-born heart is always a sufficient basis on which to found an empire, he said: "Frenchmen, come home. I pardon the crimes of the last twelve years; I blot out its parties; I found my throne on the hearts of all Frenchmen," — and twelve years of unclouded success showed how wisely he judged. That was in 1802. In 1800 this negro made a proclamation; it runs thus: "Sons of St. Domingo, come home. We never meant to take your houses or your lands. The negro only asked that liberty which God gave him. Your houses wait for you; your lands are ready; come and cultivate them"; — and from Madrid and Paris, from Baltimore and New Orleans, the emigrant planters crowded home to enjoy their estates, under the pledged word that was never broken of a victorious slave. [Cheers.]

Again, Carlyle has said, "The natural king is one who melts all wills into his own." At this moment he turned to his armies, — poor, ill-clad, and half-starved, — and said to them: Go back and work on these estates you have conquered; for an empire can be founded only on order and industry, and you can learn these virtues only there. And they went. The French Admiral, who witnessed the scene, said that in a week his army melted back into peasants.

It was 1800. The world waited fifty years before, in 1846, Robert Peel dared to venture, as a matter of practical statesmanship, the theory of free trade. Adam Smith theorized, the French statesmen dreamed, but no man at the head of affairs had ever dared to risk it as a practical measure. Europe waited till 1846 before the most practical intellect in the world, the English, adopted the great economic formula of unfettered trade. But in 1800 this black, with the instinct of statesmanship, said to the committee who were drafting for him a Constitution: "Put at the head of the chapter of commerce that the ports of St. Domingo are open to the trade of the world." [Cheers.] With lofty indifference to race, superior to all envy or prejudice, Toussaint had formed this committee of eight white proprietors and one mulatto, — not a soldier nor a negro on the list, although Haytian history proves that, with the exception of Rigaud, the rarest genius has always been shown by pure negroes.

Again, it was 1800, at a time when England was poisoned on every page of her statute-book with religious intolerance, when a man could not enter the House of Commons without taking an Episcopal communion, when every State in the Union, except Rhode Island, was full of the intensest religious bigotry. This man was a negro. You say that is a superstitious blood. He was uneducated. You say that makes a man narrow-minded. He was a Catholic. Many say that is but another name for intolerance. And yet — negro, Catholic, slave — he took his place by the side of Roger Williams, and said to his committee: "Make it the first line of my Constitution that I know no difference between religious beliefs." [Applause.]

Now, blue-eyed Saxon, proud of your race, go back with me to the commencement of the century, and select what statesman you please. Let him be either American or European; let him have a brain the result of six generations of culture; let him have the ripest training of university routine; let him add to it the better education of practical life; crown his temples with the silver of seventy years; and show me the man of Saxon lineage for whom his most sanguine admirer will wreathe a laurel rich as embittered foes have placed on the brow of this negro, — rare military skill, profound knowledge of human nature, content to blot out all party distinctions, and trust a state to the blood of its sons, — anticipating Sir Robert Peel fifty years, and taking his station by the side of Roger Williams before any Englishman or American had won the right; — and yet this is the record which the history of rival states makes up for this inspired black of St. Domingo. [Cheers.]

It was 1801. The Frenchmen who lingered on the island described its prosperity and order as almost incredible. You might trust a child with a bag of gold to go from Samana to Port-au-Prince without risk. Peace was in every household; the valleys laughed with fertility; culture climbed the mountains; the commerce of the world was represented in its harbors. At this time Europe concluded the Peace of Amiens, and Napoleon took his seat on the throne of France. He glanced his eyes across the Atlantic, and, with a single stroke of his pen, reduced Cayenne and Martinique back into chains. He then said to his Council, "What shall I do with St. Domingo?" The slaveholders said, "Give it to us." Napoleon turned to the Abbé Gregoire, "What is your opinion?" "I

31

think those men would change their opinions, if they changed their skins." Colonel Vincent, who had been private secretary to Toussaint, wrote a letter to Napoleon, in which he said: "Sire, leave it alone; it is the happiest spot in your dominions; God raised this man to govern; races melt under his hand. He has saved you this island; for I know of my own knowledge that, when the Republic could not have lifted a finger to prevent it, George III. offered him any title and any revenue if he would hold the island under the British crown. He refused, and saved it for France." Napoleon turned away from his Council, and is said to have remarked, "I have sixty thousand idle troops; I must find them something to do." He meant to say, "I am about to seize the crown; I dare not do it in the faces of sixty thousand republican soldiers: I must give them work at a distance to do." The gossip of Paris gives another reason for his expedition against St. Domingo. It is said that the satirists of Paris had christened Toussaint, the Black Napoleon; and Bonaparte hated his black shadow. Toussaint had unfortunately once addressed him a letter, "The first of the blacks to the first of the whites." He did not like the comparison. You would think it too slight a motive. But let me remind you of the present Napoleon, that when the epigrammatists of Paris christened his wasteful and tasteless expense at Versailles, *Soulouquerie*, from the name of Soulouque, the Black Emperor, he deigned to issue a specific order forbidding the use of the word. The Napoleon blood is very sensitive. So Napoleon resolved to crush Toussaint from one motive or another, from the prompting of ambition, or dislike of this resemblance, — which was very close. If either imitated the other, it must have been the white, since the negro preceded him several years. They were very much alike, and they were very French, — French even in vanity, common to both. You remember

Bonaparte's vainglorious words to his soldiers at the Pyramids: "Forty centuries look down upon us." In the same mood, Toussaint said to the French captain who urged him to go to France in his frigate, "Sir, your ship is not large enough to carry me." Napoleon, you know, could never bear the military uniform. He hated the restraint of his rank; he loved to put on the gray coat of the Little Corporal, and wander in the camp. Toussaint also never could bear a uniform. He wore a plain coat, and often the yellow Madras handkerchief of the slaves. A French lieutenant once called him a maggot in a yellow handkerchief. Toussaint took him prisoner next day, and sent him home to his mother. Like Napoleon, he could fast many days; could dictate to three secretaries at once; could wear out four or five horses. Like Napoleon, no man ever divined his purpose or penetrated his plan. He was only a negro, and so, in him, they called it hypocrisy. In Bonaparte we style it diplomacy. For instance, three attempts made to assassinate him all failed, from not firing at the right spot. If they thought he was in the north in a carriage, he would be in the south on horseback; if they thought he was in the city in a house, he would be in the field in a tent. They once riddled his carriage with bullets; he was on horseback on the other side. The seven Frenchmen who did it were arrested. They expected to be shot. The next day was some saint's day; he ordered them to be placed before the high altar, and, when the priest reached the prayer for forgiveness, came down from his high seat, repeated it with him, and permitted them to go unpunished. [Cheers.] He had that wit common to all great commanders, which makes its way in a camp. His soldiers getting disheartened, he filled a large vase with powder, and, scattering six grains of rice in it, shook them up, and said: "See, there is the white, there is the black; what are you afraid of?" So when people came to him in great numbers for office, as it is reported they do sometimes even in Washington, he learned the first words of a Catholic prayer in Latin, and, repeating it, would say, "Do you understand that?' "No, sir." "What! want an office, and not know Latin? Go home and learn it!"

Then, again, like Napoleon, — like genius always, — he had confidence in his power to rule men. You remember when Bonaparte returned from Elba, and Louis XVIII. sent an army against him, Bonaparte descended from his carriage, opened his coat, offering his breast to their muskets, and saying, "Frenchmen, it is the Emperor!" and they ranged themselves behind him, *his* soldiers, shouting, "*Vive l'Empereur!*" That was in 1815. Twelve years before, Toussaint, finding that four of his regiments had deserted and gone to Leclerc, drew his sword, flung it on the grass, went across the field to them, folded his arms, and said, "Children, can you point a bayonet at me?" The blacks fell on their knees, praying his pardon. His bitterest enemies watched him, and none of them charged him with love of money, sensuality, or cruel use of power. The only instance in which his sternest critic has charged him with severity is this. During a tumult, a few white proprietors who had returned, trusting his proclamation, were killed. His nephew, General Moise, was accused of indecision in quelling the riot. He assembled a court-martial, and, on its verdict, ordered his own nephew to be shot, sternly Roman in thus keeping his promise of protection to the whites. Above the lust of gold, pure in private life, generous in the use of his power, it was against such a man that Napoleon sent his army, giving to General Leclerc, the husband of his beautiful sister Pauline, thirty thousand of his best troops, with orders to reintroduce slavery. Among these soldiers came all of Toussaint's old mulatto rivals and foes.

Holland lent sixty ships. England promised by special message to be neutral; and you know neutrality means sneering at freedom, and sending arms to tyrants. [Loud and long-continued applause.] England promised neutrality, and the black looked out on the whole civilized world marshalled against him. America, full of slaves, of course was hostile. Only the Yankee sold him poor muskets at a very high price. [Laughter.] Mounting his horse, and riding to the eastern end of the island, Samana, he looked out on a sight such as no native had ever seen before. Sixty ships of the line, crowded by the best soldiers of Europe, rounded the point. They were soldiers who had never yet met an equal, whose tread, like Cæsar's, had shaken Europe, — soldiers who had scaled the Pyramids, and planted the French banners on the walls of Rome. He looked a moment, counted the flotilla, let the reins fall on the neck of his horse, and, turning to Christophe, exclaimed: "All France is come to Hayti; they can only come to make us slaves; and we are lost!" He then recognized the only mistake of his life, — his confidence in Bonaparte, which had led him to disband his army.

Returning to the hills, he issued the only proclamation which bears his name and breathes vengeance: "My children, France comes to make us slaves. God gave us liberty; France has no right to take it away. Burn the cities, destroy the harvests, tear up the roads with cannon, poison the wells, show the white man the hell he comes to make"; — and he was obeyed. [Applause.] When the great William of Orange saw Louis XIV. cover Holland with troops, he said, "Break down the dikes, give Holland back to ocean"; and Europe said, "Sublime!" When Alexander saw the armies of France descend upon Russia, he said, "Burn Moscow, starve back the invaders"; and Europe said, "Sublime!" This black saw all

Europe marshalled to crush him, and gave to his people the same heroic example of defiance.

It is true, the scene grows bloodier as we proceed. But, remember, the white man fitly accompanied his infamous attempt to *reduce freemen to slavery* with every bloody and cruel device that bitter and shameless hate could invent. Aristocracy is always cruel. The black man met the attempt, as every such attempt should be met, with war to the hilt. In his first struggle to gain his freedom, he had been generous and merciful, saved lives and pardoned enemies, as the people in every age and clime have always done when rising against aristocrats. Now, to save his liberty, the negro exhausted every means, seized every weapon, and turned back the hateful invaders with a vengeance as terrible as their own, though even now he refused to be cruel.

Leclerc sent word to Christophe that he was about to land at Cape City. Christophe said, "Toussaint is governor of the island. I will send to him for permission. If without it a French soldier sets foot on shore, I will burn the town, and fight over its ashes."

Leclerc landed. Christophe took two thousand *white* men, women, and children, and carried them to the mountains in safety, then with his own hands set fire to the splendid palace which French architects had just finished for him, and in forty hours the place was in ashes. The battle was fought in its streets, and the French driven back to their boats. [Cheers.] Wherever they went, they were met with fire and sword. Once, resisting an attack, the blacks, Frenchmen born, shouted the Marseilles Hymn, and the French soldiers stood still; they could not fight the Marseillaise. And it was not till their officers sabred them on that they advanced, and then they were beaten. Beaten in the field, the French then took to lies. They issued proclamations, saying, "We do not come to make you slaves; this man Toussaint tells you lies. Join us, and you shall have the rights you claim." They cheated every one of his officers, except Christophe and Dessalines, and his own brother Pierre, and finally these also deserted him, and he was left alone. He then sent word to Leclerc, "I will submit. I could continue the struggle for years, — could prevent a single Frenchman from safely quitting your camp. But I hate bloodshed. I have fought only for the liberty of my race. Guarantee that, I will submit and come in." He took the oath to be a faithful citizen; and on the same crucifix Leclerc swore that he should be faithfully protected, and that the island should be free. As the French general glanced along the line of his splendidly equipped troops, and saw, opposite, Toussaint's ragged, ill-armed followers, he said to him, "L'Ouverture, had you continued the war, where could you have got arms?" "I would have taken yours," was the Spartan reply. [Cheers.] He went down to his house in peace; it was summer. Leclerc remembered that the fever months were coming, when his army would be in hospitals, and when one motion of that royal hand would sweep his troops into the sea. He was too dangerous to be left at large. So they summoned him to attend a council; and here is the only charge made against him, — the only charge. They say he was fool enough to go. Grant it; what was the record? The white man lies shrewdly to cheat the negro. Knight-errantry was truth. The foulest insult you can offer a man since the Crusades is, You lie. Of Toussaint, Hermona, the Spanish general, who knew him well, said, "He was the purest soul God ever put into a body." Of him history bears witness, "He never broke his word." Maitland was travelling in the depths of the woods to meet Toussaint, when he was met by a messenger, and told that he was betrayed. He went on, and met Toussaint, who showed him two letters, — one from the French general, offering him any rank if he would put Maitland in his power, and the other his reply. It was, "Sir, I have promised the Englishman that he shall go back." [Cheers.] Let it stand, therefore, that the negro, truthful as a knight of old, was cheated by his lying foe. Which race has reason to be proud of such a record?

But he was not cheated. He was under espionage. Suppose he had refused: the government would have doubted him, — would have found some cause to arrest him. He probably reasoned thus: "If I go willingly, I shall be treated accordingly"; and he went. The moment he entered the room, the officers drew their swords, and told him he was prisoner; and one young lieutenant who was present says, "He was not at all surprised, but seemed very sad." They put him on shipboard, and weighed anchor for France. As the island faded from his sight, he turned to the captain, and said, "You think you have rooted up the tree of liberty, but I am only a branch; I have planted the tree so deep that all France can never root it up." [Cheers.] Arrived in Paris, he was flung into jail, and Napoleon sent his secretary, Caffarelli, to him, supposing he had buried large treasures. He listened awhile, then replied, "Young man, it is true I have lost treasures, but they are not such as you come to seek." He was then sent to the Castle of St. Joux, to a dungeon twelve feet by twenty, built wholly of stone, with a narrow window, high up on the side, looking out on the snows of Switzerland. In winter, ice covers the floor; in summer, it is damp and wet. In this living tomb the child of the sunny tropic was left to die. From this dungeon he wrote two letters to Napoleon. One of them ran thus: —

"Sire, I am a French citizen. I never broke a law. By the grace of God, I have saved for you the best island of your realm. Sire, of your mercy grant me justice."

Napoleon never answered the letters. The commandant allowed him five francs a day for food and fuel. Napoleon heard of it, and reduced the sum to three. The luxurious usurper, who complained that the English government was stingy because it allowed him only six thousand dollars a month, stooped from his throne to cut down a dollar to a half, and still Toussaint did not die quick enough.

This dungeon was a tomb. The story is told that, in Josephine's time, a young French marquis was placed there, and the girl to whom he was betrothed went to the Empress and prayed for his release. Said Josephine to her, "Have a model of it made, and bring it to me." Josephine placed it near Napoleon. He said, "Take it away, — it is horrible!" She put it on his footstool, and he kicked it from him. She held it to him the third time, and said, "Sire, in this horrible dungeon you have put a man to die." "Take him out," said Napoleon, and the girl saved her lover. In this tomb Toussaint was buried, but he did not die fast enough. Finally, the commandant was told to go into Switzerland, to carry the keys of the dungeon with him, and to stay four days; when he returned, Toussaint was found starved to death. That imperial assassin was taken twelve years after to his prison at St. Helena, planned for a tomb, as he had planned that of Toussaint, and there he whined away his dying hours in pitiful complaints of curtains and titles, of dishes and rides. God grant that when some future Plutarch shall weigh the great men of our epoch, the whites against the blacks, he do not put that whining child at St. Helena into one scale, and into the other the negro meeting death like a Roman, without a murmur, in the solitude of his icy dungeon!

From the moment he was betrayed, the negroes began to doubt the French, and rushed to arms. Soon every negro but Maurepas deserted the French. Leclerc summoned Maurepas to his side. He came, loyally bringing with him five hundred soldiers. Leclerc spiked his epaulettes to his shoulders, shot him, and flung him into the sea. He took his five hundred soldiers on shore, shot them on the edge of a pit, and tumbled them in. Dessalines from the mountain saw it, and, selecting five hundred French officers from his prisons, hung them on separate trees in sight of Leclerc's camp; and born, as I was, not far from Bunker Hill, I have yet found no reason to think he did wrong. [Cheers.] They murdered Pierre Toussaint's wife at his own door, and after such treatment that it was mercy when they killed her. The maddened husband, who had but a year before saved the lives of twelve hundred white men, carried his next thousand prisoners and sacrificed them on her grave.

The French exhausted every form of torture. The negroes were bound together and thrown into the sea; any one who floated was shot, — others sunk with cannon-balls tied to their feet; some smothered with sulphur fumes, — others strangled, scourged to death, gibbeted; sixteen of Toussaint's officers were chained to rocks in desert islands, — others in marshes, and left to be devoured by poisonous reptiles and insects. Rochambeau sent to Cuba for bloodhounds. When they arrived, the young girls went down to the wharf, decked the hounds with ribbons and flowers, kissed their necks, and, seated in the amphitheatre, the women clapped their hands to see a negro thrown to these dogs, previously starved to rage. But the negroes besieged this very city so closely that these same girls, in their misery, ate the very hounds they had welcomed.

Then flashed forth that defying courage and sublime endurance which show how alike all races are when tried in the same furnace. The Roman wife, whose husband faltered when Nero ordered him to kill himself, seized the dagger, and, mortally wounding her own body, cried, "Poetus, it is not hard to die." The world records it with proud tears. Just in the same spirit, when a negro colonel was ordered to execution, and trembled, his wife seized his sword, and, giving herself a death-wound, said, "Husband, death is sweet when liberty is gone."

The war went on. Napoleon sent over thirty thousand more soldiers. But disaster still followed his efforts. What the sword did not devour, the fever ate up. Leclerc died. Pauline carried his body back to France. Napoleon met her at Bordeaux, saying, "Sister, I gave you an army, — you bring me back ashes." Rochambeau — the Rochambeau of our history — left in command of eight thousand troops, sent word to Dessalines: "When I take you, I will not shoot you like a soldier, or hang you like a white man; I will whip you to death like a slave." Dessalines chased him from battle-field to battle-field, from fort to fort, and finally shut him up in Samana. Heating cannon-balls to destroy his fleet, Dessalines learned that Rochambeau had begged of the British admiral to cover his troops with the English flag, and the generous negro suffered the boaster to embark undisturbed.

Some doubt the courage of the negro. Go to Hayti, and stand on those fifty thousand graves of the best soldiers France ever had, and ask them what they think of the negro's sword. And if that does not satisfy you, go to France, to the splendid mausoleum of the Counts of Rochambeau, and to the eight thousand graves of Frenchmen who skulked home under the English flag, and ask them. And if that does not satisfy you, come home, and if it had been October, 1859, you might have come by way of quaking Virginia, and asked her what she thought of negro courage.

You may also remember this, — that we Saxons were

slaves about four hundred years, sold with the land, and our fathers never raised a finger to end that slavery. They waited till Christianity and civilization, till commerce and the discovery of America, melted away their chains. Spartacus in Italy led the slaves of Rome against the Empress of the world. She murdered him, and crucified them. There never was a slave rebellion successful but once, and that was in St. Domingo. Every race has been, some time or other, in chains. But there never was a race that, weakened and degraded by such chattel slavery, unaided, tore off its own fetters, forged them into swords, and won its liberty on the battle-field, but one, and that was the black race of St. Domingo. God grant that the wise vigor of our government may avert that necessity from our land, — may raise into peaceful liberty the four million committed to our care, and show under democratic institutions a statesmanship as far-sighted as that of England, as brave as the negro of Hayti!

So much for the courage of the negro. Now look at his endurance. In 1805 he said to the white men, "This island is ours; not a white foot shall touch it." Side by side with him stood the South American republics, planted by the best blood of the countrymen of Lope de Vega and Cervantes. They topple over so often that you could no more daguerrotype their crumbling fragments than you could the waves of the ocean. And yet, at their side, the negro has kept his island sacredly to himself. It is said that at first, with rare patriotism, the Haytien government ordered the destruction of all the sugar plantations remaining, and discouraged its culture, deeming that the temptation which lured the French back again to attempt their enslavement. Burn over New York to-night, fill up her canals, sink every ship, destroy her railroads, blot out every remnant of education from her sons, let her be ignorant and penniless, with nothing but her hands to begin the world again, — how much could she do in sixty years? And Europe, too, would lend you money, but she will not lend Hayti a dollar. Hayti, from the ruins of her colonial dependence, is become a civilized state, the seventh nation in the catalogue of commerce with this country, inferior in morals and education to none of the West Indian isles. Foreign merchants trust her courts as willingly as they do our own. Thus far, she has foiled the ambition of Spain, the greed of England, and the malicious statesmanship of Calhoun. Toussaint made her what she is. In this work there was grouped around him a score of men, mostly of pure negro blood, who ably seconded his efforts. They were able in war and skilful in civil affairs, but not, like him, remarkable for that rare mingling of high qualities which alone makes true greatness, and insures a man leadership among those otherwise almost his equals. Toussaint was indisputably their chief. Courage, purpose, endurance, — these are the tests. He did plant a state so deep that all the world has not been able to root it up.

I would call him Napoleon, but Napoleon made his way to empire over broken oaths and through a sea of blood. This man never broke his word. "No Retaliation" was his great motto and the rule of his life; and the last words uttered to his son in France were these: "My boy, you will one day go back to St. Domingo; forget that France murdered your father." I would call him Cromwell, but Cromwell was only a soldier, and the state he founded went down with him into his grave. I would call him Washington, but the great Virginian held slaves. This man risked his empire rather than permit the slave-trade in the humblest village of his dominions.

You think me a fanatic to-night, for you read history, not with your eyes, but with your prejudices. But fifty years hence, when Truth gets a hearing, the Muse of History will put Phocion for the Greek, and Brutus for the Roman, Hampden for England, Fayette for France, choose Washington as the bright, consummate flower of our earlier civilization, and John Brown the ripe fruit of our noonday [thunders of applause], then, dipping her pen in the sunlight, will write in the clear blue, above them all, the name of the soldier, the statesman, the martyr, TOUSSAINT L'OUVERTURE. [Long-continued applause.]

A METROPOLITAN POLICE.*

I HAVE been requested to speak to you to-day on the subject of a Metropolitan Police. That plan has already been presented, two or three years ago, to this community, and, of late, very elaborately and eloquently argued before a committee of the Legislature, by Edward L. Peirce, Esq., and still more comprehensively and in detail by Charles M. Ellis, Esq.; but it is one of vital importance to the welfare and progress of our city, and, until the object be achieved, it can never be too frequently considered and urged. Other cities have led the way in this path, years ago. The capital of the civilized world, London, many years ago, found herself utterly unable to contend with the evils of accumulated population, — found municipal machinery utterly inadequate for the security of life or property in her streets; and the national government, by the hand of Sir Robert Peel, assumed the police regulation of that cluster of towns which we commonly call London, though the plan does not include the city proper. New York, on our continent, about six years ago, followed the example; Baltimore and Cincinnati have done likewise to a greater or less extent, and so also have some of the other Western cities. The experience of all great accumulations of property and population

* A Discourse delivered before the Twenty-eighth Congregational Society, in the Melodeon, Boston, April 5, 1863.

reads us a lesson, that the execution of the laws therein demand extra consideration and peculiar machinery. The self-organized Safety Committees of San Francisco and other cities prove the same fact. Indeed, great cities are nests of great vices, and it has been the experience of republics that great cities are an exception to the common rule of self-governed communities. Neither New York, nor New Orleans, nor Baltimore — none of the great cities — has found the ballot-box of its individual voters a sufficient protection, through a police organization. Great cities cannot be protected on the theory of republican institutions. We may like it or not, — seventy years have tried the experiment, and, so far, it is a failure; and if there is no resource outside of the city limits, then a self-governed great city is, so far as my experience goes, the most uncomfortable which any man who loves free speech can live in. It is no surprise, therefore, that we ask you no longer to let the police force represent the voters of Boston. Hitherto, the police regulations in the city of Boston have been modelled on those of a small town; that is, the inhabitants themselves have called into existence a body of constables, in fact, to execute the laws of the State and the by-laws of the city. Our text, in presenting this subject to you, is this: in Boston, as everywhere else, where large numbers are brought together and great masses of property are found, a police force appointed by the voters of the place cannot be relied on to execute the laws; and, in order to secure their full and impartial execution, it has been found necessary elsewhere, and I shall attempt to show you that it is necessary here, to put the control of the police force into other hands than those of the voters of the place. That is our claim, — that the men of the peninsula, like those of other great cities, are not to be trusted with the execution of the State laws, but that executive power must be based on broader foundations. Such a course is no uncommon machinery in democratic institutions. We put the interpretation of the laws — the judiciary — not into the hands of any local municipal body, but the interpretation of the State laws is in the hands of persons appointed by the whole State. I invoke the same principle for their execution, — following old republican precedents, as I shall shortly show.

In order to sustain this claim before you, I ought to show three or four things. First, that in important particulars — *important* particulars — the law has failed of execution; that good and vitally important laws have failed of execution. Secondly, I ought to show you that this failure is due to the machinery which the city puts in motion for the execution of the laws. Thirdly, that a better machinery may be found. And, fourthly, that it is important for the welfare of the State that the attempt to find a better machinery should be made.

My first point is to show you that in important particulars, where great and grave interests are involved, the laws have failed of execution. You perceive that this involves, in fact, an indictment against the city government. It is, in reality, arraigning the government of the city for failure to do its duty. Before I pass to it, therefore, let me make one protest. I do not come here to find fault with individual policemen. I think our body of police is as good, on the average, as that of any great city I know. I think upon all trying occasions they have done their duty, as far as they have been permitted, and have always shown full capacity to do their whole duty. Neither do I come here to arraign the individuals of the city government; not, however, on account of the same excuse, but because I deem it unnecessary. They are mere puppets, fluttering before us for a little while; they are only victims of a great system, which they did not originate and cannot control. Looking over the last dozen years, considering that the Mayor and Aldermen during those years have been, in the aggregate, only a standing committee appointed by the grog-shops of the peninsula, it has been no honor, but a shame, to hold one of those offices. No man with a full measure of self-respect could accept such an office. All politics necessitates questionable compliances; but this serfdom touches a base depth. It is not however necessary, and certainly not within my plan to-day, to arraign individuals. I am merely criticising a system which throws up into unfitting places and undue importance men who have no real right to the power which they are wholly unable or unwilling to use.

To return now to my first point, I am to show you that, in many important particulars, the laws have failed of execution. I shall take, in the first place, temperance. Some men look upon this temperance cause as whining bigotry, narrow asceticism, or a vulgar sentimentality, fit for little minds, weak women, and weaker men. On the contrary, I regard it as second only to one or two others of the primary reforms of this age, and for this reason. Every race has its peculiar temptation; every clime has its specific sin. The tropics and tropical races are tempted to one form of sensuality; the colder and temperate regions, and our Saxon blood, find their peculiar temptation in the stimulus of drink and food. In old times our heaven was a drunken revel. We relieve ourselves from the over-weariness of constant and exhausting toil by intoxication. Science has brought a cheap means of drunkenness within the reach of every individual. National prosperity and free institutions have put into the hands of almost every workman the means of being drunk for a week on the labor of two or three hours. With that blood and that temptation, we have adopted democratic institutions, where the law has no sanction but the purpose and virtue of the masses. The statute-book rests not on bayonets, as in Europe, but on the hearts of the people. A drunken people can never be the basis of a free government. It is the corner-stone neither of virtue, prosperity, nor progress. To us, therefore, the title-deeds of whose estates and the safety of whose lives depend upon the tranquillity of the streets, upon the virtue of the masses, the presence of any vice which brutalizes the average mass of mankind, and tends to make it more readily the tool of intriguing and corrupt leaders, is necessarily a stab at the very life of the nation. Against such a vice is marshalled the Temperance Reformation. That my sketch is no mere fancy picture, every one of you knows. Every one of you can glance back over your own path, and count many and many a one among those who started from the goal at your side, with equal energy and perhaps greater promise, who has found a drunkard's grave long before this. The brightness of the bar, the ornament of the pulpit, the hope and blessing and stay of many a family, — you know, every one of you who has reached middle life, how often on your path you set up the warning, "Fallen before the temptations of the streets!" Hardly one house in this city, whether it be full and warm with all the luxury of wealth, or whether it find hard, cold maintenance by the most earnest economy, no matter which, — hardly a house that does not count, among sons or nephews, some victim of this vice. The skeleton of this warning sits at every board. The whole world is kindred in this suffering. The country mother launches her boy with trembling upon the temptations of city life; the father trusts his daughter anxiously to the young man she has chosen, knowing what a wreck intoxication may make of the house-tree they set up. Alas! how often are their worst forebodings more than fulfilled! I have known a case — and probably many of you can recall some almost equal to it — where one worthy woman could count father, brother, husband, and son-in law, all drunkards, — no man among her near kindred, except her son, who was not a victim of this vice. Like all other appetites, this finds resolution weak when set against the constant presence of temptation. This is the evil. How are the laws relating to it executed in this city? Let me tell you.

First, there has been great discussion of this evil, — wide, earnest, patient discussion, for thirty-five years. The whole community has been stirred by the discussion of this question. Finally, after various experiments, the majority of the State decided that the method to stay this evil was to stop the open sale of intoxicating drink. They left moral suasion still to address the individual, and set themselves as a community to close the doors of temptation. Every man acquainted with his own nature or with society knows that weak virtue, walking through our streets, and meeting at every tenth door (for that is the average) the temptation to drink, must fall; that one must be a moral Hercules to stand erect. To prevent the open sale of intoxicating liquor has been the method selected by the State to help its citizens to be virtuous; in other words, the State has enacted what is called the Maine Liquor Law, — the plan of refusing all licenses to sell, to be drunk on the spot or elsewhere, and allowing only an official agent to sell for medicinal purposes and the arts. You may drink in your own parlors, you may make what indulgence you please your daily rule, the State does not touch you there; there you injure only yourself, and those you directly influence; that the State cannot reach. But when you open your door and say to your fellow-citizens, "Come and indulge," the State has a right to ask, "In what do you invite them to indulge? Is it in something that helps, or something that harms, the community?"

I will try to show you, in a moment, on what grounds

the State decided that these numberless open doors harmed the community, and that the method to be adopted was to shut them up. The majority, after full argument in district school-houses, the streets, and the State-House, from pulpits, lyceum platforms, and everywhere else, decided that prohibition of the traffic was the only effective method. The law was put upon the statute-book. A reluctant minority went to the Legislature, and endeavored to repeal or amend it, alleging that this was not a good law; and they were voted down. Again they went, — were voted down. A third time they went, — and were voted down. They then appealed to the courts, and said, "This is not a constitutional law." The courts said, "It is." If anything ever had the decided, unmistakable sanction of a majority of the people of this Commonwealth, the Maine Liquor Law has it. After a quarter of a century of discussion, it was enacted; three times assailed, it was maintained; subjected to the crucible of the court, it came out pure gold. We have a right to say that it is the matured, settled purpose of the majority of the Commonwealth; if the majority have a right to govern, that law is to govern. Is it not so? If not, let the minority assail again the Gibraltar of the statute. But meanwhile it, like all other laws not immoral, is to be obeyed. I have not, therefore, to argue to-day whether the law is good or not, whether it is wise or not. That is settled. It is good and wise in the opinion of the Commonwealth. The era of *public opinion* is finished, that of *law* has commenced. This is the history of all legislation. Do not find fault with us for enacting, in due time, public opinion into a statute. Where did all statutes come from? Hundreds of years ago, men argued the question, "Shall one man own a separate piece of land?" They argued it, and settled that he should. That became a statute. They then began to argue the question, "Shall he transmit to his children by will?" They argued that for centuries, then said, "Yes," and enacted it. Nobody now goes behind those statutes. Hundreds of years ago, our race argued the question, "Shall a man have one wife or three?" We settled that he should have but one; it is the law of the Commonwealth.

The era of discussion and opinion is over; the era of legislation has come, — the time when the minority sits down and obeys. With all great questions, covering important interests, there is a time when public opinion stereotypes itself into statutes. Land, harvests, marriage, the laws against burglary and theft, settled themselves years ago. If I raise a harvest, it is mine; that is the law of the land. There was a time when it was a question; it is not a question now. So with temperance and the Maine Liquor Law. Time was when the question whether a man had a right to sell liquor openly, licensed or not, was discussed; we have passed that point, and reached the time when the majority — in other words, the State — decrees that these shops shall be shut.

Now let me show you, in a few words, *why* it should decree that. In order more clearly to show this, let me go back a little, and ask how did the Mayor and Aldermen, the City, meet this Maine Liquor Law? They said, "You may decree it if you please, we won't execute it. You say we shall not license anybody, but we will effect the same thing, for we will let everybody sell, except just those whom we should not have licensed." These are the exact words of the order to the police some years ago. The Chief of Police replied to a question from the Massachusetts Temperance Society, "We have directions never to prosecute a liquor-seller, unless he be one who would not have received a license under the old license act." In other words, the State says, "On mature consideration, I prohibit the sale." The City says, "I shall allow it, — help yourself!" Those whom it would not have licensed are "nuisances," as it calls them; — houses vulgar, noisy, disorderly; kept, as the Dogberry of the Board of Aldermen told us at the State House, by "imbecile old men and ancient women," — as the constable of Shakespeare's play arrested all "vagrom men." That is the position of the city. The law is intentionally and avowedly set aside. The city government announces that it does not intend to obey it; makes no effort, and never has made any, to enforce it. What is the result? The result is, that there are at least three thousand places in the city where liquor is publicly and continually sold. These consist partly of dram-shops, partly of gambling saloons, partly of houses of prostitution. They number in all more than three thousand. I am giving an under estimate of an average for two or three years. What are the results of these three thousand places of sale? Six million dollars' worth of liquor is sold to the retailers of this city annually; and three million dollars' worth is annually retailed on the peninsula. With what result? With this. They produce poverty and crime to this extent: — We arrest for drunkenness alone, on an average for the last three years, about seventeen thousand persons annually; that is, a little less than one tenth of the population. There are between twenty-five and thirty thousand persons relieved for poverty by overseers of the poor, and by the Provident Association, — poverty caused by intemperance. That is, every seventh man in the city is a pauper, helped by the community; every tenth man in the city is a criminal, arrested by the police. Let us look at that a moment. I say every seventh man is a pauper, relieved by the help of the community. Poverty, wholesome poverty, is no unmixed evil; it is the motive power that throws a man up to guide and control the community; it is the spur that often wins the race; it is the trial that calls out, like fire, all the deep, great qualities of a man's nature. That poverty is no evil,—at least, it is no unmixed evil; but poverty which is caused by drunkenness,—for I am only taking, in these twenty-five thousand persons, the poverty that is traceable to intemperance,—the poverty that is caused by drunkenness has what history? The father is a drunkard; the mother often imitates him; the self-respect of the family is lost; the home is gone; it is a scene of quarrel and degradation; the children are thrown neglected on the streets, with no food, no education, no moral sense developed,—the frightful and fruitful source of every vice known to the civil code. This feeds the gallows, fills the street with impurity, makes thieves and burglars. Out of such houses flows a constant supply for all forms of crime. Without the open and continued sale of drink, almost every hell of the gambler would be closed; he would have few victims. He would find few men in the mood to be victimized. Without open places for the sale of liquor, the houses of prostitution could not be maintained; that is the testimony of all experience in every city. To that shameless pit woman seldom sinks, except when betrayed by drink, and, even when once ruined, could not bear such a life unless nature was daily stupefied by intoxication. Nine tenths of those sent to the House of Industry are common drunkards. Intemperance is one of the most productive of all causes of insanity. "Truancy" finds its "cause of causes" in intemperance. Said the Chief of Police, three or four years ago, "Intemperance is the direct origin of more poverty, more crime, and consequent suffering, than all other causes combined." Twenty-five thousand men reduced to poverty in a year, or at least every year relieved by the public.

Now let me go to the schools. Twenty-five thousand is an average estimate of the children who attend our public schools. The city pours out a quarter of a million a year to mould those young souls, step by step, to virtue, to make them good citizens. Twenty-five thousand with one hand it lifts up; with the other, it tempts twenty-five thousand into pollution and crime. It spends four hundred and seventy-seven thousand dollars a year to do it; foı that is the cost of our police force, of our Overseers of the Poor, of our Lunatic Asylums (a large portion of whose inmates are rendered insane by intemperance), our House of Correction and House of Industry. You might as well take a third of a million of dollars, and toss it off the end of Long Wharf, — we should be richer at the end of the year. Leave all the children idle in the streets, shut up the grog-shops, shut up the schools, throw a third of a million into the water, and the city would be better off on the thirty-first day of December than she is now.

The Mayor and Aldermen, to whom you choose to give the police, take with one hand two hundred and fifty thousand dollars of your money and mine to educate twenty-five thousand children, and with the other they tear out a law from the statute-book in order to ruin twenty-five thousand adults. The inefficiency of the Mayor and Aldermen makes it exactly the same as if the cost of our school system were thrown into the dock from the end of Long Wharf. We know just as well what educates drunkards as what educates a school-boy. The Parker House, the Tremont House, the Revere House, and the Howard Saloon educate intemperance exactly as the Latin School educates youth. One educates for heaven, the other for hell; and the city government says it shall be so.

I am perfectly serious on this ground. I know the value of the common schools of Massachusetts. It makes my house worth a thousand dollars more to-day; it makes my right of free speech doubly valuable; it makes my life safer; it makes it happier and more honorable to live in this Commonwealth. That is the value of the common-school system, which at great expense educates the children of the State. By its side stands your State system for breaking up the intemperance of the city. I do not say that the Mayor or the Aldermen could prevent it all. I know well the difficulties. I only ask of any man an honest effort; I only ask for evidence that the first step is taken in that direction, — that there is a willingness, a disposition, to do it. A great deal could be prevented. The mob which broke up our Tremont Temple meeting, two years ago, reeled into it from the gorgeous grog-shops which surround the Temple. Where do they get their unblushing shamelessness and so-called respectability? They get it from the fact that your Governors, your Judges, your Senators, your lawmakers, meet week after week, and month after month, in these very places, to violate the law which they have placed upon the statute-book. No wonder they are ashamed to execute the laws which they break before the very sun and noonday of Massachusetts.

Such are the reasons for the Law. One half the criminals of the State are found in the city of Boston. We have one sixth of the population, and yet we have more than one half the criminals. We have one sixth of the population, but we pay about one half of the criminal expenses of the State of Massachusetts, — just three times our proper proportion. What does it come from? I am not to charge it on any particular corporation; I am to charge it to a system. It is the massing up of one third of the capital of the State, and one sixth the population on this peninsula. That makes a new order of things, one calling for a new machinery to check crime, — a hot-bed, where all the tendencies to crime become doubled and trebled, where the dangerous classes of the community get undue power. It is because of this peculiarity that we need a different system from what the country does. Up to a certain point our city government has always acknowledged this. For instance, in a small country town of a few thousand inhabitants they have two or three constables. Nobody knows who they are. You might visit half a dozen houses, and they could not tell you. Only once or twice in a year, on some festive or other occasion, a town meeting, a picnic, or something of the kind, is he ever seen or needed. He may execute a writ once in a while. If there is any disorder in the town, a citizen takes notice of it, reports it to a justice of the peace, and the difficulty is cured. That is a sufficient machinery for a small town. But when you have a large and dense population, great wealth invested in certain dangerous and tempting forms, you cannot trust the execution of the laws to the volunteer efforts of the citizens; you must have a large body of police constantly in the streets, ever on the alert, with grave and extraordinary powers, to watch criminals and follow them up. That has been found necessary. Now the question is whether something further is not necessary also. The returns for ten years show that forty-two per cent of the average population of this county was arrested for crime, while, in other counties, the number arrested was only one, two, or three per cent. Why this difference? Because a city necessarily induces greater temptations, greater dangers, and more frequent crimes. It needs, therefore, a more stringent machinery to execute the laws. Instead of that, in regard to this temperance law, the city government defy it. They themselves pay — or did pay till within a year or two, I will not speak of the present year, for I have not consulted the reports — about a thousand dollars a month out of the city treasury for the indulgences of the Board of Aldermen and Common-Councilmen at an illegal liquor-shop, which no one of them had a right to see without presenting it to the courts within twenty-four hours. In that disgraceful Anthony Burns and Sims experience of the city, upon which I am shortly to speak, one of the melancholy features of city sin that day was, that the men illegally called out to defy the State laws contracted a bill, within sight of the Supreme Court, within sight of City Hall, of between one and two thousand dollars, for liquor and food furnished them at an illegal grog-shop, by order of the city.

Let me leave this question a moment, and turn to another, — free speech. Free speech is so vital an element of civil life, so important a privilege, that the framers of our government were not willing to leave it to the law, — they enshrined it in the Constitution. It was so fundamental, that it could not be left to annual legislation; it was grouted and dovetailed into the very first stratum of the foundation of the State. Now, the class of men who have had the ordering of city affairs have never, for the last twenty years, attempted to protect free speech on this peninsula. Let me tell you what I mean. If a man like the editor of the Boston Post, like the Hon. Edward Everett, like Mr. Sumner, any popular person in the community, wished to hold a meeting on this peninsula, he could always do it; but if any set of men who are unpopular wanted to hold a meeting here, it depended entirely upon the mood of the mob that month whether they could hold it or not. These very walls could testify, if they had voice, how many dozen times they have seen their occupants, paying an honest price for a day's use of them, disturbed hour after hour, and finally, perhaps, in some instances, the meeting broken up, by a crowd of boys that the right hand of one policeman could have quelled; and when individuals, the very lessees of this hall, would take one of these disturbers to the courts, he was set free, and the persons who interfered threatened with a suit. You know that the trustees of the hall from which you have just removed for a season sat on one occasion until midnight, to decide whether they would dare to risk their property when the Mayor of the city had let it be known that he did not intend to defend it against the mob of the streets. You know too, or you might know, that the same anxious scene of consultation went on among the trustees of the Tremont Temple, again and again, whether they would dare to risk their building, when the city authorities had unblushingly and publicly declared that they would not protect free speech. You know also, that, when the Massachusetts Antislavery Society was mobbed out of its hall by the Mayor of the city, the members of the Legislature refrained from offering the Society the use of the State-House, though wishing to do so, because the Executive informed them that he had no means to protect the State's property against the grog-shops of the peninsula. Macaulay says, speaking of James the Second's disturbed reign: "On such occasions, it will ever be found that the human vermin, which, neglected by ministers of state and ministers of religion, — barbarians in the midst of civilization, heathen in the midst of Christianity, — who burrow among all physical and moral pollution in the cellars and garrets of great cities, will rise at once into terrible importance." It was when that class of the community found that the Mayor was willing to lead them, and that they could riot in the most fashionable drinking-saloons free of expense, that your Governor dared not trust the State-House to an orderly and legal assemblage of the citizens of Massachusetts. It was at a time when one of the most efficient of the Chiefs of Police said, "Give me thirty men, *and an order*, and I will quell that mob at once." The difficulty was not that it could not be quelled. That class which Macaulay describes never faces the law until it has bribed it. The moment the court turns its determined countenance upon them, they retire to cellars and garrets again. One of the Aldermen of the city said recently, in the State-House, that these mobs were only "watermelon frolics, — the pounding of men with the soft side of a cushion"; but it was a cushion that the Governor dared not trust to touch the State-House; it was a mob which the Mayor said, in excuse for inefficiency, that he had not force enough to control. Perhaps it would not be disrespectful to ask that these several city dignitaries would arrange beforehand, and make their lame excuses at least consistent. There is a class of whom an old proverb affirms that it needs to have "long memories."

Fellow-citizens, for the last five years, I have been able to make in New York, in perfect quiet, with the unsolicited protection of the police, the same speech which I could not make to you without being surrounded by fifty armed friends. Again and again have I proved this, during the last five years. In the city of New York, the common sewer of the continent, where wealth is massed up by uncounted millions, where the criminals of all nations take refuge, any man could speak his mind for the last five years; and if the journals threatened him with violence, he need not go begging to the City Hall, as we vainly used to do here; the authorities would take notice unsolicited, and see to it that he was protected. But at the same time, in our own city, of one quarter part of the inhabitants, it was impossible, without the aid of armed friends, to utter the same words. Why is this? It is no fault of individuals, as I said before. Three thousand places where drink is sold! Do I exaggerate when I say that each one of those places represents a voter? Mr. Ellis has said, with great force, that every one of those places represents at least ten men whom it influences, which would make thirty thousand, — and doubtless his estimate understates the fact; but I am not going to speak of those whom those places influence. I am going to speak of the voters which they send to the polls, and I certainly shall not exaggerate if I say, that each one of them influences one voter, — the owner of the shop, the keeper, the tender, or the frequenter of it. Such liquor-sellers are generally voters. If not, every one has a father, brother, servant, barkeeper, landlord, men of whom he buys his supplies, frequenters of his bar. Certainly, I do not make too large an estimate when I say that, on an average, each one of these places controls one vote. There are three thousand voters, — indeed, I should not exaggerate if I said five thousand. About fifteen thousand voters on this peninsula usually go to the polls, sometimes twenty-two thousand, though very rarely. Now, three thousand voters could always hold the balance in such a constituency, — Republican, Democratic, Catholic, Protestant, — crumbled up as an independent community necessarily is. With all these inevitable varieties of opinion and purpose, three thousand men, bound together by one idea, one interest, with one purpose in view, and demanding one thing, and nothing more, who know what they want, stand together for it, and throw their whole weight to secure it, can always hold the balance. There never was a city election which that number of votes massed together could not control. I say, therefore, without the slightest wish to be personally offensive, that the liquor-shops of Boston choose our Mayors. What is the result? The result is, that it is as much a bargain as if it were recorded in the registry of deeds, that the prominent aspirants for city office shall not execute the laws against the liquor-shops. I make no special charge against the Mayor and Aldermen, — they are as good as most of us. They want votes; it is the American failing, — most men want votes. One man wants to be Mayor, another man wants to be Alderman, a third wants to be Sheriff, and a fourth wants to be Common-Councilman. Very well; here stand the party that want something, and there stand the party that have something to sell. They have their votes to give. It is understood that they will give them to the man who will do the least to execute the Maine Law. The bargain is not acknowledged before a justice of the peace, nor recorded in the registry of deeds; but every sensible man in the city knows of its existence; and these men walk into office because those will that they shall. The liquor-dealers say, "This is the condition: shut your eyes upon us!" The consequence is, that both parties, all parties, are obliged to bow their necks to that yoke, and, with rare exceptions, there cannot be an Alderman nor a Mayor of the city elected, who is not understood to be willing to shut his eyes to that crime, and leave the law of the State unexecuted. It has been so, it always must be so while these elements of civic strength exist, and are thus tempted to exert themselves.

The reason why the law is not executed in favor of free speech is germane and sister to this; it is, that the men who are interested in these drinking-shops, and the men whose votes they can command, are of the class which hates progress and freedom, — is naturally antagonistic to them; and any designing leader can stir up such a mass, and fling it at virtue and order and liberty. Hence these consequences. Their agents, of their own natural bias, run greedily to do such agreeable work.

For the last ten or thirteen years, this has been the character of the city government. They have said to the State, "We will not execute your law." Now, law consists of four things, — a statute, a policeman to arrest the offender, a jury to try him, and a judge to sentence him. The Constitution says, we shall have judges as "impartial as the lot of humanity admits." We have them. Appointed, how? By the State. The other end of the telegraph is a man to bring the offender before the judge. What is the use of a judge? He cannot move of himself; he is powerless if you do not bring the criminals before him. But the city government of Boston, chosen by this machinery I have spoken of, says to its police officers, "Don't you furnish that judge with any criminals; shut your eyes upon them!" Then, again, if one is arrested, by any accident, what more? Why, this: the statute says that our jurymen shall be drawn from a box, in which the names of citizens of good moral character and sound judgment, free from all legal exceptions, are put. The city weeds out the jury-box on another plan. In all trials that had antislavery or temperance in them, you might be certain of one thing, — you would never see an Abolitionist nor a temperance man on the jury. If he got there, it was an accident, and there were always enough to neutralize him. It is just like the black element. We have several thousand black men in our community; you have never seen a black man on a jury but once, and that was an accident, and he was not allowed to sit, though he had been regularly drawn. Many of them are of good moral character, but their names never get into the box; or, if they get in, never come out. So of a man known distinctively as an Abolitionist; if his name goes in, it never comes out. So of a man known as a temperance man; rarely does his name come out. But liquor-dealers have always been abundant on juries; no jury was trusted alone without them. If the State furnishes good judges, and the city, at the other end, furnishes no criminals, or, when one is by chance caught, fortifies him with a jury that will disagree on his side, how is the law to be executed? As long as the city government is chosen by men whose interest is on that side, how can it be otherwise? How is the law to be executed, when you have intrusted its execution to men who do not wish or mean to execute it, — who were elected expressly not to execute it, and have the strongest motive not to do so? No matter how good individual policemen are, while such men rule them. You know when Bailie Nicol Jarvie, in Scott's immortal novel, let Rob Roy out of jail, — he was an alderman, a bailie, and let him out, — he said to Rob, "If you continue to be such a thief, you ought to have a doorkeeper in every jail in Scotland." "O no, Bailie," replied Rob, "it is just as weel to have a *bailie* in ilka borough." It answers the same purpose to have a servile and complacent Mayor and Aldermen as to have a base policeman, because they arrange the juries, and they fetter and command the police. The consequence has been, that there has been no effort to execute the law. The defence put in is, "We cannot execute the law." The Mayor said of the riots of 1860-61, "We can't put them down." The reply of his own policemen was, "Thirty of us will put them down, if you will allow us." The reply of the Abolitionist was, "When did you ever make an effort to put them down? The only time you ever stood on Tremont Temple platform and issued an order, it was obeyed; the mob recognized you as their leader." But men say at the State-House, in reply to the eloquent argument of Mr. Ellis, — Mr. Healy, Alderman Amory, said, "We cannot execute an unpopular law." Indeed! Indeed! I can remember when Marshal Tukey put a chain round your Court-House to execute a law that was hated by the Commonwealth of Massachusetts full as bitterly as Beacon Street hates the Maine Liquor Law; and I can remember when he went up to a legislative committee appointed to examine into his conduct, and inquire why a policeman of the city of Boston was acting in that illegal manner, against the statute of the State, and answered Mr. Keyes, "Sir, I know it is illegal, but I mean to do it. Help yourself!"

In 1843, Latimer was arrested by a policeman with a lie in his mouth. In 1851, Sims was surrendered by policemen acting illegally, and avowing their defiance. In 1854, Burns was sent back, and his claimants were aided by the police, contrary to the statute. Unpopular laws! The city can execute anything it wishes to, unpopular or popular. The city executes every one of its own by-laws perfectly. No man steals with impunity; no man violates Sunday with impunity; no man sets up a nuisance with impunity. As the Grand Jury said, several years ago, of these grog-shops, "The municipal authorities can remove this nuisance, or at least abate it, whenever they will. It is as much in their power as the offal in the sewers or the dirt in the streets."

Tell one hundred and eighty thousand Yankees that they cannot execute a law when they wish to! Once, by happy accident, our Mayor left the city, and an exceptional but most unexceptionable Alderman, Mr. Otis Clapp, took his place, — no trouble that day in quelling the mob. Deputy Chief Ham did it in thirty minutes. It is only the presence of grog-shop Mayors that makes mobs omnipotent. But suppose Mayors cannot execute the laws, — what then? If Berkshire should say, "We want, every one of us, to have two wives," and practise that plan, sending word up to Boston, "We cannot execute the other law," do you think we should sit down quietly, and let it go? How long?

Boston has five or six trains of railroads, — one to the Old Colony, one to Providence, one to Worcester, one to Lowell, one to Fitchburg, one to the eastern counties. All of them run locomotives where they wish to. Suppose that, on the Fitchburg Railroad, one locomotive, for a year, never got farther than Groton, — what do you think the Directors of that road would do? Would they take up the rails beyond Groton, or would they turn out the engineer? There is a law of the Commonwealth of Massachusetts, thoroughly executed in every county but ours; and here the men appointed to execute it not only do not want to, but you cannot expect them to. They were elected *not* to execute it, and they say they can't execute it. Shall we take up the rails, or change the engineer? — which?

Men say, to take the appointment of the police out of the hands of the peninsula is anti-democratic. Why, from 1620 down to within ten years, the State always acted on that plan. The State makes the law. Who executes it? The State. For two hundred years, the Governor appointed the sheriff of every county, and the sheriff appointed his deputies, and they executed the laws. The constables of the towns were allowed merely a subsidiary authority to execute by-laws, and help execute the State law. The democratic principle is, that the law shall be executed by an executive authority concurrent with that which makes it. That is democracy. The State law, naturally, democratically, is to be executed by the State. We have merely, in deference to convenience, changed that of late in some particulars, and we may reasonably go back to the old plan if we find that, in any particular locality, the new plan fails. Why not? In all other matters of State concern, as Mr. Ellis has well shown, — Board of Education, Board of Agriculture, and all the various boards, — the State has the control. You perceive this "anti-democratic" argument can be carried out to an absurdity. Suppose the Five Points of New York should send word to the Fifth Avenue, "We don't like your police; we mean to have one of our own, and it will be very anti-democratic for you to take the choice of our own constables out of our own hands." Suppose North Street should send word to the City Hall, "We have concluded to turn every other house into a grog-shop, or something almost as bad, and to appoint our own police; please instruct your police to keep out of our ward." We should not say this was democratic. We should say, that as far as the interest of a community in a law extends, just so far that community has a right to a hand in the execution of it. Now the State of Massachusetts feels an interest in the execution of the Maine Liquor Law. We have a sixth of the population and a third of the wealth of the State. Do the influences of these stop with the people who sleep on this peninsula? Does not our influence radiate in every direction? Do not twenty thousand men do business here, but not sleep here? A third of the wealth! Who owns it? We that sleep here? Not at all. These costly railroad depots, these rich banks, these large aggregates of property, who owns them? Why, the men that live ten, twenty, thirty miles outside of the city limits, and come in here in crowds the first of January, April, July, and October, to get their dividends. Men who have millions invested on this peninsula no interest in knowing whether the streets are safe! Sending their sons into our streets, — no interest in their being morally wholesome! Trusting their lives here, — no interest in their being safe!

A fortnight ago, a woman, a teacher in a country town within twenty miles of Boston, missed her father, — an honest, temperate farmer, though not a teetotaler. He came to the city to sell cattle, and had received five hundred dollars. He had been gone a week, and she came down to the city to hunt him up. She traced him from spot to spot, and finally found that the grog-shops had got hold of him, made him drunk, taken his money, kept him drunk three days, so that a convenient policeman might see him that number of times and complain of him as a common drunkard, and he had gone to the House of Correction for three months. Has that town no interest in the streets of Boston? Let me tell you again a story that I have told you once or twice before, for it holds a grave moral. A few years ago, one spring afternoon, when I left the city to deliver a lecture, I alighted from the railroad car at the foot of a hill, whose swelling side bore the most magnificent of country dwellings. Architecture and horticulture had exhausted their art. It was so unlike anything about it, I was led to ask how it came there. The man who was driving me said it was built by a village boy, who wanted to show how much money he had made in Boston in fifteen years. "He left here without a cent," said the young man; "went to Boston, became a distiller, returned with two hundred thousand dollars, — that is his residence." Do you suppose there was a Yankee boy within sight of that hillside who was not tempted to repeat this Boston experience, of rapid and easy wealth? I rode on fourteen miles, and was set down opposite one of those village homes which Dr. Holmes describes, — a square house of the Revolutionary period, — old elms hung over the lawn before it. The same driver said, "In that front room lies dying the grandson of the man who built that house. Grandfather and father died drunkards, — lay about the streets of the village drunk. That boy and I started together in life. He went with me to Lowell. We went through the mills and a mechanic trade. Never did one drop of intoxicating liquor pass his lips. Social frolic, increase of means, friendly entreaty, laughing taunts, gay hours, never tempted him. Until thirty, he stood untouched, guarded by an iron resolution. Having gathered a few thousands, he was tempted to Boston for a wider trade. He went there, — stayed six years; came home penniless and a drunkard, to lie in the very streets where his father and grandfather had lain before. He could stand up against every temptation, except Boston streets. There he lies dying, as his grandfather and father before him." Do you say that the people of these country towns have no interest in the streets of Boston? You tempt the virtue, melt the resolution and corrupt the morals of the Commonwealth, as far as your influence extends.

No interest! Let me go a little way off, and be less invidious. New York has one fifth of the population of the State on Manhattan Island. Recently, in a great national convulsion, the city stirred herself to checkmate the State. For Wadsworth, the candidate of order, of liberty, of government, the country counties flung twenty thousand majority. The demons of discord stirred up the purlieus of the city, and flung thirty thousand against him. Ten thousand, the ultimate majority, carried their candidate to Albany. What was his first blow? Seymour's first act, when he assumed the Governorship, what was it? He fulfilled his bargain. He hurled his defiance at the Metropolitan Police, which kept him and his allies, conspirators, from carrying the Empire State into the hands of the Confederacy. These are the times when, as Macaulay says, "The vermin burrowing in garrets and cellars show themselves of terrible importance." Who knows that such times may not come upon us?

I have seen the day, in that city of New York, when Rynders dictated law to the Chief of Police, and Matsell obeyed him. For twenty years I have seen in your city the mob rule when they pleased. I have seen your Mayor order his police, in Faneuil Hall, to take off their badges and join the mob which clamored down free speech in that consecrated hall. You saw, two years ago, the State government reeling before the victims of the Tremont House and Parker House. The Governor complained then, as I am told he does now, that in the whole county he had not one single officer whom he could command to execute the law. Who shall say that it is not for the interest, for the peace, for the prosperity, of the State to make this great centre of wealth and population independent of such base control? We too may have a Fernando Wood, — who knows? Our sixth part of the population of the State may attempt, in the interest of liquor and despotism, to defy the Commonwealth. It is too important a machinery to be left in the hands of the dangerous classes. We want to take it out of the hands of the dangerous classes, and put it into the hands of the Commonwealth, — nothing else. One of two things is necessary. The law is bad, — repeal it; or the law is good, — keep it. No other county would be allowed to defy the law, — why this?

The Mayor says he cannot execute it. Take him at his word. Undoubtedly, HE cannot, for he was specially chosen not to do so; but the question is, Can it be executed? What do the temperance majority of the Commonwealth claim? One trial, — nothing more. We have funded twenty-five years of discussion, any amount of toil and labor, in that statute. It never has had one trial yet on this peninsula. May we not ask simply one trial? The locomotive has never *attempted* to go beyond Groton. Why take up the rails yet? If Berkshire should say, "We can't execute your law against polygamy," what should we do? Why, appoint fresh sheriffs, not repeal the law. So in this case, let not Massachusetts kneel and say, "I too am a slave to the grog-shops of the peninsula."

We do not claim that drunkenness can be wholly rooted out. But we do claim that this law can be executed as perfectly as other laws are, if its execution be intrusted to competent and faithful hands. No crime is wholly prevented. Our crowded prisons prove that. No law is perfectly executed. But there is nothing in the Maine Liquor Law that distinguishes it from other statutes. No man claims that the *use* of intoxicating drink can be wholly stopped. But it is idle and ridiculous to say that the *public sale* of it cannot be stopped, as much as the indiscriminate keeping of gunpowder, or the opening of shops on Sunday, or the firing of muskets in crowded streets, whenever magistrates shall really wish and mean to do their duty.

A metropolitan police has been necessary in London, and now its streets are the safest in the world. In New York it has saved the city from convulsion and bloodshed. One of its prominent citizens said to me a short time ago, "You do not know how near we have been to an outbreak in this very street. But for our police, the attempt would have been made to surrender us to Southern dictation." That same civil disorder may impend over us. What is the remedy? Let the State hold her hand on the vices of the peninsula, — claim her old democratic right to execute the laws she has made, — to execute them if the city cannot, or if, by her constitution of government, she will not try to execute them faithfully.

Our plan is to have Commissioners — three or five — appointed by the Governor or by the Legislature, whichever seems best. Let them hold their offices for three or five years; they appoint, rule, and remove the members of the police force. Such a Commission would be removed, as far as anything in our civil system is or ought to be, from the control of party politics, and would be largely independent of the "dangerous classes." This peninsula needs it immediately, — the neighboring towns and cities will need it soon. The members of such a police force should hold their places during good behavior, and be removed only on charges stated in writing, to which they may have a chance of replying. Now, every fall, the liquor-dealer or other criminal, whom an honest policeman has troubled, holds up his warning finger to the Alderman of that ward, — "Remove that policeman, or don't expect my vote." What officer can be expected to do his duty in such circumstances? Fellow-citizens, during the two or three months preceding our city elections, we have, practically, no police, — none that dares execute a law disagreeable to any influential class.

The moment the liquor interest of the city see that their mixing in city elections will not secure a police force in their interest, they will probably leave the election of Mayor and Aldermen to the natural action of ordinary politics, as they did in New York, and then we shall have as good officers as our system will secure, with the present level of education. Such Mayors and Aldermen will, probably, no longer prostitute the jury-box to defend rum and shield mobs. They will have no interest to do so. They cannot so wholly corrupt the jury-box as to protect the liquor-seller. The liquor once poured into the street, according to the statute, by an honest policeman, he must be sued by its owner before a jury of the county. No Mayor could make up a jury wholly of liquor-dealers. Two or three honest men on it suffice to disagree, and no verdict, in that case, is in effect a verdict for the officer. Disagreement of juries now, which a servile Mayor arranges for, protects the indicted grog-seller; then, to use a common proverb, "the boot would be on the other leg," and disagreement of juries executes the law. But if this change be not an entire relief, we must press forward, and find a remedy for that. I have full faith in democratic institutions. Work on, and we shall yet lift them up to much higher perfection. The future is sure. Honest men rule in the end. Only show them their interest and duty, and, in due time, they will rally to do it. Ten years ago, I made an antislavery speech, painting Southern despotism, and demanding that the North should rouse herself against her tyrants. The next day, meeting the oldest statesman of the Commonwealth, he said to me,

"Your speech was all true. I knew it thirty years ago. But what can you do about it? They won't listen." I answered, "I mean to protest, — claim my rights, and denounce those who assail them, whether they listen or not." The policy has been somewhat successful. Agitate! and we shall yet see the laws of Massachusetts rule even Boston.

THE STATE OF THE COUNTRY.*

LADIES AND GENTLEMEN: I understand this is a ward meeting, — the Sixteenth Ward of New York, the banner ward for radical Republicanism. [Applause.] A very good-sized meeting for a ward meeting. [Laughter.] I am glad, for the first time in my life, to be adopted into the politics of New York city, and to address a ward meeting in behalf of justice and liberty. The text of my address is, Patience and Faith. Possess your souls in patience, not as having already attained, not as if we were already perfect, but because the whole nation, as one man, has for more than a year set its face Zionward. Ever since September 22d of last year, the nation has turned its face Zionward; and ever since Burnside drew his sword in Virginia, we have moved toward that point. [Cheers.] Now, a nation moving, and moving in the right path, — what reason is there for doubt? what occasion for despair? We have found out at last the method, and we are in earnest. Patience, all the passion of great souls, makes victory certain; when the human heart is once capable of this greatest courage, no matter what clouds may be on the horizon, now and then God lifts the cloud so as to show us the blue sky behind; no

* Substance of Speeches in New York, January 21 and May 11, 1863, — the last as one of a series of Lectures before the Sixteenth Ward Republican Association.

matter how dark political mistake or treachery may lower, the moment comes when the North says that it is all a phantasmagoria, and behind, the great heart of the nation beats true to its destiny. [Cheers.] When I stood on this platform five months ago, men said: "You must not be surprised if blood flows in the streets. Traitors are trying to take the great Capital of the North out of our arms, and the Democratic party of the State is behind them." But one fine morning there was prudent hesitation in the leading Democrat of Albany, and the Mayor of New York defeated him on his first move. [Cheers.] When the counties came to be represented, the leaders found an army with officers and no rank and file. And the Goliath of Connecticut Copperheads has been killed, not by a stripling, but by a girl. [Applause.] Or if we must add to her merits that of General Hamilton of Texas, the eloquent champion of the Union, then we can almost say that out of the mouths of girls and slaveholders God is perfecting liberty. [Applause.] Now I neither doubt nor despair. Gradually, one after another, the shams of the North fall away. It is to be a long fight, no local struggle, — only one part of the great fight going on the world over, and which began ages ago, — only one grand division, one army corps doing its duty in the great battle between free institutions and caste institutions, the world over. Freedom and Democracy against the institutions that rest upon classes. We may be the centre or only the outskirts of that struggle, but wherever caste lives, wherever class power exists, whether it be on the banks of the Thames or the Seine, whether by the side of the Ganges or the Danube, there the South has an ally, just as the surgeon's knife gives pain when it touches the living fibre. [Cheers.] And against this mighty marshalling of everything that is strong in human selfishness the democracy of the North does battle. Some of our friends are anxious that able and earnest men shall go to England, make the real state of the case known there, and so, they think, avert national collision. Instinct, Mr. Chairman, is a great matter. The ruling classes of England understand our quarrel only too well. They feel that victory for the North is ultimate ruin for them. The more of the truth you show them, the more their hearts lean to the Southern side, — their side.

Every proud man who hates his brother is our enemy, every idle man too lazy to think is our enemy, every loafer who seeks a living without working for it is our enemy. [Applause.] Every honest man, asking only for his own, and willing fairly to do his part, is our ally, whether he eats rice on the banks of the Ganges or is enrolled in the army under Hooker: never till honest men realize this can there be peace or union. Till that time union means a submission to the old slavocracy, as bitter and more relentless than ever. The South counted on two allies in the ranks of her Northern enemy: one was hatred of the negro, — the other Copperhead Democratic sympathy with the aristocracy of the South. She counted confidently on these allies, but found she had reckoned without her host. We have been accustomed to say on this platform, for the last ten years, that if circumstances should ever rouse to an antislavery purpose the rank and file of the Democracy, the victory for freedom would be as sure as the existence of God. The Abolitionists have always claimed that they had an invincible ally in that democratic prejudice against wealth and rank, and the ineradicable love which man has at the core for the rights of his fellow-man. [Applause.] When the war broke out, the first blow the South aimed at the Union, as if according to chemical law, crystallized that level of democracy into an antislavery mould, and from that hour to this it is the sheet-anchor of the Union, and while it holds the future is certain. The only reason why this element did not grope its way at once to victory was because it was led by men who did not intend to conquer. Our statesmen were only ready for the shibboleth, "Freedom, if necessary to save the Union"; it was a contingent freedom, — not freedom for itself and in any event. No one of them welcomed the war as a God-given opportunity to do justice, and secure for the nation lasting, immutable peace. Under that sort of leadership we went to battle. The generals and the Cabinet meant no more than to play a part in the great drama of justice for which their hearts were not ready. Lucian tells us of an exhibition in Rome in which monkeys had been trained to take part in a play. They played their parts perfectly, for a while, before an audience composed of the beauty and fashion of the city, but in the midst of the performance some Roman wag flung upon the stage a handful of nuts, and immediately the actors were monkeys again. Our statesmen went to Washington monkeys in human attire, determined to compromise if possible, the South flung nuts among them for eighteen months, and they were on all fours for the temptation. [Laughter and applause.] That epoch is ended. As in Cromwell's day they sloughed off such effete elements as Essex and Fairfax, we should slough off generals and statesmen; and never can we be successful till routine West Point and rotten Whiggery have been made to put on decent attire, or sent back to private life, and those put in their places who believe in absolute, uncompromising war.

This real democratic element in the North is strong enough, were it one and united, to have crushed all its foes on this continent in ninety days. There never was a time since the commencement of the struggle when, if the North had been a unit, the war might not have been ended in three months; and, so ended, it would have left slavery where it found it. But the North has never been a unit. With the North as a unit, democratic, intelligent, resolved, in earnest, the South never would have risked the struggle. But she knew that the North was divided into three great parties. One was routine, West Point, too lazy to think. [Great applause.] I resolve hunkerism into indolence and cowardice, too lazy to think, and too timid to think. The man of the past is the man who got his ideas before he was twenty, and had rather think as his father thought than take the labor of thinking himself: he is a hunker, and he will probably die such. [Laughter.] And the North had a second element, negrophobia, the Saxon contempt for a black skin, disgust with the question of the negro, hatred of him as another race, contempt for him as a slave, and weariness of the question. Outside of that was the democrat of the North, in the good sense of the term, — the man who believes in the manhood of his brother the world over, and is willing he should have his rights. Against such a North the South rebelled, — one of our hands tied up by negro hatred, and the other by constitutional scruples, and West Point on our shoulders. Against such a North the South rebelled. You remember it well, — the North that never dared to apply the line and the plummet to the ethics of its civilization, — that never dared to have a logic which would know no black, no white, when it studied its duties, — the North that, both in pulpit and in civil life, believed and obeyed the old proverb: "When the monkey reigns, let every man dance before him." [Laughter.] As long as a wicked, contemptible institution had honors and wealth and fashion to bestow, so long the pregnant knee was crooked before it. That North the South met in battle, and she mistook, as we Abolitionists did, (that is, the issue will show whether we did mistake, we hope it is so,) how far the canker had gone, how great hold this routine of hunkerism had on the body of the people: that North rallied for the struggle, poured out her money like water, and her sons with ever-growing willingness for the great battle betwixt democracy and slavery, betwixt God and the Devil, for the world and the century. The government was equally in the dark, equally undecided, equally uncertain what course to pursue, and for a long time we stumbled together. We have learned of events, and claim to know our times. The government seems neither to learn nor to forget anything. Why? Well, I think, because our rulers were educated as Whigs. The old Whig party, good as it was in many respects, virtuous in many of its impulses, correct in certain of its aspirations, had one great defect: it had no confidence in the people, no trust in the masses; it did not believe in the conscience or the intelli gence of the million; it looked, indeed, upon the whole world as in a probate court, in which the educated and the wealthy were the guardians. And so, when our rulers entered on the great work of defending the nation in its utmost peril, they dared not fling themselves on the bosom of the million, and trust the country to the hearts of those that loved it. Your President sat in Washington, doubtful what he ought to do, how far he might go. Month after month, stumbling, faithless, uncertain, he ventured now a little step, and now another, surprised that at every step the nation were before him, ready to welcome any word he chose to say, and to support any policy he chose to submit; so that matters of vexed dispute, matters of earnest doubt, the moment the bugle gave a certain sound, have passed into dead issues. You know that when the rebellion first broke forth no man dared speak out touching the negro. The South fought to sustain slavery, and the North fought not to have it hurt. But Butler pronounced that magic word "contraband," and summoned the negro into the arena. [Applause.] It was a poor word. Some doubt — I do not — whether it is sound law. Lord Chatham said, "*Nullus liber homo*" is poor Latin, but it is worth all the classics. Contraband is a bad word, and may be bad law, but just then it was worth all the Constitution [applause]; for in a moment of critical emergency it summoned saving elements into the arena, and it showed the government how far the sound fibre of the nation extended. When Fremont [loud and long-continued applause] — why won't you ever let me go on when I name Fremont? [Laughter.] I say, when he pronounced that word Emancipation on the banks of the Mississippi, the whole North, except the government, said Amen. [Applause.] The government doubted till the 22d of September, 1862. But the moment the government pronounced the word, it floated into a dead issue, and nobody worth minding now doubts or debates about the emancipation of slaves. [Applause.] It only shows you how strong the government is, if it will only act; how certain the heart of the people is to support it, if the government will only trust. If Mr. Lincoln could only be made to accept the line of the old huntsman song, —

> "Sit close in the saddle and give him his head,"

he could carry twenty millions of people with him over every barrier to victory and peace. [Loud applause.] I believe, therefore, in ultimate success, because every act of the government is more than indorsed by the intelligence and virtue of the people, — the *virtue of the people.* That is the only point at issue. To-day, your city roars with the tumult of welcome for returning soldiers. Those soldiers will find here not a Virginia eaten over with barrenness, not starving people, not empty treasuries; they will find a North untouched, — so much money that we have not to go abroad to borrow any [applause], so much wheat that we could feed the world, such ample munitions of war that your traitor merchants smuggle them to Carolina [sensation], — a traveller might journey through half the North, and if he neither spoke nor read English, he would never dream there was a war in any part of the nation, — an untouched North, while the South, mustering all her white men and all her sympathizers the world over, has not yet reached the garnered treasure of Northern strength. We have not yet put forth the first beginning of our power. In Scripture phrase, "Truly there has been a hiding of our power." If we fail, it will be because we deserve to, because we have not virtue enough to prefer the end to the means. There is no question but of the conscience and intelligence of the North. Now, I believe in that, because thus far the government has never asked for anything, nor ventured anything, that the readiness of the people has not both given and indorsed. There is my ground of hope.

I do not believe in Southern exhaustion. There may be starving men at the South, starving households, ill-clad soldiers, but there is no such exhaustion as approaches despair. The South has not yet begun to play her last card. The moment she feels exhaustion she will proclaim liberty to the negro. The moment her cause touches its downfall in the judgment of its leaders, she will call the black into her ranks, — call him by some proclamation of gradual emancipation, which will gather to her side the heartiest sympathy of the English aristocracy. England never was an antislavery nation. Her ruling classes never accepted emancipation on any basis. England herself never accepted immediate abolition on any basis. As O'Connell well said, the scheme of immediate emancipation was carried over Parliament by the conscience of the middle classes, and they do not usually rule in England. To-day, that party in the contest which offers England gradual emancipation will offer her all that her judgment approves. Before the South permits her flag to stagger, she will write on it gradual emancipation, and bring the House of Commons to her side. Many slaveholders will submit to be colonists of England where one would submit to Lincoln. General Hamilton goes to Boston, a slaveholder, and says on our platform, "I am glad that my slaves are gone if it saves the Union." If loyal men will surrender their slaves and save the Union, do you not suppose disloyal men will surrender theirs to save the Confederacy? Do you suppose the South will stop before she puts on to her banner Emancipation? The moment she utters that word, I shall admit that she feels weak in the knees, — never till then. There is no exhaustion yet that touches a traitor. The men that rebelled are the slaveholders, — rebelled under the pretence of slavery, with the real purpose of killing republican institutions and founding aristocratic institutions in their place. Slavery was the point to be protected, and the pretence that rallied the rebellion. But, now that it is afoot, its leaders throw off the mask, and, without concealment, avow at home that their object is to put this belt of the continent under the control of aristocratic institutions, for the perpetuation of that system, among others, which they love. That element has yet felt no exhaustion, — it boasts, justly, of rare military skill, and of as large armies as ordinary men can handle, — and with that element I have no plea of conciliation. I am for conciliation, but not for conciliating the slaveholder. Death to the system, and death or exile to the master, is the only motto. [Applause.] There is a party for whom I have ever the right hand of conciliation, and whenever the foot of military despotism is lifted from that party, I believe that in the South itself we shall be surprised at the weight, strength, and number of the men who still love the Union. There is a party for whom I have conciliation, and this [taking by the hand a beautiful little girl of five years old, with a fair complexion and light auburn ringlets] is its representative. In the veins that beat now in my right hand runs the best blood in Virginia's white races and the better blood of the black race of the Old Dominion [applause], — a united race, to whom, in its virtue, belongs in the future a country, which the toil and labor of its ancestors redeemed from nature and gave to civilization and the nineteenth century. [Applause.] For that class I have ever an open door of conciliation, — the labor, the toil, the muscle, the virtue, the strength, the democracy, of the Southern States. This blood represents them all, — the poor white, a non-slaveholder, deluded into rebellion for a system which crushes him, — some equally deluded and some timid and gagged masters, — the slave restored to his rights, when now, at last, for the first time in her history, Virginia has a government, and is not a horde of pirates masquerading as a State. No, the South has not yet felt the first symptom of exhaustion. Get no delusive hope that our success is to come from any such source.

* * * *

This war will never be ended by an event. It will never come to a conclusion by a great battle. It is too deep in its sources; it is too wide in its influence for that. The great struggle in England between democracy and nobility lasted from 1640 to 1660, taking a king's life in its progress, and yet failed for the time. The great struggle between the same parties in France began in 1789, and it is not yet ended. Our own Revolution began in 1775, and never, till the outbreak of the French Revolution concentrated the attention of the monarchies of Europe, was this country left in peace. And it will take ten or twenty years to clear off the scar of such a struggle. Prepare yourself for a life-long enlistment. God has launched this Union on a voyage whose only port is Liberty, and whether the President relucts, or whether the cabin-boys conspire, it matters not, — absolute justice holds the helm, and we never shall come into harbor until every man under the flag is free. [Applause.] Why do I say this? I will tell you. We are accustomed to use the words North and South familiarly. They once meant the land toward the pole and the land toward the sun. They have a deeper significance at present. By the North I mean the civilization of the nineteenth century, — I mean that equal and recognized manhood up to which the race has struggled by the toils and battles of nineteen centuries, — I mean free speech, free types, open Bibles, the welcome rule of the majority, — I mean the Declaration of Independence! [Applause.] And by the South, I mean likewise a principle, and not a locality, an element of civil life in fourteen rebellious States. I mean an element which, like the days of Queen Mary and the Inquisition, cannot tolerate free speech, and punishes it with the stake. I mean the aristocracy of the skin, which considers the Declaration of Independence a sham, and democracy a snare, — which believes that one third of the race is born booted and spurred, and the other two thirds ready saddled for that third to ride. I mean a civilization which prohibits the Bible by statute to every sixth man of its community, and puts a matron in a felon's cell for teaching a black sister to read. I mean the intellectual, social, aristocratic South, — the thing that manifests itself by barbarism and the bowie-knife, by bullying and lynch-law, by ignorance and idleness, by the claim of one man to own his brother, by statutes making it penal for the State of Massachusetts to bring an action in her courts, by statutes, standing on the books of Georgia to-day, offering five thousand dollars for the head of William Lloyd Garrison. That South is to be annihilated. [Loud applause.] The totality of my common sense — or whatever you may call it — is this, all summed up in one word: This country will never know peace nor union until the South (using the words in the sense I have described) is annihilated, and the North is spread over it. I do not care where men go for the power. They may find it in the parchment, — I do. I think, with Patrick Henry, with John Quincy Adams, with General Cass, we have ample constitutional powers; but if we had not, it would not trouble me in the least. [Laughter and applause.] I do not think a nation's life is bound up in a parchment. I think this is the momentous struggle of a great nation for existence and perpetuity. Two elements are at war to-day. In nineteen loyal and fourteen rebellious States those two elements of civilization which I have described are fighting. And it is no new thing that they are fighting. They could not exist side by side without fighting, and they never have. In 1787, when the Constitution was formed, James Madison and Rufus King, followed by the ablest men in the Convention, announced that the dissension between the States was not between great States and little, but between Free States and Slave. Even then the conflict had begun. In 1833, Mr. Adams said, on the floor of Congress: "Whether Slave and Free States can cohere into one Union is a matter of theoretical speculation. We are trying the experiment." In June, 1858, Mr. Lincoln used the language: "This country is half slave and half free. It must become either wholly slave or wholly free." In October of the same year, Mr. Seward, in his great "irrepressible conflict" speech at Rochester, said: "The most pregnant remark of Napoleon is, that Europe is half Cossack and half republican. The systems are not only inconsistent, they are incompatible; they never did exist under one government. They never can." "Our fathers," he goes on to say, "recognized this truth. They saw the conflict developing when they made the Constitution. And while tenderconscienced and tender-hearted men lament this strife between slavery and antislavery, our fathers not only foresaw, but they initiated it." They knew that these two systems would fight. But they thought under the parchment of the Constitution they could fight it out by types; they could discuss it to a peaceful solution; ballots and parties, types and free speech, would make brother States and sister States, — settle the conflict between two irreconcilable civilizations. What is the history of our seventy years? It is the history of two civilizations constantly struggling, and always at odds *except when one or the other rules.* So long as the South ruled, up to 1819, we had uniform peace. The Missouri Compromise was the first solemn protest of rising Northern civilization against the Southern. It was an unsuccessful protest. The South put it under her feet, but she did not kill it. It continued alive through the stormy days of Texas, and showed its head above water in the Compromise in 1850. And again it was strangled and put under the heel of fourteen States. But it culminated again by the irrepressible power of God's own laws, and in 1861 wrote the name of Abraham Lincoln on the topmost wall of the Republic. This was not victory. Not victory, but the herald of victory. It was seventeen hundred thousand ballots recording the strength of the rising North against the South. And the statesmanship of the South read correctly this record. She said, "I can for four or eight or twelve years buy this man, and bribe that, and bully the other. But that is a poor and beggarly existence. There is another way open to me. I agreed at the outset to abide the issue of free discussion, and I put my system on trial against Massachusetts free speech."

Seventy years ago the North flung down the gauntlet of the printing-press, and said, "I will prove that my system — freedom — is the best." The South accepted the

Constitution of the United States, securing a free press, and took the risk. She said: "There is my slavery. I believe it will abide discussion. I am willing to put it into the caldron." And Massachusetts put in her land and character and brains, and we made a "hodge-podge," as the English law says, a general mess, a bowl of punch [laughter], of all the institutions of the nation, and we said, "There is the free press, untrammelled, for one element, and whatever cannot bear that must be thrown away." [Applause.] For two generations, the experiment went on; and when Lincoln went to Washington, South Carolina saw the handwriting on the wall, — the handwriting as of old, — that the free press had conquered, and that slavery was sinking, like a dead body, to the bottom; and she said, practically: "I know I made the bargain, but I cannot abide it. I know I agreed to put myself into the general partnership, and now comes the demand for my submission to the great laws of human progress, — I cannot submit." So she loaded her guns, and turned them, shotted to the lips, against the Federal Government, saying, "There is a fortification behind the printing-press, — it is the Minie rifle." "All well," said the North; "now we will try that. [Applause.] I offered you the nineteenth century, — books; you chose to go back to the fifteenth, — armies; try it!" The South flung down the gauntlet; the North raised it, and has flung it back into the Gulf. [Applause.] Beaten in both ways, conquered on both issues, our civilization triumphant in brains, and still more emphatically triumphant in bullets [applause], the question now comes up, Which shall rule this one and indivisible country? The South said, "I load my cannon in order that I may annihilate Massachusetts." "I accept it," said the Bay State, and, her cannon being the largest and the strongest, she annihilates the South instead. [Renewed applause.] That is the argument. We should have gone to the wall had she beaten. One nation! — she goes to the wall when we beat. That is common sense; that is fair, sound policy.

We have been planted as one nation; the normal idea of our existence is that it is to be one and indivisible. We are one nation. That being taken for granted at the outset, in this battle of civilizations, which is to govern? The best. I do not think we have any claim to govern this country on the ground that we have more cannon, more men, and more money than the South. That is a bald, brutal superiority. The claim of the North to govern must be founded on the ground that our civilization is better, purer, nobler, higher, than that of the South.

The two ideas have always contended for mastery, till now by argument, by types; — now, with bullets. Our war is only an appeal from the nineteenth century of freedom and ballots to the system of the sixteenth century. The old conflict, — a new weapon, that is all. The South thought because once, twice, thrice, the spaniel North had gotten down on her knees, that this time, also, poisoned by cotton-dust, she would kiss her feet. [A voice; "No go this time!" and applause.] But instead of that, for the first time in our history, the North has flung the insult back, and said: "By the Almighty, the Mississippi is mine, and I will have it." [Applause.] Now, when shall come peace? Out of this warlike conflict, when shall come peace? Just as it came in the conflict of parties and discussion. Whenever one civilization gets the uppermost positively, then there will be peace, and never till then. There is no new thing under the sun. The light shed upon our future is the light of experience. Seventy years have not left us ignorant of what the aristocracy of the South means and plans, if it has left the Secretary of State ignorant. [Laughter and applause.] The South needs to rule, or she goes by the board. She is a wise power. I respect her for it. She knows that she needs to rule. What does Mr. Jefferson Davis plan? Do you suppose he plans for an imaginary line to divide South Carolina from New York and Massachusetts? What good would that do? An imaginary line will not shut out ideas. But she must bar out those ideas. That is the programme in the South. He imagines he can broaden his base by allying himself with a weaker race. He says: "I will join marriage with the weak races of Mexico and the Southwest, and then, perhaps, I can draw to my side the Northwest, with its interests as an agricultural population, naturally allied to me, and not to the Northeast, with its tariff set of States." And he thinks thus, a strong, quiet slaveholding empire, he will bar New England and New York out in the cold, and will have comparative peace. But if he bar New England out in the cold, what then? She is still there. [Laughter.] And give it only the fulcrum of Plymouth Rock, an idea will upheave the continent. Now, Davis knows that better than we do, — a great deal better. His plan, therefore, is to mould an empire so strong, so broad, that it can control New England and New York. He is not only to found a slaveholding despotism, but he is to make it so strong that, by traitors among us, and hemming us in by power, he is to cripple, confine, break down, the free discussion of these Northern States. Unless he does that he is not safe. He knows it. Now I do not say he will succeed, but I tell you what I think is the plan of a statesmanlike leader of this effort. To make slavery safe, he must mould Massachusetts, not into being a slaveholding Commonwealth, but into being a silent, unprotesting Commonwealth; that Maryland and Virginia, the Carolinas, and Arkansas, may be quiet, peaceable populations. He is a wise man. He knows what he wants, and he wants it with a will, like Julius Cæsar of old. He has gathered every dollar and every missile south of Mason and Dixon's line to hurl a thunderbolt that shall serve his purpose. And if he does achieve a separate confederacy, and shall be able to bribe the West into neutrality, much less alliance, a dangerous time, and a terrible battle will these Eastern States have. For they will never make peace. The Yankee who comes out of Cromwell's bosom will fight his Naseby a hundred years, if it last so long, but he will conquer. [Applause.] In other words, Davis will try to rule. If he conquers, he is to bring, in his phrase, Carolina to Massachusetts. And if we conquer, what is our policy? To carry Massachusetts to Carolina. In other words, carry Northern civilization all over the South. It is a contest between civilizations. Whichever conquers supersedes the other.

I may seem tedious in this analysis. But it seems to me that the simple statement includes the whole duty and policy of the hour. It is a conflict which will never have an end until one or the other element subdues its rival. Therefore we should be, like the South, penetrated with an idea, and ready with fortitude and courage to sacrifice everything to that idea. No man can fight Stonewall Jackson, a sincere fanatic on the side of slavery, but John Brown, an equally honest fanatic on the other. [Applause.] They are the only chemical equals, and will neutralize each other. You cannot neutralize nitric acid with cologne-water. You cannot hurl William H. Seward at Jeff Davis. [Great applause and laughter.] You must have a man of ideas on both sides. Otherwise the elements of the struggle are unequal.

Our object is to subdue the South. What right has our civilization to oust out the other? It has this right: We are a Union, — not a partnership, — a marriage. We put our interests all together in 1787. We joined our honor and our wealth. This question is not to be looked at like a technical lawyer dotting his i's and crossing his t's, and making his semicolons into colons. It is to be looked at in the broad light of national statesmanship. Our fathers, if they were honorable men, as we believe, accepted slavery as a part of their civil constitution on the ground that it was put into a common lot with freedom, with progress, with wealth, with education. If it stood its own, well; if it went by the board, so. It was an intelligible, if not an honest, bargain. They consented to be disgraced by the toleration of slavery; they consented to let the fresh blood of the young, vigorous free labor of many States build it up into longer and firmer life, only on condition that it should take its chances with all the other great national interests. It was with this fundamental understanding that the nation commenced, and the great special interests of the country are based upon it. For instance, the Illinois farmer, when he bought of the Union a thousand acres in the Northwest, he did not buy a thousand acres isolated in the Northwest; he bought a thousand acres with New Orleans for his port of entry and New York for his counting-house. And it was as much a part of the deed as if it had been so written. Now, if South Carolina can show that Illinois and New York have broken the deed, she has a right of revolution; that is, she has a right to reject it. But until she can show that they have broken the deed, she is a swindler. Illinois owns New Orleans as much as Chicago, in a national sense. So the negro who sat down and waited when Samuel Adams, who thought slavery a crime, and your Gouverneur Morris, who thought it a disgrace and a sin, said, "Wait, the time will come when the constant waves of civilization or the armed right hand of the war power will strike off your fetters," and the slave sat down and waited. In 1819, — the Missouri Compromise, — when the time had come, as John Randolph said the time would come, when the master would run away from his slave, the slave arose and said, "Fulfil the pledge; I have invested a generation of submission." We begged him still to wait, and he sat down in the darkness of despair. God alone counted the moments of his agony. At last the gun sounded at Sumter, and the slave cried, "New York and Massachusetts, fulfil the pledge of your fathers in the name of God and justice." [Cheers.] We are a nation by all these considerations. To-day, the question is, not merely whether the negro shall be free; not, certainly, whether New York and Massachusetts shall dictate to sister States; but it is, whether the free lips of New York and Massachusetts shall be protected by the laws of the nation wherever the stars and stripes float; whether this great, free, model state, the hope of the nations and their polar star, this experiment of self-government, this normal school of God for the education of the masses, shall survive, free, just, entire, able not only to free the slave, but to pay the further debt it owes him, — protection as he rises into liberty, and a share in the great State he aided to found, not one merely in its ruins.

Mr. Jefferson Davis has two hundred thousand men in arms to-day. I do not believe he ever had over three hundred thousand. Great is brag, and they have bragged three hundred thousand into six, and wooden guns into iron ones. He has got two hundred thousand in arms to-day. Before this body retreats into Mexico, — before, like his great father in the Gospel, he goes "violently down a steep place into the sea" [loud laughter and applause], — he will fight great battles somewhere. Let me grant you that we crush that army out, scatter it, demoralize it, conquer it, — where is it to go? What will become of its materials? What brought it together? Hatred of us. Will being beaten make them love us? Is that the way to make men love you? Can you whip a man into loving you? You whip him into a bitterer hate. Where will that army go? Into a state of society more cruel than war, — whose characteristics are private assassination, burning, stabbing, shooting, poisoning. The consequence is, we have not only an army to conquer, which, being beaten, will not own it, but we have a state of mind to annihilate. You know Napoleon said, the difficulty with the German armies was, they did n't know when they were beaten. We have a worse trouble than that. The South will not only not believe itself beaten, but the materials which make up its army will not retire back to peaceful pursuits. Where are they going to retire? They don't know how to do anything. You might think they would go back to trade. They don't know how to trade; they never bought nor sold anything. You might think they would go back to their professions. They never had any. You might think they would go back to the mechanic arts. They don't know how to open a jackknife. [Great merriment.] There is nowhere for them to go, unless we send them half a million of emancipated blacks, to teach them how to plant cotton. To the North, war is a terrible evil. It takes the lawyer, the merchant, the mechanic, from his industrious, improving, inspiring occupation, and lets him down into the demoralization of a camp; but to the South, war is a gain. The young man, melted in sensuality, whose face was never lighted up by a purpose since his mother looked into his cradle, — the mere wreck of what should have been a man, — with neither ideas nor inspirations nor aspirations, was lifted by the war to a higher level. Did you ever look into the beautiful faces of those Roman young men, whose ideas were bounded by coffee and the opera, — till Garibaldi's bugle waked them to life, — beautiful, because human still? Well, that was the South. Over those wrecks of manhood breathed the bugle-note of woman and politics, calling upon them to rally and fight for an idea, — Southern independence. It lifted them, for the moment, into something which looked like civilization; it lifted them into something that was a real life; and war to them is a gain. They go out of it, and they sink down a hundred degrees in the scale of civilization. They go back to bar-rooms, to corner-groceries, to plantation sensuality, to chopping straw, and calling it politics. [Laughter.]

Now, that South, angry, embittered, having arms in its hands, what is it going to do? Shoot, burn, poison, vent its rage on every side. Guerilla barbarities are but the first drops of the shower, — the first pattering drops of the flood of barbarism which will sweep over those Southern States, unless our armies hold them. When England conquered the Highlands, she held them, — held them until she could educate them; and it took a generation. That is just what we have to do with the South; annihilate the old South, and put a new one there. You do not annihilate a thing by abolishing it. You must supply the vacancy. In the Gospel, when the chambers were swept and garnished, the devils came back because there were no angels there. And if we should sweep Virginia clean, Jeff Davis would come back with seven other devils worse than himself, if he could find them, and occupy it, unless you put free institutions there. Some men say, begin it by exporting the blacks. If you do, you export the very fulcrum of the lever; you export the very best material to begin with. Something has been said about the Alleghanies moving toward the ocean as the symbol of colonization. Let me change it. The nation that should shovel down the Alleghanies, and then build them up again, would be a wise nation compared with the one that should export four million blacks, and then import four million of Chinese to take their places. To dig a hole, and then fill it up again, to build a wall for the purpose of beating out your brains against it, would be Shakespearian wisdom compared with such an undertaking. I want the blacks as the very basis of the effort to regenerate the South. They know every inlet, the pathway of every wood, the whole country is a map at night to their instinct. When Burnside unfurled the Stars and Stripes in sight of Roanoke, he saw a little canoe paddling off to him, which held a single black man; and in that contraband hand, victory was brought to the United States of America, led by Burnside. He came to the Rhode Island general, and said: "This is deep water, and that is shoal; this is swamp, that is firm land, and that is wood; there are four thousand men here, and one thousand there." The whole country was mapped out, as an engineer could not have done it in a month, in the memory of that man. And Burnside was loyal to humanity, and believed him. [Applause.] Disloyal to the Northern pulpit, disloyal to the prejudice of his race, he was loyal to the instincts of our common nature, knew that man would tell him the truth, and obeyed him. The soldiers forded where the negro bade them, the vessels anchored in the deep waters he pointed out, and that victory was planned, if there was any strategy about it, in the brain of that contraband [applause]; and to-day he stands at the right hand of Burnside, clad in uniform, long before Hunter armed a negro, with the pledge of the General that, as long as he lives and has anything to eat, the man who gave him Roanoke shall have half a loaf. [Enthusiastic applause.] Do you suppose, that if I multiply that instance by four million, the American people can afford to give up such assistance? Of course not. We are to take military possession of the territory, and we are to work out the great problem of unfolding a nation's life. We want the four million of blacks, — a people instinctively on our side, ready and skilled to work; the only element the South has which belongs to the nineteenth century. You never can mistake them. It used to be said, in old antislavery times, that if a fugitive negro saw a Quaker coat, his heart beat easy, — he knew he was safe. I think the Stars and Stripes can float lazily down and kiss the standard, all over the South, when a black face is in sight.

But I am not speaking for the negro; I am not asking now for his rights; I am asking for the use of him. I want him for the future. We have to make over the State of South Carolina, and we are not sure there is a white man in it who is on our side. Do you remember that significant telegram of McClellan from Yorktown, — and it was only the repetition of a dozen telegrams that preceded it, substantially this: — "To the Secretary of War: Sir, we have taken Yorktown; only one single white man in it." He does not think it necessary to say there were some thousands of negroes. Of course there were. They stayed where liberty was coming, and ideas, and civilization, and men who worked with their hands and their brains, as they themselves did. They recognized in the Yankee a brother mechanic. [Laughter and applause.] They said: "Here are men who don't know how to do anything but eat, and they are going. The people who are coming are men who know how to manufacture, to create, and we, the creators of the South, stay to welcome the creators of the North." [Applause.] But that one poor solitary white man, who always remains [laughter,] —just like

"The last rose of summer,
Left blooming alone,"

[great merriment,] — he is only suggestive of that other kindred and friendly race which never flies.

Colonize the blacks! A man might as well colonize his hands; or when the robber enters his house, he might as well colonize his revolver. What we want is systematic, national action. Confiscate those lands. Colonize them. Sell them with the guaranty of the government to the loyal Massachusetts man or New Yorker. Say to him, "There is a deed as good as the Union. Carry there your ploughshares, seeds, schools, sewing-machines." Carry free labor to that soil, and you carry New York to Virginia, and slavery cannot go back. I want to supply the vacancy which this war must leave in every Slave State it subdues. The Slave States, to my mind, are men and territory, and nothing else. The rebellion has crushed out all civil forms. New government is to go there. It seems to me the idlest national work, childish work, for the President, in bo-peep secrecy, to hide himself in the White House and launch a proclamation at us on a first day of January. The nation should have known it sixty days before, and should have provided fit machinery for the reception of three million bondmen into the civil state. If we launch a ship, we build straight well-oiled ways upon which it may glide with facility into its native element. So when a nation is to be born, the usual aid of government should have been extended to prepare a pathway through which to step upon the platform of civil equality. It is nonsense without. We cannot expect in hours to cover the place of centuries. It is a great problem before us. We must take up the South and organize it anew. It is not the men we have to fight, — it is the state of society that produces them. He would be a fool who, having a fever, scraped his tongue and took no medicine. Killing Davis is only scraping the tongue; killing slavery is taking a wet-sheet pack, destroying the very disease. But when we have done it, there remains behind the still greater and more momentous problem, whether we have the strength, the balance, the virtue, the civilization, to absorb six millions of ignorant, embittered, bedeviled Southerners, and transmute them into honest, decent, educated, well-behaved, Christian mechanics, worthy to be the brothers of New England Yankees. [Applause.] That is the real problem. To that this generation should address itself. You know men take their floating capital, and fund it in a permanent investment. Now the floating virtue of forty thousand pulpits, the floating wealth of these nineteen millions of people, the floating result, big or little, of Tract Societies, is to be funded, — like sensible heat, is to be transformed into invisible, latent heat; it is to pass away into the Southern capacity of being educated. The water is to sink to its level. Harvard College, whose men can think, — though so often on the wrong side, — is to go down half way, and meet South Carolina, saying her A, B, C. That is what you are to do.

It will take time undoubtedly. The nation is able to do it. The vigor and good sense and strength of endurance of these Northern classes is equal to the achievement, if we can only have leaders; but we have none.

The government looks to the people for its initiative. Lord Lyons said (substantially) in his dispatch to Earl Russell: "The Republican government dare not initiate a policy; it looks outward and asks what its opponents will consent to." That is now the condition of the government. Hence the necessity of outspoken, perpetual, constant education of public opinion. I do not believe in the government at Washington. I believe in the nation, I believe in events, I believe in the inevitable tendency of these coming ten years toward liberty and Union. But it is to be done as England did it in 1640, by getting rid gradually, man by man, of those who don't believe in progress, but live and mean to live in the past. And as man by man of that class retires, and we bring to the front men who are earnest in the present, victory, strength, and peace are to be the result. Now, for the present, I believe in Hooker. [Loud applause.] Men say he has faults, — faults which some of his predecessors did not have. [Laughter.] Perhaps he has, but in my opinion a diamond with a flaw is better than a pebble without. [Applause.] I do not set one defeat against him. I think, as Lord Bacon says, that a soldier's honor should be of a strong web which slight matters will not stick to. I believe Hooker's is of that kind. He means to fight; he knows how to fight; and those two are new elements at the head of the army. On the other side there are three elements. Lee means to fight, and knows how to fight, and he is deadly in earnest. We have had men who neither knew how to fight, nor meant to fight, — of no ability. Now we have ability to match the other side. We yet lack earnestness, ideas, a willingness to sacrifice everything, a readiness to accept the issue, courage and industry in thinking. We have now two Commanders-in-chief. They both live in Washington. The sad news reaches us to-day that one means to take the field. [Laughter.] Lincoln and Halleck, — they sit in Washington, commanders-in-chief, exercising that disastrous influence which even a Bonaparte would exercise on a battle, if he tried to fight it by telegraph a hundred miles distant. But now it is said one of them means to take the field. Heaven forbid! [Applause.] The difference between Halleck and Fremont is just this: one has not learned anything since he graduated at West Point, and does not wish to. As long as he rules, West Point, dead lumber, rules. An old adage says, "A fool is never a great fool till he has learned Latin." And so a man is never utterly incorrigible till he graduates at West Point. [Laughter.] General Halleck does not mean to undertake the labor of thinking. He is too indolent to go about to examine a new idea. It is enough for him that it was not in the text-books when he graduated. [Laughter.]

Battles were not fought so when he was taught, and if he is beaten according to the book, he is willing to be beaten. [Laughter.] The German commanders complained of Napoleon, when he first launched into the battle-field, that he violated all the rules. Now his Missouri rival occupied the nineteenth century, and thought out the issues for himself, — had the labor of meeting a new contingency. He went to the head of the army a living man, — not a dead book. I am beyond likes and dislikes. The day is too serious for antipathies or likings. All these men are nothing but dead lumber, to be thrown into the gulf, that the nation, over the path their bodies make, may march like an army with banners to liberty and peace. [Applause.] But never will this rebellion be put down while West Point rules at Washington. [Applause.] It does rule. That second Commander-in-chief cuts off everything which outgoes his own routine. There are two great classes in the army and in the state: one is, such a man as Halleck, who hates negroes, spurns novelties, distrusts ideas, rejects everything but red tape. The others are Hamilton, Butler, Phelps, and Fremont [loud applause], Sigel, who mean that this Union shall mean justice at any rate, and that if it does not mean justice it shall not exist; who know no nation except one that secures liberty. [Applause.] These are the men who are to shape the policy and guide the thunderbolts of the government. [Applause.] The cook takes an onion and peels off layer after layer till she gets to the sweet, sound vegetable. So you will have to peel off Seward and Halleck, Blair and Chase [laughter], till you get to the sound national element of civil and military purpose, the earnest belief, the single-hearted, intense devotion to victory, the entire belief in justice, which can cope with Stonewall Jackson. [Applause.] Never till then shall we succeed.

I have compared General Halleck and General Fremont.

You may take another parallel. One is Seward, and another is Butler. Seward does not believe in war, but in diplomacy or compromise. He has prophesied again and again that this war, like the divisions of former times, could be quieted in sixty or ninety days. He thought so; if he had not, he never would have risked his fame as a statesman upon the prophecy. He said by the voice of a regular army officer in the cabin of that ship which went down to dismantle Norfolk, when foreign-bred soldiers begged the American officers to stop and give them three hundred men to save two thousand cannon from the armies of the Confederates, and guaranteed to take that place and hold it three or six months, with two hundred men, — one of his class took a gentleman into the cabin and said, "You don't understand this thing; this is not a war, it is a quarrel: we have had a dozen of them; we shall get over it in sixty days." Seward believes it yet; he receives commissioners; he sends Frenchmen to Richmond to note terms; he sends letters abroad dealing with rebels as equals in fact. Butler is the first man who ever hung a rebel [loud applause], — and it ought to be recorded on his gravestone. If I were a politician and a general, I would not live an hour until I was his twin. [Laughter.] Let it go down to history, that one third of the nation burst into insurrection, and there was but one man, and he a Democrat, who dared to hang a felon. [Loud applause.] A government in arms against criminals who have wasted its treasures and filled two hundred and fifty thousand martyred patriot graves, — rebels, not belligerents. Now in the two distinctions between Halleck, routine, and Fremont, Phelps, Butler, realities, is the change needed for the future in military affairs; in the difference between Seward, the politician, and Butler, the government, is the change needed in civil affairs. If Seward is a Republican, God grant us a Democratic successor. [Laughter.] I want somebody to occupy the Presidential chair who believes in the government and in the people, — who will act without casting his eyes over his shoulders to see how far the people will support him. We need some one who believes in God and the people, — in justice and the masses. The Democrat believes in the masses; the Whig is neither one nor the other. We want leaders that initiate, — that actually lead. Friends, my belief is, that you and I are bound to create an exacting, imperative public opinion which shall compel the government to the adoption of such measures and such men. I say such men, because, though I believe in events, which are stronger than cabinets, and are bearing us onward whether we will or not, I believe also in men as harmonizing the issue of events. Let me make the Generals, and I don't care who makes the proclamations. Only let me put at the head of the advancing columns of the Union certain men that I could name, and the Cabinet at Washington may shut themselves up and go to sleep with Rip Van Winkle till 1872. [Laughter.] For I know those one blast of whose bugle-horns were worth a million men, — only put them in the heart of the rebellion, where our armies ought to be. I do not like to fight on the rim of the wheel and let the enemy rest on the hub. [Laughter.] I am no anaconda fancier. [Laughter.] I would be at the hub. I would put men, whose names you know too well, among the black masses of the Carolinas and Mississippi, and fight outward, grinding the rebellion to powder. To hurt the rebellion by bringing the negro into the war, does not mean merely troops; it means localities. When we bring the negro into the war, we fight in his home, in the Gulf States, where he ought to fight. The heart of the rebellion is where the negro is. It is there where our army should stand; if victorious, the bottom of the tub is out. And you know whose name the slave cherishes like a household word in every hovel, and at whose bidding he will rise to the Stars and Stripes. Will the *slave* fight? Well, if any man asks you, tell him no. Will he work? If any man asks you, tell him no. But if he asks you whether the *negro* will fight, tell him yes. [Applause.] If he asks you whether the negro will work, tell him yes, — work even for patriotism without wages, as he has worked at Fortress Monroe, the United States promising him $ 10 a month, keeping the first $ 3 for any stray contrabands who might join him, taking the second $ 4 for clothing the contraband himself, and the other $ 3 Uncle Sam keeps. [Laughter.]

But men say, " This is a mean thing; nineteen millions of people pitched against eight millions of Southerners, white men, and can't whip them, and now begin to call on the negroes." Is that the right statement? Look at it. What is the South's strength? She has eight millions of whites. She has the sympathy of foreign powers. She has the labor of four millions of slaves. What strength has the North? Divided about equally — that is a very poor statement for your side — into Republicans and Democrats; the Republicans willing to go but half way, and the Democrats not willing to go at all. [Laughter.] I will tell you what it is. It is like two men fighting. We will call them Jonathan and Charles. Jonathan is the North. His right hand, the Democratic party, he holds behind him. His left hand, his own tenderness of conscience uses to keep the slaves down. That is how he is to fight. No, that is not all. Upon his shoulders is strapped the West Point Academy, like a stone of a hundred weight. [Laughter.] The South stands with both hands, holding loaded revolvers, and, lest she should lose any time, John Bull is behind with additional pistols to hand the moment she needs them. Those are the two powers which are fighting this battle. Now the question is, whether in this great conflict, — not a boy's play between A and B, but the great struggle for the control of this continent in behalf of free labor, — is it not the duty of wise men to use every means within their reach? This is a contest between slaveholders and free labor, — nothing more; and in that contest the people, as in every contest against an aristocracy, are bound in their own right, in the right of their children, in the right of the great interests of the world which hang upon their success, to bestir themselves to understand, and to use the moment they see it, every weapon within their reach. I contend, therefore, that it is both constitutional and rightful, and, more than that, that it is absolutely necessary, that this government should, in the hour of its peril, call upon the four millions of blacks to aid it in a struggle which means liberty to them. I am not speaking now as an Abolitionist. I hold the hour to be a momentously serious one. Deeply in debt, with a terrible loss of blood, having fixed foul shame upon the cause of democracy by our indecision or delay, with a future before us complexed by every variety of dangers, the question is how we shall pilot the ship of state, the hope of the world, through this storm. The silver lining of the dark cloud that overhangs us is the irradicable loyalty of four millions of bondmen who hold the scale in their hands.

Throw aside all these idle quibbles: a mighty work is before us; welcome every helper. Cease to lean on the government at Washington. It is a broken reed, if not worse. We are lost unless the people are able to ride out this storm without captain or pilot. Yes, in spite of something worse at the helm. The President is an honest man; that is, he is Kentucky honest, and that is necessarily a very different thing from Massachusetts or New York honesty. A man cannot get above the atmosphere in which he is born. Did you ever see the Life of Luther in four volumes of seven hundred pages each? The first volume contains an account of the mineralogy of his native country, the trees that grow there, the flowers, the average length of human life, the color of the hair, how much rain falls, the range of the thermometer, &c., and in the second volume Luther is born. That was laying the foundation of Luther's character. Lincoln was born in Kentucky, and laid the foundation of his honesty in Kentucky. He is honest, with that allowance. He means to do his duty, and within the limit of the capacity God has given him he has struggled on, and has led the people struggling on, up to this weapon, partial emancipation, which they now hold glittering in their right hand. But we must remember the very prejudices and moral callousness which made him in 1860 an available candidate, when angry and half-educated parties were struggling for victory, necessarily makes him a poor leader, — rather no leader at all, — in a crisis like this. I have no confidence in the counsels about him. I have no confidence in the views of your son of York who stands at his right hand to guide the vessel of state in this tremendous storm. [Hisses.] That is right. I honor every man who expresses his opinion. I express mine; I would have every man express his dissent. I am saying nothing of the motives of Mr. Seward, nothing. When a man is dying, an honest mistake in the medicine is as bad as poison. The question is whether his is the statesmanship of the hour, and if it is not, then, on every theory of parliamentary government, he is bound to retire from his position and let another man occupy it. He has never uttered a prophecy which events have not falsified, nor initiated a policy which he has not himself been obliged to forego.

If the hope of the nation rested on the Cabinet he leads, I should despair; but our government is not at Washington, neither the brains nor the vigor of Washington guide the people. It only blocks the path of the real government, — the people, — the people whose substratum purpose, underlying all honest parties and cliques, is to save the Union by doing justice and securing liberty to all. At least, if all do not consciously plan this, the vast majority are willing for it. I know there are those standing to-day among us who would stretch their hands over two hundred thousand martyr graves and clasp hands with the rebels. That element is to be put under our feet, with the declaration that the helm is ours, by party right, by natural right, by the right of absolute justice; and while God gives us the power, we will use it boldly in the service of freedom and the Union. [Applause.] The whole social system of the Slave States is to be taken to pieces; every bit of it. General Butler tells us that in Louisiana it has gone to pieces. [Great applause, followed by an attempt at cheering for Butler, not fully understood.] He deserves a better cheer than that [three cheers for General Butler called for, and enthusiastically responded to] for this reason: he is almost the only general in our service who acts upon the principle that we are all right and the traitors all wrong. [Renewed applause.] Most of our other generals act upon the principle that the rebels are half right, and we are half wrong. When Butler was at New Orleans last summer, he assembled some fifty slaveholders in the parlors of the St. Charles Hotel, and said to them: "Don't you indulge the idea that there is a Democratic party in the North making a bridge back to Washington. I am a Democrat, and shall always be a Democrat; and I tell you I will burn every house in the State of Louisiana, and put every negro's right hand upon every master's throat, before I take down that banner and go home." [Loud and long cheering.] Why is General Butler idle? Who can tell? Abraham Lincoln can't; he says he knows nothing about it. [Laughter.] General Halleck can't; he says he knows nothing about it. William H. Seward can't; he says he knows nothing about it. One of the best generals in the service, the man who held the third city in the empire in his right hand like a lamb, that man comes home to the Capital, and cannot find a man in the Cabinet who will take the responsibility of saying, "I advised his recall," or will tell him the reason why he was recalled. [Three more cheers for Butler.] Why is he, one of the ablest of the very few able men this war has thrown to the surface, — why is he idle?

General Hamilton had the promise of the government at Washington, over and over again, that he might go and shut the back door of the rebellion, Texas, out of which the traitors mean to fly when they are beaten, and through which Vicksburg gets her strength to-day. Why has he not gone? Your own great fellow-citizen goes to Washington under the pledge of the President, too much in a hurry to allow him to leave Washington for six hours, stays for a week, and comes back without a command. Why? Because Abraham Lincoln is not President of the United States, or because he too ardently longs and plans to be so again. Either because the war is henceforth subordinate to a policy dictated by the next Presidential canvass, or because behind President Lincoln, curbing his purpose, making conditions which balk his designs, making him doubt the purpose and the strength of the North, standing round him in civil and military positions, are men who do not mean that this battle shall be bravely and gallantly fought through. The worst rebellion in the land is the rebellion of the Cabinet and Generals against common sense and justice. Cromwell never succeeded until the Long Parliament sloughed off every man who believed in the House of Lords, and left nothing but democrats behind. We shall never succeed until we slough off everything that believes in the past, and bring to the front everything that believes there is but one remedy, — that is, to save the Union on the basis of liberty. [Cheers.] I believe that the President may do anything to save the Union. He may take a man's houses, his lands, his bank-stock, his horses, his slaves, — anything to save the Union; the government may make every slave a free man, no matter where he is, Kentucky or Louisiana, now or to-morrow, with compensation or without. We need one step further, — an act of Congress abolishing slavery wherever our flag waves. The same war power and military necessity which made the proclamation constitutional authorizes this act as much. There is but one thing the government can't do to save the nation, and that is to make a free man into a slave; everything else is within its power.

I doubted somewhat when I heard the news from the Rappahannock, until I saw that reverses had taught the nation where its strength lay. God grant us so many reverses that the government may learn its duty. God grant us that the war may never end till it leaves us on the solid granite of impartial liberty and justice. [Cheers.] The government which has had two years of experience, of warning, and of advice, without profiting by it, must abide the consequences. In the words of the old proverb, "He that won't be ruled by the rudder must be ruled by the rock." [Applause.] If they will not be ruled by wise counsels, they must abide disaster; if they won't hear advice, they must expect reverses. What we have to teach Washington is, that such is the full purpose of the millions, and under it and in it is the certainty of success, — the millions, not the leaders. In my judgment, unless the sky soon clears, the Republican party has proved its own incapacity, — written *Ichabod* on its own brow. Judging by the past, whose will and wit can we trust? None of them, — I am utterly impartial, — neither President nor Cabinet nor Senate. Peel off Seward, peel off Halleck, peel off Blair, peel off Sumner, — yes, Massachusetts Senators as well as others. No, I will not say peel off our Massachusetts Senators; but I will say their recent action has very materially lessened my confidence in their intelligence and fidelity. I will tell you why. When the government called on New England for a negro regiment, and we went from county to county urging the blacks to enlist, one Massachusetts Colonel dared to say, down in South Carolina, in the face of the enemy, that he had rather be whipped without negroes than conquer at their side, — a Massachusetts Colonel, in that hour of emergency and critical issue. His case within twenty days went before the Senate of the United States, and the very week that his apology was filed in the War Office at Washington, Massachusetts Senators begged their reluctant brothers to make him a Brigadier-General. Yes, Massachusetts Senators, thoroughly informed and put upon their guard, against the repeated remonstrance of their fellow-Senators, insisted on rewarding the mutineer. ["Shame, shame."] A private, ignorant, uneducated, just mustered into the service, mutinied in the streets of Boston, and Colonel Lowell shot him rightfully. [Cheers.] A Massachusetts Colonel mutinied in the face of the enemy, and a Massachusetts Senator made him a Brigadier-General. Such Republicanism will never put down the rebellion.* [Cheers.]

* Colonel Stevenson said he had rather be whipped with white men than conquer with black men; and General Hunter took away his sword. When Adjutant-General Thomas went to the Southwest to muster negroes into our ranks, he lifted his index finger, and, pointing to Washington, said, "The wind blows North there," and from Brigadier to Lieutenant every man closed his lips and denied all prejudice against color. Negrophobia stabs nearer the heart of the government, has more power to wound, than Davis has. There will be none of it in our army at least, the moment

Spite of these sad, sad short-comings, I have hope. Iron, they say, cannot be made to sink in the current of Niagara. The Cataract tosses it like a chip, and bears it onward. The Cabinet is unredeemed inefficiency, — heavy as molten and doubly-hammered iron; but in the Niagara of 1863 it is tossed onward like a chip. No thanks to it, but to the Niagara which will not be resisted. Neither the calculating or stupid stand-still-ism of the Cabinet, nor the weakness nor the blunders of our own best leaders, can long delay us. In time they will punish the Colonel who treads on a negro as severely as if he had wronged a college graduate, whose home was on Beacon Street or the Fifth Avenue. The South is not strong in herself. All her strength con-

government lets its will be unmistakably known. That is the chief reason why I blame our Massachusetts Senators for conferring on Colonel Stevenson the honor of Brigadier-Generalship just at the moment he defied and denounced the policy of the government. Gross insubordination existed in General Hunter's department, — arising out of this among other causes, — the soldiers, taking courage from the temper and talk of their officers, had inflicted terrible outrages on the negroes there; at the North we were appealing to the negro to enlist. All over the land men tried to penetrate the real purpose of government in respect to the negro; — its friends, in order to help it; the negro, that he might more cheerfully do his duty. We were calling, in our peril, on a wronged race, which had been cheated of its rights again and again in every national emergency, and begging them now to trust and to help us, obliged to tell them they would have no commissions, but must serve under white officers. "Will they be men whose *hearts* are with us?" we were constantly asked by the negro. We trembled while we answered, "We hope so, we believe so." At this crisis, Colonel Stevenson, standing at Hunter's side, spits on the government's movements. It was a moment and an act which fixed the attention of the nation. It was an act which, so far as one man could, perilled a great and necessary movement. It deserved, therefore, severe rebuke. It was an act which gave the administration the very best opportunity to show the world its purpose beyond a doubt. One right, decisive word from the Senate, and no officer in the service would afterwards mistake the purpose of the administration, or dare to misuse a negro. That word was, "Colonel Stevenson, for your sists in our unwillingness to strike? Why this unwillingness to strike? Because we do not yet see John Hancock under a black skin; and until we do see him, we shall never wage an honest and utter battle. No man who does not grant to the negro his just place is fit to be enlisted in the army of the Union, or to stand in its Senate, if that Union means liberty; or if that is an exaggerated statement, certainly no man has a right to lead our Senate or our army who does not carry that idea in his heart. [Applause.]

Never until we welcome the negro, the foreigner, all races as equals, and, melted together in a common nationality, hurl them all at despotism, will the North deserve triumph or earn it at the hands of a just God. [Applause.]

services and your apology we overlook your fault; but stay a Colonel till by faithful and hearty co-operation in the new movement you earn the nation's confidence, and let every officer take warning by your fate." Such was the message we urged the Senate to send to the mutineer. Instead of that, Massachusetts Senators reward the mutineer to conciliate hunker treason.

Thus we see high-handed defiance of the government's policy enter the Senate a Colonel and come out a Brigadier. What rule for its conduct could the army take from such an example? Spit on the government, and expect promotion, — trample on the negro, and be sure of employment! Sigel, Fremont, Butler, Hamilton, Phelps, and a host of others idle, yet a negro-hater promoted on the plea of necessity to get good officers! When Mr. Sumner let personal feelings lead him to such a step, he betrayed the negro. If, as his friends allege, he allowed Hunter or Burnside — one a new convert, the other not converted at all — to dictate such a course, he forgot that we chose him, not them, our Senator, and trusted him, not them, with these grave powers. But I have the best authority for saying that General Hunter never asked of any Senator to promote Colonel Stevenson. I have the best reason for believing that he, like myself, looks on that act of the Senate as a grave error. This is only one case of a single and soon-forgotten individual, but it tests statesmen as much as large matters. Massachusetts Senators must reform on these points altogether if they expect trust in future. Let them see to it, lest, while they think they are using others for good ends, they may themselves be made tools for base ones.

But the North will triumph. I hear it. Do you remember in that disastrous siege in India, when the Scotch girl raised her head from the pallet of the hospital, and said to the sickening hearts of the English, "I hear the bagpipes, the Campbells are coming," and they said, "Jessie, it is delirium." "No, I know it; I heard it far off." And in an hour the pibroch burst upon their glad ears, and the banner of England floated in triumph over their heads. So I hear in the dim distance the first notes of the jubilee rising from the hearts of the millions. Soon, very soon, you shall hear it at the gates of the citadel, and the Stars and Stripes shall guarantee liberty forever from the Lakes to the Gulf. [Continued applause.]

THE END.

Cambridge: Stereotyped and Printed by Welch, Bigelow, & Co.

www.ingramcontent.com/pod-product-compliance
Lightning Source LLC
LaVergne TN
LVHW021233110826
845150LV00002B/320

* 9 7 8 1 4 2 5 5 6 2 2 0 5 *